SO-BLX-332

✓

PR
5366
.17
1968

Irvine, William

The universe of
G. B. S.

DATE

THE UNIVERSE OF G. B. S.

The Universe of G. B. S.

BY WILLIAM IRVINE

NEW YORK / RUSSELL & RUSSELL

ACKNOWLEDGMENTS   I wish to thank the following periodicals for permission to incorporate in this book articles of mine which originally appeared in their pages: *Foreign Affairs; The Huntington Library Quarterly; The Journal of Economic History; The Journal of the History of Ideas; The Musical Quarterly; South Atlantic Quarterly; The Trollopian; The Virginia Quarterly Review.* ¶I wish also to express gratitude to the Yale University Library for permission to quote from rare materials in the Henderson Collection, and to Mr. Charles Bolles Rogers for permission to quote from his letters to me. ¶Lastly, I wish to acknowledge a great indebtedness to my wife, Charlotte Irvine, not only for editing and correcting, but for first drafts and preliminary studies of many chapters, notably "The Music Critic," "Marriage," and "Saint Joan."—William Irvine

COPYRIGHT, 1949, BY WILLIAM IRVINE

REISSUED, 1968, BY RUSSELL & RUSSELL

A DIVISION OF ATHENEUM HOUSE, INC.

BY ARRANGEMENT WITH CHARLOTTE S. IRVINE

L. C. CATALOG CARD NO: 68-15130

PRINTED IN THE UNITED STATES OF AMERICA

CONTENTS

THE UNIVERSE OF G. B. S.

CHAPTER ONE

The Origins of a Revolutionary

Not since the days of the French *philosophes* has one of the immortals aroused so much evanescent interest. Within his own lifetime Shaw has managed to combine the exciting notoriety of a movie star with the sedate glory of a great author long dead. His quips on current events have been quoted with éclat on the front page, and his life and plays are dissected with scholarly minuteness in five-hundred-page volumes. What man ever had so many talents for the limelight? He is not only the greatest of modern dramatists but the greatest publicist since Voltaire and the greatest actor off the stage since Disraeli—for after all, he is his own most brilliant role and for more than ninety years has played himself with infinitely more gusto and success than anybody ever played John Tanner or Professor Higgins. Finally, he is a peculiarly elusive and complicated personality. Critics will always be fascinated by a writer capable of being so ingeniously explained. He has not only provided G. K. Chesterton with a most congenial subject but forced even William Archer, with his admirable Scottish gift for Aristotelian platitude and searching commonplace, into sparkling paradox and witticism. Shaw is not only clever himself; he has been the cause of cleverness in others.

During the first fifty years of his life he was a desperate revolutionist. During the last fifty he has been a British institution. If in the nineteenth century Wellington was the guardian of the English state, Shaw in the twentieth has been its official gadfly. Wellington tried to preserve an old world. Shaw has attempted to create a new one. And in part he has succeeded, for he has grown into an institution not, like many grand old thinkers, because he has become more worldly but because the world has become more Shavian. If one could explain Shaw thoroughly, one would also have explained a great deal of the twentieth century.

In a modest but genteel house, in a modest but genteel section of Dublin, George Bernard Shaw, the youngest and the only boy in a family of three children, was born on July 26, 1856. It is difficult to

[1]

realize that so modern a man was born so long ago. At that time, the steamboat and the railroad were feeble and dubious novelties. The telephone and the motor car were uninvented. The airplane was a dream, and the radio, less than a dream. Germany was not yet a nation, and *The Origin of Species* was unpublished. Dublin itself was a shabby, corrupt, pretentious little capital, which as a boy Shaw hated so grimly that fifty years later, as a famous and successful man, he could write of its evils with intense bitterness:

> If I had not suffered from these things [social injustices] in my childhood perhaps I could keep my temper about them. To an outsider there was nothing but comedy in the spectacle of a forlorn set of Protestant merchants in a Catholic country, led by a miniature plutocracy of stockholders, doctors, and landagents, and flavoured by that section of the landed gentry who were too heavily mortgaged to escape to London, playing at being a Court and an aristocracy with the assistance of the unfortunate exile who had been persuaded to accept the post of Lord-Lieutenant. To this pretense, involving a prodigious and continual lying as to incomes and the social standing of relatives, were sacrificed citizenship, self-respect, freedom of thought, sincerity of character, and all the realities of life, its votaries gaining in return the hostile estrangement of the great mass of their fellow-countrymen, and in their own class the supercilious snubs of those who had outdone them in pretension and the jealous envy of those whom they had outdone.[1]

Here was oppression and hatred for the Catholic, fear and isolation for the Protestant, and poverty for both, with a whole nation devoted to the demonstration of its evils. Here was the natural goodness of man corrupted by his environment and his institutions, a naturally gay and clever people debased by misery, made cynical by injustice and despair, and grotesquely inflated by petty rank and pretension. History might have formed this stagnant, futureless city to prove the doctrines of a reformer like Rousseau to a satirist like Shaw. Such a city might make a man callous to poverty and waste or make him wish to spend his life in removing them; it might produce either an incurable snob or a fanatical revolutionary, a hardheaded materialist or a mystical dreamer, an optimist or a cynic, a humanitarian or a misanthrope. A born dramatist, Shaw became nearly all of these—even a misanthrope. "A critic has described me, with deadly acuteness," he writes, "as having 'a kindly dislike for my fellow creatures.' Perhaps dread would have been nearer the mark than dislike; for man is the only animal of which I am thoroughly and cravenly afraid."[2]

In a very gallant book, G. K. Chesterton has presented Shaw with all the glories of Ireland and puritanism for a past, seeing in him the Irishman's aggressiveness, hard clarity of intellect, and hatred of emotional display; the Orangeman's "inhumane humanity," his tendency to "benevolent bullying" and "knocking men down for their own good"; [3] the puritan's aristocratic moral fastidiousness and contempt for the vulgar amusements of this world, his burning desire to worship God with the intellect alone and to interpose no veil or symbol, however beautiful, between his Deity and himself. It is characteristic that Shaw responded to this generous and penetrating analysis by abusing his relatives. To be sure, no man has done so more brilliantly.

And as usual, Shaw involves himself in at least a seeming contradiction. Reading through his many autobiographical writings, one gathers that his family were amiable nonentities clinging to a very tenuous gentility with the desperation of people who have no other distinction. Without money, energy, or knowledge, they prided themselves on an empty profession of Protestantism and an impecunious superiority to the vulgarly lucrative trades. "What we clung to was a tradition of landed gentry without any land—the fate of the younger sons under feudalism." [4] That side of the picture represents his Marxian ferocity against social pretension and practical incompetence. The other side, one suspects, represents family affection and his talents as a dramatist. For one gathers also that his family was the most amazing menagerie of eccentrics ever collected together outside his wildest comedies. His maternal Uncle Walter and his father were strange, Butlerian characters who had a giddy tendency to laugh at the sacred ark of family respectability, in which, incidentally, they pretty devoutly believed; and what Shaw calls the "hard facts" about his Uncle William make the character and opinions of Captain Shotover seem the most sober and prosaic reality.

Which of these two libels are we to believe? Both. The Shaws, descended of country gentry, distinguished rebels and traitors, and indubitably related to a baronet, were a strong-minded, capable clan with startling peculiarities and an almost morbid sense of their respectability, doubtless intensified by embarrassed circumstances, which had resulted from the ruin of the dramatist's grandfather "before he had provided for his widow and eleven children." [4] The family quickly recouped its fortunes, sending pioneers and police chiefs over the Empire, but Shaw's father and a few others seem to have suffered some permanent demoralization, in part perhaps simply from having remained in Dublin.

Of course Dublin had its compensations. If it lacked the wealth, it also escaped the stupid and tasteless complacency of the great, thriving English cities. It belonged to a preindustrial society which still retained a connection with the aristocratic classicism of the eighteenth century. Mr. Edmund Wilson has pointed the lesson:

> If we compare Shaw, Yeats and Joyce to, say Bennett, Galsworthy and Wells, we are at once struck by the extent to which these latter have suffered from their submergence in the commercial world. In their worst phases of sentimentality and philistinism, there is almost nothing to choose between them and the frankly trashy popular novelist; whereas the Irish have preserved for English literature classical qualities of hardness and elegance.[5]

For most people, childhood is the period of faith. For Shaw, it was one long lesson in skepticism. The credulous mind of the child awoke to the irreverent laughter of his elders. He saw paternal authority linked with drunkenness, class pride with shabby incompetence, and religion with ludicrous snobbishness and indecent mockery. All this he accepted as a child accepts, echoing the laughter he heard. And indeed the respectable Shaws were so prodigiously, hopelessly, insultingly respectable, the topers so scandalously, incessantly drunk, the eccentrics so wildly and grotesquely eccentric that intelligent sanity could maintain itself only by laughter. Moreover, the family had a sense of humor. One of his uncles told racy sacrilegious stories with careful art and abandoned gusto. Another made his life one long and equitable flirtation with virtue and damnation.

But the chief lesson in irreverence was his father. George Carr Shaw was a pleasant, middle-aged idler with red whiskers, a pronounced squint, and a weak mouth. His mother, the grandmother of the dramatist, had with the inflexible insistence of a strong-minded woman taught him to believe in his own gentility, in the gentility of the Protestant religion, and in the primary duty of keeping up a seemly show of opulence, even though at the occasional sacrifice of ordinary necessities. He lived his life accordingly, but always with that tendency to private laughter and that disinterested fascination with the forbidden, characteristic of a clever boy who has been too strictly reared. For many years he drank heavily, and being unable to ignore the situation, his family resolutely regarded it as a joke. But for young George there was a stage before laughter, when childhood's clear, definite, secure little world of convention, belief, and affection was subjected to heavy shocks:

> One night, when I was still about as tall as his boots, he took me out for a walk. In the course of it I conceived a monstrous, incredible suspicion. When I got home I stole to my mother and in an awe-struck whisper said to her "Mama, I think Papa's drunk." She turned away with impatient disgust and said, "When is he ever

anything else?" I have never believed in anything since: then the scoffer began.[6]

And of course, being set a strong example by nearly all his elders, the scoffer developed precociously:

A boy who has seen "the governor," with an imperfectly wrapped-up goose under one arm and a ham in the same condition under the other (both purchased under heaven knows what delusion of festivity), butting at the garden wall in the belief that he was pushing open the gate, and transforming his tall hat to a concertina in the process, and who, instead of being overwhelmed with shame and anxiety at the spectacle, has been so disabled by merriment (uproariously shared by the maternal uncle) that he has hardly been able to rush to the rescue of the hat and pilot its wearer to safety, is clearly not a boy who will make tragedies of trifles instead of making trifles of tragedies. If you cannot get rid of the family skeleton, you may as well make it dance.[7]

But if the elder Shaw compelled laughter, he also induced a sense of humor:

The more sacred an idea or a situation was by convention [writes his son], the more irresistible was it to him as the jumping-off place for a plunge into laughter. Thus, when I scoffed at the Bible he would instantly and quite sincerely rebuke me, telling me, with what little sternness was in his nature, that I should not speak so; that no educated man would make such a display of ignorance; that the Bible was universally recognized as a literary and historical masterpiece; and as much more to the same effect as he could muster. But when he had reached the point of feeling really impressive, a convulsion of internal chuckling would wrinkle up his eyes; and (I knowing all the time quite well what was coming) would cap his eulogy by assuring me, with an air of perfect fairness, that even the worst enemy of religion could say no worse of the Bible than that it was the damndest parcel of lies ever written. He would then rub his eyes and chuckle for quite a long time. It became an unacknowledged game between us that I should provoke him to exhibitions of this kind.[8]

Like his son, he was the slave of his sense of anticlimax. He was also capable of a high degree of comic detachment. When the bankruptcy of a customer very nearly ruined him, he found his partner's tears and the whole situation "so irresistibly amusing" [9] that he retreated to a corner of the warehouse and laughed until he was exhausted.

One may well ask how the son of such a man could ever be serious. And yet posterity has at length decided that about art and certain ideas, the mature George Bernard Shaw could be very serious. The one person he revered was his mother, who saw no humor whatever in the master-piece of comic art which her husband and his family were enacting.

Mrs. Shaw believed in freedom for the same reason that her husband believed in conformity: she also had been reared by a determined woman. Being herself a determined woman, she adhered inflexibly to the principle of having no principles in rearing her son. *Laissez faire,* austere and rational, prevailed. Bernard and his sisters received little discipline, attention, or show of affection from their parents but passed their time largely in the company of nurses and servants. Perhaps the worst result was that Bernard learned to do without happiness and affection. He also became at once dreamy and self-reliant, very shy and very superior. "The fact that nobody cared for me particularly," he says, "gave me a frightful self-sufficiency, or rather a power of starving on imaginary feasts, that may have delayed my development a good deal, and leaves me to this hour a treacherous brute in matters of pure affec-tion." [10]

Shaw tells that in early boyhood he was a great reader, a great boaster, and a great liar. No doubt he was much confused because of a boyish habit of living in a great many worlds at once. With the fierce eagerness and the swift boredoms of early youth, he was plunging in an endless riot of adventure from the untheological fairyland of the *Arabian Nights* to the sound Protestant fairyland of *Pilgrim's Progress.* A little later he was warring against villains in many ages with Sir Walter Scott and shooting Indians in many climes with Fenimore Cooper. It is not sur-prising that after slashing or slaughtering as Richard the Lionhearted or Deerslayer, he forgot in the heat of the moment that through all the glorious existences in which he lived, he remained always mysteriously anchored to that insignificant and timid individual, George Bernard Shaw of Hatch Street. "When I was a boy," he wrote simply as a very old man, "I was a coward, and bitterly ashamed of it." [11]

Perhaps more than Shaw would acknowledge, the child's daydreams were father to the man's art:

> Ever since I can remember, I have only had to go to bed and shut my eyes to be and do whatever I pleased. What are your trumpery Bond Street luxuries to George Bernard Sardanapalus? Why, such insight as I have in criticism is due to the fact that I exhausted romanticism before I was ten years old. Your popular novelists are now gravely writing the stories I told myself before I replaced my first set of teeth.[12]

But has the author of "Arms and the Man" or "Back to Methuselah" really exhausted romanticism? Certainly he has learned to dream less obvious dreams, to coat them with a bright, hard veneer of rationalism, and to evolve an ironic dialectic between the image maker and the image breaker:

> Why does the imaginative man always end by writing comedy if only he has also the sense of reality? Clearly because of the stupendous irony of the contrast between his imaginary adventures and his real circumstances and powers. At night, a conquering hero, an Admirable Crichton, a Don Juan; by day a cowardly little brat cuffed by his nurse for stealing lumps of sugar.[13]

A rather romantic explanation of comedy! At any rate, Shaw discovered this ironic conflict between romance and reality quite precociously, in part by desperate experience, in part by reading Charles Lever's satiric novel *A Day's Ride: A Life's Romance,* in which he discovered his spiritual biography.

Unkempt and sometimes unwashed, irregular and ungoverned in his habits, he was a quiet, portentous-browed infant, who busied himself with large tomes, performed children's Christmas ceremonies of melting lead and hiding rings in pancakes with a humiliating sense of going through irrational mummeries, listened importantly to the gay blasphemies of his father and maternal uncle, repeated them to the others after the manner of Lever's hero Potts with the greatest effrontery and the most mortifying failure,[14] yet persevered in a stubborn sense of his own maturity. Imperturbably he drew with crayons on the whitewashed walls of his bedroom a bright, primitive nightmare of operatic demons. Thirty years later he succeeded in resembling his Mephistopheles, but even in these early years he discovered the excitement of wearing a mask. Sharply sensitive to the slightest rebuff, he concealed his feelings under a hard and impudent manner. Delighted to find that his elders were shocked, he played his role with all the ferocious, secret gusto of boyhood.

Not in the childhood of George Washington himself was Destiny busier than in Shaw's, though her object was to produce a breaker rather than a maker of constitutions. She fussed like an overwrought nurse over his infancy, fomenting sedition and rebellion:

> My ordinary exercise whilst I was still too young to be allowed out by myself was to be taken out by a servant, who was supposed to air me on the banks of the canal or round the fashionable squares where the atmosphere was esteemed salubrious and the surroundings gentlemanly. Actually she took me into the slums to visit her

private friends, who dwelt in squalid tenements. . . . Thus were laid the foundations of my lifelong hatred of poverty, and the devotion of all my public life to the task of exterminating the poor and rendering their resurrection for ever impossible.[15]

He not only learned to hate the poverty of the poor but seems to have been born with a "natural antipathy to his native bourgeoisie worthy of Karl Marx." [16] "I remember thinking when I was a boy," he writes, "how silly it was that my father, whose business was wholesale business, should consider himself socially superior to his tailor, who had the best means of knowing how much poorer than himself my father was." [17] For Darwin he was quite prepared. "Nobody who had lived with our dog Rover," he says, "could believe that people are different from animals." [18]

But so many precocious lessons in naturalism and rebellion could not be bought without some sacrifice of the faculty for reverence. It is one of the limitations of his youthful development that he never fell under the ascendancy of a keen, disciplined mind in a position of authority. Paradoxically, he proved later that he had a capacity for hero worship, but his heroes were all rebels like himself, and he knew most of them only in the cold abstraction of books. He worshiped, but he insisted on worshiping irreverence.[19]

Young George went to church and was exposed to the horrors of the Victorian hell, because it was genteel to go to church and believe in hell. The result was a resentment so fierce that twenty years afterward he could not enter a church without almost uncontrollable repugnance. He recalls with horror "the unnaturally motionless figures of the congregation in their Sunday clothes and bonnets, and their set faces pale with the malignant rigidity produced by the suppression of all expression." [20] Religion in general he denounces as a cruel hoax betraying his earliest innocence into noxious belief and remembers indignantly a dream in which God as a kind of supernatural dentist awaited him formidably in the next room. But surely no infant ever penetrated a hoax more swiftly. He was a freethinker, he declares, before he could think. He describes himself as at a tender age listening with approval to his Uncle Walter's explanation of the raising of Lazarus as a put-up job. Prayer he used once or twice as a "protective spell" [21] against thunderstorms but otherwise only as an elegant literary exercise. But at least his sufferings were brief, for his mother released him from churchgoing before he was ten.

Religion, like everything else, was a comic melodrama which led him to revolution:

> I was christened by a clerical uncle; and as my godfather was intoxicated and did not turn up, the sexton was ordered to promise

[8]

and vow in his place, precisely as my uncle might have ordered him to put more coals on the vestry fire. I was never confirmed, and I believe my parents never were, either. The seriousness with which English families take this rite, and the deep impression it makes on many children, was a thing of which I had no conception. Protestantism in Ireland is not a religion; it is a side in political faction, a class prejudice, a conviction that Roman Catholics are socially inferior persons, who will go to Hell when they die, and leave Heaven in the exclusive possession of ladies and gentlemen.[22]

As he grew older and stronger, Shaw's nonconformity took a less abstract and philosophical turn. "Were you often in hot water as a youngster?" his biographer Pearson asked him. "I was *always* in hot water." [23] Apparently the setting fire to the commons mentioned in "Man and Superman" was autobiographical, except that Bernard, unlike Jack Tanner, confessed when another boy was blamed; but then in a long and eloquent speech—his first—he explained everything satisfactorily for everybody. He has of course been making speeches ever since, though he has been content with merely figurative fireworks.

On the whole, Shaw's was not a happy childhood. It was one in which laughter, but not affection, was spontaneous. Its details are so ludicrous that one loses touch with its underlying tone. It is probably not pleasant to grow up in a hilarious comedy. "A devil of a childhood," Shaw wrote to Ellen Terry many years later, "rich only in dreams, frightful and loveless in realities." [24]

CHAPTER TWO

A *Self-made* **Mind**

From a very early age Shaw had a puritan's and a romantic's hatred of institutions. They represent the irrationality of cloaking human mediocrity beneath the impressive front of power and authority. They impose a tyrannous restraint on the fine freedom of momentary whim and impulse.

> They substitute a synthetic morality for the inner light and stereotype conventions that should change in response to the advances of the human spirit, which he first called the Life Force and later the Evolutionary Appetite. For educational institutions particularly he has the contempt of a man who can learn everything aesthetically and nothing pedagogically, to whom schoolbooks were unreadable and school a prison.[1]

His education began auspiciously enough at the hands first of a governess and then of his clerical uncle-in-law, William George Carroll, both of whom taught him Latin with great success. He was then sent to the aristocratically Protestant Wesleyan Connexional School, which prepared for the University. Here, though tirelessly studious by nature, he took care to be a poor scholar, except in English composition, in which he got firsts without effort. His schoolmates remembered him as having told them tales out of Homer in a Shavian manner.

After he had been several years at Wesleyan, his uncle examined him and found he had learned very little. He was therefore sent to a private school at Glasthule until a change of family domicile brought up the question of his ignorance afresh. George John Vandaleur Lee, music teacher and family friend, who carried revolutionary nonconformity to the point of eating brown bread and sleeping with open windows, proposed the Central Model Boys' School in Marlborough Street. It was an appalling thought. The Model School was in theory undenominational, but it was common knowledge that most of the boys were the sons of Roman Catholics in retail trade! Nevertheless, Lee's eloquence prevailed, and Bernard underwent a snob's martyrdom for eight months, after which rebellion brought him freedom. The experience then passed into a silence from which one of the most talkative men in the world did not rescue it—even to tell his wife—for eighty years. It had entered into the very core of his being. One perceives how much Shaw's socialism is the logical result of his snobbery. He did not love the poor. He simply hated their poverty.

Bernard's formal education was concluded at a genteel Protestant commercial school, at which, having like John Tanner experienced "the birth of moral passion," he was an exemplary student.[2] But moral passion did not bring truth and certainty. Even in those days he was a skeptic in search of a faith, an intellectual in search of a philosophy, "an actor in search of a part."[3] He sought salvation in atheism, in utilitarian rationalism, in fine art, and above all in music. Summing up a gloomy picture of his early training, he exclaims, "And now, what power did I find in Ireland religious enough to redeem me from this abomination of desolation? Quite simply, the power of Art. . . . I found the religion of my country in its musical genius, and its irreligion in its churches and drawing-rooms."[4]

His teachers were the two people of those years about whom he speaks with respect—his mother and George John Vandaleur Lee. It is a brilliant compliment to the former that her son strenuously advocated the New Woman even after having known one in the flesh, for Mrs. Shaw was a Vivie Warren set down, by a spirit even more capricious than George Bernard, squarely in the middle of the nineteenth century. Miss Lucinda Gurly, the daughter of a country gentleman, lived with her father and a "humpbacked little aunt, a fairylike creature with a will of iron, who had brought up her motherless niece with a firm determination to make her a paragon of good breeding, to achieve a distinguished marriage for her, and to leave her all her money as a dowry."[5] These benevolent intentions were reversed by a marriage that was not at all distinguished, nor even romantic. Her father had taken a second wife. Lucinda did not like the prospect, and being doubtless very brave, very rational, and very impulsive, did the one enterprising thing a woman could do in those days. She married. Her aunt, enraged, promptly disinherited her, and she found herself apparently dependent for life on the slender resources of a middle-aged cipher who brought social ostracism on himself and his young wife by a neurosis for drink. She consoled herself with music.

Shaw's mother was remarkably gifted, and absolutely insensible to public opinion and the family pressure. She soon dropped the Shaws and was dropped by them. She even dropped her husband

and attached herself to a stronger man who made a musical world for her, and calmly followed him to London when he emigrated. She had no love for him nor for anything except flowers and animals. She was as incapable of love as of unkindness to animals or children, and went her way without scandal, a complete musical Bohemian without any Bohemian vices. Altogether a very unusual mother of a consequently rather unusual son: both unclassable.[6]

Trained by Mr. Lee, she proved to have not only an excellent mezzo-soprano voice but a good head for his affairs. She sang in the operas he managed and went so far toward managing them herself that in order to make the most of her assistance, he took up lodgings in the Shaw household. Lee was the kind of man whom a Vivie Warren and her son would admire. A revolutionary hated by all the music teachers of the city, he based his method on a scientific knowledge of the human throat and could predict from the tone of the voice the exact position of the vocal organs. "He not only," writes Shaw, "made my mother sing by a method that preserved her voice perfectly until her death at over eighty but gave her a Cause and a Creed to live by."[7]

Music proved fascinating to the incorrigible student of the Wesleyan Connexional School. No one insisted on teaching him. Therefore he learned rapidly. Quite unconsciously, he developed a surprising knowledge of music from Handel to Meyerbeer and Mendelssohn.

> He told me with triumph, one day [recalls a boyhood friend], that he could read notation, and brought me into the drawing room to prove his statement. We were alone, and he had approached the piano, when a maid hurried in, exclaiming:
> "Oh, Master George, you are late for dinner!"
> Master George said: "I won't have any to-day, thank you . . ."
> "Your mama is out. What will she say when she comes back and finds that you had eaten nothing?"
> But his mind was made up. . . . The maid went out and returned with another. Both girls knelt before him and implored him to take his dinner, but in vain. Eventually they went out in despair, and then Shaw placed music on the piano and played with one finger the serenade from *Don Giovanni*. He had learned to hum the air from hearing it sung, then strummed it on the piano and compared it with the printed notes.[8]

Obviously, music must have meant many things to so complex a nature as Shaw's. The most directly moving of the arts, it satisfied above all his cravings for intensity, its sharp geometry of design ministered to his love of logic, and its lovely rhythms and harmonies raised up in him unsuspected ecstasies of emotion—without, however, doing violence to the fastidiousness of the puritan, for the ear is the chastest of the senses. Or, as Mr. Shaw emends this passage:

> Handel's and Mozart's symmetry of design formed his classical taste; and from Rossini and Verdi as well as from Shakespeare he acquired the grandiose and declamatory elements hidden beneath his superficially colloquial and "natural" dialogue.

One suspects also that music created a dream world in which this romantic could enjoy romance without being pursued by his own critical laughter.

> In the music [he writes] you will find the body and reality of that feeling which the mere novelist can only describe to you; there will come home to your sense something in which you can actually experience the candour and gallant impulse of the hero, the grace and trouble of the heroine, and the extracted emotional quintessence of their love.[9]

"Yet his chosen pursuit was painting."[10] Shaw claims to be the only Irishman who ever visited the National Gallery. His visits were begun early and repeated often. He soon became familiar with the styles of the principal Italian and Flemish masters and spent his pocket money on the Bohn translations of Vasari. One of his earliest ambitions was to be a second Michelangelo, whom he aspired to rival without previous instruction in drawing. "Years later he wrote these lines:

> For know, rash youth, that in this starcrossed world
> Fate drives us all to find our chiefest good
> In what we can, and not in what we would."[11]

Shaw was always a voluminous and extraordinarily impressionable reader. He has been influenced by more books in a decade than are most authors in a lifetime.

> I was saturated with the Bible and with Shakespeare [he says] before I was ten years old. . . . Stung by the airs of a schoolfellow who alleged that he had read Locke On the Human Understanding, I attempted to read the Bible straight through, and actually got to the Pauline Epistles before I broke down in disgust at what seemed to me their inveterate crookedness of mind.[12]

A little later he read—among the poets—Spenser, Byron, and Shelley.

> Paine had been held up to me as a drunken staymaker without a redeeming trait. Voltaire and Rousseau, I was taught, were blasphemers whose deathbeds were made frightful by their certainty

of going to hell. . . . Shelley cured me of all that. I read him, prose and verse, from beginning to end. This took place at the end of my teens.[13]

At this time also Shelley gave him metaphysical and humanitarian reasons for becoming a vegetarian, which, except for strictly medicinal deviations into liver pills in old age, he has remained throughout his life. The character of Major Saranoff in "Arms and the Man" suggests that, at some time, he came to understand Byronism very well. Among the novelists, he devoured Dickens, Scott, and Dumas *père;* among the philosophers and scientists, he knew Mill, Darwin, Tyndall, and "studied the conflict between religion and science in the pages of Draper and in the *Westminster Review,* the organ of cultured agnosticism." [14] The striking fact about this reading is that it is so much concerned with contemporary controversy. Shaw's historical perspective has always been a little flat. Only in the fullness of his powers did he discover the Middle Ages and a rather Shavian Plato. He fought in the Battle of the Ancients and the Moderns without ever coming, perhaps, fully to understand his enemy.

But at least he began to fight early. When the revivalists Moody and Sankey visited the city, Shaw, then nineteen, turned a critical eye upon the meetings, and in a letter to *Public Opinion,* annihilated the forces of religion by confronting them with the vanity of their motives. The letter is not so much a thinker's as a novelist's attack on religion. It was the first time Shaw had used literary weapons to fight the battle of science.

Unable to send his son to a university, Mr. Shaw entered him—perhaps as the next best thing—in a land-agency business, a highly genteel occupation. Bernard did not carry nonconformity to the point of being a poor clerk. On the contrary, this apparently undisciplined youth discovered that he had an appetite for laborious routine. "I work as my father drank," he confesses.[15] He improved his handwriting, kept neat, accurate accounts, and learned to draw up contracts with a sharpness and acumen which were in later years the wonder and the vexation of "hopelessly unbusinesslike" [16] theatrical managers. When the post of cashier fell suddenly vacant, he proved so efficient as temporary substitute that, despite his youth, the appointment was made permanent. He bought himself a tail coat and suffered the chafing of apprentices. He was now a man of position, having attained eminence almost beyond the wildest dreams of his family. Yet he was not content. "He longed to be a Praxiteles, a Michael Angelo, or at least a Badeali" [16] and to him the Townshend land-agency business was a very little thing.

He could not get into really friendly relations with its personnel, and did not want to. He was never uncivil in the office but never happy. He knew he did not belong there. He accepted an instruction not to discuss religion in office hours.[17]

But he revenged himself by teaching the apprentices to sing opera. During a performance in the main office one of his pupils—from the height of the washstand, which represented his tower—was singing "*Ah, che la morte*" when Mr. Townshend himself suddenly appeared, creating an industrious and awful silence among the desks and tables. The pupil, living only in his art, sang on oblivious, and Mr. Townshend, unexpectedly taking fright, fled upstairs.

At this time Shaw also really learned to play the piano. It was an act of desperation. Vandaleur Lee and Mrs. Shaw had both gone to London: the first to conquer new worlds, the second to earn her living as a music teacher "and bring out her daughter as an operatic prima donna." [17] Living in lodgings with his father, Bernard was no longer in the way of hearing good music. He did not despair of producing bad. Armed with a diagram of the keyboard, he sat down to Mozart's "Don Giovanni." With magnificent courage and a conqueror's ruthless indifference to the sufferings of his fellow lodgers, he eventually won through to "a precarious and in rapid passages recklessly inaccurate command of his instrument." [17] He was also introduced to the heretical delights of Wagner by Chichester Bell, a cousin of the inventor.

Thus, keeping his cashbook neat and his accounts balanced "and despising himself for doing it," [17] Shaw arrived at the advanced age of twenty. Then one day at the office he had a shock. An apprentice, C. J. Smyth by name, remarked that every young fellow thinks he is going to be a great man eventually. It was one of Shaw's many awakenings. Suddenly he perceived that he had never thought of himself as a land agent. Obviously, he was one of the fellowship to which Shelley and Mozart and Michelangelo belonged. But alas! He was a master totally without masterpieces. He had not even decided in what art to create them. He must acquire a skill. Nature had prevented him from becoming an opera singer; "his voice was not extraordinary, nor did he yet know how to use it." [17] Painting and sculpture presented formidable difficulties. Literature, "for which he had no enthusiasm," [17] won by a process of elimination. And why not? He had always told stories well. He had written voluminous letters, partly narrative and dramatic, to a literary friend. From his reading he had learned the fascinating trick of tracing respectable actions back to their disreputable motives. The unconscious resolution to reincarnate Shakespeare was beginning to make itself felt.[18]

Having decided to become a writer, he very wisely decided also to go to London, the literary center of the English world. The miracles he looked forward to could never happen in Dublin. It represented not only the desolate provincialism and moral bankruptcy of an empty and miniature Protestantism in a misery-ridden Catholic world; it also represented the awful despotism, so hateful to youth, of the present, with its certainties of commonplace and human limitation. "When, on his resignation, Mr. Townshend offered to improve his position, he was civilly but mulishly obdurate." [19] When his father suggested a testimonial to his commercial efficiency, he flew into a rage. In any case, he remained firm against all blandishments, and in March, 1876, set off in a soft hat and tail coat to conquer the world.

CHAPTER THREE

The Days of Methuselah's Youth: A Fatal
Capacity for Business

Methuselah was a hero because he lived for 969 years. Shaw's heroism
also has a time dimension. He has survived nearly 100 years of revolution, years in which worlds rose and faded before his eyes with almost
visionary swiftness. He was born into the rural quiet of a late eighteenth-
century Dublin. His mind awakened to the full clamor of midnineteenth-
century controversy, when science and religion were locked in Titan
combat and Heaven itself was dissolving into a vista of innumerable
stars. A few years later, a little channel steamer carried him across
several decades to the London of the later seventies, where a triumphant
middle class, amid the clatter of countless piston wheels and the haze
of a thousand smokestacks, was prosaically conquering the world.

Fittingly, he arrived during a gigantic change of scenes. It was the
twilight of the great Victorian gods. Top-hatted, gay-waistcoated,
Jovian-whiskered, they were departing one by one, tremendous shapes,
to a bourn past all influence of waistcoats, whiskers, or top hats—
Dickens in 1870, Lyell in 1875, Carlyle and Disraeli in 1881, Darwin
in 1882, Matthew Arnold in 1888. The final thirty years of the century were the ending of the past and the beginning of the present.
They represent an age of transition in unparalleled breadth and complication. During these years there is scarcely a major movement of
thought, ancient or modern, not realized—with various mitigations of
the Zeitgeist—in some commanding figure. The communists are
represented by Marx, the utilitarians by Mill, the scientists by Darwin,
the transcendentalists by Carlyle, the medieval Catholics by Newman,
the stoics and humanists by Arnold, and the romantics by everybody.
Shaw is the product of this age. In forming his creed, he had all history
to choose from.

The old Heaven and the old earth were passing away, and science
and industry were constructing a new world so amusing and comfortable that, for people of a certain income, the prospect of eternal bliss

began to seem anticlimax. Men were not only ceasing to believe; they were losing the desire and the need to believe. The clergy found their most progressive congregations interested in almost everything but Christianity. The poor longed to be rich, and the rich, especially as time went on, enjoyed their wealth frankly. In a world where houses were so warm, dinners so good, and physicians so competent, nonconformist austerity was patently ridiculous. Moreover, the critical intellect, "sinking further and further," finding "'in the lowest depth a lower deep,'" was coming to rest at last, as Newman had predicted, "on the broad bosom of skepticism." [1] The literal truth of the Bible, the divinity of Jesus, the existence of God, His moral governance of the universe, the validity of conscience, even the wisdom of imposing any rational curb whatever on appetite and impulse had been called in question.

Political power, of course, was changing hands. From the agricultural depression of the seventies the English aristocracy never recovered. Canadian and American wheat ruined them as effectually as rotten potatoes had ruined Sir Robert Peel. Their impoverished and depleted ranks were filled by the new plutocracy, and the old traditions of honor, chivalry, public service, and elegant living, maintained in great purity during mid-Victorian days, were diluted by the cynical realism of "good-business" ethics.

Meanwhile, modern life was rapidly becoming a Roman circus for the delectation, and the deception, of Demos. Stark numbers—the immense growth of population alone—had made him a giant. A long series of enactments were mitigating the awful sufferings which the Industrial Revolution had laid upon him. Working hours were being reduced, and wages were increasing. Above all, the Reform Bill of 1884 had given him the vote. The result was that some of the shrewdest brains in the country began to devise methods for leading him about by the nose. The art of mass suggestion was developed. Advertisements taught him what to buy; cheap novels and lurid melodramas, what to dream about; and the penny press, what to think—or rather, what to love and hate. Already in the nineties Alfred Harmsworth had discovered that millions could be made by giving the people, for a penny, the kind of news they wanted. Accordingly, sober political discussions gave way to the lurid fascinations of scandal, crime, intrigue, and war. By the same logic, vaudeville was more admired than opera, and horse races became more important than political elections. And yet Joseph Chamberlain was doing his best to make political elections as much like horse races as possible. The issues of empire were no longer settled by stately debate in Parliament but by machine organization and sensational campaigning.

Another result of growing democracy and returning economic distress Shaw himself has summarized:

> After 1875, leaping and bounding prosperity, after a final spurt during which the Income Tax fell to twopence, got out of breath, and has not yet recovered it. Russia and America, among other competitors, began to raise the margin of cultivation at a surprising rate. Education began to intensify the sense of suffering, and to throw light upon its causes in dark places. The capital needed to keep English industry abreast of the growing population began to be attracted by the leaping and bounding of foreign loans and investments, and to bring to England, in payment of interest, imports that were not paid for by exports—a phenomenon inexpressibly disconcerting to the Cobden Club. The old pressure of the eighteen-thirties came back again: and presently, as if Chartism and Fergus O'Connor had risen from the dead, the Democratic Federation and Mr. H. M. Hyndman appeared in the field, highly significant as signs of the times, and looming hideously magnified in the guilty eye of property, if not of great account as direct factors in the course of events. Numbers of young men, pupils of Mill, Spencer, Comte, and Darwin, roused by Mr. Henry George's "Progress and Poverty", left aside evolution and freethought: took to insurrectionary economics; studied Karl Marx; and were so convinced that Socialism had only to be put clearly before the working-classes to concentrate the power of their immense numbers in one irrestible organization, that the Revolution was fixed for 1889—the anniversary of the French Revolution—at latest.[2]

Into this brave new world so rapidly unfolding, young Shaw came—and promptly resolved to lock himself up in a room. Dedicated to the project of being a genius, he had arrived in London determined never to do another "honest day's work" as long as he lived. To so austere a resolve he was not, however, quite equal. During the next three years, he made at least two brief excursions into the paths of remunerative employment. Vandaleur Lee, the music teacher who had lived at his mother's house in Dublin, tried to make his labors profitable if not honest by himself obtaining a post as musical critic on *The Hornet* and then turning the duties and emoluments over to his young friend. Shaw gave brief and terrible ear to London music, pronounced it hopelessly uninspired, and then, hearing Wagner conduct his own work at Albert Hall, outraged cultured opinion by declaring that "cacophonous charlatan"[3] to be a great composer. *The Hornet*, horrified at the potency of its stinger, hastily parted from that member, and after the nature of a feebler insect, soon succumbed. Shaw obtained work again for a few months in 1879, with the Edison Telephone Company:

> I presently found myself studying the topography of the east end of London, and trying to persuade all sorts of people to allow the Company to put insulators and poles and derricks and the like on their roofs to carry the telephone lines. I liked the exploration involved; but my shyness made the business of calling on strangers frightfully uncongenial; and my sensitiveness, which was extreme, in spite of the brazen fortitude which I simulated, made the impatient rebuffs I had to endure . . . ridiculously painful to me.[4]

Though he felt his work unworthy of him, Shaw always did it with painful thoroughness, so that he might not accept wages not fully earned. His fatal capacity for business once more reasserted itself, and he was made head of his department. In fact, he was only rescued for literature in the nick of time by the collapse of the Edison Company itself. The Bell Company, which took over, offered him a post, but heeding the omen, he fled forever from the scenes of respectability.

> I was an ablebodied and ableminded young man in the strength of my youth [he explains pugnaciously]; and my family, then heavily embarrassed, needed my help urgently. That I should have chosen to be a burden to them instead was, according to all the conventions of peasant lad fiction, monstrous. . . . I did not throw myself into the struggle for life: I threw my mother into it. I was not a staff to my father's old age: I hung on to his coattails.[5]

Nevertheless, hanging on to his father's coattails proved a rather arduous undertaking. The superficial events of those early years were a mockingly successful business career and certain musical evenings in the West End, spent in paroxysms of social dread and a carefully disembalmed evening suit. The realities were shabby clothes, four bare walls, and a table covered with foolscap—some pages neatly bescribbled; some awfully, challengingly blank. For in 1878 he was already writing a novel. Not that he had a story to tell. His own lay all in the future. But never in his life was Bernard Shaw to hesitate for want of a plot. He had a problem—himself, and he had a head seething with other people's ideas. He had read nearly all the books in the British Museum, and it had been like listening to a monologue without being able to get in a word edgewise. The very feel of a pen in his fingers sent the phrases flying through his head. To be sure, he had written innumerable articles and essays, nearly all unpublished, but they were no satisfaction, no real test of strength. Great talents must unite with a great task before a man can rise above himself to the summit of genius.

Was he a genius? Clever young men are always asking themselves this question—especially after embarrassing failures. He had learned a technique for investigating himself. In Scott, Dickens, and particularly in George Eliot, he had observed again and again that fascinating operation by which the author, selecting words like finely adapted knives and scalpels, delicately peels away the prosaic, respectable outer tegument of human nature and reveals the grotesque and undignified realities beneath. Sometimes Bernard had experimented on his acquaintances, flaying them inside his head while he listened to their complacent phrases with a Mephistophelian smile. Now he would apply this method to himself. For several years that nemesis of all clever young men— the Monster Commonplace—had been eyeing him accusingly. Now at last he would take up the challenge.

Perhaps only great men really know the terrors of the commonplace. They turn defeat into victory from a dread of being less than themselves, sharpening the fine edge of genius on the whetstone of despair. Nor is early opportunity or outward advantage any effective bulwark against the Monster. Walter Bagehot had great ability, great intellectual self-confidence, was born into wealth, and enjoyed the important initial success of being a brilliant schoolboy. And yet he has written poignantly of that period when youthful talent, first venturing out in the world, sees all its dazzling notions frowned into absurdities by impressive gray heads and all its lofty aspirations wilted under the deadening monotonies of the ledger and the cashbook. How much grimmer and longer was Shaw's vigil. He knew little but failure in his chosen career up until his twenty-seventh year, nor was he strengthened by the powerful impression of habitual success in boyhood. He had escaped the Monster by escaping Dublin—only to confront him once more in the offices of a London telephone company.

He was probably worried about London, too. Like most puritans, he was acutely conscious of the integrity and importance of his own individual soul. In the midst of so much indifferent humanity, of so much irrelevant striving and working and succeeding and failing, the clear, sharp contours of the mind and personality of Bernard Shaw grew a little vague, even a little insignificant. Surely a 350-page definition of that fanatically honest and independent individual would be extremely valuable. To write a novel was obviously a duty of spiritual clarification. The book was finished in 1879.

CHAPTER FOUR

Five Novels in a Vacuum

Immaturity seems to have come out of the void, without much relation either to England or to the year 1878. It was the twilight of the greater, the heyday of the lesser, Victorians. Arnold was at the end of his career, grown prosperous with describing the evils of the age. Tennyson was enjoying the double advantage of the large income and a beyond-the-tomb celebrity. But Meredith was writing *The Egoist;* Butler was undermining Darwin for a minute audience of Butlerites; Hardy was buryihg himself in German metaphysical gloom and the woman problem. Ouida, Rhoda Broughton, and Mayne Reed were popular; and Eliot, Stevenson, Reade, and Disraeli were at the height of their powers. With all this Bernard Shaw had as yet little connection. To form any idea of *Immaturity* in terms of literary history, one must imagine the *Autobiography* of John Stuart Mill, written, with dashes of Disraelian satire, at the age of twenty-three.

One must also remember that as a boy Shaw had read scraps of Charles Lever's *A Day's Ride: A Life's Romance* and that the novel had made "an enduring impression" on him. There he had found at least one secret autobiography written by at least two of his artistic selves. Shaw himself explains the autobiography:

> The hero was a very romantic hero, trying to live bravely, chivalrously, and powerfully by dint of mere romance-fed imagination, without courage, without means, without knowledge, without skill, without anything real except his bodily appetites. Even in my childhood I found in this poor devil's unsuccessful encounters with the facts of life, a poignant quality that romantic fiction lacked.[1]

The two artistic selves were the comic storyteller, who exploited folly with gay anticlimax, and the relentless natural historian, who recorded it in all its bleak and wretched foolishness. The comedian had already been more fully realized by Dickens, another of Shaw's masters, but the natural historian was the special achievement of Lever, who, in delineating his hero, Algernon Sidney Potts, had, as Shaw says, "discovered a new seriousness in dealing with Potts's disease." [1] One finds this same seriousness in *Immaturity*, as one finds many other qualities of *A Day's Ride* in Shaw's subsequent novels and plays. There is the same humorous, or ironic, self-revelation, including frank admission of cowardice, the same virtuosity in comic exaggeration and preposterous anecdote, the same scorn of dullness and solid mediocrity, the same romantic preoccupation with success and fame, the same studied impudence and irreverence of fathers, the same hostility between the sexes and reluctance to deal with serious love. Partially, at least, Charles Lever had invented Shavianism before Shaw.

Immaturity contains more ideas and more solemnity than *A Day's Ride*. It is undoubtedly an accurate self-portrait, painted with an admirably conscientious hand, of the youthful Shaw—or perhaps I should say, with Mr. J. P. Hackett, of both youthful Shaws—the young man who was solemn about solemn ideas and the young man who was irrepressibly facetious about solemn people. Of these two, probably the first only was meant to be in the picture, but the second peeps out also—like the tiny devil looking down from the shoulder of a pious maiden on a cathedral façade. The book is well named. Bernard Shaw gravely investigates Bernard Shaw and pronounces him "immature." This, together with a change of jobs, a decorous flirtation, and an irrelevant marriage, is the whole plot. Indeed, the characters are pinned to the vivisection table of psychological analysis so firmly that they are hardly able to wriggle, let alone act. Not that the author lacks employment, for he plays at least two parts himself, and through several long scenes must snatch off the shabby coat and trousers of a philosophical bookkeeper in order to make reply in the petticoats of an oracular seamstress. The characters utter rationalistic opinions on philosophy, ethics, religion, literature, music, and painting, and take a weighty interest in nearly everything except getting on with the story. *Immaturity* hovers between a clinical record and a diary.

In the bookkeeper Smith, the active element in Shaw's own character, the part that believed in its genius and did battle with the Monster Commonplace, is minimized and obscured. Smith feels that bookkeeping is beneath him yet performs his duties with elaborate conscientiousness and seems to hope for little more. When he angers his employer with a frank remark, he hails the event as an omen and insists on being fired. He shows a mild interest in the oracular dressmaker, writes a little poetry, and dreams of a beautiful dancer whom he has seen at the Alhambra Music Hall, but it is uncertain whether he admires her person or her art. He becomes private secretary to an Irish Member of Parliament, introduces system and order into his affairs, and then wonders anxiously whether he is justified in devoting his abundant leisure to his own studies. He exchanges decorous remarks and glances with the Irish gentleman's beautiful daughter, she marries another, and Smith goes his way, "enjoying the prospect of a long respite from love-making and very far from realizing the ineptitude with which he has conducted it." [2] In short, his resistance to his true adversary is incipient, passive, and confused. He does not know what he is fighting. He is hopelessly immature.

The novel is not very well written, yet about page 200 it improves greatly; and now and then throughout, the genius that is Bernard Shaw descends mysteriously into the stripling and takes up the pen for a few lines. The description of the Alhambra is worthy of his hand, and comic touches in the courtship of Scott and Harriet clearly presage him. One of the most attractive features of the book is the mixture of youthful gusto and clerkish conscientiousness with which the author explores the possibilities of his medium. He records the details of a sitting room in a third-class London boardinghouse as though he were making a series of ledger entries, infinitely clear and precise.

Doubtless in the full excitement of literary creation, Shaw felt that he had written a masterpiece and for some time expected wealth and fame to arrive in the next mail. Instead, a certain brown-paper package began to appear with relentless regularity and accusation of failure. One publisher expressed interest in future productions, but that was all. The case was clear. The book was not very good, and above all, it was not, except in its rigid observance of the decencies, Victorian. No one inherits an earldom, makes a fortune, nor marries a guardsman with leather breeches and a magnificent physique. No one plunges to ruin for the greater glory of innocence and respectability, nor at the age of seven undergoes the pathetic horrors and the delicious joys of a Methodist conversion. On the contrary, the hero dares to wonder what the great public bustle is about, and when all the beautiful young ladies are married off, sighs with relief instead of being heartbroken. *Immaturity* suffered the consequences and remained unpublished for fifty years. Even the mice, says Shaw, "had not been able to finish it." [3]

Between his first and his second novel, Shaw made important discoveries in the great world outside his own head. He discovered the terrible Depression of 1880, the London debating societies, the art of public speaking, and the marriage problem. He was preparing himself for socialism and becoming a formidable amateur in music. At his own request, his mother was teaching him how to sing, and he was learning "how to play the classical symphonies and overtures in strict time by hammering the bass in piano duets with his sister." [4] He also shattered his mother's nerves and ideals by playing his favorite selections from

Wagner. "She never complained at the time, but confessed it after we separated, and said that she had sometimes gone away to cry. If I had committed a murder I do not think it would trouble my conscience very much, but this I cannot bear to think of." [5] He was also pursuing his hero Smith's inquiries into all sorts of unlikely regions. A friend, justifiably concerned about the welfare of Shaw's soul, begged him to go to Father Addis of the Brompton Oratory. The Father argued a Maker of the Universe. Shaw argued a Maker of the Maker. The Father replied that one could believe in an endless series of Makers but that it is more sensible to believe in One.

> By your leave [said Shaw], it is as easy for me to believe that the universe made itself as that a maker of the universe made himself: in fact much easier; for the universe visibly exists and makes itself as it goes along, whereas a maker for it is a hypothesis. Of course we could get no further on these lines. He rose and said that we were like two men working a saw, he pushing it forward and I pushing it back, and cutting nothing; but when we had dropped the subject and were walking through the refectory, he returned to it for a moment to say that he should go mad if he lost his belief. I, glorying in the robust callousness of youth and the comedic spirit, felt quite comfortable and said so; though I was touched, too, by his evident sincerity.[6]

This quotation suggests how early Shaw had the idea of an evolving deity and a developing cosmos. Apparently, also, long before he had read Butler or Bergson, he had taken to heart John Stuart Mill's "Utility of Religion," published in 1874.

What first interested Shaw in socialism? Partly, perhaps, Mill's posthumous articles on the subject. Much more, no doubt, his own plight and personal experiences. His London workroom was the cocoon in which the neat, meticulous young land agent was metamorphosed into a gaunt revolutionist in a long black coat, green with decay, and a treacherous stovepipe always on the verge of collapse. Those who knew him in those days describe him as looking like "a fairly respectable plasterer." [7] In his musical evenings in the West End, he was meeting young men of wealth, culture, and social assurance. What he suffered from his own poverty, his own superficial education, his own narrow background and experience, he has himself indicated:

> To be on the down grade from the *haute bourgeoisie* and the landed gentry to the nadir at which the younger son's younger great-grandson gives up the struggle to keep up appearances; to have the pretence of a culture without the reality of it . . . ; to be educated

[25]

neither at the Board School and the Birbeck, nor at the University, but at some private adventure academy for the sons of gentlemen; to try to maintain a select circle by excluding all frankly poor people from it, and then find that all the rest of the world excludes you— that is poverty at its most damnable.[8]

When did Shaw himself "give up the struggle to keep up appearances?" Contrasting the solemn, fastidious tone of *Immaturity* with the jaunty, satiric tone of *The Irrational Knot,* one suspects between his first and second novels.

In *The Irrational Knot* (1880), he makes use of his musical evenings in the West End and of his experiences with the telephone company. For the first time he discusses business and politics and hints cheerfully of social revolution. Grave suspicion is cast on the social utility of elegant idleness, conventional wooing, and conventional marriage. Children, if reared in the house, become insufferable nuisances whom parents inevitably misunderstand and neglect. The respectable mantle of John Stuart Mill is lifted and the cloven hoof of Samuel Butler becomes visible.[9] The incipient socialist is unconsciously preparing himself for the revelations of George and Marx.

This time Shaw was practical enough to provide himself with a subject and a considerable stock of plot. The subject—marriage between a workingman and a young lady of rank—was not new, but it gave him a chance to get in some smashing hits against "society." And he had a splendid bludgeon—the superlogical workingman himself, who combines a keen sense of the proprieties with a rationalistic delight in demolishing them and great practical usefulness with the impregnability of undoubted cultural superiority, being an electrical inventor by trade and a musical genius for amusement.

Shaw had with some complacency observed man as God made him. Conolly represents man as Shaw would make him: a wonderful mechanical substitute who thinks, feels, loves, and forgives with unfailing rationality. In action he is of course an insufferable prig. Eleanor McQuinch cannot stand him, his wife cannot stand him, and Shaw himself is dubious at the end of the novel. Though he does move about with a certain Frankenstein energy and consistency, Conolly does not come to life. Readers will believe in walking satires but not in walking sermons.

For this reason Sholto Douglas, though equally a caricature, is much more convincing. Like many of Shaw's later creations, he is incredible, but he is alive. Though well drawn, Marian, the sentimental and complaisant wife, is drearily insipid; yet she and Conolly are an interesting early example of that opposition between rationalist and romantic which Shaw was later to discover in Ibsen and finally to elaborate in his own plays. Marmaduke Lind is an attempt at the clever, idle young man whom later Wilde distilled into pure wit in his Algy and Shaw clothed in autobiographical flesh and blood in Charteris. Eleanor Mc-Quinch has the interest of self-portraiture, being Shaw plus ill temper, a combination frequently to be found in his plays. As a matter of fact, all the characters tend to become Shaws in a crisis, and even Marian can defy Douglas at his haughtiest: "Do not try again to browbeat me into telling you a falsehood, Sholto." [10] All the characters are also broad types, lacking the psychological detail and elaborate motivation common in the modern novel. Indeed Shaw is much less interested in the causes of situations than in their dramatic possibilities. He has very little to say about why Susanna drank, but he portrays her drunkenness with great effect. He writes novels like a dramatist.

Though still a crude performance, *The Irrational Knot* is an immense improvement on *Immaturity*. Shaw's five-pages-a-day rule had worked some havoc. The dialogue, for example, contains far too many "how do you do"s, "good morning"s, and "good evening"s. Nevertheless, it is on the whole compact, forceful, and witty, building itself into many sparkling, truly Shavian scenes.

The Irrational Knot was too revolutionary even for the unsoundest publishers. Now two brown paper parcels came back relentlessly in the mail, until it became difficult to find the necessary pennies to send them off again. The Monster Commonplace smiled hideously. Apparently Shaw could endure that smile. Could he still believe in his genius? He has denied that he ever hoped, and it is customary to quote the line from "Caesar and Cleopatra": "He who has never hoped can never despair." But surely he who has never hoped and never despaired never wrote five novels. Rebelling against invariable failure, the will may give itself up to brief paroxysms of hopeless industry, but it does not persist altogether without hope. Shaw had learned enough already to know that he could learn almost infinitely more. He set grimly to work on *Love among the Artists*. Composition was interrupted by the smallpox, contracted in the epidemic of 1881. It was his first grave illness, and as Mr. Pearson observes, "a humiliating exposure of his mortality." [11] Moreover, he had been vaccinated and was guaranteed immune for life. Shaw revenged himself on mortality by a lifelong hostility to doctors and medicine.

Love among the Artists undoubtedly reflects the bitterness of repeated failure. Owen Jack, the hero, is a great composer long neglected by an ignorant public.

I have never . . . [he bursts out] composed one page of music bad enough for publication or performance. I have drudged with pupils when I could get them, starved in a garret when I could not; endured to have my works returned to me unopened or declared inexecutable by shopkeepers and lazy conductors; written new ones without any hope of getting even a hearing for them; dragged myself by excess of this fruitless labor out of horrible fits of despair that come out of my own nature; and throughout it all have neither complained nor prostituted myself to write shopware.[12]

The theme of the novel embodies such a declaration of faith as one might expect from thwarted genius: great artists believe in themselves; uninspired craftsmen do not. The uninspired craftsman is Adrian Herbert, a romantic, who is modest, gentle, and conventional; the great artist, Jack, a realist, who is proud, eccentric, insulting, and brilliant. But Jack is by no means the mere mouthpiece of Shaw's discontent. Extremely ugly and impishly delighting in his ugliness, austere in his personal habits, scrupulously honest, fanatically independent, kind toward those whom he admires and harshly contemptuous of all others, morbidly sensitive and even timorous yet brutally frank, puckishly fond of stirring up turmoil, patient in the pursuit of his art yet infinitely impatient in all else, Jack is by far the most complicated character Shaw had thus far attempted—a remarkably faithful portrait of a fragment of himself and a good deal besides, all seen with admirable detachment and illustrated with much verve and considerable distinctiveness.

The other characters are not remarkable, except perhaps Mrs. Beatty, a truly Shavian comic figure, who defends extraordinary prejudices with extraordinary logic.

Love among the Artists shows at once more skill and less spirit than *The Irrational Knot*. This is particularly true of the dialogue, which is more smooth and natural but less compact and pointed. From the speeches of Charles, the drunken soldier, one observes that Shaw is already beginning to acquire his wonderful command of cockney, which he owes in part to philological studies made at this time with his friend Lecky. He has also learned much about scene construction and is beginning to make some use of anticlimax and dramatic reversal. In Chapter Six, for example, the lovers' quarrel and the encounters between Mrs. Beatty, her husband, and Mary Sutherland want only some cutting and highlighting to be truly excellent.

Love among the Artists is also interesting as an early attempt at a "Candida," which, together with nearly a dozen other subjects, deals with genius. Both works try to answer the question: "What is the fate of genius in the world?" Both set up, in the two principal male characters, an opposition between implausible genius and plausible mediocrity and between a life devoted exclusively to art and one partially diverted by marriage. But *Love among the Artists* is an architectural platitude. Even the dullest reader sees at a glance that eventually Herbert will achieve a respectable failure, and Jack, a terrifying success. "Candida" presents an opposition which is at once much more dramatically conceived and much closer to the center of the problem. Morell and Marchbanks have about them "the grandeur of generality." They imply volumes about success and genius. Jack and Herbert are less illuminating, largely because they belong to a design less well considered.

Love among the Artists is filled with irrelevancies, with characters that have little to do with the action and with action that has little to do with the characters. Above all, it is filled with irrelevant young ladies. The young author is sufficiently interested in girls to admit them in considerable numbers into his story, but he has a puritan prejudice against their causing young men to fall in love, and hence the theme of artists in love, suggested by the title, fails to condense into anything clearer than a bare indication of the "poet's secret" with which "Candida" concludes—that artists do not need love.

The new novel was sent off—and the brown parcels returned more frequently than ever. It was uncanny. Clearly his novels were better than many he had read by reputed authors. Or were they? Of course they had some minor faults. . . . But if they had minor faults that he could see, might they not have major faults that he could not see? He began to think about another novel.

Besides attending all the socialist and philosophical meetings in London, young Shaw apparently had time to frequent the prize ring, of which he soon characteristically acquired "inside knowledge," as well as the skill of an amateur. Frank Harris reluctantly concedes that he was for many years a very passable boxer. At any rate, in his next novel, *Cashel Byron's Profession* (1882), he deserts the brushes and the easel for the gloves and the sponge bucket. A superrational young lady of rank and fortune demonstrates her rationality by marrying a professional fighter who has learned the principles of Shavianism—including the doctrines of antivivisection, the spontaneity of genius, and the necessary enmity of parents and children—from his experiences in the ring. "I believe," explains the heroine to her cousin, "in the doctrine of heredity; and as my body is frail and my brain morbidly active, I think my impulse towards a man strong in body and untroubled in mind a trustworthy one. You can understand that; it is a plain proposition in eugenics." [13] And a plain proposition, also, in Shaw's later creed of the Life Force, according to which a mysterious vital urge, entering into inorganic matter eons ago, produced life and has guided its evolution upward. This force manifests itself in human consciousness chiefly in terms of subrational instinct and impulse. At the close of the novel, Lydia is clearly in the hands of the Life Force. The children are a success, but the marriage is indifferent. That it lasted a day is a stupendous miracle. Surely no ex-prize fighter ever showed more physical restraint.

The truth is that Shaw had not learned from experience. He has allowed that superlogical electrical inventor, Conolly, after nearly ruining one story, to don petticoats and scramble into the principal role of another. The reader might endure Lydia Carew's priggishness, appalling as it is; but surely he cannot endure her loquacity. And by filling her full of cogs and springs instead of motives and feelings, Shaw has completely avoided the whole problem of her struggle with the Life Force, which might have been interesting. Cashel Byron is agreeable, if one could only keep one's mind off his lugubrious fate, and the author shows natural skill in making prize fighting—as later he made prostitution and munitions manufacturing—a blind from which to attack more respectable professions. But perhaps the most successful parts of the book are the scenes from low life, particularly Mrs. Ned Skene's anecdotes of the prize ring. It is surprising that Shaw can slip directly from the sparkling comedy of Mrs. Skene to the desolate gravity of Lydia Carew. But a solemnity about ideas is the temptation of theorists. Shaw's sense of humor had not yet soaked through his whole mind.

Stevenson, with typical enthusiasm, has discovered great merits in the novel, but I cannot dissuade myself from the conviction that it represents a falling off from the previous two. It is less witty, less distinguished, and less concentrated. Moreover, it contains some appalling offenses against the reader's patience, of which Lydia Carew is only the weightiest. There are minor Lydias, Alice Goff and Lucian Webber, and there is a six-page posthumous letter of parental advice from Lydia's father, the unwearied didacticism of which establishes the importance of heredity more effectually than does anything else in the book. How may this retrogression in a promising young author be explained? In my opinion, by the fact that he had no audience. Shaw exorcised the Demon Commonplace by an act of faith. He told himself, very firmly, that he was a genius and took up the pen. Such a man loses the valuable sense of a reader peering critically over his shoulder. Indeed, having failed to interest editors, he dare not think of such a reader. Consequently, he is not sufficiently on guard against himself. He does not test and retest his ideas and phrases. Lacking the spur and momentum of applause, he does not hoist himself up by the bootstraps and write and rewrite—

not merely with care but with as fresh a mind as possible—for the eighth, ninth, and tenth times. *Cashel Byron* seems to me the work of an isolated talent, the kind of novel that a clever young man might write on a desert island.

Late in 1882, Shaw read Henry George's *Progress and Poverty.* The intellectual heavens opened up, and he saw that poverty is the fundamental evil in human life. Shortly after, he read Karl Marx's *Capital,* and again the intellectual heavens opened up, even more profoundly than before. Again he saw the fundamental evil of human poverty, depicted with an awful statistical vividness, and he perceived that the remedy was Marxian socialism. Henceforth a dedicated man, he determined to "produce a novel which should be a gigantic grapple with the whole social problem." "When I had finished two chapters of this enterprise—chapters of colossal length, but containing the merest preliminary matter—I broke down in sheer ignorance and incapacity." [14] The two chapters, written in 1883, were later published as a complete novel, *An Unsocial Socialist,* in which Marxism and the novelistic art are joined in a strange *mariage de convenance.* Shaw does indeed grapple with the whole social problem—in an ungovernable fury of irreverent didacticism. A bargeman illustrates the subsistence law of wages; a shepherd exposes capitalistic greed hiding behind Malthus's doctrine of population. A lecture on bourgeois medical ethics is intruded at a deathbed, and another on exchange value at the graveside. In headlong flight from two parsons and a dozen policemen, the hero pauses to summarize to his wife with admirable clarity and completeness the whole contents of *Capital* and "The Communist Manifesto." There is also an economic history of the nineteenth century, together with a moving account of the miseries of the exploited classes and the saga of that economic Mephistopheles, the great predatory capitalist.

The last of five bitter failures, *An Unsocial Socialist* is one of the gayest books Shaw ever wrote. The paradox is easily explained. Gaiety is his natural artistic idiom. Moreover, he had found a faith. He was exuberantly happy in a dazzling new certainty. In a sense, Marxism accounts for both the strength and the weakness of the book. *An Unsocial Socialist* is the story of Sidney Trefusis, a wealthy young man who, stricken with remorse for his father's economic virtues, deserts his newly married wife and devotes all his money and talents to the destruction of capitalism. From this point the story becomes a fairy tale. Like Robin Hood, the hero goes to live in a forest and there transforms himself into a goblin called Jeff Smilash, who, gifted with magical powers of impudence, wit, and bad grammar, lives a merry life confounding the rich in argument and converting the poor to Marxism. But this is not all. There is a girls' college nearby, and Smilash is a goblin with glimmerings of Ibsenite emancipation and alarming tendencies toward free love. Moreover, he can change himself into the elegant Trefusis at will. What might not be expected from such materials? Shaw himself is justly proud of the early chapters, but the powerful initial enchantment rapidly pales; the reader yawns. Why? Because the author cheerfully sacrifices art to economics. Plot is a mere convenience. People rush to London or to Lyvern merely to fly into a rage or to make a few clever remarks. There is no close development of motives, no genuine psychological entanglement. The characters fade into the most insipid shadows, leaving Trefusis, who alone remains vivid, to preach his Marxism on and on in a capitalistic society hardly worth the effort of destruction.

Indeed, between the earlier and the later parts of the novel, there is a sharp break—a lapse of time, a change of place and mood. Sylvan fairy tale becomes Marxist-Ibsenite social drama. Marriage as well as poverty proves to be a problem in the modern capitalistic state. All the young ladies of Miss Wilson's school are now extremely unhappy, either because they have married or because they have not. Trefusis, whose wife has been murdered with pneumonia by a ruthless novelistic hand, prescribes a cure for each young lady in turn and finally marries the ghost of one, who in the earlier fairy tale had been a delightful female Shaw. And yet the later part of the novel is not entirely without recommendation. Shavian intellectual drama is obviously struggling to be born. There is a titanic "discussion" scene, in which, between intervals of shooting the heads off marble busts in his study with a pistol, Trefusis once more puts, for two mildly bewildered aristocrats, the whole of Marx into a few thousand well-chosen words and even explains middle-class temperance (for other people) according to the iron law of wages.[15] There is another remarkable scene, in which the Shavian heroine proposes to the Shavian hero, on the condition that the marriage be scrupulously loveless.

In fact, Shaw seems to have invented Shavian love after protracted and conscientious failure in depicting any other kind. Every resource of Victorian melodrama is frantically utilized to bring men and women together under romantic circumstances, yet romance obstinately refuses to take place. The young people talk with each other so formally that any intimacy strikes one as utterly incredible. One is told that Sir Charles married his wife because of her voluptuous beauty, yet he seems susceptible to nothing but the sharpness of her tongue. The familiar pattern of the Shavian "love scene" already begins to show itself. Shavian antisentimentality was born of the despair of Shavian sentiment.

An Unsocial Socialist is, in a peculiar sense, a complete Shaw, an epitome not only of all his literary vices and virtues but of nearly all his ideas and poses. There are the familiar Butlerisms (before Butler), and there is suddenly, as though at the touch of an enchanter's wand, nearly the whole Alice's Wonderland of his later theories. There is Marxism— already with the Fabian reservation that socialism must come gradually.[16] There are lectures on the famous Shavian tenets that Shakespeare will be outdated by the socialist revolution; that genius deserves no special payment because genius costs its possessor no labor; that rich men, even when they want to, cannot possibly give their wealth to the poor; and that capitalism and free trade will eventually turn England into a mere luxury resort inhabited by the idle rich and their servants. There are ferocious Shavian-Millite attacks on bourgeois marriage, with its ridiculous assumption that two people of opposite sex can actually remain in love with each other throughout life. There is the familiar Shavian-Marxist maneuver of demonstrating how individual virtue or justice is impossible in an individualistic society. There are glimmerings of the doctrine, fundamental to the Life Force creed, that in mating the human female pursues the male. Henrietta, Trefusis's deserted wife, hunts him with the lachrymose ferocity of a lioness bereft of her cubs. Finally, there is the authentic Shavian impudence and effrontery. With cold rationality, Trefusis adopts in every situation precisely that course of action best calculated at once to gain his ends and to infuriate conventional heads and hearts. Moreover, he is absolutely unscrupulous. Commenting on his own work, Shaw explains:

> The hero is remarkable because, without losing his preeminence as hero, he not only violates every canon of propriety, like Tom Jones or Des Grieux, but every canon of sentiment as well. In an age when the average man's character is rotted at the core by the lust to be a true gentleman, the moral value of such an example as Trefusis is incalculable.[17]

In short, he is willing, at least on paper, to throw even morality overboard, if in so doing he can hit hypocrisy and timid conventionality on the head.

An Unsocial Socialist strikingly resembles a great work of Shaw's maturity, "Man and Superman." Both Trefusis and Tanner are impudent and furious rationalists. Both are young capitalists devoted to the extinction of their class. Both are hunted by desperately biological females. The first point of resemblance, at least, may be easily explained. Trefusis and Tanner are similar portraits of the official and institutional Shaw which the world and the newspapers know so well. But Trefusis, because he is depicted within the larger and more intimate frame of the novel and by a more youthful and naïvely revealing hand, affords many glimpses of the elusive, secret Shaw. His relations with women are particularly significant. Why has Shaw adhered so persistently to the idea that the female always pursues the male? Partly, of course, because he loves paradox and because there is considerable truth in his contention. But also because, especially as he grew famous, he was the kind of man that women pursue. Like Trefusis, he was one of those independent, mercurial, little-sensual natures, whose instinct of sex refines itself into forms of social amusement and intellectual excitement, who prefer a sense of momentary power over a woman to a sense of permanent possession, who like very much to fascinate an attractive lady for an hour and very little to accept the responsibility of her affection for a lifetime.

These five novels, written in solitude and for the most part hidden away from the sight of the world, represent a kind of embryonic development toward genius, in which the simple and rudimentary Shaw develops gradually, with some capricious deviation into fish and fowl, toward the wonderful and complete Shaw, with all his peculiar talents and ideas upon his head. In these few years the solemn stylist is changing into a hilarious wit. The modestly antlered Millite rationalist is acquiring—within the ample womb of his respectable London garret—a strange Schopenhauerian proboscis, terrible Butlerian horns, and a fiery breath and inward furnace of Georgite and Marxian combustibles.

Not only a genius but a world also is struggling to be born—a world filled with ingenious devices of satirical ambush and torture, where realists overcome romantics, socialists confound capitalists, and rationalists instruct everybody; where, perhaps too frequently, Shaw meets Shaw and platitude never enters. Unfortunately, it is a world as yet not platitude-proof, as yet not wholly rescued from the chaos of artistic ineptitude. Especially in his last novel, Shaw gives ample proof that he possesses the power of creation, but—still an apprentice deity—he has not yet acquired the technique. He has not learned the language of his world, how to organize it into closely logical scenes, how to make it delineate those admirable characters—in whom the probable is sometimes rendered fantastic and the fantastic sometimes probable—with sufficient energy to keep them securely in flesh and blood until the end of the performance. Much of this he was to learn, as a dramatic critic, by watching others.

CHAPTER FIVE

A Thinking Machine and a Prophet

Shaw's biography cannot be written as a single narrative about a single man. There are many Shaws—Shaw the author, Shaw the critic, Shaw the metaphysician, Shaw the socialist, each with his particular adventures and achievements, his particular development and inward logic. The biographer finds himself committed to a *Shaw and His Circle*, of which every member is a separate Shaw. He also finds himself writing the history of England.

Between his first and his second novel, the youthful Bernard had, as I have already intimated, discovered British politics, at that time in a posture of spectacular disaster. Having begun magnificently in 1875 with the purchase of the Suez Canal and come to a grandiose climax in 1878 with the Congress of Berlin and "peace with honor," Disraeli ended his ministry miserably and prosaically the following year in financial depression and "foreign incidents." His Moslem allies were massacring Greek and Bulgarian Christians in the Balkans, and British troops were being massacred by insignificant Zulus and Afghans in obscure corners of the globe.

The agricultural depression, beginning with bad harvests in 1874, had quietly ruined the old aristocracy, then spread to finance and industry, until by 1880 unemployment, starvation, and despair had sounded depths hardly known before or since. Even Disraeli could not escape the fallacy that he had caused these catastrophes. Nor did Gladstone develop scruples in the interests of truth. Having some time before firmly announced his retirement, that statesman had kept one eye on the Greek classics and the other on the political situation. Now he came forth from his study, roaring vengeance against unspeakable Turks and Tories and purring promises of succor and protection for unemployed workmen at home and helpless Christians abroad. He was swept triumphantly into office. The ensuing years were to see an incalculable development of the labor and socialistic movements. History was preparing itself for George Bernard Shaw.

It was also preparing George Bernard Shaw for history. The nineteenth century was an age of reason faced with a world of problems. It was therefore also an age of debating societies. Indeed the nation itself was still ruled by a debating society, for the House of Commons possessed minds independent enough to be changed and consequently tongues eloquent enough to change them. And Parliament was but the apex of a vast pyramid of discussion. All London, all England debated in those days. For decades *The Times* was filled with the announcements of meetings, and they are described at length in such works as the *Autobiography* of John Stuart Mill and the novels of Disraeli. Science, religion, art, literature, history, politics, the living habits of the mastodon, and the legislative powers of Anglican convocation—everything was debatable. Some groups consisted of tradesmen and laborers; some, like the Metaphysical Society, represented exclusively the Olympus of contemporary fame. Some dined, some did not. Little men tried to make themselves feel important by adopting elaborate parliamentary procedure; important people tried to be easy by dispensing with all formality. Some meetings were sleepy and dignified, some boiled with excitement, and not a few ended in physical combat.

The story of Shaw's activities in the debating societies is as copious and intricate as the intrigues of the Guelphs and the Ghibellines or the political affiliations of a Bosnian bomb thrower. He confined himself by no means to politics and philosophy. In F. J. Furnivall's Shelley, Browning, and New Shakespear Societies, for example, he began to acquire that knowledge of the polite upper middle-class mind and that mastery of the techniques of shocking, baffling, and unhinging it which he later used with such effect in his plays and criticism.

Some time in the winter of 1879 Shaw attended a meeting of the Zetetical Society, an organization of advanced young middle-class intellectuals dedicated to the worship of Mill, Malthus, Darwin, Spencer, and lesser deities. Shaw took a seat and listened—but not for long. Soon his temples began to throb and his mouth to grow dry with a desire to speak and a fear that he might find an opportunity to do so. He did. With an air of impudence and a dizzy head, he rose on precarious legs, babbled hazily for a few minutes into tiers of intent faces, and then sat down. No one seemed to think he had been conspicuously bad, but vanity convinced him that his remarks had been utterly fatuous. He resolved on the spot to become an effective speaker. At later meetings he spoke incessantly and soon became feared as much for his volubility as for his wit. Indeed the Zetetical, a heavy and skeptical society, doubted his sanity with implacable obstinacy—until a lady in an aesthetic dress lectured on art. "I wiped the floor with that meeting," says Shaw, "and several members confessed to me afterwards that it was this performance that first made them reconsider their first impression of me as a bumptious, discordant idiot." [1]

He joined other societies, continued to speak, developed coolness and fluency; from an old Alsatian opera singer, Richard Deck, he learned "how to articulate and emphasize his consonants for public delivery." [2] He also began to teach himself the art, which he later mastered so thoroughly, of acting the role of his own most ardent admirer and supporter. During the principal speech, he would hand up to the chairman a card upon which was written, "Mr. Bernard Shaw would like to ask a question." At his earliest opportunity, the chairman would shout, "Mr. ———!" Shaw would then instantly arise and put a question calculated to "make a worm turn and a rabbit fight." [3] Thus he became infamous. As time went on, he acquired a dangerous taste for large, turbulent public halls, so that when after an arduous day of writing he went out to seek his pleasure, he ranged the debating societies as another man might range the gin shops.

He was actuated only in part by the thirst for life, knowledge, and power. The political appetite for power over others was probably secondary to the ethical appetite for power over himself. At this time he was a Sholto Douglas who wanted to be a Conolly, a Saranoff who wanted to become a Bluntschli. He was a complexly objectionable and amiable, an intricately impulsive, excitable, and inhibited young romantic who was determined to convert himself into a smooth, efficient, dispassionate machine for thinking ideologies, making speeches, and manipulating people. He wanted to play the parts of both father and son in a new education of John Stuart Mill. With a minimum of aid from others, he taught himself how to write, sing, and speak in public. Later he acquired a broad knowledge of art, drama, literature, economics, and sociology; and developed his own spelling, punctuation, diet, mode of dress, manners, tact, committee personality, and literary style; so that by a prodigious effort he actually became the fabulous machine, and infinitely more than the machine, that he aspired to be. Perhaps it is regrettable that he did not aspire to be more of a human being, that so much self-discipline did not lead to humane self-control. For Shaw's self-control, though elaborate, complex, and efficient, was comparatively superficial. He was an anarchist who disciplined his talents. The result is that though he did succeed wonderfully in becoming Bluntschli, he never ceased to be Saranoff.

It is a fact of great importance that Shaw learned to think in an atmosphere of eager and passionate discussion. Perhaps he was too self-willed to learn in any other school. Perhaps in any other school his peculiar powers would not have attained the same perfaction. Nevertheless, it is unfortunate that his education provided no safeguard against the excess of his virtues. The result was that a rhetorical mind became yet more rhetorical, and the talents of the market place were developed into sophistical refinement. There is hardly a truth and hardly an error to which he has not given brilliant and epigrammatic expression; hardly a creed and hardly a cause which he has not set forth in strong and partisan argument.

One evening at the Zetetical Society, as Shaw sat in trembling fear of the urge to speak, a young man arose, who, though actually not more than twenty-one, looked like a middle-aged French provincial actor.

> He had a fine forehead, a long head, eyes that were built on top of two highly developed organs of speech (according to the phrenologists), and remarkably thick, strong, dark hair. He knew all about the subject of debate; knew more than the lecturer; knew more than anybody present; had read everything that had ever been written; and remembered all the facts that bore on the subject. He used notes, read them, ticked them off one by one, threw them away, and finished with a coolness and clearness that seemed to me miraculous. This was the ablest man in England: Sidney Webb.[4]

Here was the Conolly, the Bluntschli he secretly longed to become. Shaw hastened to make the acquaintance of the ablest man in England. "Quite the wisest thing I ever did," he says, "was to force my friendship on him . . . and to keep it." [4]

At that time Sidney Webb had a post in the Office of the Surveyor of Taxes. He had finished his formal schooling at sixteen, had gone to night school, and passed every imaginable examination on every imaginable subject—including those for the Civil Service—with fantastically high grades. In spite of official duties and many recondite avocations, he was shortly to pass with brilliant success his examinations for the L.L.B. degree in law. His future life was to be a prosaic and doctrinaire fairy tale: he was to win a rich and handsome young lady by being a socialist, to marry her with great scandal to her relatives, to live with her a life of ideal romance among statistics and blue books, and eventually to conquer the world in a strangely austere manner—by accumulating facts and writing formidable treatises on difficult subjects.

When he met Shaw, Webb was a Millite.[5] In fact, he was a kind of John Stuart Mill brought up to date, for like Mill he possessed an infinite capacity for rapid mental labor and—what is the greatest luxury of a scholarly existence and the most brutal weapon of learned controversy —a faultless memory. His intellectual life was not a long, weary, sedentary struggle in which learning hurried breathlessly a book's throw ahead of forgetting. Rather, knowledge, precise and sure, raced triumphantly forward with apprehension. The result was that his mind came

to resemble a vast card index with a convenient system of cross reference. And fortunately, there was another unpatented device attached—
an efficient and cautiously realistic thinking machine. But Webb was a
good deal more than mind and fact. Later, he was to show himself an
astute man of action.

Shaw's instinct was a shrewd one. Associating with Sidney Webb
was like swimming in an ocean of fact. No element could have been
healthier for a young man so full of words and ideas. "As I am and was
an incorrigible mountebank, and Webb was one of the simplest of
geniuses, I was often in the centre of the stage whilst he was invisible in
the prompter's box." [6] Webb was very much at home in the prompter's
box; his specialty was influencing people. Undoubtedly, he had a good
deal to do with forming Shaw's politics and certainly made them sounder
than they would have been otherwise. Perhaps he also made them nar-
rower, for in comparing Shaw with Morris and Ruskin, one is always a
little surprised that so great an artist could have allowed so little scope
to the artistic principle in his social thought.

In 1883 Shaw met Sidney Olivier at the Land Reform Union and
brought him into the Zetetical Society. Like Webb, he became one of
Shaw's lifelong associates. It is natural that, being a Millite, he should
have joined a Millite society. Indeed, the event is probably significant in
calling attention to the importance of that society in Shaw's own development, for though he has spoken rather patronizingly of the Zetetical as
having been swept into "the blind cave of eternal night" [7] by the newer
issue of socialism, yet the friends, the ideas, the issues, and the point of
view which he encountered in that somewhat solemn association of
young men remained with him throughout life. The battles of science
against religion, of evolution against prejudice, of the emancipated
against the womanly woman, he fought as fiercely in 1909 as in 1879.
He was, as I shall try to show more fully later,[8] nearly as much a utilitarian at sixty-three as at twenty-three. In fact, the greater part of his
intellectual development can be explained in terms of the utilitarianism
of the seventies and the romanticism which was at once an accompani-
ment and a reaction to it.

In a letter to Archibald Henderson, Olivier gives an interesting indication of how Shaw struck a critical and cultivated young man at this time:

> Needless to say we delighted in Shaw's society—his talk was a
> continual entertainment; and he regarded it, we tolerantly con-
> sidered, as his duty to talk wittily, if only for practice. And the
> transparent generosity and liberality of his character had an ir-
> resistible charm. But Webb and I were university graduates, I from
> Oxford, and we often judged Shaw's education and his appreciation

of academically and socially established humanities to be sadly defective. . . . On the face of his conversation I thought his apprehension and sympathies in regard to a good deal of the springs of human conduct perversely shallow and limited, and his controversial arguments often cheap and uncritical: an attitude of priggish superiority which he no doubt fully appreciated, and at which he poked fun (in the character of Cokane) in his first play, "Widowers' Houses." [9]

One night, ranging the dens of his peculiar vice, Shaw passed Memorial Hall in Farringdon Street. A meeting was evidently going on, for he could hear the speaker's voice and occasionally the multitudinous whispering and coughing of a great crowd. On the notice board there was a placard:

LAND NATIONALIZATION.
MEMORIAL HALL,
FARRINGDON STREET,
On Tuesday, September 5th, 1882
Under auspices of
THE LAND NATIONALIZATION SOCIETY.
Professor
F. W. NEWMAN
will preside.[10]

Shaw entered. The huge room was packed. Far off on the platform a short, stocky man was speaking. He had a great, shiny bald dome, a sandy, spade-shaped beard, and an unmistakable American accent. The articulation was precise, the voice clear but not deep or melodious, and yet sometimes, when pronouncing certain emotive words, like "liberty" or "poverty," it dropped suddenly to a full, booming resonance and shook the listening mind like a harp string.

One gathered that history was in a situation of stupendous crisis, that a miracle was needed, and as the sharp, earnest voice continued, one became convinced that a miracle would occur. The nineteenth century was a time of unprecedented material wealth. Never in the purple ages of Nineveh or Rome had there been such palaces, such marts, such cities. A few vigorous, somewhat trite Macaulayan periods painted flatteringly the splendor of modern London. But—and here the precise voice dropped—never had there been such poverty. Poverty was the monster, the sphinx,[11] not to answer whose riddle would bring destruction to the world. True, it was a thousand-year-old monster, and the question had long been insistent, but now the peril was acuter, vaster, and therefore critical. But the miraculous answer trembled on the lips of the speaker: art, literature, wisdom, happiness all lay beyond the iron gates of logic and political economy; and those gates were to be unlocked by the magic key of social justice.

The speaker was Henry George. Up to this time Shaw had known poverty only in terms of the commonplace and the shabbily oppressive. He was now in the presence of a man who had known it in terms of the spectacular and the terrible. The life of Henry George had been a grim, fantastic adventure from which, with considerable calm, he had drawn a prosaic and complicated moral. An American, he had grown up in the noise, bustle, and puritanism of the Eastern seaboard; he had sailed the seven seas and touched at the shores of other worlds. In California, where the nineteenth century was spread thinly over the top of a sleepy Spanish past and a magnificent wilderness, he had been prospector, printer, and reporter. He had succeeded and failed many times, and once in San Francisco, when his wife was with child, he found himself in such extremity that he walked up to the first prosperous-looking citizen he met and demanded five dollars. Since then fame and a precarious competency had intervened. His book *Progress and Poverty*, finished in spite of dire need and adversity, had pained San Francisco and astonished the world. Henry George had now gone forth to preach the bible which he had written.

British trade-unionism, timidly liberal till the close of the seventies, became in the early eighties aggressively socialistic. That revolution of attitude, say Beatrice and Sidney Webb, is due to Henry George more than to any other single influence.[12] Certainly the *Zeitgeist* could not have chosen a more effective medium. "You sound like Wendell Phillips reporting St. John the Baptist," remarked Charles Dana to a neophyte whom he had sent to interview the prophet of the single tax.[13]

That Shaw himself was much impressed by George's lecture there can be no doubt.

> It flashed on me then for the first time [he says], that 'the conflict between Religion and Science,' . . . the overthrow of the Bible, the higher education of women, Mill on Liberty, and all the rest of the storm that raged round Darwin, Tyndall, Huxley, Spencer, and the rest, on which I had brought myself up intellectually, was a mere middle-class business. Suppose it could have produced a nation of Matthew Arnolds and George Eliots!—you may well shudder. The importance of the economic basis dawned on me.[14]

To discover in a single night that Mill, Darwin, Tyndall, Huxley, and Spencer were a mere middle-class business—what a revelation! It was the first, or perhaps the second, of Shaw's many gay and witty conversions.

In the act of prostrating himself before an idol, Shaw always had a good look for clay feet. On another occasion he writes of George's lecture:

> I knew he was an American, because he pronounced 'necessarily' —a favourite word of his—with the accent on the third syllable instead of the first; because he was deliberately and intentionally oratorical, which is not customary among shy people like the English; because he spoke of Liberty, Justice, Truth, Natural Law, and other strange eighteenth-century superstitions; and because he explained with great simplicity and sincerity the views of the Creator, who had gone completely out of fashion in London in the previous decade and had not been heard of there since. I noticed, also, that he was a born orator, and that he had small, plump, pretty hands.[15]

Wonderful—that the acolyte could distinguish so sharply between the prophet and the message! But then, clever, superior young men are always much more respectful of ideas than of thinkers.

At any rate, he bought a copy of *Progress and Poverty* and read it. In this book Henry George offers an explanation and a solution for the paradox: Why does increasing economic progress bring increasing poverty? In new communities like San Francisco, where industry was little developed, wages were high and fortunes comparatively modest. In old communities like London, where capital and production were almost unlimited, unemployment was often widespread, wages were in many trades close to the starvation point, and individual fortunes, though few, were enormous. Why? Fundamentally because of the pre-eminence of land, and consequently of the law of rent, in capitalistic economy. Rent determines wages and interest because, fundamentally, land is essential to every kind of production and therefore landowners always take first share. Where rent is high, as in old established communities, interest and wages are notoriously low. The mere presence of people, their activities and demands make ground valuable. Society should receive the value which it creates. In short, landowners should pay a tax equal to the total rent, or "unearned increment" of wealth, which they receive. Then, all other taxes could be abolished, the government would have unlimited funds for unlimited public service, the increasing wealth that goes with increasing civilization would devolve upon the community as a whole—and poverty would be eliminated.

The common socialistic criticism of George is that he does not go far enough. And certainly he does expect miraculous results from very mild medicine. An unearned increment does not accrue to landed wealth alone, nor would the payment of large sums in economic rent to a fallible government necessarily produce utopia. On the other hand, much land has undoubtedly gained value out of all proportion to any useful or social effort made by its owners. Like Mill and others before him, George has indicated a major source of unearned increment. George is significant not so much because he thought as because he believed. He is significant because, with deep feeling and a persuasive voice, with vigorous rhetoric and obvious logic, he convinced great masses of people that poverty is a curable evil.

Shaw was among those masses. He plunged into economic study and socialistic agitation. Characteristically, he elevated poverty into a theological doctrine, making it the original sin from which all other human ills proceed. In fact, he considered physical well-being so much more fundamental than spiritual that, in several of his plays, he has placed himself in the paradoxical position of applauding guilt in order to disparage poverty. By promoting security and prosperity among his munitions workers, the Machiavellian Andrew Undershaft confers benefits greater than those of religion itself, and Mrs. Warren, fairly bursting with unspiritual pride, defies her daughter to maintain that a career of laborious poverty is superior to one of prosperous vice, such as she herself can look back upon. Enough bread and butter will save the world. A curious faith for a puritan, perhaps—and yet not so curious, when one considers the history of puritanism. Shaw's reasons were partly puritanical, partly humanitarian. Poverty is refined and very slow torture. It is shabby, dirty, humiliating, degrading. It is disgusting aesthetically; it offends the puritan sense of neatness. Moreover, it is irrational. It presents a spectacle so obviously wasteful, so acutely distressing that he could not bear to think of it as a permanent condition due to the infirmities of our nature. In short, poverty offers a challenge to faith. Finally, it constitutes an impeachment of human, and therefore Shavian, dignity. This is probably fundamental. It explains why he hated the poor nearly as much as their poverty, and poverty, hardly less than mere unthinking comfort and complacency.

George had of course provided Shaw not only with a religion but with a sword. The sword was the law of rent, which from the *Fabian Essays* to *The Intelligent Woman's Guide* became the basis both of Shaw's social theory and of his polemic against capitalism. What he quickly dispensed with was George's patent medicine, the "single tax" on land. Like many others, he decided George did not go far enough. Shortly after reading *Progress and Poverty,* he went to a meeting of the Social Democratic Federation. There George was destroyed in a parenthesis. Shaw arose to protest and was told condescendingly to read *Capital.* He did so forthwith and found, when he announced the fact, that his advisers were awe-struck, as they had not read it themselves.[16]

And thus he underwent another illumination. His intellectual life at this time was a vista of perpetual dawns and sunsets, so that he lived in the excitement of incessant fresh dedication. Marx had replaced George on the precarious Olympus of Shavian faith.

CHAPTER SIX

On *This Stone. . . .*

By 1884, when Marx, though dead, was still largely unknown and un-hated, Shaw was a thoroughgoing Marxist. In many respects *Capital* was peculiarly suited to be a Shavian bible. It is long, difficult, anti-bourgeois, revolutionary—a book that everybody talks about and no-body reads, that only the determined attempt and only the reckless de-fend. It is in Shaw's mood—full of the passion of the intellect and the gusto of generous denunciation. Finally, it offers satisfaction—super-ficially at least—to the two contradictory impulses of Shaw's mind, the critical and the visionary. It enables a man to dream and at the same time to feel brutally realistic. Out of hard fact and cold logic, it con-structs a ladder to the clouds. Marx is a "scientific" socialist. He speaks of despotism and slavery as economic necessities during certain periods of history and sneers at the "*justice éternelle*" of Proudhon. To many his scathing criticism of capitalism appears as but an inverted picture of utopia. The link between our present and his future is dialectical materi-alism. Marx's peculiar fascination consists in seeming to prove that a utopia is scientifically inevitable. But of course such determinism is simply another kind of predestination. Marxist theory is also an elabo-rate parody of Calvinism, with its own triumphant certainties of election, God's will, final judgment, and heavenly bliss. It appealed not only to the romantic and the rationalist in Shaw but to the puritan as well.

Exactly how far Marx is deterministic is of course a problem. Mr. Sidney Hook makes him something of a pragmatist. His position can-not be understood without reference to the dialectical materialism which he developed by inverting Hegel. That philosopher tried to show that the content of history is logical; Marx, that the content of logic is historical:

> From objective *conditions,* social and natural (thesis), there arises human *needs* and *purposes* which, in recognizing the objective possibilities in the given situation (antithesis) set up a course of *action* (synthesis) designed to actualize these possibilities.[1]

Marx believes that in social theory complete objectivity is impossible. Every body of thought reflects the interest of a class. We understand the past and present not simply by observing them but by studying them in terms of some purpose which we set up in the future. A valid doctrine must have an objective and a subjective moment. It must correspond at once to outward facts and to inward needs. To be proved valid, it must result in successful action. Marxism is the theory and practice of revolution.

Marx's interpretation of history is an illumination arising from his revolutionary purpose. The fundamental fact about a society—what more or less drastically conditions its art, literature, religion, politics, and legal structure—is its mode of production, which determines the distribution of economic power among the classes. As production develops, economic power gets out of adjustment with legal structure, which is the formalized expression of earlier economic relations. A struggle ensues between the class which has legal power and that which has economic power. At length there is a revolution. The first class is overthrown by the second, which then dominates the state in its own interests. History is a series of class struggles.

Modern capitalism began to grow up within the hard shell of feudalism. The discovery and colonization of the New World, trade with the East, general improvement in the means of exchange brought about an amazing development of commerce and industry, which shattered medieval legalism and gained the middle class ever more political power. Economic necessity, or the search for profits, mothered an infinite series of new inventions both social and mechanical—an increasing division of labor, larger scale enterprise, and finally, machines, which in a sense have created the modern world. Machinery is costly; therefore it shifts the ownership of production goods from the workers to the capitalists, making the latter indispensable to the former and dividing society into two hostile camps. Machinery is intricately related to other machinery; therefore it gives rise to the factory system and huge industrial cities, concentrating great numbers of laborers in one place, so that they are led to form unions and revolutionary organizations. Finally, machinery is tremendously productive; therefore capitalism must be continually searching for new markets, spreading its goods, its system, and its problems over the globe. At length the whole world will be divided into the two hostile armies of capital and labor. Capital dominates the political state, the police, and the professional classes. On the other hand, competition is constantly reducing the capitalists in number, enriching tremendously the few that survive and forcing the many that fail into the ever increasing and therefore ever more miserable proletariat. Moreover, periodic crises occur when the productive power of the community, out of harmony with existing property laws, floods the market with goods which the general public has not money to buy. Thus profits are at once the sustenance and the poison of capitalism. They lead it to destruction. More and more the workers perceive that, actually, they have all the power and capitalists all the wealth. Eventually, in the midst of a great depression, they revolt. The capitalistic state collapses, a dictatorship of the proletariat forms the communistic state and as that state becomes unnecessary and withers away, evokes its Hegelian opposite, the classless society.

Shaw's novel *An Unsocial Socialist* (1883), begun soon after his conversion to Marxism, shows him to be a fairly orthodox, if somewhat frivolous, Marxist. Certainly the hero conducts the class war in a very extraordinary fashion. At times he seems to be trying to awaken a workingman's consciousness not among the proletariat but among the aristocracy. One suspects that he has a middle-class prejudice against throwing bombs. Occasionally he threatens catastrophe, but in the rather distant future and always with disarming gaiety. Indeed the new religion has increased rather than diminished Shaw's epileptic tendency to laughter.

After a brief novelistic honeymoon of waging the class war against an exclusive young ladies' seminary, Shaw had to settle down to sober matrimony. Uncongeniality of temperament manifested itself almost at once. In March, 1884, shortly after the Marxist paper *Justice* began to appear, the editors felt it their duty to publish a letter headed "Who is the Thief?" and signed "G. B. S. Larking." Mr. Larking is clearly a respectable member of the lower middle class in a rhetorical state of bewilderment. He feels that in the sacred name of justice the editors have said some very harsh things about our modern bourgeois civilization, which has made us all what we are, including this clever Dr. Marx himself. According to that gentleman's theory of surplus value, the capitalists alone are thieves. But sometimes competition drives profits down to almost nothing. Then the workers get far more of the "plunder" than the capitalists, and the consumers, far more than either. The writer is stricken with an appalling thought. The consumers are ourselves— our wives, our daughters, even the editors of *Justice*. Are we all thieves? Mr. Larking concludes with a pious defense of hearth, home, and country, declaring with fervor that "Britons never shall be slaves." The letter was of course from Shaw. It attacks not the ideas but the temper of Marxism. The Social Democrats are not wrong. In a sense they are worse than wrong. They lack humor. "Who is the Thief?" is a solemnly hilarious satire of a solemn fanaticism. Essentially, it is a comic artist's criticism of Marx. It may also reflect the mood of a man who, as Chesterton says, is so sure of the new truth he has discovered that he must show his exultant high spirits by stretching and twisting it and standing it on its head.

Yet two months later Shaw committed what proved to be a profoundly un-Marxian act: he joined the Fabian Society. The blackness of the heresy was not at once evident. For the Fabians, then wallowing happily in a fiery ideological chaos, were as likely to become Marxists as anything else. To join them was not in itself reprehensible, but to attempt to resolve their bewilderment at once by providing them with a heretical constitution was certainly very serious. The Fabians themselves require a word of historical explanation.

Nineteenth-century socialism is said to pass through two phases— a utopian and a "scientific." The first, begun about 1830 by such men as Owen and Fourier, aspired by education, rational decision, and voluntary cooperation to establish miniature static utopias in the immediate future. It was idyllic, nonpolitical, and in its leadership, middle-class. "Scientific" socialism, beginning in 1848 with the publication of the "Communist Manifesto" by Marx and Engels, was based on the economic interpretation of history and saw in contemporary society forces which in time would inevitably produce socialism. It emphasized evolution and revolution rather than any utopia to which those forces might lead. Holding that labor would eventually overthrow capital, it identified itself with the workingman. It was exclusive, violent, and Machiavellian. To this later phase of socialism might be added as an alternative what Mr. Archibald Henderson calls "practical socialism," which became an articulate creed in Mill's later writings. Practical socialism was evolutionary, gradualistic, latitudinarian, constitutional, argumentative, and frequently middle-class.

Even in sociology, ontogeny sometimes recapitulates phylogeny. The Fabian Society is an instance. It developed from utopian to practical socialism, with the mildest suggestion of Marxian characteristics intervening. Founded in 1883 as the Fellowship of the New Life, a communistic society dedicated to somewhat vague moral, religious, and social ideals, it belonged at the outset, in mood and type, to the earlier phase of socialism. Indeed, it was directly linked with that period by a significant event. The granddaughter of Robert Owen was invited to the first meeting. What is perhaps even more significant—she did not come. Everybody, in fact, was cautiously utopian. Thomas Davidson, who had spent a lifetime resisting with Scottish common sense an almost overwhelming desire to enter a Phalanstery or a Brook Farm, founded but did not join the Fellowship. The members themselves, poised on the very brink of utopia, cast back many a nostalgic glance at the tinseled and shabby Philistia which, perhaps, they were soon to leave forever. Meanwhile a few bolder spirits were proposing to regenerate human nature in Brazil, in Southern California, in Topolo-bampo. After some debate it was decided—no doubt with universal relief—that

> the members would pursue their present callings in the world, but they would always aim to make the community as far as practicable self-contained and self-supporting, combining perhaps to carry on some common business or businesses.[2]

In short, they would forsake Philistia and have it too.

The utopian phase of the society was embryologically rapid. Decades of socialistic phylogeny were compressed into a few months of Fabian development. The word "socialism" appeared more and more in the minutes. Soon it became clear that while some members felt that their first objective should be moral perfection within a small communistic society, others felt that socialistic revolution in the great world outside would be much quicker and more practical. Finally a spilt occurred. On December 7, 1883, the Fellowship of the New Life became a separate body and so continued until 1898. The Fabian Society was born on January 4, 1884. It comprised a majority of the old common organization, and indeed some, like Havelock Ellis, belonged to both. The spirit of the club was to be suggested by its name, which was of course derived from that of the Roman general, Fabius Cunctator. Like him, they would go slowly. They would take the long road to utopia.

On the whole, they did not go very slowly. They soon decided to do away with the competitive system, to reconstruct society, and incidentally, to study social theory, labor problems, and the entire structure of contemporary institutions. They appointed a pamphlet committee. Within three weeks the first *Fabian Tract*, written by W. L. Phillips, the only "genuine working man"[3] among them, had been published. It declared that capital reveled in luxury on the great bulk of the national income, that labor subsisted at a point just above starvation on the remainder, and that Christian prayer would not remedy the situation. Thus far the Fabians had neither ideas nor facts. Webb and Shaw were soon to provide both.

The minutes of the May 16 meeting are followed by a penciled note in Shaw's handwriting: "This meeting was made memorable by the first appearance of Bernard Shaw."[4]

At this time Shaw was a prophet seeking not only a religion but a church. He had abruptly joined the Georgites, found himself unable to dissuade them from their cardinal doctrine, and as abruptly left. He was on the point of joining the Marxist Democratic Federation, which was composed largely of workingmen. Then he heard of the Fabian Society. The name attracted him. He decided to become a member.

"I was guided," he wrote, "by no discoverable difference in programme or principles, but solely by an instinctive feeling that the Fabian and not the Federation would attract the men of my own bias and intellectual habits who were then ripening for the work that lay before us." [5] In other words, he joined the Fabians because they were not laborers but middle-class intellectuals. This was a natural choice. It may reflect some traditional Shaw snobbery, perhaps some personal fastidiousness, for he has always loved mankind more in the abstract than in the concrete. It may also reflect the intellectual's desire to join a small organization in which he would be encouraged to think and learn rather than a large one in which he would be encouraged simply to shout and yell. One has only to compare Shaw's experience with Morris's to see that the former was wiser and more fortunate. Shaw felt that he was associating himself with the leaders, rather than the followers, of the popular movement; or as he puts it, with typical paradox, "The middle and upper classes are the revolutionary element in society; the proletariat is the conservative element, as Disraeli well recognized." [6]

In a larger sense, Shaw was choosing, no doubt unconsciously, between revolutionary extremism and constitutional meliorism, between Karl Marx and John Stuart Mill. Throughout this period, though with many countermarches, he was moving from the first to the second. Less and less he burned with revolutionary fanaticism and saw the catastrophic vision. More and more the cautious tendencies of his nature, the direct influence of Mill, the indirect influence of Webb and others, and the practical necessities of British political life made him the almost irreproachable Fabian that he became. His sense of humor made Marxism repugnant. Respectability—and common sense —made Millism attractive.

But the history of Mill's socialism is very long and very English.

CHAPTER SEVEN

Fabian Scriptures, Old Testament

At the beginning of the nineteenth century, noisy little jungles of atomic capitalism were growing up on the picturesque detritus of feudalistic society. At the end of the century, a great industrial state was moving rapidly toward socialism. In this swift development, doctrinaire socialistic thought undoubtedly played a great part—and particularly the thought of Karl Marx, for he is startling disproof of his own theory that conditions determine ideas. Long after many of the conditions which he describes had practically ceased to exist, his ideas of them went far to cause the cataclysm in which they were supposed to result. Marxian doctrines, working through able and determined disciples, actually brought about a Marxian revolution in a country where the necessary Marxian forces had never existed.

But of course modern England is by no means the work of armchair revolutionists. In fact, the history of English socialism itself is often written with far too much attention to the socialists. The spectacle of the London slums, for example, converted almost as many middle-class intellectuals to socialism as did Karl Marx. To interpret a British intellectual movement exclusively in terms of ideas is to ignore British character. Broadly, British socialism resulted from the attempt to solve the problems of the industrial revolution in terms of the British democratic tradition. The expanding franchise, the legalization of trade-unions, universal education, agitation for the rights to subsistence and to the whole produce of labor were but successive steps. The movement toward equality changed democratic individualism into democratic socialism at the strategic moment.

If socialism is the product of industrialism and democracy, the intellectual movement most clearly identified with those two forces at the beginning of the nineteenth century was the radical utilitarian, which had for two hundred years been the very projection into thought —an extremely uncongenial element—of the English middle-class mind. Its skeptical empiricism, employing great theoretical subtlety to keep theoretical considerations at a minimum, expressed the middle-class distrust of ideas and reverence for facts. Its preoccupation with utility reflected the commercial materialism which in the nineteenth century turned political economy into a theology. Politically, utilitarianism was an individualistic creed with this peculiar weakness—that it made the individual a blank, a *tabula rasa,* upon which circumstances wrote their story.

It is chiefly in this sense—in hitching their wagon to circumstances—that the middle class became what Shaw called them, the only genuine revolutionists. It ,is a commonplace that most revolutionary socialism is a critical modification of middle-class utilitarian economics. What is not so clearly understood is that the Fabians, like the advanced radicals led by Morley and Chamberlain, stemmed not so much from the revolutionary utilitarianism of Thompson and Marx as from the evolving and expanding utilitarianism of John Stuart Mill.

At the beginning of the century, this tradition was represented by a remarkable body of men. The Benthamites were vastly learned, fantastically laborious, romantically benevolent, and sternly practical. Up to that moment, history had been a morass of ignorance and stupidity. To transform it into a garden of logic, men needed only to become Benthamites. Yet no one has railed at human folly more bitterly than Bentham. Did he expect a superrational philosophy to be adopted by a race of fools? To be sure. In the last resort, he founded his hopes on the conviction not so much that men are rational as that his own ideas were irresistible. Truth, like the mustard seed, grows miraculously.

According to Bentham, man seeks pleasure and avoids pain. Benthamite philosophy would simply teach him to follow his nature more intelligently. He must acquire good habits and pertinent knowledge. He must study logic and learn to think clearly. Above all, he must become adept in Bentham's own moral calculus, adding up pleasures and pains to sapient preferences. Man's final end should be at once his own personal good, or utility (a preponderance of pleasure over pain), and the greatest good of the greatest number. But are these two goods in any sense the same? Bentham seems to have believed that in a scientifically ordered society they should be nearly identical. Taking self-interest for granted, he would prod it into justice and honesty by threatening legal pains ingeniously calculated. He would surround it with such a political environment as to guarantee both particular virtue and general harmony. In other words, he would reform the individual by first reforming the state. But rather paradoxically, Bentham would confine his reform chiefly to rationalizing legal structure and limiting legal authority. He felt that every man is the best judge

[52]

and abettor of his own interest and should therefore have all possible freedom in which to pursue it.

Government, then, should be largely an efficient police department, backed by rational laws and swift justice. But who is to keep the police efficient and the justice swift? Everybody, of course—with the aid of a little ingenious machinery. In this sense Bentham's philosophy is nearly all criminal code and his theory of government nearly all panopticon. Government had been a conspiracy of thieves. It could become a virtuous conspiracy only by being democratically reconstructed in such a way that the major rogues who governed would be under the rigid surveillance of the minor rogues who were governed.

For England Bentham proposed universal male suffrage, annual parliaments, and a variety of detective devices. A good government should provide the four benefits of subsistence, abundance, equality, and security. Even economic equality, Bentham felt, was desirable, for in the enjoyment of wealth, as in the produce of land, there is a law of diminishing returns. Equal incomes mean a maximum of economic satisfaction. Yet drastic equalization would destroy the public sense of security and must therefore await the leveling effects of time. And indeed a self-made generation of merchants and manufacturers, many of whom had raised themselves by great labor and suffering, were not likely to believe in any easy legislative escape from poverty.

Utilitarian economics were constructed by Malthus and Ricardo. In their speculations Bentham's enlightened criminal becomes that cultural Neanderthal, early nineteenth-century economic man, who "desires wealth and prefers his own interest." [1] He lives of course in a world of unlimited competition, but competition leads only in a restricted sense to any utopian equilibrium of infinitely alert and energetic egotisms. Its cheerful aspects—the productivity of an increasing division of labor and the harmonies of supply and demand—had been exhibited by Adam Smith.

The utilitarians, studying the scene before them, concentrated not unnaturally on the dismal. It is grimly significant that Darwin derived his ideas of the jungle from Malthus's explanations of "civilization," as economists then referred to the industrial system. According to Malthus, population tends to increase more rapidly than the food supply and is checked mainly by disease, famine, and war. Thus economic life becomes an impersonalized gladiatorial combat in which the winners are rewarded with the ineffable pleasures of affluence and respectability and the losers punished with the pains of poverty, disease, disreputability, and death. Moreover, as Malthus explains, a more ˈequable distribution of goods can bring only temporary relief. Ultimately, it would lead not to universal comfort but to universal poverty. Population would simply increase until everybody was living at subsistence level.

Malthus had transformed the science of wealth into the science of poverty. When there are always too many mouths, distribution becomes a cheerless problem. Yet it was also an unsolved problem, and therefore both Malthus and Ricardo thought about it. What Malthus thought was more accurate and cautiously inductive, but what Ricardo thought was more influential. The whole produce of the earth may be divided into rent, profit, and wages. Adam Smith had explained the share due to each largely according to supply and demand. But that principle, Ricardo saw, accounted only for superficial fluctuations in revenue, not for the division of revenue itself. He found the key in Malthus's law. It explained the dearness of land and the cheapness of labor. The pressure of population brings poorer and poorer land into use and at the same time confers a scarcity value on good land. The rent of a piece of land is the difference between its return and that of the poorest land under cultivation. On the other hand, there is always an oversupply of labor. Wages are the economic counterpart of those efficacious checks of war, disease, and famine—but particularly of the last. In short, wages tend constantly to the subsistence level. They will be just sufficient to enable the essential number of workers to maintain and reproduce themselves. Profit is what remains after wages and rent have been subtracted. But as rent increases with the increasing scarcity of land, the rate of profit must diminish.

The revenue due each factor of production had now been defined, but not the value of the goods which that revenue could buy. Ricardo believed that value is conferred on objects by utility, scarcity, and labor. Assuming that, practically, all kinds of labor are equal and uniform, he decided that the exchange value of an object is regulated by the amount of labor necessary to obtain it. But if all exchange value is determined by labor, it follows that workers spend but a part of their day reproducing the cost of their wages. They spend the remainder in creating surplus value, that portion which goes into rent and profit. Ricardo's system is a rather anxious paradise for landlords, a luxurious gymnasium for capitalists, and a protracted limbo for workers. Nor was the real world he saw before him much different. He had genuine sympathy for the poor. Nevertheless, the only live people in his whole economic system were the capitalists. They thought and acted. The landlords were mere beribboned, luxury-consuming paunches; the workers, mere capital-producing robots.

Ricardo's utilitarian penchant for social mathematics and identical units of humanity enabled him to give economics an invaluable logic and precision. His errors were so exact that they suggested truths to other men. Indeed, his whole theory was so headily clear and abstract that a number of people got a number of astonishing ideas. Great wealth in private hands can never be justified by mere economics. Ricardo had presented an extremely aristocratic system with none of the cultural or spiritual justifications of aristocracy. He had made it baldly obvious that those who do all the rough, physical work of the community receive very little of what they produce. With amazing swiftness, his robots came to life and demanded their rights. It is significant that by far their most able and influential defender was William Thompson, a "pupil of Bentham." [2] He adhered to the "greatest-happiness" principle but interpreted it in terms of equality rather than security. Labor produced everything. Therefore it should have everything. The difference between him and the utilitarians is private property. The difference between him and Marx is the communistic state and the historical point of view. Thompson's influence on Marx, and therefore on all "scientific" socialism, is considerable.

The midcentury representative of the utilitarians was John Stuart Mill. In large part, his work was but the continuation throughout life of an amazing education, in which the teachers were all geniuses and the student was always discriminatingly worthy of his teachers. He remained a utilitarian to the last, though circumstances made of that philosophy of circumstances something very different from what he had started with. Bentham's *Treatise on Legislation* had burst on the youthful Mill with the force almost of a religious illumination. A little later the Coleridgeans taught him that Bentham's logic was incompatible with a historical sense. History produces a great deal besides prejudice and stupidity. Institutions evolve according to human needs. They are oppressive in so far as they encumber or thwart the development of the contemporary ethos. In so far as they guide and strengthen it, uniting thereby reason with habit, they are infinitely superior to any Benthamite substitute of abstract logic. Auguste Comte showed him that sociology could be a science, guided him in the formulation of its peculiar method, taught him a philosophy of history, and impressed him with the growing importance of the state. The Fourierists and the St. Simonians instructed him in the evils of unrestricted competition and opened up a hope of economic justice and prosperity through voluntary cooperatives democratically governed. From De Tocqueville he learned the opposite truth that extreme democracy may mean a crude tyranny of the masses, who dislike and would gladly suppress any deviation from their own dead level—and particularly the useless vagaries of intellectual eccentrics. Through the extraordinary breadth of his later education, Mill had come to see, more clearly than any other radical, the full scope of the Victorian political problem: How can the individual be protected from the evils of competition and yet retain reasonable economic, political, and civil freedom? Or, stated in the light of De Tocqueville's *Democracy in America:* How can justice for the many be reconciled with liberty for the few?

Like most Victorians, Mill compromised—and compromised more than he thought. He rejected the extremes. Communism, he felt, offered more liberty at the bottom, and less at the top, than capitalism. Manual workers would be freer from want, freer to choose their occupations and places of residence. On the other hand, intellectual workers would be less free from the tyranny of opinion. Moreover, equality of income, which he considered the distinguishing feature of communism, is the noblest, but also the least practical, mode of distribution, since it presents the weakest stimulus to self-interest.[3]

But though Mill's attitude of mind remained individualistic to the end, his opinions became socialistic. He adhered loyally to the principles of competition and free enterprise but restricted them almost into insignificance. He would legislate a nine-hour day and better working conditions within the factory.[4] He would permit trade-unions and collective bargaining, thereby eliminating the individual competition of laborers for wages.[5] He would nationalize "a property in canals and railways"[6] and all land—or at least the unearned increment in rent.[7] He advocated an extreme inheritance tax[8] and the encouragement of all kinds of cooperatives.[9] Indeed, voluntary cooperatives seemed the solution to his dilemma. An individual could join a cooperative and enjoy all the benefits of collectivism without surrendering his right to resign at any time and recover his full freedom. Unfortunately, as Sir Leslie Stephen observes, a state made up of gigantic cooperatives does not leave much scope for individual freedom.[10]

In any event, Mill was determined to be at once progressive and cautious. Population must constantly be watched and people taught to keep down their numbers. The situation must be studied at each stage of the process. Successful experiment must be built on successful experiment. Much more than the Benthamites, Mill believed in evolution, in historical continuity—and here he reinforced the influence of Marx in the development of socialistic thought. His compromise would work itself out in a time dimension. In his *Autobiography,* he calls himself a socialist and looks forward to the eventual achievement, by constitutional means, of a socialistic democracy.

Like Voltaire, Mill exercised the powerful influence of a transitional figure in a transitional age. Men like Thompson and Gray knew their minds too well to affect sound men at a confused juncture of affairs. Mill weighed both sides of the question judicially. He stood now upon one side and now upon the other. He acquired his authority as the official representative of Benthamite individualism and then used it to preach something very like socialism. And while events were making politicians like Chamberlain and intellectuals like Morley socialists in practice, Mill's cautious and prolonged interrogations went far to make them such in theory.

Within the framework of the utilitarian tradition, there was little to stay this development. In the Benthamite theory of individual life, there was no strength or vividness with which to resist the pressure of the modern state. Benthamite man was an automaton motivated by egotism, a standard unit fitted for nothing so much as group treatment. Nor could John Stuart Mill himself, genuinely elevating as he sometimes was, quite create a soul beneath the shiny steel ribs of this robot. It was a vacuum into which impressions rushed like atoms and tried to arrange themselves into a mind. Moreover, Benthamism had joined with Darwinism in emphasizing that character is the product of environment and had so dealt a mortal blow to what Shaw calls "perhaps the strongest moral bulwark of Capitalism," the nonconformist "belief in the efficacy of individual righteousness." [11] The utilitarians had defended freedom as an economic utility. When that utility became dubious, freedom itself—at least in the old sense—became dubious.

To be sure, Benthamite premises had from the first been fraught with socialistic conclusions. Universal suffrage, identical units of humanity, and the greatest happiness of the greatest number imply economic equality and collectivism. Faith in political machinery implies a highly developed bureaucracy and the all-embracing, corporative state. Finally, the utilitarians did more than any other body of men to create that state. They took the lead in clarifying laws, abolishing privilege, extending the suffrage, and promoting administrative efficiency. Between Bentham's distrust of government and Webb's faith in it are fifty years of Victorian political respectability.

Thus, by the most decently minute variations of shade, black became white—or white, black—in fifty years. Of course not all Benthamites became socialists. The older type of Radical was an important political factor, even in the trade-unions, as late as 1880.[12] But atomic individualism evolved into modified socialism. The position of progressive leadership that Bentham had occupied in the thirties, Mill occupied in the seventies. Harrison was a Comtist, Morley a Gladstonian Liberal, and Chamberlain a Unitarian, but all were Millites and moderate socialists, and the most powerful was the most socialistic. Chamberlain was the leader, as Mill was the prophet, of the later Radical party.

CHAPTER EIGHT

In the Wilderness

Shaw had no sooner entered the Fabian Society than he provided it with a new constitution in the form of a terrifying "Manifesto," the second *Fabian Tract*, which begins with "Wealth cannot be enjoyed without dishonor," and ends with "We had rather face a Civil War than such another century of suffering as the present one has been." [1] What lies in between is a unique snapshot of Shavian social intelligence in the year 1884. It is the photograph of a revolutionary sunrise, surprisingly pale, in which the early pink of Millite utilitarianism is only here and there shot through with the angry red of Marxism. About this time Shaw was defending Marx from the Millite attacks of his friend Sidney Webb. But the latter was an old hand at slipping into a citadel. In any case, the "Manifesto" points to Mill even more than to Marx and George—and particularly in the following items:

1. That it is the duty of each member of the State to provide for his or her wants by his or her own Labour.

2. That a life-interest in the Land and Capital of the nation is the birth-right of every individual born within its confines; and that access to this birth-right should not depend upon the will of any private person other than the person seeking it.

3. That, under the existing system of leaving the National Industry to organise itself, Competition has the effect of rendering adulteration, dishonest dealing and inhumanity compulsory.

4. That since Competition amongst producers admittedly secures to the public the most satisfactory products, the State should compete with all its might in every department of production.

5. That such restraints upon Free Competition as the penalties for infringing the Postal monopoly, and the withdrawal of workhouse and prison labour from the markets, should be abolished.

6. That Men no longer need special political privileges to pro-
tect them against Women; and that the sexes should henceforth
enjoy equal political rights.

7. That no individual should enjoy any Privilege in consideration
of services rendered to the State by his or her parents or other
relations.

8. That the State should secure a liberal education and an equal
share in the National Industry to each of its units.[2]

The first clause seems a clear restatement of Mill's St. Simonianism; [3]
the second, so far as one can judge, is very close to the suggestion made
in the *Political Economy* of equal properties with limited inheritance; [4]
the third is reminiscent of Mill's extended quotation of Louis Blanc
in an article on socialism; [5] the fourth suggests the conception, set
forth in "Liberty," of private and governmental competition in education, as well as a brief passage in the *Political Economy;* [6] the fifth
exaggerates the point of Mill's discussion of the Post-office Tax in the
Political Economy; [7] the sixth is an ironical statement of an idea to be
found throughout the "Subjection of Women"; the seventh and eighth
are also Millite and radical commonplaces.

Of the following, the first points to Marx and the class struggle; the
second, to George and land nationalization:

That the most striking result of our present system of farming out
the national Land and Capital to private persons has been the
division of Society into hostile classes, with large appetites and
no dinners at one extreme and large dinners and no appetites at
the other.

That the practice of entrusting the Land of the nation to private
persons in the hope that they will make the best of it has been
discredited by the consistency with which they have made the
worst of it; and that Nationalisation of the Land in some form is
a public duty.

In general, the "Manifesto" is not a model of consistency. Competition, for example, is attacked and defended in successive items. Altogether, the ideas seem mostly Millite, but the indignation is Marxian.

Fabian Tract No. 3, also by Shaw, is addressed "To provident Landlords and Capitalists, a suggestion and a warning." The Fabian Society, it declares, has in view the establishment of 'a socialistic order
in which all members of the upper class will actually be compelled
"to work for their own living." Shaw urges that, in order to escape this
calamitous indignity, the proprietary classes

support all undertakings having for their object the parcelling out of waste or inferior lands amongst the labouring class. . . . The peasant proprietor, having a stock in the country, will, unlike the landless labourer of to-day, have a common interest with the landlord in resisting revolutionary proposals.[8]

In short, Shaw translates Book Two, Chapter Thirteen, of Mill's *Principles of Political Economy* into Shavian humor. "At the foot of the title page, in the smallest of type, is the following: 'Note.—Great care should be taken to keep this tract out of the hands of radical workmen, Socialist demagogues and the like, as they are but too apt to conclude that schemes favourable to landlords cannot be permanently advantageous to the working class.' " [9]

On January 2, 1885, Shaw was elected to the Executive Committee of the Society, on which he served until his voluntary retirement in 1911. Socialism had not, any more than literature, destroyed his inartistic capacity for business, and now that he might use that capacity to destroy business—in the capitalistic sense—he was eager to exercise it. Moreover, he was acquiring not only the speaking habit but also the "committee habit." He was learning how to be open-minded and impassive under sharp personal criticism, how to manage people with his curious inverted tact of disguising truth as humorous insult. He never developed the dignity, the stability, and the Carlylean silence of a leader, yet as time went on his wit—and perhaps his fierce red whiskers —got him far more fear and respect than does portentous solemnity the more conventional executive.

Shortly after Shaw's election to the Executive Committee, two delegates emerged from the fastness of Fabian middle-class respectability to attend the Industrial Remuneration Conference. One of these was Shaw. He made a speech, which he began as follows:

> It is the desire of the President that nothing shall be said that might give pain to particular classes. I am about to refer to a modern class, burglars, and if there is a burglar present I beg him to believe that I cast no reflection upon his profession. I am not unmindful of his great skill and enterprise; his risks, so much greater than those of the most speculative capitalist, extending as they do to risk of liberty and life, or of his abstinence; nor do I overlook his value to the community as an employer on a large scale, in view of the criminal lawyers, policemen, turnkeys, gaolbuilders and sometimes hangmen that owe their livelihoods to his daring undertakings. . . . I hope any shareholders and landlords who may be present will accept my assurance that I have no more desire to hurt their feelings than to give pain to burglars: I merely

wish to point out that all three inflict on the community an injury of precisely the same nature.[10]

Capitalists in the audience must have pricked up their ears. Swift's irony is hardly more imperturbably grave. Nine years later, Shaw was to use precisely the same satirical strategy in "Mrs. Warren's Profession."

The Fabian Society was now of course in grave danger of becoming the Shavian Society. Had it ever possessed a character of its own? The Fellowship of the New Life had skimmed off some of the more violent individualists. What remained might well seem at first glance harmless members of the middle class—with at most a very mild blending of Bohemianism and intellectuality. Percival Chubb was a young clerk in the Local Government Board. Ramsay MacDonald worked in a warehouse. Edward Pease was a member of the Stock Exchange and apparently the driest of utilitarians. Frank Podmore was more remarkable. He was interested in Nietzsche, *Madame Bovary,* and sex.

"There are two distinct elements in the F.S.," writes a feminine member, "the practical and the visionary—the first being much the strongest." [11] She adds that she belongs to the first. This practical lady was Mrs. Hubert Bland, well known under her maiden name of E. Nesbit as a novelist for juveniles. Many people, including H. G. Wells and Havelock Ellis, have described her as beautiful and charming, but nobody has accused her of being practical. That formidable Bohemian, Mr. Noel Coward, who knew Mrs. Bland when age might have been expected to modify her eccentricity, describes her as "the most genuine Bohemian I ever met." [12] The facts bear him out. In the very depths of the eighties, she eschewed corsets and alternated between the flowing aesthetic gowns of the Pre-Raphaelites and the Jaeger clothing of G. B. Shaw. Before the bulging eyes of her suburban neighbors, she bicycled in "radicals," or serge bloomers, and came to the Fabian meetings with a large box of tobacco and cigarette papers under her arm. H. R. Millar, the artist, remembers the container as—by an added refinement—a corset box! In the pages of E. Nesbit's biographer, the Fabians begin to acquire color.

Her husband, Hubert Bland the journalist, is described as an overpowering personality, surpassed in magnetism only by Shaw himself. Huge, muscular, meticulously befrocked and formidably bemonocled, ferociously and tirelessly contentious beneath the elaborate formality of his debating manner, Bland impressed or antagonized some of the most eminent men of his time and summoned brilliance and animosity to half a dozen of the best pages in H. G. Wells's autobiography. He was, says the latter, "a sort of Tom-cat man," who defended with passionate persistence the strictest Victorian sexual code in order to lend piquancy to his own illicit amours, about which he boasted under cover of reporting scientific experimentation. "I am," he told Mr. Wells, "not so much Don Juan as Professor Juan." [13] His socialism, he insisted, was but a return to the communism of the Middle Ages. He was, somewhat like Oscar Wilde, an able mind in search of exciting and impressive masks in the worlds of politics and art. He was a radical innovator on romantically conservative grounds, an exotic eighteenth-century buck in an age of prudish respectability, an inveterate Bohemian in an impeccably got-up, Tory-gentleman setting.

Neither Bland nor his wife, nor the group of people associated with them, were mere Philistine putty in the hands of any man. They received Shaw with very dubious homage, yet they could not long resist him. Mrs. Bland's early comments on him are illuminating:

> G. B. S. has a fund of dry Irish humour that is simply irresistible. He is a very clever writer and speaker— Is the grossest flatterer (of men women and children impartially) I ever met, is horribly untrustworthy as he repeats everything he hears, and does not always stick to the truth, and is *very plain* . . . and yet is one of the most fascinating men I ever met. Everyone affects to despise him. 'Oh its only Shaw?' That sort of thing you know, but everyone admires him all the same. Miss H——— pretends to hate him, but my own impression is that she is over head and ears in love with him.[14]

Everybody fell in love with him in somewhat the same way. Philistine or Bohemian, all became more or less Shavian. They became practical, determined, irreverent, mildly Machiavellian, and violently discourteous. Conventional reformers were terrified.

But Shaw not only brought in his own talents, his own tone, his own program; he brought in his own members. Within the next two years his close friends, Sidney Webb, Sidney Olivier, and Graham Wallas, had all joined. Their influence was not, like his, instantaneous. For some time the history of the Society continued to be an irony to its name. The Fabians believed in research and education before violence, but they also felt that a very little research and education would lead to a tremendous "smash-up of existing society." [15] Like Shaw throughout this early period, they were full of undigested Marx and George, even of Owen and Proudhon. They denounced capitalists as thieves, talked anarchism, revolution, and utopia; and Shaw himself debated labor notes *vs.* passbooks.

I remember being asked satirically and publicly at that time how long I thought it would take to get Socialism into working order if I had my way. I replied, with a spirited modesty, that a fortnight would be ample for the purpose. When I add that I was frequently complimented on being one of the more reasonable Socialists, you will be able to appreciate the fervor of our conviction and the extravagant levity of our practical ideas.[16]

This intellectual ferment was complicated by personal animosities, of which the chief, according to H. G. Wells, was that between Pease and Bland. "The larger purposes of the Wallases, Webbs and Shaw," he writes, probably with some exaggeration, "had to defer continually to the dark riddle of 'what the Blands will do about it.' . . . Rumour moved darkly and anonymous letters flittered about like bats at twilight."[17] Oddly enough, the principal peacemaker was Shaw, who by skillful insult and dexterous flattery maintained an atmosphere of gaiety and good humor if not of mutual trust. Doubtless, so far as the standing quarrel was concerned, he agreed with Pease but liked the Blands. He had an actor's fondness for impressive exteriors and complicated poses, and as his infinite patience with Frank Harris suggests, he could even relish sheer noise. Bland was more than sheer noise. The friendship was apparently not in the least complicated by the mischance that Mrs. Bland, unhappy at the disloyalties of her husband, fell in love with his friend. By amusing and heartless cruelties, Shaw modified her emotion to a frank and gay friendship, in which they continued until her death.

Toward the end of 1885, the Social Democratic Federation undertook an experiment in practical Marxism which, more than anything else perhaps—as Shaw himself emphasizes—convinced the Fabians that in British politics Marxism would not do: the Federation accepted Tory funds to pay the expenses of two candidates in the 1885 elections and, with Marxist cynicism, made no secret of the alliance. The public was horrified. The candidates suffered a crushing defeat, and the Federation, which had "loomed hideously in the guilty eye of property,"[18] became almost insignificant. The Fabians were quick to see the point. They repudiated the Federation and condemned its revolutionary tactics.

With the advent of Webb, the first true Fabian joined the Fabian Society. Marx had "convinced me," writes Shaw, "that what the movement needed was not Hegelian theorizing but an unveiling of the official facts of Capitalist civilization, which Webb had at his fingers' ends."[19] The cautious Millite seems at the time to have feared the violence and extremism of the Society, and Shaw won him only after prolonged argument. The victory was significant. The Fabians had identified themselves with the modern statistical approach, and the ratiocinating card-index file had become a socialist. For apparently, like a true Englishman, Webb did not quite know what to do with his facts. Shaw taught him to make them serve socialism, and Mrs. Webb, who had read Spencer and Comte, to make them serve sociology.

Webb's fears about the Society were justified. Soon after, the Fabians were joined by one Mrs. Wilson, an attractive and dashing Kropotkin anarchist. "A sort of influenza of Anarchism soon spread through the society." [20] The Fabians again seethed with revolution. And then revolution knocked at the door.

The depression which had unseated Disraeli in 1884 culminated under Gladstone in 1886. The unemployed were numerous and desperate. Hollow-cheeked men paraded "with red flags and banners inscribed with Scriptural texts to fashionable churches on Sunday." Mr. Champion told a great meeting in Lincoln Fields that "if the whole propertied class had but one throat he would cut it without a second thought, if by so doing he could redress the injustices of our social system." Mr. Hyndman declared on the Thames Embankment that "there would be some attention paid to cases of starvation if a rich man were immolated on every pauper's tomb." Provincial windows were being broken throughout the realm, but thus far the police had been able to keep those of London intact.

Then, on February 8, 1886, a Sugar Bounty meeting in Trafalgar Square was swamped by great numbers of the unemployed. Orators from the Democratic Federation seized the opportunity to take over and harangue the crowd. Afterward, everybody adjourned to Hyde Park. Through a mistake, the police were sent to *The* Mall instead of Pall Mall, and while they "were shivering in St. James's Park," the crowd passed before the unguarded windows of the fashionable clubs. Rich men gathered behind the polished glass to watch with idle curiosity. The temptation was more than hunger and misery could stand. Much polished glass was shattered, and a couple of shops were looted. Hyndman, Champion, Burns, and Williams were arrested and tried, but as Hyndman and Champion were gentlemen and the foreman of the jury was a socialist, all the prisoners were acquitted, and the unemployed felt they had won the right to meet in Trafalgar Square.

Still imperfectly Fabian, the Fabians reacted to these revolutionary events in the most diverse ways. Mrs. Wilson and her friends threw theoretical bombs in drawing rooms. A few genuine Fabians—Bland, Hughes, Podmore, Stapleton, and Webb—published a lengthy statistical study of the crisis, recommending experiments in tobacco culture and perhaps even military service as a means of absorbing the unemployed. Yet others, whose ambition was not bounded by a blue book or a drawing room, mingled with workingmen and dreamed wistfully of violence. They disapproved of revolutions, but they did not want to be indoors when one occurred. These Fabians were Shaw, Graham Wallas, and Mrs. Annie Besant.

They had earned reputations as open-air speakers, and naturally they attended some of the meetings now held continually in Trafalgar Square. One was announced for November 18, 1887, afterwards known as "Bloody Sunday." Great contingents of sympathizers were to assemble in various parts of the city and then march on the Square. Meanwhile shopkeepers round about Trafalgar had complained to the police that they were losing customers—not so much because of the gatherings themselves, Shaw hints, as because of the terrifying newspaper accounts of them. Accordingly, the police forbade the meeting under an act empowering them to regulate processions. Feeling mounted to a new pitch. London seemed to hang on the very brink of civil war.

Revolution brought out all of Shaw's conscientious legalism. First, he read carefully the act under which the police had prohibited the march, satisfied his conscience that the prohibition was illegal, and then, accompanied by Annie Besant and William Morris, joined the northern contingent assembling on Clerkenwell Green. There he made a speech, urging the people to be orderly and resolute. At length the procession formed. Morris took a position at the head, but Shaw modestly fell in where he happened to be. In spite of his gentlemanly protest that she not run the risk of a melee, Mrs. Besant, who admired him greatly, placed herself at his side. Finally Mr. Stead, editor of the *Pall Mall Gazette,* shouted "To the Square!" in the proper revolutionary manner. Drums beating and banners waving, the procession moved forward. Surely even Fabian hearts could not but warm to Shelley's faith in irresistible numbers and the mystic will of the people?

In a short time Shaw and his companion were amazed to meet great streams of "the people" in terror-stricken flight, pursued and bludgeoned by a very small number of police. It was the time for a hero or a martyr —or a fool. Shaw remembered that he was a gentleman. He urged Mrs. Besant to vanish. She did so. Then he joined the bystanders. "A man rushed up to him crying, 'Shaw: give us a lead. What are we to do?' 'Nothing,' said Shaw. 'Let every man get to the Square as best he can.' " 21

The heroes of the day were John Burns and Cunninghame Graham, who, a phalanx of two, charged the police. They were sentenced to six weeks' imprisonment, all of which Graham spent in the infirmary.

For Shaw, the experience was just humiliating enough to be instructive. Afterward, his political thinking revealed a great deal of faith not in the people but in the police:

> He was sometimes reminded by the more pugnacious comrades that mobs do not always run away: history records their victories. How about the French Revolution for instance? On such occasions Shaw would reply by asserting that the French monarchy could have crushed the revolution if it had not been foolish enough to believe that Marie Antoinette's gambling debts were more important than the wages of its soldiers, who did not fraternise with the mob until their pay was four years in arrear.[22]

And when the mob did win, the results were even worse than when they ran, for they simply smashed things and then chose worse rulers than those who had oppressed them. The steady though cautious faith in the ability of humble men to govern themselves which breathes from the pages of the Webbs' *History of Trade Unionism* finds no counterpart in Shaw. He believed in government for the people but not by them. His vision of equalitarian democracy was haunted by a mob scene. "The Fabian wisdom," says Shaw, "has grown out of the Fabian experience."

Like a willful Victorian girl on the verge of engagement, the Society flounced and fumed into one emotional extreme after another during these years yet allowed the true character of its feeling to appear more and more clearly. Mrs. Wilson and her fellow anarchists objected so violently to the learned moderation of the study on unemployment that the paper appeared not as an official *Tract* but as a report for the information of members. Yet almost immediately sobriety returned, and the Society again did something profoundly Fabian. It announced a public conference, deliberately renouncing its "political sectarianism" by inviting its cousins, the Radicals and the secularists. The preparations represented a meticulous compromise between respectability and revolution. The invitation cards were impeccably smart and colored blood-red. The prospectus set off socialistic sentiments with a design by Crane. Fifty-three societies sent delegates. There were three afternoons and evenings of discussion. William Morris, Sidney Webb, Charles Bradlaugh, and many others spoke. The conference elicited howls of derision from the Marxists and achieved the dignity of being reported by *The Times*. Yet it did not make history. It was little more than a declaration of respectability and a first step in educating the Liberals.

Shaw and his friends now introduced a resolution that the Fabians organize themselves as a political party to achieve state socialism by parliamentary means. The debate was so violent that the Secretary was told afterwards that the Anderton Hotel would no longer be available for meetings of the Society. The vote was forty-seven to nineteen. Led by Morris and Mrs. Wilson, the nineteen anarchists died so hard that the majority decided they must be still very dangerously alive, and to preserve unity hastily founded the Fabian Parliamentary League as a separate body. But the anarchists were really dead, for within the next few weeks all dissenters either became conformists or left the Society. The League itself died with the death of opposition and was then more modestly resurrected as a Political Committee, which aspired merely to influence the older parties and to run candidates in municipal elections.

In expelling Mrs. Wilson and her followers, the Fabians perfected their attack against the anarchists, who held that money and monopoly should be abolished, everybody should receive the product of his labor, and land should be left to its occupiers. "We demolished Anarchism in the abstract," says Shaw, "by grinding it between human nature and the theory of economic rent." [23] Human nature cannot cooperate spontaneously on a grand scale. Socially created value can be justly distributed or wisely invested only by society itself. The appropriation of economic rent by the state leads logically, as I shall explain, to Fabian state socialism.

Shaw probably led the attack against anarchism, for his *Fabian Tract* on "The Impossibilities of Anarchism," though published later, was written in 1888. More brilliant and epigrammatic than most of his economic essays, it is a shrewd and able criticism in his best utilitarian vein. Like Mill, he thinks little of human nature as it exists but has great hopes of what it may become. He observes that the only way to guard individual liberty is "to convince men of the immorality of abusing the majority power, and then to make them moral enough to refrain from doing it on that account." [24] The essay is filled with a stern, unsentimental revolutionary eloquence.

The Fabians were free at last to be themselves. Sidney Webb's "Facts for Socialists," published in 1887 as *Tract No. 5*, is their first typical publication. Bristling with graphs and statistics, it analyzes the British national income. Webb hardly argues at all; he simply quotes. The most respectable and distinguished British statisticians are made to prove a scandalous injustice in the distribution of British wealth. The most respectable and distinguished economists—but especially Mill and his disciples McCulloch and Cairnes—are made to indicate the drastic character which reform must take. Never has revolution been so cautiously and anonymously urged.

Tract No. 5 is also remarkable for making the first mention of the "rent of ability," which, as I have already pointed out, Webb derived from Mill. Whether or not he would grant exceptional men exceptional opportunities of development, he would not, according to this doctrine, offer them the incitement of an exceptional reward.

CHAPTER NINE

Fabian Scriptures, New Testament

Speaking authoritatively in a *Fabian Tract,* Shaw describes the Radicals with magnificent condescension as mere gas-and-water socialists capable at best of being little more than blind Fabian tools.[1] One suspects the animus of blood relationship, for in creed and policy the Fabians were obviously much closer to the Radicals than to any other political sect. They constantly attended Radical clubs and were friendly with Radical editors like W. H. Stead and H. W. Massingham, to whose periodicals they had access. Even more significant, they were much closer to the Radicals than to the Marxist Social Democrats, with whom they early fell into hostilities.

It is true that Shaw himself has explicitly denied the dominant influence of John Stuart Mill on the Fabians, calling attention to the influence of George and Marx on himself and that of Comte on Olivier [2] —and, one might add, on Beatrice Webb. No doubt the Fabians owed a good deal to George, Marx, and Comte—possibly even to English Hegelians like Green and Bosanquet.[3] But they were anti-Georgeite in opposing private ownership of the means of production, anti-Hegelian in opposing mere theory and abstraction, anti-Marxist in opposing revolution and violence, anti-Comtist in opposing dictatorship and class privilege. Basically, their program was that of Mill—a cautious and evolutionary progress toward socialism within the limits of the democratic state. And Shaw himself relates how, at a meeting in which he read a paper advocating the nationalization of land, Henry Sidgwick, a Millite, rose indignantly to protest. Webb then astonished and confounded the Millites by citing Mill against them.[4] It was a symbolic event in the history of utilitarianism. Webb understood, as the conventional followers of Mill did not, that with all its triumphant rational finality, Benthamism was evolving into something that was not quite Benthamism.

Like a good historian, Webb had grasped the significance of his own past. Both he and his wife had been reared in the utilitarian tradition.

Mrs. Webb's two grandfathers were Benthamite M.P.'s, and her mother spent her later years moving in a peculiarly Victorian dialectic between Malthus and the Greek Testament.[5] Sidney Webb and his father were acknowledged worshipers of Mill,[6] and the son seems in his youth to have recapitulated, in the metamorphic manner of a later generation, Mill's own development from individualism to socialism.[7] Understanding what had happened, he saw in Mill the model and symbol of all such gradual development. Having presented in the *Fabian Essays* the immediate objectives for which both Radicals and socialists were working, Webb writes:

> This is the programme to which a century of industrial revolution has brought the Radical working man. Like John Stuart Mill, though less explicitly, he has turned from mere political Democracy to a complete, though unconscious, Socialism.[8]

Shaw contributed most of the Fabian wit, theory, and brilliance. Webb contributed what he had learned from experience and inherited—the principle of gradual evolution and the utilitarian tactics and strategy which proved so admirably suited to it.

In general, the Fabians and the Radicals resembled each other in that they both approximated the position of the later John Stuart Mill. They differed in that, despite common utilitarian backgrounds, they approached this point from opposite directions—the Radicals from the ideas of the earlier Mill, the Fabians chiefly from those of Owen, George, and Marx. Moreover, the later Radicals, though socialistic, were imperfectly and partially so. Frederic Harrison was primarily a Comtist. Chamberlain was an imperialist and the friend of Tories. Morley was devoted to mere liberty and republicanism.

Converted to socialism by such unorthodox or partial utilitarians as George and Marx, then sobered by Webb, Wallas, and others to the cautiously socialistic utilitarianism of Mill, the Fabians were steeped in utilitarian literature and ideas. Character, they held, was a putty molded by circumstances. The key to polity was therefore the control of circumstances. And here the Fabians were much more thoroughly utilitarian than the Benthamites. They attempted not simply to prod a select upper middle class with police clubs into a utopia of affluence and respectability but to create that utopia for everybody by the manipulation of nearly every important condition of life. They intended not only to release and channel self-interest but to abolish poverty and legislate the means of an active and happy life for all. In fact, this post-Benthamism has moved F. G. C. Hearnshaw to even more than his habitual capitalistic indignation:

The last and most characteristic utterance of its [Fabianism's] prime was the *Minority Poor-Law Report* of the latter year [1909], a document in which the causes of destitution were elaborately classified under five heads, not one of which had any relation whatsoever to any defects of character! Drunkenness, laziness, gambling, improvidence, or debilitating vice, it appeared, were not causes of pauperism; they merely determined who should be paupers! The obvious perversity of this misguided document— which advances ludicrous arguments to show that only one of the two blades of a pair of scissors does any cutting; that only environment, and not human nature at all, determines destiny— revealed the superficiality of the Fabian diagnosis, and the quackery of the Fabian panacea.[9]

I need hardly add that no one is guiltier of such quackery than Shaw. It is a commonplace that in nearly all his plays,[10] as in the "Minority Poor-Law Report," evil resides not in men but in their social relationships.

Maintaining the malleability of human nature and the importance of circumstances, the utilitarians had always insisted on the supreme efficacy of education. Equally convinced, the Fabians were equally active in educational reform. Together with Lord Haldane, Sidney Webb brought about the London University Act of 1898, and was himself largely responsible for the Education Acts of 1912 and 1913.[11] Shaw is perhaps the only Fabian who has vilified education.

The Fabians not only stemmed from the Benthamites but resembled them strikingly. Family history repeats itself. Both sects were middle class and utilitarian in temper and outlook. Both were therefore materialistic, discreetly skeptical of religion, largely indifferent to aesthetic values. Believing in the psychological principle of rational self-interest, both aimed at social and political justice through universal suffrage and representative democracy. As philosophical reformers imbued with new and radical ideas, both were inevitably small groups of intellectuals full of gusto for prodigious mental labor and scientific inquiry. In fact, Wallas and the Webbs realized more fully than the Benthamites themselves the Benthamite ambition to be empirical—and here the influence of Comte, working directly (and indirectly through Mill) must be acknowledged. Dedicated to planning and thought rather than large-scale political action, both groups practiced the same tactics of wirepulling and "infiltration." The Fabian influence on legislation after 1906, as Ernest Barker points out, closely parallels the Benthamite influence after 1830. The Fabian doctrine that the state annex "socially created values" is the Benthamite doctrine that it promote "the greatest good of the greatest number," adapted to a new conception of the state and of society.[12] The Fabians are but latter-day Benthamites compelled by the logic of history to war against Benthamism.[13]

Bentham and Shaw, who have temperament as well as tradition in common, resemble each other amusingly in their views on orthodox religion. For churches, priestcraft, and theological dogma, both feel an impregnable contempt. But they agree even more strikingly in their mode of attack. Religion is reduced to a question of social utility. Bentham sums up the whole supernatural machinery of Ten Commandments, Heavenly Judge, and eternal punishment in Hell as an outmoded criminal code and police system badly administered. If God had understood Benthamism, he would have been an infinitely better Deity. If Jesus had known economics, says Shaw, he would have been a great constructive force in modern life.[14] As it is, Christianity is simply an inferior type of narcotic. For his rationalistic criticism of Christianity, however, Shaw is probably indebted to John Stuart Mill rather than Jeremy Bentham.

Like good Benthamite economists, Webb and the Fabians took as their starting point economic rent, advocating the transfer of all "unearned income" to society. But the socialization of values implies a receiver and an agent—the state. The law of rent made the Fabians state socialists, as British tradition made them democratic and constitutional socialists.

In these tendencies, Mill, as I have said, anticipated them. Webb was of course much less suspicious of the state but would by no means make it all-powerful. In fact, his *Constitution for the Socialist Commonwealth of Great Britain* suggests Mill's final vision of the future brought into the sharp focus of carefully elaborated practical detail. He was fifty years nearer to their common vision, and where Mill could only prophesy, Webb could define and plan. He marks out spheres for the trade-union and the cooperative, for municipal and national enterprise. He indicates how the voluntary cooperative offers a means whereby a cultivated minority may provide for those tastes which Mill feared mass opinion might suppress. He elaborates a system of checks and balances whereby individual freedom can be guarded. His impressive proposal of a twofold parliament, political and social, with appropriate interconnections, is but the integration of the socialistic with the Benthamite state.

Both Mill and Webb felt that not only must the powers of the state be increased but democracy must be made more articulate, more expressive of the multiform differences of public interest and opinion. Yet whereas Mill sought more adequately to express the variety of

[72]

political opinion by such systems as Hare's and made only tentative suggestions for the representation of economic interests, Webb would, as in his twofold parliament, systematically introduce democratic control into economic as well as into political life. A man should be represented not only as a citizen but as a producer or a consumer, perhaps as a religious believer and a seeker after knowledge.[15] Again, though opposed to the initiative, referendum, and other devices of direct and extreme democracy, Webb is less fearful than Mill of the ignorance and passion of the masses. *The History of Trade Unionism* indicates genuine faith in the ability of common men to choose for themselves adequate and reliable leaders. Both Webb and Mill believed that the future belongs to democracy, but the cautious, practical reformer of the nineties was more optimistic than the rationalistic philosopher of the sixties.

The influence of Mill on the other Fabians is less clear and explicit. The case of Shaw is perhaps typical. Like many others, he swore by Mill the individualist without apparently ever quite discovering Mill the socialist. Yet long after becoming a Fabian, he continued to be influenced, both directly, and indirectly through the plays of Ibsen and other Continental dramatists, by "Liberty" and perhaps "Utilitarianism." His dramatic ethics derive in considerable degree from Mill. In *The Quintessence of Ibsenism,* for example, he speaks of reason, or utility, though in itself inadequate, as one of the factors on which a sound ethical theory might be based. And indeed many of his plays —"Arms and the Man," "Mrs. Warren's Profession," "Candida," "Caesar and Cleopatra," "Getting Married, " "Major Barbara," and "The Shewing-Up of Blanco Posnet"—are in large measure but rationalistic criticism of conventional morality or dramatic illustrations of what rational conduct might be.

Shaw fully exploits the comic possibilities of utilitarianism, applying its standard under incongruous and paradoxical circumstances. His suggestion of polygamy and his advocacy of benevolent and regretful execution for minor crimes imply the utilitarian calculus of pleasures and pains. Indeed, with some exaggeration one might maintain that Shaw discovered the dramatic potentialities of the Benthamite robot. In Ned Conolly he introduces him into fiction and in Bluntschli puts him on the stage. "Arms and the Man," except for one or two pleasant lapses into sentiment, reduces war and romance at their most theatrical to the crassest considerations of bourgeois utility. What Mandeville did in the eighteenth century, Shaw did in the nineteenth: he translated utilitarian dullness into epigram and paradox.

Negative evidence also strongly underlines Shaw's utilitarianism. Why are his economics so little influenced by his art? Why, as a penetrating critic of painting and music and a brilliant prose writer destined soon to become a great dramatist, does he appear so little attracted to the ideas of Ruskin and Morris? Undoubtedly those ideas are to be found in his writings, but not sufficiently to indicate any considerable influence. In his political views, Shaw exhibits the utilitarian indifference to aesthetic values. He is impressed with the suffering and the injustice, not the ugliness and vulgarity, which machinery creates. Far from wishing to make the middle classes uncomfortable merely in order to make the world beautiful, he is willing to turn beauty itself into a soapbox from which to preach comfort for everybody.

It is wonderful that a movement apparently so modern and international as socialism could have been made into anything so English and conservative as Fabianism. Fabian politics were democratic yet tempered with English emphasis on trained and experienced leadership. They were so cautiously constitutional as hardly to offer, in the opinion of many, a tangible promise of complete socialism. Again, Fabian economics began with the law of rent because, as Ernest Barker points out, economic injustice had in England been traditionally associated with the great territorial holdings of the aristocracy; so that, in part at least, the Fabians presented the very English paradox of a small group of advanced reformers making their strongest attack on a typically eighteenth-century monopoly when the nineteenth century was nearly over. The Fabians fell short of British tradition only in their failure to retain a spiritual content in the principle of individual liberty and to express their doctrine in the political symbolism which has had so much power over English imagination. In their traditional as in their untraditional characteristics, they were utilitarian and Millite.

CHAPTER TEN

Marx, the Earlier Biography of a Shavian God

Shaw learned economics chiefly from George and Jevons; Fabianism, chiefly from Mill and Webb; but Marx converted him to socialism. He also learned economics by defending Marx—unsuccessfully.

In October of 1884, Shaw took part in a controversy which ultimately involved Hyndman, Wallas, and a number of other prominent socialists and which illustrates the reception accorded Marxism, then almost unknown, in England. It was of course inevitable that Marx, with his emphasis on class war, violent revolution, and the purely partisan character of the state, should not have gained a great following in a nation traditionally devoted to legality and compromise. Nevertheless, the vigorous attack made at that time against his value theory probably led, particularly among the Fabians, to an underestimation of other parts of his system. The Marxists were unfortunate in their champions. Shaw early went over to the enemy, and Hyndman, the Marxist leader, tried to conquer by sheer weight of the grand manner. In spite of his defection, Shaw continued to be a just and generous critic.

The controversy began when Philip H. Wicksteed, a Unitarian minister, published in the socialist journal *To-day* a criticism of Marx's value theory from the point of view of Jevonian economics. The attack is clear, courteous—and damaging. Wicksteed begins by pointing out that Marx accepts Ricardo's subsistence law of wages without accepting Ricardo's cause—the constant pressure of population. Marx feels that the cause is rather to be found in his own value theory. He assumes, with Ricardo, that objects will exchange for the amount of labor required to reproduce them. Labor itself, then, is worth only the work necessary barely to maintain and reproduce it. If a man working ten hours a day creates the value of his subsistence in six hours, and the interest and depreciation on capital in two, he works two more merely to enrich his employer. Thus, paying for everything at its value, the capitalist actually receives more than he puts in.

But is labor the source of value? In order to exchange, says Marx in his Hegelian idiom, articles must have elements of likeness and unlikeness, the first to create the measure for exchange, the second to create the desire.[1] The element of likeness is labor, not concrete —because all such labor differs—but abstract. To get at the value of an object, one must strip it of all the particular use values with which human effort has endowed it and regard it as a mere jelly of abstract labor. With regard to manufactured goods, Marx's argument seems especially strong, for there labor does directly affect exchange value. An invention which saves labor time undoubtedly cuts price.

Yet surely, says Wicksteed, a coat is valuable not because it is made but because it protects its owner. Not abstract labor but abstract utility determines value. The price of manufactured goods can be satisfactorily explained only by two laws formulated by W. S. Jevons. According to the law of indifference, the units of a homogeneous commodity exchange equally. According to the law of the variation of utility, each successive increment of a commodity satisfies a less urgent need and therefore has less utility and value. It follows from these two laws that "the last available increment of any commodity determines the ratio of exchange of the whole of it."[2] Assume that hats and coats are equally necessary and that eight hats can be made in the same time as one coat. Hats will then be made until there are so many that one hat is worth only one eighth as much as a coat. Then coats will be made also.

In short, the force of demand at the margin of supply determines exchange value. Moreover, the value of an object varies with the amount of labor it contains only when labor force can be directed to that or to other objects freely. And to one object labor force cannot be freely directed—to the production of labor force itself, unless one "lives in a country where slave-breeding is possible."[3] Therefore, the exchange value of labor does not depend on the amount of work necessary to maintain and reproduce it. As an explanation for the subsistence law of wages, the theory of surplus value collapses. Marx must fall back on Malthus—or nothing.

Wicksteed certainly refutes the labor theory of value, but he does not prove that Marx cannot get along without Malthus. One of the most striking passages in *Capital* explains that wages go down not because modern civilization is too poor but because it is too rich, not because population increases more rapidly than the food supply but because it increases more rapidly than employment.[4] Machinery renders labor increasingly superfluous. Certainly here right lies with Marx rather than with Wicksteed.

Had he chosen to give battle, Hyndman, as the communist leader, might have made a powerful, if not a satisfactory, reply; but he preferred simply to declare "the presumptuous insect Wicksteed" beneath his notice.[5] Nevertheless, the proprietors of *To-day*, whose socialism was still something less than an act of faith, felt that Wicksteed must be answered and urged Shaw to undertake the task. Though he knew nothing of Jevons and only as much of Marx as one can glean by reading him, he consented, on the condition that his opponent be permitted a final rebuttal.

The opening of the article presents the unique spectacle of an uncertain and hesitant G.B.S. It is clear he already suspects that, so far as the value theory is concerned, great Marx is dead. He does not mention the oversight of abstract utility in *Capital*. He frankly recognizes the ability of Wicksteed, a noted scriptural critic, who, "in search of fresh Bibles to criticise," has seized on the bible of socialism.[6] But he will be destroyed later on by some "more competent hand" than Shaw's. Meanwhile, there are weak points in his armor. For example, his use of algebra. Ever since a little boy at school proved to him that one equals two, Shaw has suspected anyone who begins with "Let x equal a." Warming to his work, he now tries to render the law of variable utility absurd by demonstrating—what Wicksteed was perfectly aware of—that the utility of successive mouthfuls of beef may vary from infinity to zero. He concludes with an orgy of literary virtuosity, in which, with the most dazzling rapidity and the most shameful disregard of his own abstemious principles, he cooks whole cows and devours them ravenously, juggles Bibles and brandy bottles by the dozen, and at length turns the Reverend Mr. Wicksteed himself into a dipsomaniac for purposes of the most casual illustration.

Apparently the blinding fireworks of his opponent left Mr. Wicksteed quite unruffled. He clears up a few ingenious confusions which Shaw has introduced into the discussion and praises him for his literary ability. If he shows a twinge of resentment, it is at the joke against mathematics. He observes that because of his boyhood experience, Shaw concluded that

> there was "a screw loose somewhere"—not in his own reasoning powers, but "in the algebraic art;" and thenceforth renounced mathematical reasoning in favour of the literary method which enables a clever man to follow equally fallacious arguments to equally absurd conclusions *without seeing that they are absurd.*[7]

The blow must have struck home, for, quite characteristically, Shaw sought Wicksteed's friendship. He was obviously a man from whom something could be learned. Shaw was right, for through Wicksteed he obtained admission to a circle which the prosperous stockbroker

Beeton had begun inviting to his house for economic discussion. Shaw held on to his entry "like grim death" until the group expanded some years later to become the Royal Economic Society. This club bore a formidable resemblance to a university seminar, yet though usually willing to learn anywhere except in school, Shaw speaks of it with surprising enthusiasm:

> During those years Wicksteed expounded "final utility" to us with a blackboard except when we got hold of some man from the "Baltic" (The London Wheat Exchange), or the like, to explain the markets to us and afterwards have his information reduced to Jevonian theory. Among university professors of economics Edgeworth and Foxwell stuck to us pretty constantly, and W. Cunningham turned up occasionally. Of course, the atmosphere was by no means Shavian; but that was exactly what I wanted. The Socialist platform and my journalistic pulpits involved a constant and most provocative forcing of people to face the practical consequences of theories and beliefs, and to draw mordant contrasts between what they professed or what their theories involved and their life and conduct. This made dispassionate discussion of abstract theory impossible. At Beeton's the conditions were practically university conditions. There was a tacit understanding that the calculus of utilities and the theory of exchange must be completely isolated from the fact that we lived, as Morris' medieval captain put it, by "robbing the poor." [8]

As the quotation indicates, the discussion was dominated by Jevonian thought. Nevertheless, one suspects there must have been frequent conflict between the rival systems of Jevons and Mill, since not only was Graham Wallas a member of the group but also Alfred Marshall,[9] who later, particularly in value theory,[10] worked out a synthesis of his two great predecessors. At any rate, Shaw himself was obviously eager to learn Jevons and followed Wicksteed to the very walls of algebra itself. These he apparently would not—or could not—scale.

Meanwhile another and on the whole more dubious path had opened to heresy against Marx. During these early years the Fabian Society, though it comprised only forty members, managed to create the noise and turbulence of a much larger organization. A small group, feeling the need of studious quiet, formed in 1885 the Hampstead Historical Society. Its members were chiefly Shaw, Webb, Clarke, Olivier, Wallas, Bland, and Mrs. Besant—in short, the authors of the *Fabian Essays;* and since out of their discussions those essays grew, both they and their club require a word of description. The Hampstead Historical was not only an inner committee of the leading Fabians but a committee of those who were later to become famous. Indeed, Mrs. Besant was already famous, having undergone the spectacular martyrdom of a chancery suit, in which her atheism had lost her the custody of her two children. She was also a magnetic personality and an unparalleled speaker. Wallas and Olivier were formidable for their knowledge and debating skill; Clarke, for his ill temper; Bland, for his great size, his "fierce Norman exterior," and his voice like an eagle's scream.[11]

Like the Fabian Society, the Hampstead Historical was dominated if not by the ideas, certainly by the temperament, of Shaw. The only defense against Shaw was to be like him: everybody was brilliant, alert, candid, contentious, and insulting. The atmosphere must have been rather like that of Shaw's plays. He himself was grateful for the Shavian frankness of his friends. "My colleagues knocked much nonsense, ignorance, and vulgar provinciality out of me," he says, "for we were on quite ruthless critical terms with one another."[12]

For several years Shaw attended one night in alternate weeks the Beeton group and the Hampstead Historical Society. If the first was essentially a university seminar with, the second was a seminar without, a professor. Doubtless the professor would have been an inconvenience, for although the Society was eager to get at truth, it also had a practical object in view: it wanted to discover a sound economic basis for socialism. Marx was the natural point of departure, particularly because at the moment Shaw was in an attitude of imminent apostasy, which he dissimulated under a jaunty and unscrupulous defense of the whole communist doctrine. Marx's system was terrifyingly huge and complex, but as an engine for the destruction of capitalistic theorists, it was, Shaw himself had discovered, a severe disappointment; it was always breaking down.[13] The fundamental question was that of the revolutionary rights of the workers: Do they, or do they not, have a right to the whole produce of their labor? Marx replies by drawing an obvious moral from Ricardo and fortifying it with the supersubtle metaphysics of Hegel. In substance, he argues that if labor alone confers value on an object, then the whole wealth of the community belongs to the laborer, not only the subsistence wages which he actually receives but the surplus value which wrongfully goes to the employer because of his private monopoly of the means of production.

The Hampstead Fabians fought Ricardo with Ricardo—or at least Ricardo plus Marx with Ricardo plus Mill. According to Wallas, Webb and Olivier had scored brilliantly in the Civil Service examination for economics because of their acumen in applying Ricardo's law of rent. With this weapon and Mill's rent of ability, they now attacked Marx. Instead of taking surplus value "in a lump," they divided it into the

[79]

three rents of land, tools, and brains.[14] If a man worked with the worst land, tools, and brains, he might make no more than he consumed; therefore, abstract labor does not create surplus value.

Shaw's Jevonian approach to the problem was more modern and precise, nor did he fail to perceive that the classical law of rent, quite as well as the doctrine of surplus value, could be turned to the advantage of socialistic economics. In 1887, when the first English translation of *Das Kapital* appeared, he published in successive weeks articles on Marx in *The National Reformer*. In the first, he criticizes the value theory from the classical point of view; in the later two, from the Jevonian.

Economics has called forth relatively little of Shaw's characteristic poetry of the intellect. These essays do not possess great literary merit, yet they are occasionally brilliant, always sensible, and sincerely in search of the truth. The first treats the prophet and his religion in their broadest aspects. When *Das Kapital* came out, says Shaw, it was hailed by many socialists as the scientific basis for a millennium, a revelation in which not to have faith was to be damned as "unscientific." To stir such enthusiasm, either the book or its author must be extraordinary. Marx's personal life was certainly not so. There is "nothing picturesque" about many years of research among blue books. "When the last word has been said about the book, no more will be needed about the man." [15] But the third volume of the book is not yet published, and Friedrich Engels himself admits that the fragment extant "leaves unexplained a difficulty apparently fatal to the whole Marxian theory." Extreme Marxolaters are therefore in an acutely ridiculous position. " 'Scientific Socialism' means cashing a promissory note of Mr. Engels, dated 'London, an Marx' Geburtstag, 5 Mai, 1885,' " when Engels had promised to bring out the third volume. The Marxists have never understood rent. In the first book of *Capital*, Marx

> treats of labor without reference to variations of skill between its parts; of raw material without reference to variations of fertility; and of the difference between the product of labor and the price [wage] of labor power, as "surplus value" without reference to its subdivision into rent, interest, and profits.

But if his economics are weak, Marx is infinitely stronger than his economics. He has discovered the law of social development. "An unsleeping sense of the transitory character of capitalism, and of the justice of equality, is the characteristic spirit of Marx." Private property is but a phase of social development, like slavery or serfdom. To Ricardo and De Quincey, the nineteenth century was as safe and solid as the wall of China. To Marx it was "a cloud passing down the wind, changing its shape and fading as it goes." Some economists feel we have had enough private enterprise but "lean towards a collegiate scheme which combines the weak points of feudalism and collectivism. Mr. Ruskin prescribes moralized feudalism, but gives no details as to the moralizing process." Marx looks toward the future. He would not abandon the machine because it has brought new problems. Mill, too, was forward-looking, but his students hardly learned this lesson. Marx's students never forgot it. For though his ideas may not be sound, they have magnificent scope, and he uttered them with an imperturbable conviction. A quip or two about his value theory will not destroy Karl Marx.

The criticism is vague but just. The economic analysis is that of Mill and Ricardo. Shaw correctly perceives that Marx's great contribution is to the evolutionary conception of society. Opinions will of course differ regarding Shaw's estimate of Marx's greatness. Mr. Barzun does not think him great at all. In *Capital*, according to that critic, his indignation and his sarcasm are puny beside the awfulness of his facts.[16] Certainly more restraint would have been more eloquent. Nevertheless, Shaw is himself a proof for his contention that Marx has exerted a powerful influence on gifted men. Perhaps through ignorance of biographical facts, Shaw underestimates the power of Marx's personality. Essentially, he was a kind of unamiable Bentham, who, though he had not himself a talent for the limelight, could dominate clever men who did.

The second article repeats in another form the attack on Marx's value theory made by Wicksteed three years before, except that whereas Wicksteed deals with the value of both labor and commodities, Shaw deals here with the latter only. Naturally, his article strongly reflects the influence of the evenings at Beeton's.[17] It is clear that Shaw's pen is new to close economic discussion. The article attempts to be extremely simple and clear, but some slippery transitions and perhaps some economic confusion have rendered it in places vague and obscure.

The third article, though written only a week later, indicates a notable advance in clarity and sureness of both thought and expression. For the first time Shaw seems thoroughly at home with his subject. He frequently cites chapter and verse. He seems to know more about Marx and more about Jevons. This paper continues the attack on Marx's value theory, dealing now with its relation to labor rather than to commodities. In *Capital*, a sharp contrast is drawn between use value and exchange value in order to show how the worker, not having access to the means of production, must sell his labor as a ware in the market. To do so, says Shaw, is practically to sell its total for its final utility, its use for its exchange value. Marx explains the transaction by his theory of surplus value. In a twelve-hour day, the worker reproduces his own subsistence in the first six and gains for his employer in the remaining six. Marx fully understood the facts, but his theory fails to explain them. The employer and the worker do not stand over against each other like the buyer and the seller of an ordinary commodity. The employer has no absolute need of the worker. He can work himself. But the worker, if he means to live, must have access to land and capital, of which the employer enjoys a monopoly. Moreover, "unskilled labor-power differs from all other commodities in that its production, instead of being an effort or a sacrifice, is a pleasurable act to which man is driven by an irresistible instinct." [18] In short, the supply is increased until each unit can be bought for what will keep it precariously alive. Again, failing to see the difference between labor and goods, Marx tries to account for the peculiarity of labor power by seeing differences where none exist. For example, does not a steam engine, just as much as a man, produce surplus value? If not, why are highly mechanized industries no less profitable than those which employ proportionately more workers? Indeed, to non-Marxists, is not the expression "surplus value" itself a contradiction in terms?

Nevertheless, Shaw "never took up a book that proved better worth reading than *Capital*." [19] Marx's errors are more easily explained than his greatness.

> A born materialist . . . he attempted to carve a theory with the tools of the born metaphysician. . . . In his time, too, the germ of the truth about value lay in the old supply and demand theory, which was historically anti-popular, whereas the labor theory of Ricardo had a delusive air of being the reverse. Again, the question of the value of labor force was inseparable from the population question; and that, too, he disliked as a recognized staple of capitalist apologetics. [20]

The polite hostilities between Wicksteed and Shaw in 1884 had expanded into a violent and embittered controversy between catholic and protestant Marxists, in which, by speech, debate, letter, review, and article, Hyndman and his colleagues poured vague and lofty contempt upon Jevons's sunspot theory while Shaw, Wallas, and Wicksteed poured deadly Jevonian criticism into the shattered superstructure of Marx's value doctrine. Of all this Shaw gives an amusing account in "Bluffing the Value Theory," published in the May, 1889, number of *To-day*. The article contains nothing new about Marx and is chiefly interesting because it indicates that while attacking the economic basis of Marxism, Shaw was building up that of Fabianism:

> Commodities of the same kind and value are products, not only of labour force, but of raw material which varies greatly in ac-

cessibility and adaptability, as every farmer and mine owner knows. Under Socialism we should obtain these for their average cost of production; but individualistic free competition can never permanently reduce the prices of manufactured goods below the cost of their production from the least accessible and most refractory raw materials in use: the resultant profit to the proprietors of the more favourable raw material being economic rent, the main source of "surplus value." Without a thorough grip of this factor it is impossible to defend Socialism on economic grounds against rival systems.[21]

In short, rejecting the attempt to found, on a dubious labor theory of value, the claim of a single class to the whole product of its industry, Shaw establishes on a sound theoretical basis the claim of the whole community to economic rent, which he generalizes to include all forms of value resulting from special ability or a favorable position in society. This argument is elaborated in his contribution to the *Fabian Essays*, published in the same year with "Bluffing the Value Theory."

To be sure, both Shaw and Marx, as Mr. Maurice Dobbs has pointed out, were attempting to formulate the same principle: that socially created values should accrue to society as a whole.[22] Shaw's formulation had the advantage of being free from obvious fallacy; Marx's, that of exerting greater rhetorical force.

Like nearly everything else in Marx's system, surplus value is made to be an expression of the class struggle and a means of intensifying the class consciousness of the proletariat. One suspects the influence of *Past and Present*. Beginning like Carlyle with the hypocrisy of "cash payment is the sole nexus between human beings," Marx tries to discover in the very laws which govern the sale and purchase of commodities the underlying tyranny of the middle class: political freedom hides social bondage. As Shaw remarks in his third review of *Capital*, the laws of value and distribution do certainly reflect the antagonism between labor and capital, but not nearly so starkly as Marx represents. In fact, he has formulated not so much a theory of value as a theory of exploitation. The very crudeness of the argument, as Shaw points out in "The Illusions of Socialism," explains its power over the uneducated mind.[23] He overlooks not only the rents of land and capital but the rent of ability too. Crude physical labor is the one great reality in his economic world. Through the palpable phenomena of that world, abstract labor flows like a metaphysical fluid. Marx's economics appeal to class interest among the workers; Shaw's, to disinterested reason among all classes. Though more accurate theoretically, Shaw's are less realistic in the pragmatic sense that they probably deterred Fabians from recognizing the importance to socialism of labor as a class movement.

Perhaps because he had exhausted all his careful justice in the heat of controversy or because he wanted to give an unusual judgment the spice of exaggeration, Shaw's more mature pronouncements on Marx tend to overrate him as an artist and underrate him as a thinker. "Marx's *Capital*," he wrote in 1901, "is not a treatise on Socialism; it is a jeremiad against the *bourgeoisie*, supported by such a mass of evidence and such a relentless genius for denunciation as had never been brought to bear before." [24] The same tendency is evident in a lengthier comment made in 1921:

> The moment Marx shewed that the relation of the bourgeoisie to society was grossly immoral and disastrous, and that the whited wall of starched shirt fronts concealed and defended the most infamous of all tyrannies and the basest of all robberies, he became an inspired prophet in the mind of every generous soul whom his book reached.[25]

For Shaw the religion of Marx, in the strict sense of drastic class war and violent revolution, was a brief fanaticism, which, having blazed fiercely for a few weeks, died down and then smoldered malevolently for a lifetime. His sense of humor, his sense of legality, his aversion to violence, fatalism, and mechanism were against it. His hatred of Philistinism, his puritan predilection for the honesty of root-and-branch reform, his growing distrust of democracy and gradualism were for it. The result was a periodic and un-Fabian tendency to revolution. In fact, the story of his nostalgic flirtations with Marxism is but the tale of his Fabian defections told positively.

CHAPTER ELEVEN

"Educate, Agitate, Organise!"

What the late thirties had been for the middle class, the late eighties were for laboring men. Electoral reform gave many of them the vote, the Local Government Bill offered them a new field of influence, returning prosperity gave them hope and comfort, and the trade-union movement gave them power. Socialism was becoming possible. Therefore socialism was in the air. It was a time when a compact group of educated, determined young men, trained in economics, practiced in public speaking, gifted in writing, and apt at political maneuver, might "educate, agitate, and organise" with telling success. In short, it was a period in which Fabians might make history.

"Educate, agitate, organise!" was the motto of the Society. Apparently they placed least emphasis on the last, for though pretty closely unified in opinion and attitude, they were surprisingly loose and individualistic in formal organization. A favorite saying of Webb's was that "the activity of the Fabian Society is the sum of the activities of its members." [1] When branches began to grow up in provincial cities, they were permitted to be completely independent of the London group. Moreover, the Fabians made little attempt to amalgamate with other collectivist associations or to form a political party. They put their faith in ideas rather than numbers. With Mill's conversion before his mind, Webb felt that a little education would change Liberals and Radicals into socialists almost as logically and inevitably as two and two make four. Swayed by his own romantic conceptions of genius and the class struggle, Shaw inclined to believe that great thinkers and not large parties produce revolutionary changes. Fabian constitutional rationalism caused Fabian leaders to hope a little too much for a broad movement inspired by a sense of justice and to fear too much a narrow class movement impelled by economic interest. Webb himself confesses that they failed at first to see the political significance of the trade-unions. [2] Later, they may indeed, as Shaw declares, have preferred to aid the labor movement rather than lead it. [3] At any rate, they chose to educate rather than organize. The result was that they created the doctrine of British socialism but not the political structure. The latter was chiefly the work of Ramsay MacDonald, who, though a Fabian at the time, attached himself through the Independent Labour Party to the trade-unions and led them toward socialism with a program of Fabianism plus religious fervor.

Fabian "education" proved to be a benevolently Machiavellian combination of propaganda which inevitably reminds one of the conspiratorial philanthropy of James Mill and Francis Place. History is always at its best when it repeats itself, for then it is ironic. What the Radicals had done sixty years before to the Whigs, the Fabians now did to the Radicals—and in less degree, to everybody else. Precisely as the Whigs had been drifting in the thirties, the Radicals were drifting now. They were between philosophies—progressives with a limited and contradictory vision of progress. Some, like Morley and Chamberlain, were already moving along the road to socialism. Others, like Roebuck, were more conservative than Disraeli. But the Fabians were not at all confused. They had a formidable theory of the future. Shaw was nearly as full of ideas as Bentham, and Webb was as full of facts as Mill and as full of stratagems as Place.

The Fabian method was to "permeate," to inculcate socialistic opinions anonymously. Members of the Society joined Radical clubs, trade-union and cooperative branches, Liberal and even Tory associations, where they became as active and influential as possible. Soon headquarters, whether Radical or Tory, were besieged with a bewildering stream of resolutions in favor of the eight-hour day, slum clearance, gas-and-water socialism, and the heavy taxation of unearned increment. The Holborn and Strand Liberal associations became virtually Fabian. Hampstead and Highgate were astonished at their own radicalism. Fabians not only inspired Fabian resolutions in Liberal minds but, as Liberal delegates, carried them to regional conferences and even wrote them up as Liberal exploits in Liberal journals and newspapers. Indeed, the whole Fabian assault on unsuspecting capitalism suggests, in spite of the sageness of Webb, the gay audacity and melodramatic resource of a college prank. As a matter of fact, Olivier and Wallas were at this time not long out of college, and most of their principal confederates were also quite young.

The Fabian conquest of the press was typical. They rejected the idea of a separate periodical publication like the *Justice* of the Social Democratic Federation, on the ground that workingmen can afford only one paper and want at low cost something much more elaborate than a small socialistic society could finance. The Fabians therefore decided to "permeate" the Liberal and Radical press.

Their most brilliant exploit was the "collaring" of the newly founded *Star* in 1888. Twenty Fabians sent twenty eloquent postcards, suggesting to the editor that the whole metropolis was aflame with Fabian socialism. Then other Fabians offered their services. They quickly found places in every department of the journal and before the year was out, according to Shaw, had H. W. Massingham, the assistant editor, writing pure communism. *The Star* had suddenly become a pirate ship. It sailed the journalistic main belching—even from the music and literary columns—a murderous fire on the money-laden barks of capitalism, until the proprietors, awakening to the real character of their crew, cleared them out to the last man. But by this time the Fabians had persuaded *The Daily Chronicle* that a column devoted to labor would appreciably increase circulation, and by 1892 they had persuaded *The Daily News* likewise, "although five years ago the editor would as soon have thought of setting aside a column for Freethinkers." [4]

But much as they valued the press, the Fabians valued lecture and debate even more. Having lectured and debated themselves into a wide knowledge of history, social theory, and advanced economics, they naturally hoped to lecture and debate a great many others into an earnest conviction of constitutional socialism. Outside of Mrs. Besant, their greatest master of forensic art was Shaw himself. A true college professor under the skin, he commonly taught himself a subject by delivering lectures on it, and as his interests were keen and varied, he rapidly became a formidable education machine, ready at any moment to lecture at any length on anything from the latest music to the earliest socialism. For years he devoted a good part of every Sunday and many weekdays to speaking in Hyde Park, on street corners, and in out-of-the-way halls and meeting rooms. He developed a taste for low audiences—and quarrelsome ones. The consequence was an indefatigable readiness and lucidity, which on one occasion enabled him, in the midst of a driving rain, to fascinate six stolid and dripping policemen, sent to keep order among a large crowd that never gathered. Other Fabian lecturers were but lesser heroes of the same Homeric pattern. In 1888, the Society delivered over seven hundred lectures.

This work must not be conceived simply as an exhilarating and somewhat strenuous adventure. Shaw has written with sympathetic understanding of how difficult it was for a sensitive man like William Morris to face rough and sometimes hostile audiences. In some degree all the Fabians, middle class to the core, must have felt this difficulty—and particularly Shaw, who carried on far more street-corner agitation than his fellows. As I have said, he had a taste for noise and turmoil. He enjoyed loud audiences as he enjoyed loud people —like Frank Harris—and he knew how to handle both. But he was also shy, sensitive, proud, and even snobbish. Later he confessed that he felt, quite as keenly as Morris, the humiliations of the gentlemanly agitator. During the Dod Street disturbances, each of the three socialistic societies agreed in the interests of martyrdom to furnish a victim for arrest at a meeting which had been forbidden by the police. Probably Shaw suffered one of the most exquisitely uncomfortable moments of his life when he learned that his offer to be the Fabian victim had been accepted by his fellow members. At the last minute he was saved by the police themselves, who decided not to make any arrests. His respectability remained inviolate.

Fabians did not shirk the benefits they inflicted on the world at large. They continued to lecture each other—and not only on economics and politics but on art, literature, and science, particularly in their relations to socialism. Many of these lectures were prodigies of information and austerity, but the mightiest ever delivered among them was fittingly achieved by Shaw, who, making as it were a tremendous three-times forensic circuit of Victorian London, brought forth nearly the whole of *The Quintessence of Ibsenism* before an awe-struck audience.

Occasionally the Fabians invited in outside speakers, some of whom, like Morris and Bosanquet, were among the most eminent men of the time. But only socialistic celebrities were absolutely sure of respect. Almost too highly civilized, the Fabians were not free from sudden and elaborately premeditated accessions of barbarism. There was a calculated *Schrecklichkeit* in their war of instruction against capitalism. Having discovered after their expulsion from Anderton's Hotel that the red plush and gold lace of Willis's Rooms could be very cheaply hired, they seized the opportunity to invite with spiderish courtesy into that most respectable of parlors a succession of eminent Liberal and Radical politicians, who came to instruct and remained to be assassinated. One of these was Richard Haldane, whose visit has been immortalized in an article entitled "Butchered to Make a Fabian Holiday." He was an easy, confident, purring lion, much given to slumming in the queer, amusing lecture rooms of faddist societies. Lured into the Fabian den, he poured forth Benthamite wisdom for more than an hour with the utmost good humor—and then discovered that what he had taken to be utopian lambs were ravening wolves formidably fanged with the sharpest logic and the latest economics. After prolonged carnage, "the Chairman called upon Mr. Haldane to reply. Hideous mockery! the chairman knew that Haldane was *dead!*" [5] Education by murder, though brutal, proved effective. Haldane eventually became a member of the Labour Party.

To his great loss, Asquith declined to undergo the ordeal, though once he stooped to address the Workingmen's College. At the end of the speech, Shaw snapped viciously at his heels, while the other Fabians strained at the leash with slavering jaws. But Asquith snubbed them and so never learned that the Liberals were inevitably doomed, though he lived to see the day—as well as to find his own ultimate damnation in the political satire of *Back to Methuselah*. But many other Liberals had, like Haldane, the good fortune to become both sadder and wiser. "We were," writes Shaw with immense satisfaction, "the recognized bullies and swashbucklers of advanced economics." [6]

The Fabians were of course too practical to devote themselves exclusively to the conquest of the press or the education of Cabinet ministers. They soon made an assault on the government of London, concentrating their most formidable lecturers on the powerful Liberal and Radical Workingmen's clubs, and in 1889, the year of the first County Council Election, achieved the solid advantage of a Progressive majority. In 1888 Mrs. Besant and the Reverend Stewart Headlam were elected to the London School Board. In 1892, Webb and five other Fabians were elected to the County Council, and later Shaw became a Vestryman and a Borough Councilor. "The generalship of this movement was undertaken chiefly by Sidney Webb, who played such bewildering conjuring tricks with the Liberal thimbles and the Fabian peas, that to this day [1892] both the Liberals and the sectarian Socialists stand aghast at him." [7] Perhaps the generalship was a little too brilliant. It fell short of that perfect anonymity so characteristic of Place and so necessary to the quiet and continued exertion of power. At any rate, the fine Fabian hand was rather speedily discovered, and with extraordinary discrimination, *The Speaker*, a leading Gladstonian organ, denounced the Fabian creed as "a mixture of dreary, gassy doctrinairism and crack-brained farcicality, set off with a portentous omniscience and flighty egotism not to be matched outside the walls of a lunatic asylum." [8] Clearly, Webb and Shaw were appreciated! The Society's coat of arms itself, representing those two eminent men rampant, does not more adequately suggest how much two personalities have given their stamp to nearly all Fabian thought and action.

Unfortunately, the discovery of the Fabian red herring precipitated the issue of socialism into local politics and probably delayed some necessary municipalization. Nevertheless, the Fabians had won a strong position, and though stubbornly opposed, achieved a significant work in sanitation, slum clearance, municipal enterprise, and particularly in education. Promptly on his election to the Council, Webb was made Chairman of the Technical Education Board, and as that body had power over nearly all metropolitan education except that in Greek and theology, he was able to do much "to bring secondary and university education within the reach of the working people of London." [9] He also gave direction and scientific basis to municipal reform in general by his remarkable pamphlets, supplementing "Facts for Socialists," *Fabian Tract No. 5*, with *No. 15*, "English Progress Toward Social Democracy," and *No. 8*, "Facts for Londoners," which led to the "voluminous statistical publications of the London County Council." [10] From 1892, a group of Fabians remained continuously on the Council, and working in close harmony with the Labour contingent headed by Burns, largely shaped the policy of the Progressive Party in London affairs. The consequence was an era almost as significant for London as Chamberlain's mayoralty had been for Birmingham.

The Fabians also had some very practical plans for national politics. In 1888, Webb drafted what he thought the Liberal program ought to be, had it privately printed under the title "Wanted a Programme," and circulated it widely throughout the country, taking care it should reach the Liberal leaders. Shaw describes its launching as a bit of Fabian pressure politics at their most swashbuckling:

> Webb gave me the Program in his own handwriting as a string of resolutions. I, being then a permeative Fabian on the executive of the South St. Pancras Liberal and Radical Association (I had coolly walked in and demanded to be elected to the Association and Executive, which was done on the spot by the astonished Association—ten strong or thereabouts) took them down to a meeting in Percy Hall . . . where the late Mr. Beale, then Liberal candidate and subscription milch cow of the constituency (without the ghost of a chance), was to address as many of the ten as might turn up under the impression that he was addressing a public meeting. . . . I asked him to move the resolutions. He said they looked complicated, and that if I would move them he would second them. I moved them, turning over Webb's pages by batches and not reading most of them. Mr. Beale seconded. Passed unanimously. That night they went down to The Star with a report of an admirable speech which Mr. Beale was supposed to have delivered. Next day he found the National Liberal Club in an uproar at his revolutionary break-away. But he played up; buttoned his coat determinedly; said we lived in progressive times and must move with them; and carried it off.[11]

Ultimately, the Liberals came forth with the Newcastle Program of 1891. It contained Webb's proposals, as well as nearly everything else under the sun. How much its acceptance was due to Fabian agitation and how much to the competition of the strongly socialistic politics of Chamberlain, who had recently come out for old-age pensions, is difficult to say. Certainly the "London radicals" had impinged on the Gladstonian consciousness. He seems to have regarded them as dangerous demogogues who must be promised the moon so that their votes might be used to bring about Irish Home Rule.

As a matter of fact, the Newcastle monster deceived no one—Webb and Shaw least of all. Shaw claimed credit for it, but he had no hopes of it. The Fabian "Election Manifesto of 1892," one of his most compact, sober, and eloquent political writings, makes this very clear. The "Manifesto" is nothing short of a reversal of Fabian policy and an open declaration of war against the Liberals.

It begins by cataloguing the crimes of the two dominant parties. The Liberals have avoided English problems by appearing to solve Irish ones. What is really necessary is the redistribution of rent and interest and the "Disestablishment and Disendowment of Idleness." [12] But of course there is a conspiracy of silence on this question, because only endowed idleness can afford to sit in the House. In the last analysis, even advanced Radicals like Morley and Chamberlain will vote for property and against labor, because they possess property. Therefore, the primary issue of the election is the payment of Members, which would permit labor to be represented by labor. This the Liberals seem to promise in the Newcastle Program, but the workingman has little reason to trust them. In exchange for a great labor vote, they have passed a few socialistic measures and offered support to a few labor candidacies in safe Tory constituencies. Labor will command real power only when it organizes and finances its own party and finds able men of its own class to represent it. Meanwhile, it must exert all possible pressure on the Liberals.

Clearly, this document marks a new development in the history of the Fabians. They have turned their efforts from a general to a narrow class movement. Socialism must be achieved not primarily by reason and argument but by brute votes and constitutional class struggle. Having given up all hope of a permanent alliance with the Liberals, the Fabians have recognized the importance of the labor and cooperative movements, which they aspire not to lead but simply to educate.

Essentially, the "Manifesto" outlines the tactics and immediate objectives of a new Labour party. But why so sudden a change of policy? The reasons were probably many: the devious stubbornness of Gladstone, the confusion of the Liberals, the ambiguous defections and alliances of the Chamberlain Radicals, the triumph of unskilled labor in the Dock Strike of 1889, and probably even Webb's marriage in 1892 with Miss Beatrice Potter, who had recently finished a historical book on the cooperative movement. That pretty and serious young lady, reared in the lap of the greater capitalism, which regarded cheap labor, like cheap water, as one of the natural resources of a vicinity, had in the course of a very studious youth recapitulated the history of her century and moved from the extreme individualism of Herbert Spencer to the Fabian socialism of Sidney Webb. Then, with admirable femininity, she had married the somewhat prosaic truth she had discovered. It is the fairy tale of the solitary princess translated into Victorian economics and blue books. They lived happily with statistics ever after—and the history of ordinary mortals was visibly changed thereby.

The Liberals won the election but not with sufficient strength to carry through Home Rule. Gladstone would hardly undertake anything else. The Fabians simulated rage, and when, in spite of Campbell-Bannerman's explicit pledge, the government made no effort to raise the wages or improve the working conditions of its own employees, Webb and Shaw published in *The Fortnightly Review* the famous "To Your Tents, O Israel." They examined each government department in turn, explaining existing conditions, what had been promised, and what had been done—which was practically nothing. The article amounted to a declaration of war, and several prominent Fabians, including H. W. Massingham, resigned from the Society.

Massingham did not completely dissociate himself from his former friends, for he joined several of them shortly after in writing for *The Fortnightly* a symposium on "What Mr. Gladstone Ought to Do," which was in large part a continuation of the Fabian attack on the Liberals. Shaw's contribution is another masterpiece of political prose, which, were it not written so precisely in the language of immediate issues, would certainly have found its way into his collected works. It combines a brilliant portrait of Mr. Gladstone with a shrewd and witty scolding to voters. The Victorian parliamentary Achilles is depicted in his characteristic milieu:

> The chief difficulty in dealing with Mr. Gladstone as a statesman arises from the fact that his statesmanship . . . has nothing to do with his popularity. . . . It is as an artist, an unrivalled platform artist, that Mr. Gladstone is popular. . . . The tree-felling, the lesson-reading, the railway journeys punctuated with speeches, the feats of oratory and debate, the splendid courtesy and large style, the animated figure with the blanched complexion lighted by the great eyes, the encyclopaedic conversation, the elastic playing with an immense burden of years: all these bring rounds of applause louder and longer than any merely theatrical actor can hope for. Mr. Irving in the Lyceum is but the microcosm. Mr. Gladstone in England is the macrocosm. . . . Mr. Irving is deservedly so popular as an artist that it is unpopular to deny that he is a connoisseur in

literature as well. And Mr. Gladstone, too, is so popular as an artist that it is unpopular to deny that he is a great political thinker as well.[13]

Actually, Gladstone has long since ceased to think. On all questions except Home Rule, he is a hopelessly prejudiced Tory.

But the voter perceives no inconsistency between Liberal professions and Tory measures:

> He declares that he is for "measures, not men"; but as he is no judge of measures, and is able to judge men, according to their command of political claptrap, just enough to feel impelled to back them against one another in the political arena much as he would back a horse or a prizefighter, he is really always for "men, not measures," unless the measure is one for relieving the rates, when he will sell his vote with shameless promptitude for a penny in the pound.[14]

About this time William Morris made a pathetic and desperate effort to bring the three tiny socialistic organizations together. A working unity was to come shortly from another quarter, but Morris did not see this. And yet his had been a life of discoveries. For thirty years he had with brilliant success devoted the talents and energy of a Philistine, as well as the genius of an artist, to the purpose of beautifying an ugly century. Inevitably he had studied the causes of this ugliness and found them partly in poverty but chiefly in the Industrial Revolution. The modern factory was a pandemonium of joyless labor in which the standardized tyranny of the machine thrust itself between the artistic instincts of the workman and the artistic desires of the consumer, to turn out ugliness which could satisfy only vulgar luxury or desperate necessity. Morris decided that the only remedy was to replace machinery with artistic handicraft and a luxurious, spendthrift capitalism with a restrained, beauty-loving communism. When most of his associates were becoming the most respectable of Philistines, Morris became a socialist.

His conversion was not exhilarating. For nearly forty years his friends had taught him to regard himself as a noisy, irrepressible boy of genius called Topsy. When he stepped into the street and mingled with workingmen, he suddenly found himself looked on as a magnificent and bearded sage of sixty. He was only fifty, and he didn't like being a sage—especially on dirty street corners and in ugly, stuffy halls. Morris went about the business of stirring up revolution in a mood of mild melancholy and depression, varied with spasmodic bursts of enthusiasm. But he struggled manfully, and as head of the Socialist League and later of the smaller Hammersmith Society, he became the most impressive figure in British socialism.

Perceiving at length that the period of agitation was over, he was eager to effect the unity necessary to practical action. In 1893 he succeeded in bringing about a conference between Shaw, representing the Fabians, Hyndman, representing the S.D.F., and himself, representing the Hammersmith Society. The conversation was beautifully harmonious so long as socialism was not discussed. But when the drunken Secretary, the only representative of the proletariat, awoke to bring the meeting to order, Hyndman and Shaw proved irreconcilable. The final result was a decorous manifesto in which all the original Fabianism and Marxism had been watered down to platitude and ambiguity. Unity existed for a while as a pious fiction but never as a reality. These early societies had not a sufficient following, sufficient political strength, to have a genuine stake in unity. The responsibilities of practical politics had not yet overtaken them.

Morris was one of the few men with whom Shaw differed respectfully. They shared a passion for art and a passion for equality, but within these two spheres they stood at opposite poles. Morris believed in the necessity of revolution, Shaw—though with occasional doubts—in the necessity of constitutionalism. Morris would turn the clock back against the Industrial Revolution. Shaw could not conceive of deliberate economic retrogression. He sympathized with Morris's interest in handicrafts and reckoned pleasure in work as one of the values created by production. Nevertheless, he insisted that such pleasure must be reconciled with the use of machinery. Poverty, not ugliness, is the fundamental evil of modern society. Bread and butter is a necessary condition to the satisfactions of the soul.

It is clear that Shaw enjoyed immensely playing a Fabian Mephistopheles to Morris's Jove. But though by sticking pins of epigrammatic caution into Jove's simple and explosive revolutionism, Mephistopheles frequently triumphed on the debating platform—as in this world—still revolutionism gained in the long run, for Mephistopheles was in this case very impressionable. Probably Shaw tended toward Marxism in his later years partly because he had listened critically to Morris in his earlier:

> When [William Morris] . . . told the workers that there was no hope for them save in revolution, we [the Fabians] said that if that were true there was no hope at all for them, and urged them to save themselves through parliament, the municipalities, and the franchise. Without, perhaps, quite converting Morris, we convinced him that things would probably go our way. It is not so certain to-day as it seemed in the eighties that Morris was not right.[15]

[94]

Doctrinaire differences did not prevent these two men from appreciating each other. At the beginning of their acquaintance, Morris astonished Shaw by declaring that he knew *An Unsocial Socialist* and later on scandalized him with the flattering announcement, in the midst of a speech, that "in economics Shaw is my master." [16] But Shaw was always making pleasant and amazing discoveries about Morris, whom apparently he, like other socialists, regarded as a venerable antiquity impervious to the advanced ideas of the day. Morris was the kind of man for whom Shaw reserved all his courtesy and charm—he was massive, vivid, eccentric, and terrifying. He stunned the complacent by bursting into thunderous rages and refuted the contentious by pulling single hairs out of his moustache and growling, "Damfool! Damfool!" When he recited his poetry, he would mark "its swing by rocking from one foot to the other like an elephant." [17]

For *The Earthly Paradise, Atalanta's Race,* and *The Life and Death of Jason,* Shaw accords handsome praise to "an idle singer of an empty day"; but *Pharamond* is too much: "The title repeated that irritating nineteenth century cliché 'love is enough' (which is not its moral) and therefore suggested a very idle singer of a damnably empty day to anyone who had just read Marx and was raging for justice, not for love." *Sigurd the Volsung* is the greatest epic since Homer, for epic was "child's play" to Morris, but what "really called up all his mental reserves for the first time" was socialism. Having thus destroyed at a single blow both the epic and the respectable Morris-worshipers who pushed Morris's radicalism into a dark corner, Shaw pays solid tribute to the painfully written lectures which "survive as the best books in the Bible of Socialism." [18]

CHAPTER TWELVE

The Fabian Essays in Socialism

Shortly before Christmas in 1889, the Fabians climaxed their golden age with the publication of the famous and oft-reprinted *Fabian Essays in Socialism,* which were written by the seven members of the Executive Committee. Seldom does a book by so many authors survive—as a book. *The Fabian Essays* have done so for two reasons: they express, cogently and clearly, the fundamental doctrine of an important political organization; and they constitute a distinguished and on the whole unified treatment of the problems of socialism. For though they are not the product of a single mind, at least they are the product of a single discussion, being the outcome of a year's coordinated study in the Hampstead Historical Society. *The Fabian Essays* are something between inflammatory political propaganda and the *Festschrift* of a professorless seminar of gifted young men and women.

Shaw was the editor, and doubtless the high literary quality of the volume is due in considerable degree to his strenuous criticisms and revisions. Being unable to find a firm that was "fair to labor," the Fabians themselves undertook the task of publication. Walter Crane designed the frontispiece; May Morris, the cover; and Mrs. Besant, herself a veteran publisher, managed the business details. *The Fabian Essays* were received with neither the uproarious acclaim of *Progress and Poverty* nor the total indifference of *Das Kapital.* They achieved the moderate success of a moderately revolutionary volume. Within a month one thousand copies had been sold; by 1932, upward of seventy thousand.

In plan the book is divided into three sections. The first, presenting "The Basis of Socialism," is treated in four essays—"Economic," by Shaw, "Historic," by Webb, "Industrial," by Clarke, and "Moral," by Olivier. The second section, dealing with "The Organization of Society," contains two essays—"Property under Socialism," by Wallas, and "Industry under Socialism," by Mrs. Besant. The third section, dealing with "The Transition to Social Democracy," also contains two—"Transition," by Shaw, and "The Outlook," by Bland. The obvious weakness of this

[96]

plan is that it contains too much history in too many places, and that weakness is intensified by the tendency of nearly every author to explain his subject historically. The Fabians achieved unity of thought without division of labor.

Revaluating the work in his 1919 Preface, Webb singles out "The Economic Basis" as that which survives most creditably. He is undoubtedly right. Shaw's essay is a little masterpiece of popular polemics —a *Discours sur l'Inégalité* translated into economics and socialism, in which successive Adams or Robinson Crusoes illustrate with pointed clarity and eloquent moral appeal the laws of rent, wages, population, and final utility. Like most popular documents, it is a product of the *esprit géométrique*. The argument is abstract, deductive. Principles are explained without reference to mitigating facts and circumstances; yet these are conscientiously and very deftly introduced at the conclusion, so that, without any substantial sacrifice to truth, the vivid clarity of the first impression is preserved. Shaw has since regretted that his economics are not statistical and inductive in the newer fashion, but more facts would only make this essay less convincing to its readers.

In "The Economic Basis," Shaw again founds his argument on the law of rent. Capitalism turns the earth into "a great gaming table," on which early comers win enormous prizes by laying their stakes, as exclusive property claims, at the most likely places.[1] Later comers get lesser prizes, until nothing is left, so that the latest comers of all, who are the immense majority, must labor desperately for the lucky minority in order to maintain life. Here Shaw sharpens the laws of rent and wages on the law of final utility. The riches of the earth are strictly limited. Therefore their final utility tends to be high. The units of labor are infinite. Therefore their final utility approaches zero. Thus according to the present system, overpopulation brings about a surfeit of luxuries for the few and a dearth of necessities for the many. Shaw follows Ruskin in designating a national income so composed and so distributed as "illth" rather than wealth. The winners in this cruel gamble have found it convenient to relegate justice to heaven, persuading the losers to drown "the sense of worldly inequality in the contemplation of our equality before God." [2] But people are no longer content to believe in a capitalistic Deity. They perceive with John Stuart Mill that if God is benevolent, He cannot be omnipotent and so is not responsible for worldly inequality. The final resource of individualism is to erect nature, "red in tooth and claw," into a superstition. But on the human plane, the Darwinian struggle for survival preserves idlers, kills workers, and spreads poverty. Socialism would eliminate this horrible injustice by making the riches and the fertility of the earth a common inheritance. It would reward men according to their labors.

[97]

As Mr. Thomas Knowlton has pointed out, Shaw explains the law of rent in his "Economic" essay in phrases very similar to those used in *Progress and Poverty*. He introduces a first settler to "an unbounded Savannah," as George introduces him to a "vast green plain." [3] Undoubtedly, the law of rent would not have gripped Shaw's mind so strongly had not George's eloquence gripped his imagination. Shaw simply extends the conception of rent to include the socially created incomes on all kinds of property and then considers how that property can best be administered to realize its full social income. If the state is to receive and distribute wealth, why should it not invest, own, and produce also, so that it may not only annex all "unearned increment" to the community but free the industrial machine from the restrictions of the profit motive and the economics of scarcity. The chief difference between George and Shaw is that one believes that social injustice stops with land values and the other believes that it begins with land values. Largely as a result of this difference, one is a socialist and the other is not.

In building state socialism on an amplified law of rent, Shaw and Webb made perhaps their most distinctive contribution to socialistic economics, formulating a doctrine which appeals, not like Marxism, to the proletariat primarily but to nonowners generally and indeed to all classes in the community.

To evolutionary socialism, history is basic, and therefore the second essay, by Webb, is in a sense the most important in the volume. It lays down the conditions under which social progress can be achieved. Changes must be first, democratic; second, gradual; third, moral, in the sense accepted by the mass of the people; and fourth, peacefully constitutional. Once more the influence of Mill is particularly striking. The language is vigorous and in places epigrammatic, but the organization is too redundant to produce the dramatic clarity of Shaw's contribution.

William Clarke's essay on the growth of industrialism is again tersely phrased but poorly organized, telling the same story several times for separate industries. Clarke takes many hints from Marx. He emphasizes that economic causes are primary, that an institution by its very functioning creates an opposition which will eventually destroy it, and that the imperialistic competition for world markets threatens world peace. The analysis is, as Webb says, acute and prophetic. Clarke's point is that competition no longer governs economic activity. We have our choice of paying high prices to irresponsible trusts or low prices to a responsible government committed to the appropriation of rent for the collective good. With Fabian caution, however, Clarke declares that England is not yet ready for socialism.

Writing on the moral aspect of socialism, Sidney Olivier asserts that society regards as moral those actions that tend to preserve and strengthen it. Naturally, morality is continually surviving its usefulness. The virtues of a military age become the vices of an economic. And as with actions, so with institutions. Private property does society not only great economic but great moral damage, inasmuch as it leads rich and luxurious idlers to praise thrift and industry to the masses, thus creating a debilitating hypocrisy in the center of the national life. Olivier's argument suggests the influence of Spencer and Comte. He is followed very appropriately by Wallas, who writes on property rights under socialism. Wallas's essay is remarkable, however, not because it lays down any broad philosophical principle but because, in the name of efficiency, it urges government ownership of the objects of both production and consumption. Food, for example, should be prepared not in small quantities in the home but in huge quantities in great public restaurants.

The three concluding essays revert to the problem of the transition to socialism. Writing on "Industry under Socialism," Mrs. Besant advocates that socialized production should be initiated by the municipalities. They should first organize cooperative industry and exchange among the unemployed, then gradually buy up land and the instruments of production until they control nearly all economic activity except mining and other "special natural resources," which should be exploited by the central government.[4] In his 1919 Preface, Sidney Webb singles out Mrs. Besant's solution of the unemployment problem as one of the follies of Fabian youth and recommends instead the plan developed by his wife and George Lansbury in the "Minority Poor Law Report" of 1908.

Shaw's second essay in the collection, which is only surpassed by his first, treats Mrs. Besant's subject in a much broader manner. "The Transition to Social Democracy" has the disadvantage of being another history, but it is a very remarkable history, beginning with the Middle Ages and ending in the future and covering the development not only of production and trade in the strict sense but of their moral and philosophical concomitants. It is an epic written in the language of satire. In the sixteenth century, says Shaw,

> English adventurers took to the sea in a frame of mind peculiarly favorable to commercial success. They were unaffectedly pious, and had the force of character which is only possible to men who are founded on convictions. At the same time, they regarded piracy as a brave and patriotic pursuit, and the slave trade as a perfectly honest branch of commerce, adventurous enough to be consistent with the honor of a gentleman, and lucrative enough to make it well worth the risk.[5]

There is aphorism and telling statement. Compressing Malthus, Shaw writes, "Private property, in fact, left no room for newcomers"; and summing up the early economists, "All their most cherished institutions and doctrines succumbed one by one to their analysis of the laws of production and exchange." [6]

Hubert Bland's concluding essay, "The Outlook," is perhaps the thinnest in the volume. Nevertheless, it does predict that socialism will never be accomplished by "permeating" the Liberals. There must be a powerful socialist party.

In his 1908 Preface, Shaw declares that the *Fabian Essays* were published with the double purpose of making socialism respectable for the voter and practicable for the Prime Minister. But could these two purposes be reconciled? Shaw himself had his doubts. Root-and-branch socialism *with* party politics was still not respectable, and evolutionary socialism without party politics had yet to prove itself socialism—in the ultimate sense. Hoping that it would so prove itself, the Fabian authors, by implication at least, set up two programs. The first, to be accomplished in the immediate future, consisted of universal education and universal suffrage, the payment of Members of Parliament, the gradual appropriation of rent and interest, a minimum wage and maximum working day, a complete system of old-age and unemployment compensation, and the municipal ownership and operation of municipal services. The other program, to be accomplished ultimately, consisted of government ownership and operation of nearly all the instruments of production and a system of distribution which would eliminate all interest and rent, including the rent of ability. In allying itself with Liberals and Radicals to achieve the first program, a socialist party ran the risk of never being able to carry out the second, for compromise diverts attention from ultimate objectives and antagonizes the followers most devoted to these objectives, as Shaw himself explains at length in "The Illusions of Socialism." [7] Moreover, compromise is almost infinitely slow, for while a minor reform remains to be effected, the reformer finds it very difficult to urge a major one. As it approaches its goal, gradualism tends to become stationaryism, and for this reason, as I have already indicated, Shaw gave to Marx a lifelong second thought.

In his 1919 Preface, Sidney Webb finds the *Essays* at fault in their history, in their neglect of the unions and the cooperatives, and in their treatment of transport, agriculture, banking insurance, international remittance, unemployment, and questions of individual liberty within the corporative state—deficiencies which he and Mrs. Webb had rapidly corrected by the publication of *The Co-operative Movement in Great Britain* in 1890, the *History of Trade Unionism* in 1894, and *Industrial Democracy* in 1897. As the work of young and inexperienced men, the *Fabian Essays* were naturally somewhat thin and vague on matters of practical administration.

The strongest attack on the new volume came from the conservative writer and novelist W. H. Mallock, in the February, 1894, issue of *The Fortnightly Review*. He contends that not ordinary labor but exceptional ability is the chief producer of wealth, that it therefore has a moral right to large income, and that it would not continue productive unless stimulated by the prospect of accumulating a fortune based on interest and rent. Shaw's reply was prompt and adroit. He grants that ability often makes a great contribution but denies that it should be rewarded in strict proportion. In fact, it is not so rewarded. Though capitalism greatly inflates the price of ability, it often pays unproductive capacity far more than productive. Brewery operators make more money than inventors. Society tends to pay capable men the minimum that will still keep them working hard. Probably most of them will prefer the security of socialistic civil service to the uncertainties of private enterprise.

Though he argues with some force that able men should receive a high reward, Mallock fails utterly to show why idle men should receive rent and interest, which are the principal objects of Fabian attack. His psychological argument, though carried absurdly far, is much stronger than his moral. In arguing that exceptional ability requires an exceptional return to be fully productive, he touches a weak point in Fabian armor. The Fabians are optimistic about the problem of motivation. Shaw's reply, that history is full of instances of clever people working hard at low pay for idle and foolish people, is at once formidable argument and dexterous rebuttal.

Shaw's account of the victory is modest: "Mallock, whose *New Republic* once seemed the last word in daringly advanced thought, was a brief candle, guttered down long before I blew him out." [8]

CHAPTER THIRTEEN

The Fabian Sunset

Though unparalleled prodigies of permeation still lay ahead, the Fabians had now all but fulfilled their primary mission. They had shown that socialism, at least as they conceived it, need not be revolutionary. They had made it as respectable, as cautiously legal, and as traditionally British as the Tory Party or the Church of England. They had spread their ideas far and wide through the Radical and Liberal associations, and after the great dock strike of 1889, they had recognized—late according to their own estimate but years before the trade-unions themselves—the importance of these organizations and of the cooperatives to socialism. In 1890 they had carried on a successful agitation among the workers in the industrial North, urging the need of forming a parliamentary party. In *The Fortnightly* article "To Your Tents, O Israel," they had declared open war on the Liberals, and in Shaw's "Election Manifesto of 1892," they had with great effect advocated a policy and tactics for a new labor party. They had thus brought about a situation in which they were slightly out of date. Education, agitation, and permeation had become secondary, for the lines of battle were now clearly drawn. What was needed was a workingmen's party. Why didn't the Fabians themselves try to form it?

Simply, of course, because the Fabian past ideologically, psychologically, and practically had not prepared them for such a future. For one thing, their leaders were not politicians. Sidney Webb was the closest approximation. He was a skilled government official and a shrewd wirepuller behind the scenes. Yet he was much more the absorbed and sedentary student, who, far from possessing the qualities of a popular leader, had like his master Mill a snobbish contempt for the people. Shaw was even more conspicuously a member of the middle-class intelligentsia, a Bohemian who might lead but could certainly not be followed. These two dominating personalities had imposed on the Society an attitude beyond which it was unable to develop, despite the brilliant men and experienced politicians which it contained.

M. Edouard Pfeiffer says that the Fabians were actually relieved when, in 1894, the Independent Labour Party swallowed up their branches, because provincial membership had consisted largely of laborers.[1] A society so unsympathetic to the masses is not likely to understand or arouse them, and in this respect Fabian middle-class rationalism limited Fabian imagination and therefore Fabian propaganda. Apparently their leaders—and particularly Webb—conceived the influential workingman as a kind of philosophical tailor like Francis Place, whose head might be captured by a table of statistics and whose heart might be allowed to take care of itself. Above all, the Fabians forgot that most workingmen were religious. Even the Webbs' *History of Trade Unionism* seems somewhat to neglect the role of the evangelical sects in the growth of socialism. Later on, the Fabians recognized their mistake and elected the Reverend Stewart Headlam to the Executive Committee. Ironically, they did not themselves lack zeal and fire. Their idiom was simply not that of religion and piety but of logic and argument, of graphs and statistics. They did not, as Ramsay MacDonald says, have the vitalizing quality of "seeing spirit in everything." Their talents, their methods, their ideology and economic theory gave them power over the reason of the few rather than over the passions and interests of the many.

Again, paradoxically, the subsequent Fabian decline may have been due partly to the Fabian success. Fame and maturity separate men. In the anonymity and irresponsibility of a somewhat advanced youth, the Fabian leaders had remained a close-knit association. Later, each, carried along by the dynamics of his own career, was inevitably something else before he was a Fabian. Olivier became a colonial administrator in the Indies; Wallas, a professor of economics; Shaw, a critic and playwright; the Webbs, publicists and students of ever broader sociological problems. The Fabians grew weak through the brilliant diversity of their success.

They were rapidly supplanted by their own offspring. In 1894, the Fabian branch societies became the socialist core of the Independent Labour Party. The men who contributed chiefly to its rise—Hardie, MacDonald, and Henderson—were, as one might expect, Fabians who objected to Fabianism on religious grounds. They felt it was too little a creed and too much a system of economics. Under their leadership, the I.L.P. became at once more evangelical and more Marxist, more conscious of God and more conscious of class, than the Fabians. For several years the new socialist organization tried in vain to enlist the cooperation of the trade-unions, whom prosperity had made conservative, but in 1899, disgusted with the duplicity of the Liberals, the Trade Union Congress resolved that its Parliamentary Committee should confer with the socialist societies to devise ways and means for increasing labor representation at the next Parliament. In spite of its mere seven hundred members, the Fabian Society was invited to send two delegates. Bernard Shaw and Edward Pease were appointed. In February, 1900, the conference duly formed a Labour Representative Committee, on which, however, ostensibly because of their small numbers, the Fabians were permitted to have only one member. The choice fell on Pease. Shaw attributes his exclusion to Hardie's prejudice against bourgeois brains.[2] The result was that although one of those ultimately responsible for the Labour Party, Shaw was never closely associated with it.

That party itself was founded at this time. The mouse actually swallowed the elephant. The trade-unions accepted the leadership of the I.L.P. and of Ramsay MacDonald. In 1900 MacDonald and Hardie became the first socialist Members of Parliament.

Meanwhile the Fabians looked on benignly at their own eclipse. While branch societies were deserting and stampeding all around them, they continued calmly to educate, agitate, and permeate as never before; in fact, throughout the nineties, their achievements in national as well as in city government were so brilliant that they could be said to be declining only in a relative sense.

But now the scene shifts from the meeting rooms of the Fabians to the drawing room of the Webbs, a formidable, bookish apartment in which the hero of middle-class intellectualism had enthroned the princess of Benthamite millions. Having passed a brief honeymoon in the North collecting data on trade-unions, they had returned to London, and with austere utilitarian indifference to vulgarity of ornament and unfashionableness of neighborhood, selected a house precisely suited to their income and convenience. Here they wrote *The History of Trade Unionism* at the dining-room table, and as time went on, converted their drawing room by turns into a sociological laboratory, a socialistic incubator, and a chamber of state. Sometimes dinners were meticulously planned scientific experiments in which combinations of the most widely divergent types, whom the wildest chance would never have thrown together under natural conditions, were carefully marshaled, set in motion, and their reactions observed and tabulated. Just enough food was served to prevent anguish and outcry, not enough to distract attention from talk. On other occasions, dinners were the sowing seasons of an equally scientific agriculture, in which bright young people of all classes were assembled and the germs of socialism deftly dropped into their minds. The process was too scientific to require deception. The clever young people accepted socialism, succeeded—and gradually socialism became not only respectable but genteel. It is a question whether it did not also become innocuous. Again, there were small, select, quiet dinners. They were seminars for statesmen. Arthur Balfour and Lord Roseberry became intimate friends of the Webbs, and apparently Haldane, Lloyd George, and the youthful Winston Churchill were well acquainted with them. Balfour's Poor Law owes much to Beatrice, and Lord Roseberry's famous Chesterfield speech, much to Sidney's "Policy of National Efficiency." The relation between Fabian doctrine and Lloyd George's politics after 1906 has several times been pointed out.

Shaw had by then become a literary lion and prowled and roared among the Webb's guinea pigs, greater and lesser, with infinite gusto. It was the sunset of prosperous Philistinism, when genius stalked the streets and red Turkey carpets of London unchecked. A magnificent example of his species, Shaw had become very carefully and elaborately a law unto himself. He made no democratic distinctions, purring benignly while viscountesses crowded about to stroke his mane. He was apt to be a little strenuous about going in to dinner, striding ahead and declaring to his partner, "Nobody takes precedence of me!"

It was during these years that Webb, backed by faithful Fabians, was leading the London County Council, by the most circuitous and elaborately premeditated route, deeper and deeper into social revolution, particularly in the field of education. Shaw too had embarked on a miniature political career of his own. Through a deal made between the Fabians and their opponents, he was in 1897 elected "without election" to the Vestry of St. Pancras, which administered the local government of a quarter of a million Londoners. Once more the practical ability which had made him a model cashier in a land-agency business was called into requisition. For six years the author of "The Philanderer" and "Arms and the Man" plunged avidly into housing, electric lighting, and food inspection, for the last of which he put metaphysical considerations aside and in spite of vegetarianism attended inquests on tuberculous cattle. He was industrious, painstaking, shrewd, and assiduously regular.

Opinions of his performance are divided. John Burns declares him a solid success. His fellow Fabian Edward Pease somewhat acidly pronounces his work chiefly valuable to himself, as an enlightening experience for a great author. Sir David Davies reports that his fellow Vestrymen "respected him enormously for his earnestness and industry, were somewhat amused at his constant endeavours to obtain publicity, but were not aware that they had a genius among them." [3]

What Shaw thought of them appears in a letter to *The London Daily Chronicle:*

They commit crimes against society for which they would get twenty years penal servitude if they committed them as individuals against private property instead of as public representatives against the common weal. But they do it from the loftiest, kindliest, most self-sacrificing reasons; and all remonstrance strikes them as being half ludicrous, half cynical, and altogether a breach of good sense and good manners.[4]

And in the same letter he observes, "If a dramatist in a world like this has to go to books for his ideas and his inspiration, he must be both blind and deaf. Most dramatists are." [4] These passages indicate how directly Shavian drama derives from Shavian experience. Shaw's characters, like his fellow Vestrymen, nearly always feel justified in their actions. His plays are therefore a criticism of moralities as well as of people. A signal instance of this is "Candida," in the Preface to which he emphasizes that he entered sympathetically into the point of view of every character.

But such sympathy was impossible in real life. If many Vestrymen were like Burgess, Shaw could hardly have refrained from occasionally causing their crimes and their complacency to explode in their faces. It would seem he only gradually developed the capacity for anonymous industry and secret management which distinguishes the perfect committeeman of the Webb model.

Again, not being primarily interested in a public career, Shaw had not, like Disraeli, the incentive to make himself dull and sound enough to reassure voters. When invited in 1899 by the Battersea Liberal and Radical Association to stand for Parliament, he refused, but at the urging of friends he stood in 1904 as candidate for the Borough of St. Pancras in the London County Council. He was soundly beaten. Explanations are bewilderingly numerous, but it emerges that as a candidate he was even more dubious than as a committeeman—and for the same reasons. Mr. Henderson says that Shaw failed because he failed to pay the customary one-thousand-pound bribe to the ward boss. Shaw himself declares that he outraged nonconformist bigotry by a generous and heroic defense of church schools. An intimate friend suggests that he lost because he insisted throughout the campaign that "he and Voltaire were the only two really religious people who had ever lived." [5] He was given to disastrous seizures of frankness, humor, and brilliance. He seems to have larked a good deal in the St. Pancras election and to have met defeat with relief and pleasure.

Besides plays and masses of art, music, and dramatic criticism, Shaw continued to write prolifically on economic and political subjects. In 1896, when the triennial International Socialist Workers and Trade

Unionist Congress met in London, he drafted for the occasion *Tract No. 70*, "Report on Fabian Policy." It is a clear, brief, incisive restatement of the old policy of permeation, gradualism, toleration, and compromise. The Society does not ask the English people to become Fabians, but it does urge them to broaden their constitution so as to make inevitable the economic justice of socialism. It declares for representative and against direct democracy, repudiating the referendum and similar devices. It disclaims any distinctive opinions on marriage, religion, or other questions irrelevant to socialism and encourages its members to join other political organizations. It would not entirely eliminate private enterprise, recognizing its value in undertaking experiments and blazing new paths. It opposes alike strict equality of income and the right of the individual to the whole product of his labor.

Later on, Shaw himself was to declare for strict equality. In a lecture delivered at this time, however, he urged one important exception to a leveling policy. The appropriation of rent and interest to the state under commercial production would automatically produce approximate equality of income. Therefore, the rent of ability might be left to its individual possessors, since they would not be sufficiently numerous to constitute a privileged class. The effect would be simply that a few persons "of very delightful artistic talent" would have a little extra money to spend.

In 1904 Shaw produced *The Common Sense of Municipal Trading*, which, as he himself seems to feel, is his most solid and statesmanlike writing on a political subject. Feeling that the soundest beginnings are small and the solidest gains are piecemeal, the Fabians have taken a peculiar, though always critical, interest in municipal enterprise. Close, compact communities faced with immediate evils are more likely to pioneer wisely than large, loose communities faced with remote evils.

The virtues of Shaw's *Municipal Trading* are political rather than literary. It is not, like "The Economic Basis of Socialism," eloquent and provocative. Both in language and in idea it is clear, considered, and close-knit. The possibilities of municipal socialism, says Shaw, are unlimited, but progress has been slowed by one of the most desperate conflicts of interest since 1832—that between the workingman, who demands all sorts of municipal benefits, and the rate payer, who has to foot the bill and is at the same time badly squeezed by his landlord. The author will suggest ways to minimize this conflict. A municipality has immense advantages over a joint-stock company. It can borrow all the money it needs at four per cent; it can sell goods and services at almost cost prices; it can hire expert management very cheaply because it offers its employees a relatively stable way of life. And because it aims at the good of the whole community—or total, rather than marginal, utility—it can undertake projects like road and street building, which private companies find unprofitable.

On the other hand, a municipality is not self-sufficient or able to establish monopolies in all kinds of business. Even the London civic orchestras do not require musical instruments in such quantity as to warrant the city's manufacturing them. Thus municipal may expand private enterprise. So long as the latter observes a "fair" wage policy, the two can compete with benefit to the social utility of both. Of course, in services like garbage disposal, which requires little capital and much unskilled labor, a municipality cannot compete with the sweating contractor, who underpays his men so badly that they are forced to send their wives and children to work. Yet the sweater's service is not so cheap as it seems. It eventually lands many of his men in the workhouse, where they must be maintained in old age at the public expense. It is also usually inadequate and therefore entails a large invisible bill for health. In fact, whereas community enterprise aims always at the public good, much private trade, such as that in liquor and gambling, is at least in part antisocial.

Individualists are constantly crying out, Shaw continues, in terrified protest against municipal competition. They have little to fear. At present, the press, the law, and popular prejudice are all on their side. Community enterprise meets with approval only in such industries as do not pay in the commercial sense. Moreover, in power and transport it suffers because it cannot pass beyond highly restricted local boundaries. In housing it suffers because politics compels it to build too cheaply for the rich, and decency, to build too expensively for the poor. It suffers also from the general handicap that it must form a sinking fund to pay off on its total investment within a single lifetime. Moreover, Vestrymen would rather declare reductions for rate payers than build up an adequate reserve capital. Thus, the common cry of the private capitalist that the municipality uses his own money in the rates to drive him out of business is unwarranted. Such public enterprise as competes with him is usually profitable and therefore lightens rather than increases his tax burden. Indeed the small shopkeeper is much more often forced out of business by great chain firms financed with money which he pays to his landlord, for all capital derives from rent and interest. Nevertheless, municipal socialism is weakened by the injustice of its revenue system. The rates fall much too heavily on the very poor and on those of the indigent who insist on adequate housing. An income tax should be substituted and total exemption allowed those unable to maintain themselves above a minimum standard of comfort.

In conclusion Shaw frankly recognizes the weaknesses of municipal democracy. Most people are mere lodgers in their township and have little interest in its affairs. Consequently, the small shopkeeper, who knows little and goes nowhere, dominates local politics. As a voter he puts his kind in office, and as an official, he helps his friends and supports a mayor who promises parsimony and a yearly banquet with champagne. For a cure, Shaw prescribes more propaganda and education, and voting by mail.

The chief weakness of *Municipal Trading* is that it is too little suspicious of the typical egotisms and dishonesties of a corporate body. It assumes too optimistically the natural goodness of human communities. On the other hand, it contains remarkably little of Shaw's special pleadings. One feels that it is a very complete discussion, that it does not pass over difficult problems. Wells insists that in their predilection for municipalities the Fabians never recognized that modern government requires large administrative units. Shaw at least frankly declares that much enterprise is beyond the scope of the municipality. Finally, in its freshness of illustration and sureness of judgment, *Municipal Trading* clearly reveals a firsthand knowledge of the political scene it describes.

CHAPTER FOURTEEN

The Nineties

Working at the British Museum Library one day in 1885, William Archer, a confirmed freethinker and a successful critic of the arts, happened to observe a "young man of peculiar colouring . . . poring over Karl Marx's *Das Kapital,* and an orchestral score of Wagner's *Tristan und Isolde!*" [1] It was of course Shaw. Inevitably, the two became acquainted. As their friendship improved, Shaw's costume decayed. The significance of that decay was not lost on Archer, who as a Scot understood the difference between frugality and indigence. Being already dramatic critic of *The World,* he was asked to criticize pictures as well. After some weeks of uncongenial labor, he managed to hand the post over to Shaw. Shaw's first year of journalism earned him one hundred seventeen pounds sterling. At last his literary career had been established on a lucrative basis.

Solvency came just in time. In 1881, Mrs. Shaw had been compelled at last to give up the respectability of a house in Victoria Grove, and for a while she and her son had lived in a variety of flats and lodgings. Her daughter Lucy, three years older than Bernard, had apparently not been able to give much aid, though she sang for some time in Gilbert and Sullivan and then in a light opera called "Dorothy," which her brother discusses at some length in his music criticism. Her voice, rendered indestructible through Vandaleur Lee's method, was the only one able to withstand the rigors of Dorothy's soprano part and its interminable run in the provinces. By 1885, when Mrs. Shaw and her son had come to rest in the second floor at 29 Fitzroy Square, George Carr Shaw died in Dublin, and the weekly pound from him ceased to come. It was then that genius began to yield its first meager returns.

Shaw's initial act as a solvent man was to purchase a new wardrobe, which together with some rather dashing tweeds included a brown wool knitted garment resembling heavy underwear. Invented by a German doctor named Jaeger, it was designed at once to be peculiarly healthy and superlatively utilitarian, replacing as a single piece of clothing the complete Philistine regalia. Shaw shook society to its foundations by wearing this masterpiece of sartorial Benthamism into fastnesses sacred to the long black coat and the tall silk hat. When "Widowers' Houses" was played in 1892 and Fabians yelled for the author, he appeared before the footlights in another of Dr. Jaeger's triumphs, a combination coat and waistcoat of dazzling silver-gray stockinet. When the boos had quieted down, he out-Wilded Wilde by making a speech in which he patronized and insulted the audience so skillfully that they burst into general applause. Shaw persisted in his shiny, crinkly stockinet ensembles for some time, though his fellow Fabian Olivier, with whom he went on long walks, protested that conversation was impossible with a man who sounded like a giant cricket when he moved. Eventually, Shaw lapsed into the comparative restraint of brown furry tweeds and hobnailed boots, which he thought best adapted to his long critical hikes through stone-floored picture galleries.

As time went on, Shaw wrote criticism for an ever greater variety of journals—on literature for *The Pall Mall Gazette,* on painting for *The Star,* on music for *The Daily Chronicle,* and on everything for Annie Besant's *Our Corner.* It was in his relations with editors that he developed his famous code of Shavian intercourse, which features rational insult and antiseptic good humor. W. E. Henley, whom he looked on as "a tragic example of the combination of imposing powers of expression with nothing important to express," had him do music criticism for *The Scots Observer* but persisted in interpolating insults against Wagner and socialism. Shaw stopped contributing, and when a letter of remonstrance came, replied with sudden savagery that though Henley's head was bloody but unbowed, his pen was at the service of the police and the upper classes. Henley asked him for no more articles and was amazed that at their next meeting, instead of glowering through him, Shaw greeted him with the utmost friendliness. On another occasion, Shaw was invited by Nevinson of *The Daily Chronicle* to do a column of music criticism. As a good socialist, he demanded trade-union wages, which were above what *The Chronicle* usually paid. The result was a formal exchange thoroughly in Shaw's manner:

DEAR SIR,

I am directed by the editor to inform you that he will see you damned before he gives you more than five pounds for the article in question.

Shaw answered in kind:

DEAR SIR,

Please inform the editor that I will see him and you and the whole *Chronicle* staff boiled in Hell before I will do it for that money.[2]

On this basis of clear mutual understanding Nevinson paid the union wage, and Shaw became a regular contributor. Of course he was generally regarded as a freak and often compared to such essential spirits of the hour as Whistler and Wilde. As a matter of fact, he is far more broadly and complexly typical of the nineties than either of them. They represent chiefly the age of the imperturbable monocle and the fantastic costume, of exquisite sensation and excruciating scandal, when a few people had already become naughty enough to commit a sin and a great many still remained Victorian enough to be genuinely horrified by it. Shaw represents something much more significant. To understand him, we must take a very broad view of the nineties.

On the sands of multifarious transition, the Victorian middle classes had built themselves a very comfortable house of mental formulas. *Laissez faire* demonstrated the natural right of free enterprise, and Ricardo's law of wages, the inevitability of indigence. The Calvinistic virtue of thrift sanctified the wealth which resulted from the first and explained away as just punishment the suffering which resulted from the second. Victorian convention conveniently relegated woman. to a sanctum of helpless purity and established the universal superiority of the male.

In the region of metaphysics and theology, Kant's distinction between the *Vernunft* and the *Verstand,* while it hardly served as a peace treaty, did mitigate the warfare between science and religion and permitted many a comfortably intelligent citizen to make the best of both worlds. Firmly based on matter, protoplasm, and "organized common sense," midcentury science seemed, by the sedulous accumulation of small facts, to be moving soundly and cautiously toward omniscience. The doctrine of progress postponed all really disagreeable problems into the future, upon which a "far-off divine event" shed a reassuringly rosy glow. The decline in the rate of interest was almost imperceptible. Altogether, except for occasional toothaches of religious doubt and general disillusionment, the Victorian lived briefly in a middle-class paradise of security and comfort.

Throughout this period, romanticism was a decorous but pervasive force. It raised an alluring mirage above the dusty path of utilitarian progress. It humanized working conditions, undermined morals, and vulgarized literary taste. In Tennyson's poetry it multiplied forsaken maidens looking out of lush autumnal landscapes and transported

Philistine heroes to the Middle Ages; it lurked as a latent impressionism in Browning, sharpened his taste for the bizarre, grotesque, and eccentric; intensified the religious nostalgia of Arnold; and suffused the hero worship of Carlyle. Especially among the poets, it fostered a Dantesque cult of woman which elaborately confused the spiritual and the sensual.

In the transition from Tennyson and Browning to Rossetti and Swinburne, the deified ladies became rapidly less heavenly. Sentimental religiosity moved toward hedonistic irreligiosity. Late nineteenth-century romanticism became a cynical revolt against middle-class respectability, as early nineteenth-century romanticism had been an indignant and righteous revolt against aristocratic decorum. Revenging themselves for half a century of ugliness, the aesthetes rapidly divorced art from all the midcentury values—from the real, the objective, the useful, the moral. Whereas the earlier romantic mistook his dream of the outer world for a reality, Pater reduced the outer world itself to a dream—and locked it up in the iron box of subjectivity. Literature became the painfully careful recording of infinitely fleeting sensations of aesthetic enjoyment. It is amusing that Pater's ideal was Flaubert, in whom the art was so protracted and the enjoyment so fleeting that life, instead of being a swift poetic ecstasy, was a lengthy and prosaic torture of anxious labor. Art was heaven and hell to Flaubert, but mostly hell. Oscar Wilde discovered a world of wit and epigram by standing Victorian respectability very precisely on its head.

Wilde declared the Victorians had sold their birthright for a mess of facts. Poetry must treat the unreal. But the later romantics were by no means uniformly hostile to realism. Toward the end of the century, novelists, tired of playing sleight of hand with Victorian sex convention, were trying to discover the beast in the Philistine. Romantics are often quite willing to love truth—provided it is stranger than fiction. Frequently they crave it in its ugliest forms as an emotional necessity, for being escapists, they alternate between phases of illusion and disillusion. These phases may alternate on a very large scale. At the outset of the nineteenth century, illusion predominated; at the close, disillusion.

Romantic disillusionment at the end of the century proceeded primarily from a cause not in the strict sense romantic. In the seventies and the eighties, Victorian faith felt the full impact of scientific discovery. Thoughtful young men, reared from childhood in the old certainties, found themselves at intellectual maturity in a world in which those certainties were impossible. In an age constantly tempted to romantic emotionalism, Hardy and James Thompson in the eighties, like Matthew Arnold in the fifties, felt their loss romantically; and again like

Arnold, they were thrown back with all the greater force on the bare material promise of their time. The capacity to hope and believe had already suffered severe shocks and was declining. Moreover, now that there was nothing beyond it, that wonderful world of the Great Exposition began to seem, like the Crystal Palace itself, a rather stale wonder, and all those confident dreams—in spite of their modest, prosaic plausibility —either unattainable or undesirable.

Romantic disillusionment proceeded also from the inadequacies of political romanticism. The loud failure of liberalism in 1848 awakened dreamers throughout Europe, and the Machiavellian success of Louis Napoleon in 1851 and of Bismarck in 1870 strengthened a reaction toward the disillusioned romanticism of *Realpolitik*. Moreover, the steady refusal of any millennium to emerge on the attainment of wider suffrage, wider education, or any other democratic panacea led many to grow critical of democracy itself—and such criticism was particularly common among literary artists, who had long in vain offered their guidance to a great, noisy, indifferent public. They were revenged by their successors, many of whom, like Wilde, withdrew into a tiny, exotic hothouse world, in which beauty was the only value.

Others would escape from Philistia by destroying it. They invoked the superman. He represents the literary conception of original genius translated to the field of politics and action. His mainspring is revolt. His values are diabolonian. Like Blake, his advocates inverted heaven and hell. Like Carlyle, they emphasized passion, instinct, the primitive social relationship of command and obedience. The superman must be satanic, poetic, vital, and heroically despotic. But he must also know the world, and in so far as his purpose requires, he must possess the Apollonian virtue of self-control. He who would conquer the world must first compromise with it. In their criticism of democracy and bourgeois materialism, the heroic philosophers—and particularly Nietzsche—were giants. In their constructive program, they were decadent poets—vague, romantic, grandiloquent, reluctant to define for fear of not being sufficiently titanic. Essentially, they were Bohemians who escaped from fact by worshiping it—and by romanticizing it, in its past sense of heroic achievement and its future sense of overwhelming power. And yet, romantic escapists though they were, these men represent, as Mr. E. R. Bentley points out, a genuine craving for excellence in a world where excellence was being submerged in an ocean of mediocrity.[3]

The eighties and the nineties were an age of masked revolution. The late Victorian mind was in sharp opposition to the Victorian achievement. The aesthetes attacked the middle-class formulas in the name of beauty; the hero-worshipers, in the name of excellence;

the utilitarians, in the name of social justice. For utilitarianism, emphasizing democracy and equality, had moved down in the social scale and identified itself with the working classes. In so far as it was a developing doctrine, Benthamite individualism had become Fabian socialism, as I have attempted to explain. But as the philosophy of the superman borrowed from evolutionary science, so the socialistic movement was affected by late romanticism. Ruskin and Morris attempted to join the values of beauty and artistry to those of utility and efficiency, and in "Time and Tide" Ruskin tried to join a conception of social justice with one of moral and political leadership. Unfortunately, his whole system was regressive, looking back to the medievalism of status and a static society.

Perhaps the most remarkable characteristic of political thought at this time is that in its more popular and literary phases, it tended to separate the problems of justice and leadership. The socialists were largely preoccupied with justice. Their conception of leadership reflected the limitations of their Benthamite past. It lacked heroism, grandeur, imaginative appeal. The romantic superman, on the other hand, was nearly all heroism and grandeur. Moreover, he represented a primitivistic protest against the whole problem of justice. As the product of a competition in brute strength and animal cunning, he seemed left no practical method of emergence in a civilized state. Unfortunately, the twentieth century was to prove that even civilization was an illusion.

This is the period in which Shaw became Shaw. If, as he says, he has kept a thousand years ahead of the times, he has done so after the manner of clever men of the eighties and nineties. Nearly every movement of these complicated decades translated itself into his clear, practical intelligence. The eighties made him a socialist. The nineties made him a "mystic"—a rather Benthamite mystic in the cult of the superman. His superman was somewhat inferior as an *objet d'art*, but he had admirable mechanical works inside, and many years later Shaw discovered that the blueprints fitted Joseph Stalin remarkably well.[4] Thus, though in some degree he made his specifications fit the measurements of social justice, he never made them fit the ampler measurements of democracy. Indeed Shaw kept his ideas on democracy and on heroic leadership curiously separate. They were alternative theories rather than parts of a larger theory.

Another development of the scientific-utilitarian movement was pragmatism, which, following implications already clear in John Stuart Mill's "Utilitarianism," reduced truth itself to considerations of utility. In 1878, Charles Pierce pointed out that "our beliefs are really rules for action" and that to develop the meaning of a thought "we need only determine what conduct it is fitted to produce." [5] Pragmatism had two tendencies. Emphasizing "practical," or scientific, utility, it plunged philosophy even more deeply into the facts of experience. Emphasizing subjective, or religious, utility, it freed thought from the tyrannies of monism and strict logical consistency and permitted it to adopt the metaphysics best calculated to marshal the inward strength of the individual. Butler and Meredith represented characters testing ideas in action. Bergson and Shaw illustrated the tendency to identify truth with will and power. Related to pragmatism was the late romantic emphasis on instinct and impulse, characteristic of nearly all the writers of the eighties and nineties.

The age was one of youth without innocence. The Victorian dream was rapidly fading, and young men found themselves faced, at the threshold of life, with the awful possibilities of infinite freedom and an indifferent universe. Many lost their heads. There was much reckless fiddling while Victorian conventions burned. Some again, like Richard Wagner in Germany, were obsessed with a hunger for life and a fascination with death. Others, like Randolph Churchill, flung themselves into action. Some, like Oscar Wilde, desperately explored the world of hedonistic sensation. Some, like Francis Thompson, fled before eternity; other faced it, like Gerard Hopkins. Many a promising young artist died with a rosary or a whisky glass in his hands. Aubrey Beardsley devoted the fierce energy of a brief and feverish lifetime to immoral art and then on his deathbed begged that in the name of the church all of his work be destroyed. History had summoned a new generation to shatter the grave and plausible illusions of its elders. Quite naturally, writers like Wilde and Shaw were always contrasting the wisdom of youth with the folly of age.

But lost innocence revenged itself. Many young men of the eighties and nineties passed through the extremities of experience without ever acquiring the maturity which experience confers. They saw vanity in everything without ever having overcome the vanity of childhood and were disillusioned about ultimates without having outgrown the simplest naïvetés. They seem to have known dissipation before they knew normal life, and they explored the elaborate self-consciousness of pose and mask without ever coming to understand ordinary sincerity.

It was an age of intense and forced inspiration. The muse was a bizarre, oriental exhalation, rushing out—too often—like some Aladdin's genie from an absinthe bottle. And yet, having cast aside moral form, late Victorian artists—in part perhaps simply because they felt the weight of too much freedom—subjected themselves the more elaborately to aesthetic form. The nineties were a decade of style and technique—fortunately for Shaw, because the idiom of the nineties, with its wit, paradox, and rhetoric, proved to be his native tongue.

Indeed the nineties were the period in which Shaw arrived at artistic maturity. And though, like G. K. Chesterton, he reacted sharply against the decadent aestheticism and the sensuous violence of that time, yet its brilliance, its swift elusiveness, its magnificent posing, its sophisticated sensationalism, its many-sided romanticism all entered deeply into his genius. But how deeply? When he first appeared on the literary horizon, he was frequently likened to Whistler. His own remarks on this comparison are significant:

> Whistler came to grief . . . because he gave himself up to clever smartness, which is abhorrent to the average Englishman. As for me, I have never for a moment lost sight of my serious relation to a serious public. You see, I had an advantage over Whistler in any case, for at least three times every week I could escape from artistic and literary stuff, and talk seriously on serious subjects to serious people. For this reason—because I persisted in Socialistic propaganda—I never once lost touch with the real world.[6]

In short, he was saved from being a Bohemian because he often had to be a Philistine. Unfortunately, the one character did not moderate the other very much. Between the reckless gaiety of the wit and the fierce earnestness of the doctrinaire socialist, there was not much scope for judicial calm.

CHAPTER FIFTEEN

The Art Critic

From 1885 to 1889, Shaw attended every picture exhibition in London and wrote regularly on art in *The World*. In the late nineteenth century, English painting was as usual suspended between its characteristic extremes of lyric color and detailed realism tending to caricature, both of which, according to Elie Faure, inhibit any profund sense of plastic form.[1] Turner was losing the world of articulate shapes in luminous storms and whirlwinds. Ruskin was demanding that men who seemed fatally incapable of learning to draw emulate the magnificent draftsmanship of the primitive Italians. Rossetti was painting valentines, sonnets, and romances; Watts, cold and plausible Michelangelos; and Burne-Jones, Tennysonian Mantegnas and Botticellis. Infinitely laborious, Madox Brown was filling yards of canvas, inch by inch, with a multitude of disjointed and rather ugly facts. With the beautiful idealism of his line, Aubrey Beardsley was eternalizing the soiled linen of the nineties.

Meanwhile a revolution had taken place in French painting. Manet, Pissarro, Renoir, Monet, and others had left the studio and gone out into the open air to paint. The result was a harsh, loud technique, which largely eliminates modeling, makes shadows faint and luminous, sometimes throws form into sharp outline, and sometimes dissolves it in a vibrant brilliance of color. It is perhaps not surprising that these painters emerged from the intellectual civilization of their studios to discover in the bosom of nature the latest modern philosophy, for daylight, ever waxing and waning, changes the outer world into a shimmering dream and varies it from second to second in a manner that is infinitely fleeting and unique. In the nineties, even the sun had become Pateresque.

Shaw wrote art criticism with indefatigable industry, brutal frankness, and elusive conscientiousness. He read the proper books, including those of Ruskin—whom he ultimately considered unreliable except where religion afforded a clue—but he thought it the critic's first duty to look at art. For years he was as inevitable as the pictures at an exhibition, and at the same time he refreshed himself regularly with the great masters at the National Gallery and at Hampton Court. Among the latter he particularly admired that painter of supermen Michelangelo and the fourteenth-century artists, like Bellini and Filippo Lippi, who inspired the stark, crude realism of Madox Brown and Holman Hunt. The merit of all these men is that they studied life and tried to represent it without sentiment or illusion. Michelangelo had an additional virtue:

> I never shall forget climbing an enormously high, rickety framework, in company with Anatole France . . . in order to get a closer look at the Delphic Sibyl. We were close enough to touch it with our hands; and I was surprised to discover that, instead of losing, it gained impressiveness on nearer view. The grand, set face made a tremendous impression upon me. For the first time, I fully realized that Michael Angelo was a great artist, and a great man as well—because his every subject is a person of genius.[2]

Shaw declares that in the development of his mind and art Michelangelo played a considerable part. "Michael Angelo, you see, taught me this —always to put people of genius into my works. I am always setting a genius over against a commonplace person."[2]

Apparently Shaw did not begin his career in art criticism as an unqualified admirer of realism.

> I remember once, when I was an "art critic" [he writes in 1897], and when Madox Brown's work was only known to me by a few drawings, treating Mr. Frederick Shields to a critical demonstration of Madox Brown's deficiencies, pointing out in one of the drawings the lack of "beauty" in some pair of elbows that had more of the wash tub than of "The Toilet of Venus" about them. Mr. Shields contrived without any breach of good manners to make it quite clear to me that he considered Madox Brown a great painter and me a fool. I respected both convictions at the time; and now I share them. Only, I plead in extenuation of my folly that I had become so accustomed to take it for granted that what every English painter was driving at was the sexual beautification and moral idealization of life into something as unlike itself as possible, that it did not at first occur to me that a painter could draw a plain woman for any other reason than that he could not draw a pretty one.[3]

Shaw's admiration of realism suffered from another limitation, and this was a permanent one. The puritan in him could take nothing but a regretful view of the nude. In 1901, with an optimism both Victorian and premature, he asserted as a chief advantage of photography over painting that it presented the nude in a manner too vivid to be endurable in art. Ingres' fabulous "La Source" inspired him with only one idea: "Imagine having to make conversation for her for a couple of hours." [4] But for reality fully clothed, Shaw early developed a passionate devotion, which was all the stronger, probably, for the somewhat uncomfortable lesson inflicted by Frederick Shields. Shaw liked to learn pragmatically, by getting his aesthetic fingers burned.

In discovering artistic good, he also discovered artistic evil. It was simply another form of universal evil, that is, of Victorian convention. Socialism had taught him that the Philistine kept his hand tightly in his pocket. Modern painting taught him that he kept his head in a cloud of sentimental illusion. And what was middle-class sentimentality but romanticism? Shaw had found a new antagonist. Praising the realism of Madox Brown, he writes:

> This love of life and knowledge of its worth is . . . whole Alps and Andes above the common market demand for prettiness, fashionableness, refinement, elegance of style, delicacy of sentiment, charm of character, sympathetic philosophy (the philosophy of the happy ending), decorative moral systems contrasting roseate and rapturous vice with lilied and langorous virtue, making "Love" face both ways as the universal softener and redeemer, the whole being worshipped as beauty or virtue, and set in the place of life to narrow and condition it instead of enlarging and fulfilling it. [5]

His summing up of three figures in contemporary art rescues something of romanticism in the person of Watts: "Madox Brown was a man; Watts is at least an artist and poet; Leighton was only a gentleman." [6] One is reminded of the damnation of Adrian Herbert in *Love among the Artists*.

In disparaging the prettiness of Leighton, Shaw is led to overlook, with puritan austerity, a good deal of ugliness in Madox Brown. His harsh and garish colors, his laborious, piecemeal realism, his general lack of harmony and design not only escape censure but become virtues. He is compared favorably with Rembrandt, whose realism ceases where his atmosphere begins. But Shaw does not pretend to be just or accurate: "Accuracy only means discovering the relation of your will to facts instead of cooking the facts to save trouble." [7] In short, he is a pragmatist. He wants not so much to discover truth as to increase it. He magnifies the crude veracity of Madox Brown and decries the polished sentimentality of Leighton because thereby he hopes more effectually to teach the public to admire truth. Nevertheless, his early warfare against romanticism was not as ruthless as his later. Less venturesome than he was a few years afterward, he did not sacrifice undoubted genius to his cause. His criticism of Rossetti is severe but just:

> When Rossetti's work was first assembled at the Fine Arts Club, and, very soon afterwards, at the Academy, their wealth of color, poetic conception, and the fascination of the faces with which the canvases were crowded, dazzled all those to whom the work of Rossetti was new. But our eyes are now used to the sun; and, at Christie's, Rossetti's want of thoroughness as a draughtsman, and the extent to which his favorite types of beauty at last began to reappear as mere Rossettian conventions, with impossible lips and mechanically designed eyebrows, came with something of a shock upon many who had previously fancied him almost flawless.[8]

Shaw was artistically conscienceless only on high philosophical grounds. Otherwise, he was aggressively incorruptible. He was continually being fired from newspapers and journals because he refused to allow his criticisms to be padded with puffs. The low wages which he received in no way prevented him from taking a very high view of his office and function. At the cost of prodigious mental exertion, he was always improving his best, and by the time he was well embarked on music criticism, his best had become amazingly good. "Daily journalism," he declares, "is a superhuman profession." [9] Good criticism, he decides, is rarer and more difficult than good creative writing.

Shaw's journalistic fun is also commendably serious. It depends in considerable degree, as Chesterton observes, on the fact that truth is often stranger than fiction. As Shaw himself .puts it:

> There is an indescribable levity—not triviality of mind, but levity— something spritelike about the final truth of a matter; and this exquisite levity communicates itself to the style of a writer who will face the labour of digging down to it. It is the half-truth which is congruous, heavy, serious, and suggestive of a middle-aged or elderly philosopher.[10]

One may well doubt whether a whole truth is always amusing, and a half-truth, always heavy and serious. Indeed Shaw himself frequently urges a half-truth in a plausible and witty manner because he feels the public is too complacently convinced of the opposite half-truth. Sometimes, without much regard for truth, he simply shocks and dumfounds. But he nearly always shocks and dumfounds in such a way as to provoke thought. Even his wildest hilarity has usually an element of seriousness in it.

And here it is necessary to recognize how immensely more important he is than such men as Whistler and Wilde. Undoubtedly he learned much from them. His experiments in Jaeger clothing, his sedulous cultivation of pose and idiosyncrasy, his thunderclap announcements to the press, all suggest a debt to the great masters in self-advertisement. But Shaw has far surpassed them. They were the sensation of a decade. He has been the sensation of a half-century—chiefly because he has both more humor and more gravity than they. While he has taken his masks less seriously than they did theirs, he has taken his purposes more seriously, and his purposes have been deeper. People would have stopped laughing at Shaw a long time ago, did he not represent something serious. Shavian epigram is in one sense but the rhetorical form of Fabian permeation.

Shaw's anathema against romanticism apparently excluded the Pre-Raphaelites—and particularly Burne-Jones, whose sentimental and mannered art he esteemed very highly. Burne-Jones was of course a great friend of Morris. One is tempted to suspect that Shaw placed Burne-Jones so high because Morris was a socialist—and also a Shavian hero. And because he read Morris in his earlier years, Shaw occasionally sounds like a Pre-Raphaelite and an aesthete.

In order to drink at the fountainheads of Pre-Raphaelitism, Shaw in 1895 made a pilgrimage to Italy with twenty-seven members of the Art-Workers' Guild. Unfortunately, the experience turned him unexpectedly into a hopeless Philistine. The loudness and vulgarity of his companions, their provincial Ruskinisms, their mistakes in French grammar, the stinginess of their tips threw him into a state of morbid, snobbish embarrassment, which only a violently comic letter to Morris could relieve. This document is crammed with epigrammatic blasphemies against Italian art. Milan Cathedral confesses architectural bankruptcy in a wilderness of white marble and is decidedly inferior to St. Paul's. The exterior of St. Mark's in Venice would be ideal for a railway station. He would like Italian churches if they were free of living humanity—particularly hawking and spitting priests with their perpetual colds. He also defends the honest British tourist against the Italian congregation.

Shaw threw himself wholeheartedly into the battle to secure acceptance for impressionism, "because, being the outcome of heightened attention and quickened consciousness on the part of its disciples, it was evidently destined to improve pictures greatly by substituting a natural, observant, real style for a conventional, taken-for-granted, ideal one." [11] His method was as usual eager and brilliant special pleading. He saw very clearly the central danger of impressionism: "Once I had a discussion with an artist who was shewing me a clever picture of his in which the parted lips in a pretty woman's face revealed what seemed to me like a mouthful of virgin snow." [12] The mouthful of snow turned out to be a mouthful of teeth, as one actually sees them. But having normal eyesight, Shaw knew better and said so. If truth is agreed to be in the eye of the beholder, then the beholder begins to see all sorts of strange things. Moreover, the myopia of a great painter, whether due to spiritual pride or a want of spectacles, may lead to endless folly and chauvinism among his imitators: "We soon had young painters with perfectly good sight looking at landscapes or at their models with their eyes half closed and a little asquint, until what they saw looked to them like one of their favorite master's pictures." [13] Convention may thus crystallize folly and error into a rigid form. It may cramp originality and misguide industrious talent. But in general, impressionism stands for greater freedom, and Shaw feels that modern genius needs more freedom rather than more control. Like John Stuart Mill, he believes that truth will win in the battle with error.

Replying in *The Sanity of Art* (1895) to Max Nordau's *Entartung*, Shaw wrote a definition of the nature and function of art which rises magnificently above the impressionistic and anarchistic tendencies of the essay itself:

> The claim of art to our respect must stand or fall with the validity of its pretension to cultivate and refine our senses and faculties until seeing, hearing, feeling, smelling, and tasting become highly conscious and critical acts with us, protesting vehemently against ugliness, noise, discordant speech, frowzy clothing, and re-breathed air, and taking keen interest and pleasure in beauty, in music, and in nature, besides making us insist, as necessary for comfort and decency, on clean, wholesome, handsome fabrics to wear, and utensils of fine material and elegant workmanship to handle. Further, art should refine our sense of character and conduct, of justice and sympathy, greatly heightening our self-knowledge, self-control, precision of action, and considerateness, and making us intolerant of baseness, cruelty, injustice, and intellectual superficiality or vulgarity. The worthy artist or craftsman is he who serves the physical and moral senses by feeding them with pictures, musical compositions, pleasant houses and gardens, good clothes and fine implements, poems, fictions, essays, and dramas

which call the heightened senses and ennobled faculties into pleasurable activity. The great artist is he who goes a step beyond the demand, and, by supplying works of higher beauty and a higher interest than have yet been perceived, succeeds, after a brief struggle with its strangeness, in adding this fresh extension of sense to the heritage of the race.[14]

In short, art is a way of living, a highly self-conscious discipline aiming at an illumination and intensification of life itself, and not only aesthetically but morally. Shaw has translated Morris, Ruskin, and the *fin de siècle* into a higher and yet very Shavian common sense and amplified Pater's hard, gemlike flame into a more serviceable lamp of truth and virtue.

Always progressive, Shaw became a fanatical devotee of photography, in which he became proficient in the late nineties. Photography was a pariah among the arts. It promised to be revolutionary. It seemed to minimize technique and maximize realism and ideas. No more was necessary. Shaw announced the imminent desiccation of painting as an art. But not the total desiccation. The camera could not represent the supermen of Michelangelo until nature produced them, nor did it need to attempt the "pious edifications" of Raphael, Kaulbach, and Delaroche.[15] All else it could equal or surpass. Shaw envisaged a composite art in which poser and photographer would cooperate to produce every effect of expression and design.

CHAPTER SIXTEEN

The Music Critic

When T. P. O'Connor discovered the piratical character of the Fabian crew which he had allowed to steal aboard his journalistic venture *The Star*, he was confronted with an embarrassing problem. He hated to injure even criminal sensibilities by an act of summary dismissal. He therefore consented with much relief when Shaw, no longer allowed to publish political leaders six hundred years ahead of the time, suggested he write two columns a week on music instead. Shaw did music criticism for *The Star* from 1888 to 1890 and for *The World* from 1890 to 1894. In 1932 the articles for *The World* were republished in three volumes; in 1939 those for *The Star* were republished in one. As musical criticism, these articles maintain a uniformly high level. As artistic prose, they progress from the relatively formal and utilitarian to the racily colloquial and epigrammatic. As an expression of personality, they ascend from the merely human to the genuinely Shavian.

When Shaw became a music critic, members of that occult and fashionable profession were much amused. The fellow was a socialist and a freethinker. His manners were incredibly eccentric. It was even doubtful whether he was a gentleman. Obviously, he could not succeed as a London music critic. And surely he was too witty and frivolous to know anything about music.

Actually, of course, he had been steeped in it from early childhood; scores faintly familiar to others he could sing in their entirety long before he thought of turning his knowledge to commercial account. Unlike "the average critic, with his feeble infusion of the musical dictionary and analytical program, the man who has no opinion and dare not express it if he had, who is afraid of his friends, of his editor, of his own ignorance," [1] Shaw was very sure both of his knowledge and his opinion and delighted in ramming both down the throat of the British reader. He understood not only the techniques of all sorts of instruments and voices but their physical basis in mechanical or physiological structure. With daring omniscience, he detects the slightest variation from legitimate scores, the slightest faults in voice technique, the slightest errors in Italian accent or English pronunciation, the quality and excellence of every instrument in a great orchestra. "Last Saturday," he remarks, " I heard a new note in the orchestra, and traced it to the first flute, Mr. Fransella, whom I have not, as far as I know, had the pleasure of hearing before." [2]

How seriously should all this formidable omniscience be taken? "I do not mind confessing," says Shaw himself, "that I do not know half as much as you would suppose from my articles; but in the kingdom of the deaf the one-eared is king." [3] Nevertheless, he stands solidly behind his pronouncements, numerous and explicit though they are: "Don't be in a hurry to contradict G.B.S. as he never commits himself on a musical subject until he knows at least six times as much about it as you do." [4]

Though he was not above parading his knowledge, Shaw was thoroughly on guard against it. When it tended to minimize common sense and natural sensitivity, when it acted as a mechanical force obscuring imaginative insight, he disowned it. Referring to his technical ignorance of the ballet, he writes, "If I were equally ignorant of the technical differences between a tonal fugue and a quadrille, I should be a better musical critic than I am; for I should not so often be led astray from the essential purpose of art by mere curiosity as to the mechanical difficulties created by certain forms of it." [5]

Shaw also brought to music criticism an extremely un-Shavian virtue: he had saved for music all the reverence of a highly irreverent nature. "Among the pious I am a scoffer," he declares, "among the musical I am religious." [6] Of his responsibility as critic he writes, "I should be a very poor critic indeed if I did not take my function to be as religious a one as man can discharge." [7] The result is that in his musical criticism more than any other writing he shows genuine artistic conscience, a consuming puritanical passion for artistic perfection, the slightest infringement against which brings down whole thunderstorms of censorious wrath. He is the malignant personal enemy of every fallible musician. Usually he punishes quite impartially, but not always. Indeed he declares that justice is unattainable and truth is not a mean between extremes but "quite the most extreme thing I know of." [8] His professed attitude is once more relativistic and pragmatic. He writes for immediate effect, in a gay and passionate effort to make audiences insist on better music and musicians and composers produce it. He coddles, bullies, lauds, insults, gadflying everybody to do his best. His criticism is propaganda for Wagner, for realistic costuming and staging, for precise and intelligent execution, for a dozen other causes and partial truths neglected at the moment.

Inevitably, therefore, the articles date, but this seems hardly a disadvantage, for Shaw makes yesterday so interesting that today becomes a little dull. In these pages, as vividly as the characters in a novel, appear Joachim the impeccable violinist and the musical snob, Mme. Patti the lovely-voiced Philistine with the thirst for money and floral applause, the male choirs singing "in the true English choral fashion, as if to call attention to their being a fine body of men," and the Philharmonic, which, "English to the backbone, never knows when it is beaten . . . going on for years in a chronic state of ignominious defeat, without for a moment losing a sense of superiority which Napoleon at the height of his fortunes probably never enjoyed." [9]

Gradually the picture expands. We perceive that in the eighties and nineties music in England, like religion in Ireland, was a badge of class distinction. Elaborate ceremonies of Bach and Handel were attended by thin ranks of gentry, vast legions of "deadheads," and a sprinkling of professional critics, more or less critical. Among the initiate, Mozart and Beethoven were underestimated; Spohr and Mendelssohn, overestimated. Grieg and Berlioz were just beginning to be recognized; Wagner was just beginning to be reviled. That, whatever his faults, the latter had invented a new kind of music drama, revolutionized orchestration, devised a technique by which the interval of musical memory for the listener could be greatly extended, that he had evolved a philosophy uncannily prophetic of the century to follow was very little suspected. In fact, says Shaw, it was as easy to find a man who had explored the sources of the Congo as one who had so much as heard "Parsifal." What everybody had heard and understood were Gilbert and Sullivan, which, being light, pretty, and literary, suited English taste perfectly. Therefore Shaw often snubbed them—and was deeply influenced by them.

In fact, the greatest difficulty with music in England was the English themselves. Shaw had learned to know them as politicians, as artists, and now as musicians. The result was conclusive: he pronounced them irreclaimable Philistines—and firmly resolved to reclaim them.

> If our popular art was really the expression of the national character, England would long ago have been annexed as a convenient coaling station by Portugal. Fortunately, Englishmen take their business and their politics very differently from their art. Art in England is regarded as a huge confectionery department, where sweets are made for the eye and ear just as they are made for the palate in the ordinary "tuck-shop." [10]

To be sure, he is not much easier on the French. They are shallow and mundane but musically efficient. He speaks of a Frenchman who conducted the overture to "Tannhäuser" without understanding one bar of it, "but who 'worked-up' the finish with a truly Gallic glitter and grandiosity." [11] As a devotee of Bach, Mozart, Beethoven, and Wagner, Shaw naturally reserves his admiration for the Germans, and probably much of his prejudice in favor of that nation springs from his love for their music. "Mr. Villiers Stanford," he writes, "is too thorough an Irishman to be an ideal Bach conductor . . . he lacks the oceanic depth of German sentiment that underlies the intense expression of Bach's music." [12] Needless to say, Shaw is by no means uncritical. He speaks of ridiculous costumes and obsolete stage machinery at Bayreuth and, on another occasion, of "the German tendency to coarse singing and wooden declamation." [13]

The musical articles give a picture not only of the age but of Shaw himself. In fact, they reveal him in the very process of becoming himself. In the earlier numbers of *Corno di Bassetto* he does not differ widely from other men. He actually apologizes for bad manners and even expresses mild remorse for the literary murder of a fellow critic. In the first volume of *Music in London,* he declares, "The critic who is grateful is lost." [14] In the third volume, after wrecking wanton critical destruction from Italy to Ireland, he grumbles, "It has taken me nearly twenty years of studied self-restraint, aided by the natural decay of my faculties, to make myself dull enough to be accepted as a serious person by the British public." [15]

We also get an occasional glimpse of Shaw at the concert. He likes to go with an interesting woman yet nearly always neglects her shamefully. When the music begins, he is completely absorbed. When it ceases, he plunges into the composition of his article instead of conducting her downstairs for refreshments. When the performance is uninteresting, he sneaks away by himself and leaves her to find her own cab. And yet the ladies thought him fascinating, for he got them to improve his manners and to explain "society" to him. He is full of "inside" knowledge about society, as about everything else, though perhaps not quite the kind of inside knowledge that society itself might expect. He refers flamboyantly to "Kensington society, which combines the philistinism of old Bloomsbury with the frivolity of old Brompton." [16] He makes expert lightning calculations at the Grosvenor Club: "Here I found a nob or two, a deadhead or two, and a vast majority of solid snobs. No celebrities, no literary lot, no journalistic lot, no artistic lot, no Bohemian lot, nothing (to speak of) except plain snobbery, more or less choice." [17] This is the society column written by a revolutionist.

Shaw was by no means content to tell composers how to compose, musicians how to play, stage managers how to produce, and audiences how to feel. He also told financiers of music how to venture and manage and the government how to legislate with reference to musical problems. In his spirited yet offhand comment, the English, a placid and political people, discovered with amazement that music was a burning political issue and might at any moment explode into social revolution. The natural enemies of art, he declares, are "the baker and the landlord." [18] Until the first has supplied the community and the second been done away with, true artistic culture will not be possible.

The plight of music in England is but another example of the poverty, artistic and material, in which capitalism results. Most musicians are drawn to a country which supports music by public funds, because there they can be sure of steady employment. Great stars are drawn to a capitalistic country, because there they can command high prices by appearing seldom. Consequently England, like America today, could afford only a single opera company and had to conduct it on a costly monopolistic basis. In order to channel the available private wealth into one solvent enterprise, Sir Augustus Harris, the impresario, had to control all singers and all potential opera houses, though until his great success in later life he made use only of one company and one house. Analyzing the situation at another time, Shaw declares that the dissemination of wealth and education has created a great new audience of musical beginners. They are up to Donizetti but not up to Wagner. Shaw suggests that there should be three kinds of national theater: one for the musically advanced, one for the musically retarded, and one—with a great promenade down the center—for the snobs.

But state opera backed by state socialism was only the distant and and ultimate goal. Shaw did not leave his Fabianism in the foyer of the theater. He had always in view a dozen immediate and lesser objectives, which ranged from cheap seats and a drastic reduction in the number of child actors to municipal bands and provincial music festivals for the benefit not of hospitals but of music itself. In a tone of suave superiority, he addressed his suggestions, in the guise of shrewd and profitable advice, directly to the impresario. Readers of *The Star* and *The World* must have suspected that the soundest business was talked in the music column.

One is not surprised that music should have brought out in Shaw the wit and the dramatist or even the economist and the shrewd man of business; but one is a little surprised that it should reveal a man of deep and even romantic feeling or one so much concerned with mere immediate truth and justice.

Shaw insists that the performance of music should always be governed by the score and the intention of the composer. Sir Charles Hallé is preferable to Rubenstein as a pianist because he plays more Beethoven and less Hallé.[19] Albani's "acting has the sincerity which . . . so often leads her straight to the right vocal treatment of purely dramatic music." [20] He listens to a performance with the anxious jealousy of a dis-

placed prima donna. He is furious at the common deletions and interpolations made for the convenience of the artist—in general is reluctant
to eliminate anything from any work except the repetitions of Bach,
which he considers wearisome to modern taste. He nags incessantly at
errors in tempo and rhythm and alternately grovels in despair and
thunders with rage at the mechanical and unimaginative interpretations
of professional, workaday musicians. "It will be necessary," he sighs
after a concert by the Philharmonic, "to invent some exceptionally
poignant form of insult to flog it up to the mark again." [21]

Though firmly convinced that London audiences deserve the worst, he
nevertheless insists that they be given the best. Artists must always be
deeply conscious of the sacredness of their art and never fall below the
level of their best performance. The vagaries of prima donnas rouse him
to furies of puritanical rationalism. They must have no whims, no temperament, no nerves, no stupidity. They must never get fat. They must never
end on a high note for sensational effect when Mozart's score designates
a low one. They must renounce all applause, floral and vocal. In short,
they must live in a vacuum of pure reason and pure art, giving themselves up entirely to making the proper sounds in the proper way. Sheer
zeal and power of screaming are not to be mistaken for music: "My dear
young lady, pray *dont*. Your voice is not a nail, to be driven into my
head." [22]

On the other hand, he cannot resist gusto and passion when they burst
spontaneously from a great artist. He is hugely delighted with Mme.
Nilsson, who, in the middle of "Il Trovatore," was so carried away with
enthusiasm at the singing of an aria by a patriarch tenor that she slapped
him on the back with a hearty bravo. Artistically, he is head over heels in
love with Giulia Ravogli, who acted Carmen so ferociously that a trom-
bone player in the orchestra dodged with involuntary fear. "If anybody
else," says Shaw, "were to sing the florid passages in Bertoni's aria in *Or-
feo*, or the lilt in the tavern scene of Carmen, as she sings them, how that
person would catch it in this column! But in the presence of such a millionaire in artistic force as Guilia, Bertoni and Bizet lose their rights." [23]
But perhaps Shaw's greatest favorite is Sophie Menter, who on more
than one occasion "left Weber and Schumann for dead on the platform." [24] In fact, he does not mind a little freedom with a composer
whom he dislikes. He has long been amused by the spectacle of the ane-
mic Schumann sung by the magnificently virile Sophie Menter. It is, he
declares, "like bringing a sensitive invalid into the fields on a sunshiny
day and making him play football for the good of his liver." [25] In such passages, the dramatist can already be seen in the music critic.

The operatic stage is one hundred years behind the dramatic. Impre-
sarios fail to realize that opera is not only music but drama. Nothing that

contributes to the effect at which the composer aimed is irrelevant to a good performance. He never forgave the peculiarly broken-down sofa on which Orpheus had to die at Covent Garden. There must be the right kind of bats in "Die Fledermaus," the right kind of lightning in "Die Walküre." Everything matters, from the waistlines of the soloists to the unshaven chins of the chorus. "The Egyptian priests looked more like a string of sandwich men than ever," he complains.[26] Poor diction is particularly infuriating. One perceives that Shaw the dramatist learned cockney by abominating it. He was fond of translating, with deliberate and painstaking rage, the most solemn parts of sacred music into the typical phonetics of London singers:

Eoh kum let hus hadore 'im.

Diction frequently leads the discussion to dramatic poetry, and one observes with some surprise that the most eminent deprecator of Shakespeare is also a bardolator. He is full of carefully thought-out ideas about how Shakespeare should be produced, acted, and recited—and full of admiration. He concludes a discussion of Marlowe's blank verse with the words, "Marlowe's line was not mighty: blank verse did not become mighty until the lines had grown together into the great symphonic movement of Shakespear's final manner." [27] Mere mind may be Shaw's language, but there are other languages which he can understand—and understand very deeply.

As a critic of music interpretation, Shaw betrays no observable bias. Ordinarily, he is almost pedantically insistent on technical correctness, yet he can tolerate the failings of Alexander Bull:

> Each performance has the same odd appearance of being his first attempt; and though he makes less faults than most professional violinists, yet there is something strange about them, because they are not the usual faults. He solves the ordinary player's difficulties by natural magic, and then falls into new difficulties of his own which an ordinary player would solve offhand. But his tone is so fine and nervous, and so full of sudden and unexpected inflexions; and his playing is so unflaggingly imaginative that I receive a much more vivid and musical impression from him than I do from Joachim.[28]

In general, Shaw counsels restraint within the limits of the score and the proper nature of the instrument. A performance on the piano should not be an orgy, nor should a pianist try, like Paderewski, to be a blacksmith.[29] On the other hand, he demands that the Rienzi overture be played "so as to give concussion of the brain." [30]

As a journalistic commentator, Shaw necessarily wrote much more on the performance than on the composition of the music. Nevertheless, the skeleton of a musical theory and history might be deduced from his pages. If the composer's intent is the test of good performance, what is the test of the composer himself? First, feeling. "There is a great deal of feeling, highly poetic and highly dramatic, which cannot be expressed by mere words—because words are the counters of thinking, not of feeling—but which can be supremely expressed by music." [31] Want of feeling condemns Rossini: "I cannot say 'Rest his soul,' for he had none; but I may at least be allowed the fervent aspiration that we may never look upon his like again." [32] Second, thought. Poor Schubert feels "that if he only hurries fast enough he will presently overtake Mozart and Beethoven, who are not to be caught up in a thousand miles by any man with second-rate brains, however wonderful his musical endowment." [33] Third, there must of course be genuine inspiration, which might be described as the tension between a mind and an an idea, or, as Shaw puts it, "a definite poetic intention adequately and characteristically expressed." [34] This intention must be controlled and sustained. Mozart, for example, leads his inspiration, "makes its course for it, removes obstacles, holds it in from gadding erratically after this or that passing fancy, thinks for it, and finally produces with it an admirable whole, the full appreciation of which keeps every faculty on the alert from beginning to end." [35] Finally, Shaw emphasizes that there are no permanent laws of musical syntax. "The severity of artistic discipline is produced by the fact that in creative art no ready-made rules can help you." [36]

A composer who "borrows" his ideas cannot belong to the first rank— and Shaw's musical memory is diabolically sharp, perhaps deceptively so. Part of a Brahms composition "is a ridiculously dismal version of a lately popular hornpipe . . . it certainly deserved a merrier fate than burying alive in a Brahms quintet." [37] Saint-Saëns's violin concerto in B minor is made up of "trivially pretty scraps of serenade music sandwiched between pages from the great masters." [38] He gives no quarter to academic composers. "The writing of a piece in three movements in sonata form does not add a cubit to its stature." [39] Even genuine inspiration can debase itself by extravagant or insincere expression. "Tchaikowsky could set the fateful drum rolling and make the trombones utter the sepulchral voice of destiny without any conceivable provocation." [40]

In general, Shaw's conception of the role of music is just and broad. Since it is a means of expressing human feelings and ideas, music is inevitably related to life and should be so judged—particularly opera, which is a dramatic imitation of human action. Among operatic composers, Verdi must be assigned a lesser place because, except in "Otello," he does little more than set the police intelligence to beautiful melody. Wagner is greater, chiefly because he brought opera much closer to life technically and because he has "a philosophic intellect of first-rate force and dexterity." [41] But the greatest of all is Mozart. Shaw devotes a whole article to describing, with immense gusto, such a performance of "Don Giovanni" as he has dreamed of but never seen. Clearly he considers that opera all that an opera should be—great as music and as a dramatic representation of human life.

Shaw's remarks on musical history are for the most part brief and incidental. Criticizing a piano concert, he interposes, "Do you know that noble fantasia in C minor, in which Mozart shewed what Beethoven was to do with the pianoforte sonata, just as in *Das Veilchen* he shewed what Schubert was to do with song?" [42] But in a remarkable article, written in 1901 and appended to *Corno di Bassetto*, he embarks on a lengthy discussion of Italian opera which indicates that he had studied closely the evolution of musical forms. The difference between Verdi's "Ernani" and "Aïda," he observes, for example, is not, as critics assert, the influence of Wagner but that of Boito, Beethoven, and Mendelssohn. "The utmost that can be said to connect him [Verdi] with Wagner is that if Wagner had not got all Europe into the habit of using the whole series of dominant and tonic discords as freely as Rossini used the dominant seventh, it is possible that Falstaff might have been differently harmonized." [43] And tracing more broadly the development of Italian opera, he continues:

> Verdi, stronger and more singly dramatic, broke away from the Rossinian convention; developed the simpler Cavatina form with an integral codetta instead of a separated cabaletto; combined it fearlessly with popular dance and ballad forms; and finally produced the enormously popular, because concise, powerful, and comparatively natural and dramatic type of operatic solo which prevails in *Il Trovatore* and *Un Ballo*. A comparison of this Italian emancipation shews in a moment the utter unthinkableness of any sort of connection between the two composers. [44]

Lashing out ferociously at all musical imperfection, Shaw speedily made himself the enemy of many of the musicians and nearly all the critics in London. Not knowing quite how to refute him, they condemned him for his virtues and denied him a knowledge of music because he was clever and amusing. Managers patronized him heavily—and refused to send him complimentary tickets. Nevertheless, a few recognized him for what he was. Edward Elgar, then a youthful and struggling music teacher, relished his sharp and witty criticism so much that many years later he could quote passages from it to the author.

Shaw was destined to be a Wagnerite. Wagner was romantic in his metaphysics, equalitarian and socialistic in his politics, dramatic and literary in his music, and revolutionary in everything. That Shaw was romantic, socialistic, and revolutionary, I need hardly emphasize. That he was also dramatic and literary in his approach to music, many passages indicate: "I gained penetrating experiences of Victor Hugo and Schiller from Donizetti, Verdi, and Beethoven; of the Bible from Handel; of Goethe from Schumann; of Beaumarchais and Molière from Mozart; and of Mérimée from Bizet, besides finding in Berlioz an unconscious interpreter of Edgar Allan Poe." [45]

In 1898, while convalescing from a severe illness, Shaw wrote *The Perfect Wagnerite*. By that time nobody could pretend to belong to the upper middle class without having heard *The Ring*. Wagner's music had become fashionable, but most of his political ideas were still revolutionary. That a prophet of socialism should unwittingly be deified by the economically unregenerate was the kind of opportunity Shaw was always looking for. *The Perfect Wagnerite* gravely throws this irony in the face of respectable readers. It explains orthodox Wagnerism as revolutionary anarchism and translates that doctrine with awful immediacy into the idiom of the English suburban mind.

To be sure, Wagner is not all revolutionary anarchism. Shaw also had availed himself of the worshiper's privilege and, as much as possible, made his god over in his own Shavian image. Nevertheless, he presents the elements of a fairly reliable interpretation of *The Ring*. The dwarfs he identifies quite correctly with "predatory, lustful, greedy people" and enriches the parallel with suggestions of the class struggle and the sweatshop operator. The giants represent "patient, toiling, stupid, respectful, money-worshipping people," and the gods—who do not differ in kind from men—"intellectual, moral, talented people." [46]

Wotan's career is the tragedy of a brilliant political leader who finds he can maintain his ascendancy only by sacrificing his integrity to his interest and his highest purposes to maintenance of the *status quo*. If he would be secure, he must wrest from the giant Fafnir the ring of the Niebelungen, symbolizing apparently economic power. To this end and to free himself, if only vicariously, from the shackles of his own laws, he brings forth by Mother Earth the race of the Volsungs and ultimately Siegfried, who is the hero, or superman. Mischievously, Shaw sees in Siegfried the Russian anarchist Bakunin, who, together with Wagner, was a leader in the Saxon uprising of 1848. But the youthful and exuberant superman does not very much suggest the middle-aged and battle-worn connoisseur in revolution, nor does Wagner very often see anyone but himself as the hero of an opera.

The concluding work of *The Ring*, the "Götterdämmerung," Shaw simply refuses to take seriously. Here, in his opinion, significant social criticism descends into mere Shelleyan romanticism, the drama of ideas into mere conventional operatic stage fustian. That a pint or two of love potion should make Siegfried forget Brünnhilde and his own high purpose, that Brünnhilde herself, who represents the creative will of Wotan, should descend to jealousy and murder, is completely unworthy of the basic symbolism of *The Ring*. As a matter of fact, Wagner had begun with the "Götterdämmerung," or "Siegfrieds Tod," and had subsequently written "Das Rheingold" and "Die Walküre" as an explanation. But according to Shaw, the explanation explained too much and demanded a new conclusion, which the later Wagner, disillusioned with the failure of 1848 radicalism, was totally unable to write. Shaw then shows how strict Fabian doctrine would greatly have sharpened the social criticism of the early operas and confesses that the super-Fabianism which should conclude them cannot yet be foreseen.

Wagner himself attempts to reconcile the "Götterdämmerung" with the earlier operas by the philosophy of Schopenhauer, whom he read soon after completing his libretto. Undoubtedly the "Götterdämmerung," culminating in cosmic suicide, does lend itself to a Schopenhauerian interpretation. Undoubtedly also, Wagner was by nature something of a Schopenhauerian. But to translate the whole *Ring* into metaphysical will is simply to introduce elaborate metaphysical bewilderment.[47] As dramatic art, the tetralogy is both uneven and inconsistent. As an expression of idea, it is fairly clear though unsystematic. Its final meaning, according to Mr. E. R. Bentley, is that heroism is not enough; it represents the annihilation of will by love, the need of sacrifice to restore "the innocence of becoming."[48] In more or less coherent fashion, it summarizes all Wagner's ideas and reveals him a socialist, a hero-worshiper, a nihilistic sensualist, and a *fin de siècle* Christian.

Of these elements, two, it seems to me, are dominant and essential— the heroic revolutionism and the romantic glorification of love and death. Wagner's approach to life is essentially that of an artist in whom inspiration is closely linked with eroticism; and the sense of achievement, with the applause of a Wagnerian audience. He became a revolutionist because he felt that only a revolution could raise the masses to an understanding of his operas. Later he became a mystical searcher after nirvana because both the revolution and his operas seemed destined to fail. His exaltation of death proceeds directly from his eroticism, which by frustration and an unhappy early marriage had been conditioned to a pleasure in suffering. For Wagner, death becomes identified with the consummation of the sexual act and again with the supreme ecstasy of a nihilistic sensualism. It is also his particular variety of "the blue flower," a refuge from the trials and disappointments of the world. At its most vulgar, it is a romantic badge worn by an aged Philistine who wishes, half sincerely, for an escape from the noise and strain of a monotonously successful life. Shaw is perfectly aware of the romanticism and the eroticism, but he prefers to treat them as the pardonable nonsense of a great man.

Of the characteristically romantic oppositions on which Wagner's political thought is based—Kultur *vs.* polyglot metropolitanism, German heroism *vs.* Jewish capitalism—Shaw says almost nothing, nor did they cause him any alarm when they reappeared mildly in the German neopaganism of 1914 and more violently in the Nazism of 1932. It is characteristic that he continued to combat nineteenth-century menaces in the twentieth century. With all his rationalistic emphasis on the dangers of romantic illusion, he sees them always as consisting in sentimentalizing convention and conformity rather than in glamorizing anarchy and rebellion. To be sure, he is here as on other occasions vigorously on both sides of the question, but by way of ultimate emphasis he seems to believe that we cannot have too much freedom or too little morality. And this attitude is strengthened by an endorsement of the Wagnerian superman.

If he finds some fault with Wagner's drama and his ideas, Shaw finds hardly any with his music. Wagner did not open a new epoch but culminated one inaugurated by Mozart and Beethoven, in which music became steadily less formal and more dramatically expressive of human emotion. Wagner greatly elaborated the device of applying musical themes to dramatic character. He got magnificent effects by combining notes never before sounded together. He made music as never before articulate and dramatic and surpassed all others in accommodating instrumentation to the human voice. His signal merit was that he created a genuine music drama.

In a footnote to *The Sanity of Art* (1898), Shaw observes that Richard Strauss has gone far beyond Wagner in realism and discord. He "actually makes a feature of unresolved discords, just as Wagner made a feature of unprepared ones." [49] Yet the same "authorities" who lost their tempers about Wagner were now yelling with rage against Strauss. And in twenty years he would seem as conventional as Mozart. It was the chief function of Shaw's criticism to shorten, for other composers besides Strauss, that twenty-year interval.

CHAPTER SEVENTEEN

The Quintessence of Ibsenism

For more than a hundred years English drama, like Wagner's Brünnhilde, had been slumbering peacefully, guarded by the jealous fires of middle-class puritanism. To be sure, the fires had not kept out vice so much as genius. Victorian authors had preferred the plebeian respectability of the novel to the aristocratic iniquity of the drama. Moreover, both science and romanticism had strengthened the novel by making it more historical and realistic, whereas science had not yet reached the theater, and romanticism had weakened the drama by making it, especially at the beginning of the century, too lyrical and subjective. Lord Byron had been unable to get more than one real person—and that himself—on the stage at once; and all nineteenth-century dramatists were so hypnotized by the gigantic reputation of Shakespeare that they attempted not only to imitate his impossible technique of putting whole novels on the stage but actually to reproduce the Elizabethan rather than the modern world and so wrote, as Charles Lamb said, for antiquity rather than for posterity.

They were also discouraged from writing about contemporary life by the great tradition of heroic acting, which, coming down from the eighteenth century, had been partly inspired by Shakespeare and partly necessitated by the size of the old, dimly lit theater. The secondary art had thus gained ascendancy over the primary. Great actors either hacked up Shakespeare to fit their own talents or hired nonentities to whack them out a tailor-made part from whole cloth. They dominated the English theater until well into the nineties, when Shaw asserted the rights of the dramatist by carrying on a personal war against Sir Henry Irving.

History had long been preparing for that attack. The first step was taken in France during the thirties and forties, when the bourgeois of Paris began to tire of the turgid swashbuckling of romantic historical drama. It was then that Eugène Scribe saw he could make a good deal of money by giving them neat, well-made little packages of melodrama done up in contemporary middle-class costume and setting. Soon plays were flowing from his pen as swiftly as Fords from an assembly line.

Their immense success proved the public preference for simple plots and contemporary life.

In the fifties the next step was taken. Scribe had usually added to his concoction just a drop of thought and realism, like a dash of angostura bitters. Dumas *fils* and Augier perceived that ideas themselves could be a sensation and truth a novelty. Naturally, they were cautious. Dumas was a liberal, and Augier was a conservative, but both represented the middle-class point of view, and both were careful to prove only the morally obvious about fascinatingly disreputable people—as, for example, that prostitutes or dissolute husbands are not very useful citizens.

Yet the spirit of the time and of the theater was leading both authors, tacitly at least, to question accepted morals. It is a principal tenet of romanticism that society is a villain, and it is a natural tendency of melodrama, in its search for sensation, to deal in moral paradox. Just as romantic dramatists had turned heaven and hell upside down in the name of truth and glorified brigandage in the name of freedom, so in the name of a much more prosaic humanitarianism Augier and Dumas pitied, condemned, and sensationalized the libertine, the adulteress, and the undutiful mother. As far at least as the audience was concerned, the free morals of the nineties began as a shudder of pleasant horror at the top of decorous midcentury spines.

But genuine intellectual drama is not prepared for simply by the titillation of conventional spines. It requires also some disturbance in the gray matter of unconventional heads. This disturbance was provided first by the Germans, and particularly Hebbel, who in the midcentury outlined the drama of ideas; and then by Ibsen, who in the seventies and eighties realized it. Refining Scribe's well-made play into something yet more naturalistic and concentrated and using it to set forth problem situations much more drastic and complicated than those of Dumas and Augier, Ibsen criticized contemporary moral conventions and moral character from the point of view partly of the new sciences of biology and psychology, partly of John Stuart Mill's social philosophy, and partly of romantic anarchism. As a matter of fact, his social drama was but the middle stage of the Ibsenite quest, which began and ended in the mocking dilemmas of his own soul.

Ibsen's "Doll's House" appeared on the London stage in 1889. Meanwhile, English drama had been moving slowly in his direction. Baronets began, as William Archer observes, to develop an alarming turn for stage villainy. Lesser actors wrested a precarious livelihood from pirated Scribe and Dumas in English settings—and indeed the English theater had always been more or less concerned with contemporary life. In the seventies Tom Robertson modernized dialogue and staging technique and in "Caste" touched on contemporary social problems. By the end of the eighties the English stage was ready not for ideas but at least for big words and the posture of thought. The result was that Ibsen's "Doll's House" produced universal horror and execration, and Pinero's "Second Mrs. Tanqueray" general applause and wonder. Pinero was safe. He did not know when he was thinking and when he was frowning. Indeed, the dramatists of the nineties had invented a new and balder Victorian Compromise: they were simply both for and against. Jones and Pinero mixed up the New Woman with the old ideas and used the new ideas as a device of complication in the old melodrama. Oscar Wilde upheld the Victorian conventions in his plot and tore them down in his dialogue. Nevertheless, these men—and particularly Wilde—wrote better drama than had been known in England for more than a hundred years.

In 1891, Ibsen's "Ghosts" was performed on the London stage. An attack against the inward spirit of virtue was bad enough, but a violation as well of the outward form—of the decencies themselves—was intolerable. Sexual disease depicted on the stage! If "A Doll's House" had created a scandal, "Ghosts" provoked a holy war. All the most respectable newspapers poured forth all their foulest language of abuse. Clement Scott, writing in *The Daily Telegraph*, compared the play to "an open drain; a loathesome sore unbandaged; a dirty act done publicly; a lazar-house with all its doors and windows open." [1] Such an outburst of exasperated virtue Shaw could not pass over. In a lecture to the Fabian Society, he had only the year before claimed Ibsen as a socialist. There was now obviously no other course than to write a book in his defense. Besides, he merited further study, for Shaw had become convinced that in the drama proper, Ibsen—as in music drama, Wagner—was the most significant development of the nineteenth century. And Shaw had two acts of an Ibsenite play burning in his pocket.

The year 1891 was undoubtedly one of the most significant in Shaw's life. He not only wrote much brilliant musical criticism, erupted political manifestoes, and completed a remarkable play, but adopted a great many new ideas, which he expressed in *The Quintessence of Ibsenism*. George and Mill had taught him that man is rational. Now he learned from Schopenhauer, Ibsen, and others that man is irrational. He also learned that man is not only an economic but a religious animal. The change was less fundamental than it seems. Shaw remained a materialist, a socialist, and even a rationalist. He simply broadened the basis of his attack on midcentury civilization, occupying the positions not only of the utilitarian socialist but also of the romantic individualist.

In *The Quintessence* Shaw begins by outlining some basic Ibsenism. Much of it is of course even more basically Shavian. There are, he says, two kinds of spiritual pioneers: those who teach that the currently immoral is moral, and those who teach that the currently moral is immoral

—in short, those who say "yes" and those who say "no." In general, Shaw favors the first, for moral progress consists in the repudiation of duties. At first men's conduct was limited by superstitious fear, then by reason, which itself, however, came to mean "syllogism worship with rites of human sacrifice." [2] Here of course "reason" signifies that philosophy which very ingeniously "banished brains from the universe"—and pity as well —by explaining progress in terms of blind atomic competition. The Benthamites had explained economic progress by such competition, and with his doctrine of the survival of the fittest, Darwin had exalted *laissez faire* into a natural law of organic life. As a socialist, Shaw is not content to find the kingdom of God within himself and therefore still less can he accept cosmic capitalism, with its Malthusian concomitant of the mass torture and murder of failures, in the world without. The success of the labor movement in itself refutes such a theory. Indeed, that success and all progress, he feels, can only be understood as the work of a World Will, or Life Force, whose highest manifestation is man and whose ethical intimations, as later writings make clear, proceed from human impulse and instinct. Thus Shaw's creative evolution issues directly from his socialism, and by a very rational process he comes to deny reason as a guide to life. Schopenhauer, he points out, has taught us that if we were genuinely reasonable, we should all commit suicide. Only the will to live keeps us alive, as will in general moves us to action, though reason has first to translate will into orderly purpose. The triumph of modern moral philosophy is its freedom, which teaches us that we do things because we want to. The triumph of modern religion is creative evolution, which deifies man and sets up no law above his own individuality.

So far Shaw seems pretty clearly an anarchist. We cannot have too much liberty. Actually, he does not face the issue so squarely. He praises self-control in the artist Marie Bashkirtseff, and in speaking of the development of institutions, he suggests that moral progress consists in the supersession of one set of duties by another.[3] Later he hopes, like Blake, that men may eventually learn moderation from their headaches.[4] In other words, if morality remains with us, it must be an evolving morality. We must learn to submit it critically to the test of experience. We must judge it as it contributes to the greatest happiness of the greatest number. And indeed one great tendency of Shavian drama is not to free us from obligations but to lay a heavy social obligation upon us. Thus he is enthusiastically for freedom and rather decidedly against it.

The fundamental cause of this confusion is that Shaw does not sufficiently recognize the dualism of human nature. That civilization requires civilized conduct; that such conduct cannot commonly be the spontaneous result of whim, biological urge, or virginal self-trust but in the long run requires positive effort informed by that curious complex of habit, feeling, and critical thought we call conscience; that conscience is frequently in conflict with the primitive tendencies of our nature; that every degree of civilization from the shallowest respectability to the most heroic virtue requires some victory of conscience over impulse, Shaw is always extremely reluctant to grant. Any theory of human nature built upon the practical moral problem seems to him crude and artificial. In *The Sanity of Art* (1895) he writes:

> The ingrained habit of thinking of the propensities of which we are ashamed as "our passions," and our shame of them and our propensities to noble conduct as a negative and inhibitory department called generally our conscience, leads us to conclude that to accept the guidance of our passions is to plunge recklessly into the insupportable tedium of what is called a life of pleasure.[5]

The narrowness of Victorian conscience made him hostile to conscience itself, as the hollowness of Victorian convention made him hostile to convention and law. Sometimes he strikes at law and undermines conscience by emphasizing the hostility between them. In *The Sanity of Art*, for example, he points out that laws are so convenient men often cling to them long after they have become hopelessly outmoded and sharply opposed to the dictates of conscience. They are moral crutches which prevent men from ever learning to think or to act. Shaw declares that virtue is to be achieved through thought and will and then resolves both to passion, or emotion. A true romantic, he tries to see as much harmony and as little conflict as possible in human nature. To be sure, by employing the single word "will" to cover momentary impulse, biological instinct, and the kind of steady effort necessary to carry out a rational or moral design, he achieves, like Schopenhauer, further unity —and confusion. The practical consequence of his ideas is sometimes impulse without morality and sometimes morality without principle. The second, as G. K. Chesterton observes, usually takes the form of

> . . . a worried and conscientious anarchy. . . . For it refuses to trust in traditional experiments or plainly trodden tracks; every case must be considered anew from the beginning, and yet considered with the most wide-eyed care for human welfare; every man must act as if he were the first man made. Briefly, we must always be worrying about what is best for our children, and we must not take one hint or rule of thumb from our fathers. Some think that this anarchism would make a man tread down mighty cities in his madness. I think it would make a man walk down the street as if he were walking on eggshells.[6]

[141]

In the next section of *The Quintessence,* Shaw sets up between the realist and the idealist an opposition which he declares—and on the whole rightly—to be implicit in Ibsen's plays. A realist is a man who "dares to love and trust" and who sees the facts without illusion. Shelley is his outstanding example. And yet Shelley's readiness to love and trust caused him to have a great many illusions about pretty girls, other men's wives, the common man, democracy, and the immediate political future of a very conservative nation. Those who dare to love and trust are seldom those who see facts without illusion. Again, Shelley's realism about women and marriage, which Shaw particularly admires, would seem to consist chiefly in yielding to temptation. Probably nineteenth-century sex convention made too little concession to the instincts. Yet hardly any convention, nor very much sanity either, could survive long in a nation composed of such realists as Shelley.

Shaw has two separate definitions for the word "ideal." An ideal represents a future possibility, or it is a pleasant mask put on an ugly fact, as the doctrine of personal immortality is a pleasant mask put on the ugly fact of death. Shaw emphasizes the second meaning, which he asserts—and again I think rightly—to be that most frequently implied in Ibsen. Thus in Ibsen's plays—and in Shaw's also—an ideal usually represents an illusion and tends to be characteristic of conservatives. Progressives are usually realists. Even more than Ibsen, Shaw sees progress as essentially a tearing away of veils in order to get at facts. Apparently new purposes spring quite spontaneously out of fresh facts. Shaw's violent antagonism to Victorian convention, and therefore to Victorian illusion and romanticism, led him at this time, like other nineteenth-century rationalists, to emphasize the dangers rather than the virtues of the imagination as a means of arriving at truth. Though himself brilliantly imaginative, he regarded the visionary faculty as essentially romantic, as a means by which lyric poets and sentimental women escaped from the pressing problems of sex and socialism into ivory towers which were after all so much Victorian capitalistic real estate.

Following up his distinction between realist and idealist, Shaw makes another between the modern and the womanly woman. The first, exemplified by Marie Bashkirtseff, is realistic, rationalistic, independent, and emancipated. The second, exemplified by great numbers of her sex, is idealistic, pure, submissive, self-sacrificing, and parasitic. She is not an end in herself but a mere instrument for man's sensuous enjoyment. Yet instead of this ugly fact, she has been taught to see first the strenuous fiction of romantic love, which is satirized in "Arms and the Man," and then the idealistic mask of the pure and indissoluble marriage, which is dealt a shattering blow in "Candida." In general, love

[142]

is an appetite, and marriage, in so far as it is at all admissible, should be a rational bargain between clear-sighted egotists. Shaw's distinction between the modern and the womanly woman fits his own plays even better than Ibsen's. The latter's women are less satirically womanly and less rationalistically, more romantically modern.

This whole discussion of pioneers, realists, idealists, and modern women is essentially a Shavian elaboration of the ideas of Ibsen's middle period. But Ibsen was more complicated than Shaw thought. The expansive vest of the *petit bourgeois* covered the warm heart of a romantic optimist and the strong will of a Protestant fanatic. From under the tall hat of a Pillar of Society looked out the emancipated intellect of a methodical skeptic. Shaw is quite right that most of Ibsen's heroes are idealists. They try to live according to an idea; and since that requires a strong effort of will, Ibsen is also interested in the will. More broadly, he deals with ideas in their double relation to the world without and the mind within. The idea is tested by its applicability to human society and the man by his application of the idea—especially when it seems less and less an adequate picture of reality. Thus Ibsen's plays are usually dramas of self-deception and awakening.

His first period emphasizes will and idea in relation to the individual. In Brand the two are one. His idea is that will is the key to life. Ibsen concludes his investigation of the individual will in "Emperor and Galilean," coming to a halt before the old dilemma of free will and necessity, which as a skeptic he cannot resolve by an act of faith.[7] Turning then in his second period with "The Pillars of Society" to the world without, he begins to test contemporary social conventions by the "realistic" values of truth and freedom. But again the skeptic triumphs, this time over the romantic optimist, and in the self-satire of "The Wild Duck," he rejects truth and freedom as the ultimate conditions of human intercourse. His third period begins with "Rosmersholm." Here he returns to the problem of the will but gives it an ethical rather than a religious formulation. Having himself been an arduous worker with little time for happiness, he quite naturally establishes a dichotomy between virtue and significance on the one hand and happiness and freedom on the other. The strong man strives ruthlessly toward happiness or greatness but is held back by the dead conscience of the fossil man inside of him.

The difficulty is, of course, that Ibsen's conception of happiness remained too narrowly romantic and utilitarian. He could not expand it to contain the elements of virtue and achievement chiefly because, as a skeptic, he could not decide where moral activity should tend. He never succeeded in mediating between happiness and virtue on a higher level than that of bourgeois common sense.

As a social and political thinker, Shaw attempted quite naturally to explain his subject in terms of his social and political period, setting up truth and freedom as the permanent values of Ibsen drama. His definition of that drama is, with some humorous exaggeration, a very neat summing up of his thesis. An Ibsen play, he says, is "one in which the leading lady is an unwomanly woman, and the 'villain' an idealist, who brings forth evil by virtue of his determination to do nothing wrong." [8] He uses this dictum with great ingenuity to explain Ibsen's whole development from "Brand" to "When We Dead Awaken." It is fairly satisfactory for Brand, whose determination to achieve his ideal works far more harm than could the most active malevolence. But already in "Peer Gynt" it becomes misleading, and here Shaw's loose conception of the will also leads him astray. He regards Peer as at once a modern success man and an idealist who compensates for the failures of his will with romantic self-deception. But Peer is not in any sense an idealist. He is simply the example of a man who sacrifices will, together with all high or steady purpose, to idle dreams and casual pleasure, as Brand sacrifices all pleasure and affection to will. "Emperor and Galilean" Shaw sees as a drama not so much of the will as of faith and understanding, which in large part it is. He is chiefly interested in the mystic Maximus, who inculcates the divinity of man and the glorious evolution of the World Will. Clearly, "Emperor and Galilean" is one of the earliest sources of Shaw's religion of the Life Force.

As it appeared in 1891, *The Quintessence of Ibsenism* concluded with a review of the plays from "The Pillars of Society" through "Hedda Gabler." Here of course Shaw is at his best. He attempts no critical estimate but simply explains and defends, emphasizing how one drama grows naturally out of another. One sees that, waging unremitting war on conventional idealism, Ibsen has from "The Pillars of Society" to "An Enemy of the People" dealt with worthier and worthier victims in more and more searching and poignant situations. In "The Pillars of Society," Shaw dwells with pleasure on Hilmar Tönnesen, who is an excellent example of the comic Shavian idealist. From "An Enemy of the People" through "Rosmersholm," he is less satisfactory because he does not see that Ibsen is repudiating his own values and once more shifting his interest from society back to the individual. Throughout this discussion Shaw stresses Ibsen's attitude toward particular problems, such as marriage and democracy.

In 1913, stirred at last by the piracies of American publishers, Shaw brought out another edition of *The Quintessence of Ibsenism,* in which he interpolated some additions to the original text, explained the last four plays, and appended two chapters on Ibsen's thought and dramatic technique. The analysis of the new plays is excellent. In accord with his original thesis, Shaw regards all the protagonists as idealists. He does a little less than justice to the "sickly conscience," which he does not sufficiently see is set off against happiness. He interprets "Little Eyolf" too much as Ibsen's conversion from rugged individualism to Fabian socialism, just as he had interpreted "Hedda Gabler" too much as a revolutionary indictment of the upper middle class. In morals, he remains as much a naturalist as ever and seems to feel that men can improve themselves in any way except through their own efforts. Apparently, they have very little power to realize their ethical ideals, which are simply pretexts by which they do what they want with a clear conscience.

Shaw declares Ibsen has introduced three features new to the theater before the late nineteenth century. First, he has surprised people into thinking about themselves, even into laughing at themselves. Second, he has injected ideas and discussion into the well-made play. Third, he has made plot as well as character realistic. Shakespeare represented real people leading melodramatic lives. Ibsen represents real people living real lives: "Our uncles seldom murder our fathers, and cannot legally marry our mothers; we do not meet witches; our kings are not as a rule stabbed and succeeded by their stabbers; and when we raise money by bills we do not promise to pay pounds of our flesh." [9] Even Ibsen is a little too homicidal in his last acts. The post-Ibsenites are more realistic because they do not murder their failures and derelicts. Mme. Ranevsky is more tragic than Hedda Gabler.

In all this there is some truth—rather provincial truth. Shaw might have waited until he had seen the twentieth century before pronouncing so confidently on the eventlessness of modern life. Moreover, he seems in some danger of mistaking the humdrum for what Aristotle called the universal. If nothing happens outside, much less is likely to happen inside. Only rather "melodramatic" lives contain the extremities of passion, temptation, and remorse. Shakespeare understood this, and so did Ibsen, for he is by no means so prosaically "suburban" as Shaw would make him out.

To say that Ibsen introduced discussion into conventional drama is accurate only with reference to the nineteenth century. "Hamlet" contains more discussion than "Rosmersholm." The difference is rather that in Ibsen ethical exploration and ethical criticism predominate, whereas in Shakespeare moral choice and moral struggle predominate, though the latter are by no means absent in Ibsen any more than the former are absent in Shakespeare—or in Homer or Sophocles. In Shakespeare the tragic phenomenon is usually a disintegration of character following some great moral failure. In Ibsen it is usually an illumination of the mind and conscience following actions too narrowly moral or too daringly "idealistic." In Shaw himself—as with Vivie Warren and Barbara Undershaft—it is also an illumination. But Shaw is much more a comic than a tragic writer, and being convinced that the outward constitution of society is more important than the inward moral posture of the individual, he is much more concerned with ideas than with the psychology of moral struggle. His characters tend to be not so much moral individuals as the intelligent spokesmen of creeds and ideologies.

What Shaw learned from Ibsen was a religion of the Life Force, an attitude toward "ideals," realism in character, plot, and dialogue, and a method of exploring and explaining ideas in terms of dramatic situations, together with a stock of situations ready-made, from which he later drew for some of his best plays. What he added to Ibsen was more wit, more rhetoric, more didacticism, more ideas, a more formally symmetrical scene structure, and a technique which seeks a point of vantage from which to pour irony and satire on the audience.

CHAPTER EIGHTEEN

The Life Force in Action

The Shaw biographer is constantly in danger of forgetting that his subject is a human being. Fascinating ladies like Mrs. Hubert Bland serve to remind one of the fact. Shaw was by no means so much the sexless walking brain as popular legend—and Frank Harris—have made him out. Frank Harris seemed so vivid and virile to himself that he found everybody else pale by contrast. It is perfectly true that Shaw has expressed a puritanical repugnance to the primitive and undignified fact of human lust, that he has criticized God for combining the sexual with the excretory organs, that in his *Back to Methuselah* Eve makes a wry face when the serpent whispers in her ear the secret of reproduction. Puritan cleanliness, puritan pride and logic have always been against the grosser instincts as against the grosser habits. Not that Shaw "associated sexual intercourse with delinquency" or "Original Sin." [1] He is perhaps more severe with smoking than with fornication. "When I returned from the Carpentier-Beckett fight," he wrote in 1924, "I had to change every stitch of clothing before I could approach anyone without an apology." [2]

His feeling against sex was by no means so intense, nor was sex an acquired habit. In fact, he agrees with Rousseau that "his blood boiled with it from his birth." [3] He cannot remember when he did not dream about women, and his imaginary amours were so magical that he long remained "celibate through a surfeit of beauty and an excess of voluptuousness." [4] But a puritan virtue infused with such romanticism could not be permanently safe. Eventually, Shaw yielded to the flesh with a will. He was too busy to be incontinent, but some of the abundance of genius is to be seen in his sexual, as in his other, experience. "You certainly do warm both hands at the fire of life," his friend Webb once mildly observed to him. [5]

Like most puritans, Shaw was misled largely through his virtues. His psychological curiosity about women, his urge to improve them, to dominate them for their good, his love of novelty and excitement, his desire to declare his freedom from Victorian prejudice and convention—all contributed to make him an incorrigible flirt and philanderer. What made him a lover as well also derives in part from his puritanism—his loneliness, his hunger for affection (which was all the greater for being hidden behind the flamboyant masks to which his shyness and reserve condemned him), his craving for sympathetic recognition and some sharing of the solitary and mystical experience of genius and inspiration:

> He for God only, she for God in him.

He valued the sexual act itself "because of its power of producing a celestial flood of emotion and exaltation." [6] In short, he was drawn to the New Woman, but for the old reasons.

Of course Shaw began, as usual, not with the physical but with the metaphysical. Some of his love affairs were hardly love affairs at all, and one of the earliest was so tenuously mystical that the lady—May Morris—seems not to have known that it occurred until many years later, when she asked Shaw to write a memoir of her father for the latter's collected works. Shaw, then aged and respectable, responded with a brief account of the poet and a lengthy account of a heavenly betrothal with his beautiful daughter. Her comment was simply, "Really, Shaw!" But she published the memoir.

As a socialist and a writer, Shaw was a frequent guest at the Morris house:

> One Sunday evening after lecturing and supping, I was on the threshold of the Hammersmith house when I turned to make my farewell, and at this moment she came from the diningroom into the hall. I looked at her, rejoicing in her lovely dress and lovely self; and she looked at me very carefully and quite deliberately made a gesture of assent with her eyes. I was immediately conscious that a Mystic Betrothal was registered in heaven, to be fulfilled when all the material obstacles should melt away, and my own position rescued from the squalors of my poverty and unsuccess. . . . I did not think it necessary to say anything. To engage her in any way—to go to Morris and announce that I was taking advantage of the access granted to me as comrade-Communist to commit his beautiful daughter to a desperately insolvent marriage, did not occur to me as a socially possible proceeding. . . . I made no sign at all: I had no doubt that the thing was written on the skies for both of us. [7]

Then the beautiful daughter stunned him by marrying another socialist. He leaped to the conclusion that the Mystical Betrothal had been the figment of a very susceptible imagination. Not at all. Shortly after, he became ill with overwork and was invited to recuperate at the house of the young couple, completing thus an idyllic *ménage à trois*, which "was probably the happiest passage in our three lives":

> But the violated Betrothal was avenging itself. It made me from the first the centre of the household; and when I had quite recovered and there was no longer any excuse for staying unless I proposed to do so permanently and parasitically, her legal marriage dissolved as all illusions do; and the mystic marriage asserted itself irresistibly. I had to consummate it or vanish.[8]

Shaw vanished. And of course May Morris never owned up to the Mystical Betrothal. Nevertheless, her husband's account of the *ménage à trois*, according to Mr. Pearson, bears out Shaw's, and he told Holbrook Jackson "that after completely captivating his wife Shaw suddenly disappeared, leaving behind him a desolated female who might have been an iceberg so far as her future relations with her husband went." [9] The episode bears more than a casual resemblance to the plot of "Candida" and may have been an experience out of which two works of art were created.

Shaw received his punishment shortly after. He made a brilliant conquest of Mrs. Annie Besant, who had long been high priestess to the archatheist Bradlaugh. Like most atheists, she combined an infinite capacity to believe with very little discrimination about what to believe. A mere dogmatic atheist is not in herself remarkable, but having a fine contralto voice, an electric platform manner, and an unexampled flow of oratory, Mrs. Besant also possessed a tremendous power of inspiring belief—or disbelief. Naturally, she had no sense of humor. At a first meeting she was offended by Shaw's levity, and when he ventured to lecture on socialism in her stronghold at the Dialectical Society, it was generally predicted that she would annihilate him. But even annihilation, he felt, could be instructive. He fired off his speech as well as he could and sat down. There was a brief silence. The terrible Mrs. Besant did not rise, and at length another speaker led the attack. Her ally had no sooner finished than Mrs. Besant blasted him from the platform. Shaw had debated his way into her heart. For him she gave up Bradlaugh and atheism and became a Fabian socialist.

To Shaw's brains and Webb's facts was now added the impassioned eloquence of Mrs. Besant. They were henceforth unbeatable on the platform. Ultimately, of course, she became one of the Fabian essayists and also founded *Our Corner*, a socialist newspaper of her own, on which she appointed Shaw art critic and for much of the time paid him out of her own pocket, until he understood the situation and refused further money. So long as there was work to be done, life with Annie was a thrill and a satisfaction. But when work gave out, Shaw discovered that there were two Mrs. Besants. Mrs. Besant on the platform was as exciting as a sibyl in an ecstasy, but Mrs. Besant off the platform was an affectionate and motherly bore. Small talk with a high priestess proved impossible, and humor was an offense against the solemnity of life. There remained piano duets, which belonged to the ritual of her new god. Being a conscientious and industrious woman, she carefully practiced her part beforehand and so played all the right notes without feeling while he played all the wrong ones with great fire. This was of course not to be endured. Shaw began to absent himself in the evenings. The situation became very ambiguous and Mrs. Besant very sad. At length in an unlucky moment Shaw demanded a clarification. Being still tied legally to her husband and therefore unable to marry, she drew up an elaborate document listing the conditions under which she and Shaw would live together as man and wife. He must sign at the bottom.

"Good God!" he exclaimed after glancing it over, "this is worse than all the vows of all the Churches on earth. I had rather be legally married to you ten times over." [10]

Unwilling to be content with less, she demanded her letters back. He gave her what he could find but would not accept his own. A high priestess to the last, she insisted that the whole correspondence undergo a solemn ceremony of suttee. It is said that her hair turned gray and that she thought of suicide. For a while she languished without love and without faith. Then she was asked to review Helen Blavatsky's *Secret Doctrine* and found just the religion she had always been looking for. Theosophism combined the melodramatic secrecy of a barbaric priesthood with the exhilarating publicity of the propaganda platform. She abandoned the Fabians, and one day Shaw read in a newspaper that she was a Theosophist. Rushing to her office, he exposed Madame Blavatsky in a single breath. But Mrs. Besant felt that exposures were irrelevant to faith. Then Shaw played his trump.

"Why need you go to Thibet for a Mahatma?" he demanded. "Here and now is your Mahatma. I am your Mahatma." [11]

But for her, Great Shaw was dead. Many years afterward, she realized her dearest subconscious longing and played mother to Krishnamurti, a Messiah of her own.

"Only twice in my life have I been sexually infatuated," Shaw told Pearson, "once as a young man and once in middle life." [11] He blundered into his first adventure at the rather late age of twenty-nine and in a manner not uncommon to shy, preoccupied young men. At about the time when he shed the decayed plasterer and burst forth the rational man in tweeds, he was invited to tea by one Jenny Patterson and "virtually raped. . . . I permitted her, being intensely curious on the subject. Never having regarded myself as an attractive man, I was surprised; but I kept up appearances successfully." [12] But for the common, garden-variety diet of monogamous sexual love, especially with Jenny Patterson, Shaw had too fastidious a stomach:

> Though for nearly two years [he wrote in a short story which deals with the experience] the lady had no reason to complain of my fidelity, I found the romantic side of our intercourse, which seemed never to pall on her, tedious, unreasonable, and even forced and insincere except at rare moments, when the power of love made her beautiful, body and soul. Unfortunately, I had no sooner lost my illusions, my timidity, and my boyish curiosity about women, than I began to attract them irresistibly.[13]

The trouble was, Jenny Patterson was not only "sexually insatiable" but appallingly jealous. Shaw lived over and over the early scenes of "The Philanderer" years before he wrote them. Jenny was of course Julia Craven.

The role of Grace Tranfield was vaguely that of the actress Florence Farr, whom he first met at one of the annual soirees of the Hammersmith Socialist Society. She was a good-looking, good-natured, easy-going young woman, "with semi-circular eyebrows" and a great deal of assorted talent. She composed music, wrote books, investigated the ancient Egyptians—and acted very competently. If she could have been electrified into a passion for self-perfection, for rebuilding herself artistically from the toes up, she could have become a great actress. In short, she appealed to Shaw's constructive and didactic instincts. He loved her—in part simply because she was beautiful and complaisant, in part because of what she might become. He wanted to dominate her, to create her, to turn the soft, living flesh into the hard marble of an artistic idea. As with Jenny he lived "The Philanderer," so with Florence Farr he lived "Pygmalion." They soon became intimate.

> All her men friends fell in love with her. This had occurred so often that she had lost all patience with the hesitating preliminaries of her less practised adorers. Accordingly, when they clearly longed to kiss her, and she did not dislike them sufficiently to make their gratification too great a strain on her excessive good-nature, she would seize the stammering suitor firmly by the wrists, bring him into her arms by a smart pull, and saying 'Let's get it over,'

allow the startled gentleman to have his kiss, and then proceed to converse with him at her ease on subjects of more general interest.[14]

Of course Jenny immediately scented danger, confronted her rival in Shaw's presence, and there was a horrible scene—substantially that of the first act in "The Philanderer." Shaw kept his temper—and his disgust. A storm of letters and telegrams broke upon stony silence. They never saw each other again. From her he first experienced the acute and oppressive sensation of being pursued by a female. Characteristically, she lingered in his memory chiefly as a theory. She typified the Vital Woman. Julia Craven was a photograph, somewhat touched up. Ann Whitefield was a quintessential abstraction, sublimated by comedy. Jenny Patterson became an important aspect of the Life Force.

Meanwhile, Shaw vented his feelings to Florence Farr:

> Not for forty thousand such relations will I forego one forty-thousandth part of my relation with you. Every grain of cement she shakes from it falls like a block of granite on her own flimsy castle in the air, the work of my own imagination. The silly triumph with which she takes, with the air of a conqueror, that which I have torn out of my own entrails for her, almost brings the lightning down upon her. Imagine being told—but I cannot write it. Damnation! triple damnation! You must give me back my peace.[15]

There ensues a considerable correspondence, stretching from 1891 to 1906, when Florence Farr, stricken with cancer, went out to India to find religious peace and to die. Shaw's letters are at once a dramatic dissertation on how to be an actress and an intimate revelation of two characters. With Florence Farr, apparently, he came for the first time to know the full intellectual and emotional companionship of love. She was highly susceptible to poetry and sentiment. Therefore he gave free rein to his strong latent inclination to both, adding now and then just a touch of blarney. He was Peter Keegan as well as Professor Higgins.

Early in their affair, rather irrelevantly, Florence married. Nothing daunted, Shaw wrote, "We are mere acquaintances, my dear Mrs. Emery, just as we were that day at Merton. And so we are FREE— to begin it all over again. I am a beggar once more; and once more I shall come into my good fortune." [16] There are also passages of abject despair—unique in Shaw for their lyric beauty—which tell us how the unsuccessful novelist felt when he went about in the disguise of a decayed plasterer:

I have fallen in with my boyhood's mistress, Solitude, and wandered aimlessly with her once more, drifting like the unsatisfied moon. Tears have dropped from my heart—tears of mortal disappointment, reminding me of days when disappointment seemed my inevitable and constant lot. I have lost faith in all the achievement and confidence since that time: whatever my dreams may have been, I have slept where I was born, in the valley of shadow.[17]

But that mood comes seldom. He has long since suspected his true stature, and now brilliant and habitual success confirms him. He is intoxicated with the *certainty* that he is a great man:

When you tell me that I best know what I am, I assent, not with humility, but with towering head striking against every star and raising great bumps on them; so that astronomers reel amazed from their telescopes. Cubits high and fathoms deep am I the noblest creature you have yet met in this wood of monkeys where I found you straying.[18]

He explains that there are two kinds of genius: "One is produced by the breed throwing forward to the godlike man—exactly as it sometimes throws backward to the apelike. The other is the mere monster produced by an accidental excess of some faculty." [18] He adds that he belongs to the first order. And certainly he does, though there is something of the talking monster about him.

The rest of the correspondence is Pygmalion and Galatea. A silk purse is all the better—if it can be made of unlikely materials:

Your ability to act must only be a mere consequence of your ability to live. . . . For the born actress I have a certain contempt: for the woman who is a consummate artist I have a deep fellow feeling. The one is sham: the other a reality completely expressed. . . . In my own art I am ready, if only time be given me, to answer for the workmanship to the last comma.[19]

But the words of the master somehow do not create the artistic soul in the pupil. They do not electrify her to the great dedication:

You have an idea that because the first hundred pounds of steam are not acting, but simply mere brute grip of the audience, they are inartistic. So they are; but they are necessary, and should be automatic with all experienced public performers. With your voice and looks and intelligence you would seldom be out of an engagement if only you would work as Wynne Matheson works. She would put as much nervous force into saying "My lord: the carriage waits," as you would into "Give *me* the daggers!" [20]

[153]

The master's words develop more violence, more shock. Professor Higgins himself is not more brutal: "You have brains and imagination— the means of deceiving yourself, without faith, honor, heart, holiness —the means of saving yourself." [21] And once he bursts out, "I declare before creation that you are an idiot!" [22]

A warmhearted and popular actress cannot permanently embrace an iceberg of merciless criticism. So much could not be expected of an amiable woman with semicircular eyebrows. Florence took to giving special recitals in which she chanted Yeats's poetry to a very special kind of lyre. Finally Yeats wrote "The Land of Heart's Desire" for her, and she faded out of Shaw's life into a Celtic twilight in which a somewhat old-maidish Shelley wrote her letters full of sentimental adoration for herself and querulous complaints about everybody else.

With the beautiful and dashing Mrs. Patrick Campbell, who entranced London in "The Second Mrs. Tanqueray," Shaw carried on a schoolboy tease-and-insult flirtation. They used to talk to each other like this:

SHE. What about God?

HE. *I* am God.

SHE. Don't be silly.

HE. What would you be without your face?

SHE. I'm not going to talk to you any more.

HE. Scorn me, scorn me; I don't mind. Two hundred years hence, the world will say you were my mistress, and ———— was our son![23]

CHAPTER NINETEEN

Mr. Archer Discovers a Kingdom

By this time Shaw had achieved nearly everything but his destiny. Yet the dramatist had of course been latent from the first. Five stillborn novels had probably undermined artistic self-confidence, but he had found an outlet in creating the G.B.S. of the music column and the speaking platform. In fact, Shavian drama invented itself when Shaw walked into a debating society. Public debates were intellectual dramas in real life, and—especially when the opposition was weak—he had longed to create one entirely for himself in which he could make all the speeches on both sides. Finally he did. But argument seldom brings opposing thinkers to a unified and consistent point of view. And therefore, explaining himself after the event and perhaps more simply than his practice warrants, Shaw has declared that drama is not a unity but a conflict revealing character and exposing ideas.[1] None of the ideas is absolutely true. They are simply the ideas of the characters and, for the moment at least, of Shaw, who identifies himself with each character in turn. As logic is historical in Marx, so in Shaw truth is forensic and dramatic.

He had been interested in the stage from a very early age. He could remember vividly the acting of Barry Sullivan in his prime. Yet the stage seems to have been the only platform—outside, perhaps, of the pulpit—which Shaw never thought of mounting. The vast thundercloud of his genius might have brooded over London indefinitely, had not William Archer quite innocently set it bellowing and flashing with the electricity of a significant idea. Having heard that his friend was the author of five novels, Archer confessed that he himself had the itch to write plays, and though poor at dialogue, he was a master of construction. Shaw admitted that he wrote incomparable dialogue. Archer proposed collaboration and outlined one of his best plots, all very neat and clear, with a good deal of the action coming, à la Scribe, by telegraph. There was to be a garden scene on the banks of the Rhine, a capitalistic villain, tainted gold, and finally a grand gesture of throwing the tainted gold back into the Rhine.

Wagner in modern dress! Shaw agreed to collaborate. For some time Archer saw him writing diligently at his desk in the British Museum. After about six weeks Shaw declared that he had used up all the plot. He needed more. With some annoyance Archer explained that the plot was an organic whole; to add to it would be like adding extra arms and legs to a statue. He asked to see what Shaw had written. But that proved to be a secret securely preserved in the inscrutability of a neat commercial shorthand, and when with excruciating slowness Shaw had translated a few pages orally, Archer perceived that his plot had not been used up but simply ignored. Moreover, since the play as so far completed seemed quite unlike anything Scribe, Augier, or even Ibsen had ever written, Archer gave it up. So did Shaw—for seven years.

But all roads led him to the dramatic stage at this time. Socialism led him to Ibsen, and musical criticism led him through Wagner and the opera to a renewed interest in Shakespeare, and Shakespeare apparently led him to dramatic criticism and once more to Ibsen and the new drama. The new drama, like the new opera and the new socialism, became another cause to fight for. In the Independent Theatre, it had a very tangible and visible citadel, which was valiantly defended by J. T. Grein, in spite of awful admonitions from the box office. Having fired off a great deal of foreign genius in the faces of the British public, Grein was eager to shoot off some domestic. Shaw asserted that such could be found. Still Grein could find none. "In this humiliating national emergency," says Shaw, "I proposed to Mr. Grein that he should boldly announce a play by me. Being an extraordinarily sanguine and enterprising man, he took this step without hesitation." [2]

There is of course another reason why Shaw took up once more the two acts of his unfinished manuscript:

> There is an old saying that if a man has not fallen in love before forty, he had better not fall in love after. I long ago perceived that this rule applied to many other matters as well: for example, to the writing of plays; and I made a rough memorandum for my own guidance that unless I could produce at least half a dozen plays before I was forty, I had better let playwriting alone. [3]

The play was "Widowers' Houses" (1892). Shaw declares that as first produced it contained some juvenile extravagances which cheapened its effect, though the text was otherwise as it now stands. In its final form, it is, though a first work, one of the most powerful plays until then produced in the nineteenth century. It reveals that while Jones and Pinero were learning their art by producing innumerable mediocrities and Wilde was triumphing in his by hanging his dinner con-

[156]

versation on conventional plots, the greatest dramatist of the period had been growing up silently inside of a witty music critic.

"Widowers' Houses" presents at once the whole problem of Shaw's dramaturgy. Very simply, it is the problem of an author who wanted to tell his audience what they didn't want to hear. This was work for a satirist, and as a great satirist Shaw combined with supreme powers of amusing 1890 audiences an almost misanthropic antagonism to their essential values and opinions:

> I had no taste for what is called popular art, no respect for popular morality, no belief in popular religion, no admiration for popular heroics. As an Irishman I could pretend to patriotism neither for the country I had abandoned nor the country that had ruined it. As a humane person I detested violence and slaughter, whether in war, sport, or the butcher's yard. I was a Socialist, detesting our anarchical scramble for money, and believing in equality as the only possible permanent basis of social organization, discipline, subordination, good manners, and selection of fit persons for high functions.[4]

But Shaw was not quite misanthropic. He wanted passionately to interest his audience because he wished to convert it. And to this end he possessed the gift of the dramatist: "I have encountered no limit but my own laziness to my power of conjuring up imaginary people in imaginary places"—and finding pretexts for theatrical scenes between them.[5] Moreover, he was a great comic artist. Seldom has so much laughter been joined with so much seriousness—and the one has procured a hearing for the other.

Physiologically, laughter is probably a means of releasing tension after the sudden disappearance of some physical threat. Psychologically, it is a means of putting disagreeable or challenging thoughts—or, as Freud points out, the more or less subconscious accusations of conscience—at a distance. One may escape from a puzzling set of intellectual relationships by discovering among them some neat and startling incongruity, which may be quite accidental and unimportant, representing mere verbal cleverness, or significant and essential, representing a genuine truth or evaluation. Of course the "escape" into significance is seldom, especially nowadays, a complete escape, or relief from tension. Though crude and violent outbursts close the mind and induce conceit in oneself and contempt for others, quiet merriment opens up the mind, encourages flexibility, detachment, and the amiable reception of unwelcome truths. The great comic artist allows only limited indulgence to the crude relief of loud laughter and maintains thought at high tension. He strikes a bargain with his audience, granting that a social foible or a social convention is funny if they will allow it to be evil. But in proportion as he presses an accusation home, his audience looks for means of escape. Clever spectators apply his indictment to everybody but themselves. Stupid spectators loudly laugh his quips into a crude *ad hominem.* Obviously, the second reaction is common with Shaw. His audiences usually avoid laughing at themselves by laughing at the author. But while they stay to laugh, there is always the possibility that they may really understand the joke and so, achieving the gay detachment of higher laughter, arrive at Shavian theory or even some broader truth. Shaw offers revolution tempered by epigram.

Shaw did not become Shaw at once. He began as the pupil of Ibsen. "Widowers' Houses" adds to the tight construction and the bold realism of that author the grim humor and harsh accusation of satire. It combines the method of "Ghosts" with the subject matter of *Oliver Twist.* For whereas Jones and Pinero were problem dramatists constantly in search of a problem, Shaw found that he introduced new problems with every stroke of the pen. They worked up portentous sex titillations by cautiously paring at the edges of Victorian convention. He produced frenzies of rage and horror by showing people what was under their noses.

Perhaps because of Ibsen's influence, "Widowers' Houses" is artistically one of the more satisfying of Shaw's plays. The whole of its complex and satiric significance is held securely within the framework of a simple, coherent plot. In the first act, laid in a small Rhineland hotel, a middle-aged bachelor and a young doctor with aristocratic connections and vulgar manners fall in with an elderly gentleman of formidable respectability and his daughter, a ferocious young tigress who, like Ann Whitefield, uses the innocent mask of the womanly woman to further her own bloodthirsty ends. There is some wicked satire of the British tourist; and then in a brilliantly executed comic reversal, the young tigress, under pretense of injured virtue, maneuvers the doctor into an embrace, in which he is discovered by his friend, Cokane, and her father, Sartorius. Suspense is subtly developed. Sartorius seems strangely eager for the match, strangely reticent about his profession, and strangely insistent on the written consent of young Dr. Trench's aristocratic relatives. We perceive, however, that he is a solid and authentic member of the middle classes, with middle-class standards, code, and piety.

The next act takes place some time later in his suburban house. Dr. Trench, triumphantly armed with approving letters, encounters Sartorius's discharged agent Lickcheese, who reveals that his late master is one of the worst slum landlords in London. The scene is fiercely ironic. Begging the young doctor to intercede for him, Lickcheese pleads his virtues as an agent:

> Look at that bag of money on the table. Hardly a penny of that but there was a hungry child crying for the bread it would have bought. But I got it for him—screwed and worried and bullied it out of them. I—look here, gentlemen: I'm pretty well seasoned to the work; but there's money there that I couldn't have taken if it hadn't been for the thought of my own children depending on me for giving him satisfaction. And because I charged him four-and-twenty shillin' to mend a staircase that three women have been hurt on, and that would have got him prosecuted for manslaughter if it had been let go much longer, he gives me the sack. Wouldn't listen to a word, though I would have offered to make up the money out of my own pocket—aye, and am willing to do it still if you will only put in a word for me.[6]

Sartorius's case is now skillfully generalized so as to become the target for a typically Fabian attack on all exploiters and receivers of economic rent, including Trench's fashionable aunt, Lady Roxdale, who holds seven per cent mortgages on Sartorius's property and is quite willing to see her poor nephew marry his rich daughter. Trench is aghast at Lickcheese's revelation, and while Cokane acts as a sort of brainless Greek chorus of Philistine hypocrisy, presses for further explanation. Lickcheese concedes, "I don't say he's the worst landlord in London: he couldn't be worse than some; but he's no better than the worst I ever had to do with." [7] And a little later, with some violence to his character as a benighted scamp, he protests, "I'm poor; that's enough to make a rascal of me." [8] In other words, poverty is the root of all evil.

At this point Blanche Sartorius enters and is left alone with Trench. Without giving her a reason, he insists that when they are married they must live on his small income. She flies into an appalling rage, and we see that, so far from being a lady, she is not even a human being. Shaw says that he discovered her in real life one dark night savagely pommeling another woman in the street. But even more directly than from real life, she derives from the Victorian womanly woman. She brilliantly satirizes that pure and brainless ideal by being its terrifying opposite. The opposite proves to be a monster of intelligence and ferocity, who gradually became a recognized type of Shavian womanhood and the generic original of Julia Craven and Ann Whitefield. She is certainly a powerful counteractive to romance in a love scene. And of course she does not give up all for love. When Trench lays down his conditions, she bursts out:

You depended on your family to get you out of your engagement; and they did not object: they were only too glad to be rid of you. You were not mean enough to stay away, and not manly enough to tell the truth. You thought you could provoke me to break the engagement: that is so like a man—to try and put the woman in the wrong. Well, you have your way: I release you. I wish you had opened my eyes by downright brutality—by striking me—by anything rather than shuffling as you have done.[9]

When at length her father appears, Trench challenges him with the infamy of his profession. Observing that his young friend has not much of a head for business, Sartorius explains with pious, Pecksniffian regret that the poor cannot be given well-furnished lodgings, because, being so very poor, they simply burn up the furniture for firewood. Cokane, now also present, breathes something about Malthus, and then Sartorius applies the clincher. Dr. Trench himself derives his income from slum mortgages. He could not possibly get seven per cent elsewhere. Stricken in both conscience and pocketbook, Trench collapses in hopeless bewilderment and meekly accepts Blanche and the seven per cent. The play might have ended here, but theatrical convention required another act. Blanche therefore uncovers a satanic pride and refuses Trench.

The third act exposes fresh horrors of slum landlordism, which, with the aid of some coincidence, is further connected with the love story. Blanche and Harry are once more brought together, and after an erotic combat in the best Shavian manner, come to an understanding. Trench acquiesces—though bitterly and with rather more understanding than his brains would seem to warrant—in the *status quo* which wrings him seven per cent out of the sufferings of tenement lodgers. In short, there is, as Mr. Bentley says, a happy ending Shavianized. The young people live happily ever after, at heavy expense to their moral characters.

Shaw himself speaks of this play as "unpleasant" and "grotesquely realistic." He is certainly right. The characters consist of a monster, a cockney rascal, two fools, and a kind of satanic Pecksniff. The manners depicted are uncompromisingly vulgar. The central theme is one of the worst abuses of metropolitan life described with a savage irony and clear, cold concentration totally unlike the sentimental conventionality and the diffuse, halfhearted realism of the average English "problem play." "Widowers' Houses" contains a good deal of sparkling comedy but not enough to reconcile an audience to so much harsh realism. Shaw's purpose, like Ibsen's, was to shock and construct. In fact, "Widowers Houses" may be regarded as the first example of Shavian tragedy, which Shaw defined eleven years later as "the being used by personally minded men for purposes which you recognize to be base." [10] In this sense Harry Trench, like Vivie Warren in a later play, is a tragic protagonist. Unfortunately, it is perhaps not always easy to distinguish between Shavian tragedy and Shavian greatness, for as the first is being used by selfish men for base purposes, the second is being used by the Life Force for biological purposes. The difference between the base and the biological is not always clear, as we shall see when we come to "Major Barbara."

Grein had been looking for a bomb. Shaw had suddenly handed him a very large bomb with a very short fuse. Grein was not particularly happy but went forward with rehearsals. They were anxiously attended by the author, who, then in his stockinet phase, moved about chirping like a cricket and looking like a gigantic silver-gray beetle without shards. These rehearsals were one of the great experiences of Shaw's life—and probably of Grein's also, for Shaw was not the man to keep his experiences to himself. Some three years later he wrote: "The author of a play is the only person who really wants to have it well done in every respect, and who therefore has every drawback brought fully home to him. The man who has had that awakening about one play will thenceforth have his eyes open at all other plays." [11]

Before the first performance, an interview with the press was printed, as for all celebrated authors.

"Sir," Shaw sternly told the interviewer in the idiom of Dr. Johnson, "[my play] will be nothing else than didactic. Do you suppose that I have gone to all this trouble to *amuse* the public? No, if they want that, there is the Criterion for them, the Comedy, the Garrick, and so on. My object is to instruct them."

The interviewer then questioned him concerning the title, on the meaning of which everybody was speculating.

"I have been assured," returned the author formidably, "that in one of the sections of the Bible dealing with the land question there is a clause against the destruction of widows' houses. There is no widow in my play; but there is a widower who owns slum property. Hence the title. Perhaps you are not familiar with the Bible." [12]

According to Archer, both the timid interviewer and the dictatorial celebrity were the projections of Shaw's imagination.

The play was not a success, but it did what no play has done before or since. It made an English audience behave very much like a French one. "Hernani" itself did not arouse more contention and controversy. Socialists yelled stentorian approval and nearly everybody else booed. After repeated demands from the audience, Shaw came out and made a speech. He assured his listeners that their reception of the play pleased him, for he did not wish it to be taken lightly. It represented actual middle-class life, though he hoped for the time when it should no longer do so. In conclusion, he trusted that "the critics would carefully discriminate between himself and the actors who had so zealously striven to carry out his intentions." [13] The applause was universal. The audience could distinguish between socialism and manliness.

"Widowers' Houses" was a nine-days' wonder and then vanished from the boards amid ear-splitting howls and shrieks from the newspapers, which rightly regarded the play as an attack on the middle classes. They also saw in it a slavish imitation of Ibsen and particularly of "An Enemy of the People," which likewise deals with tainted goods and social guilt. Undoubtedly, "Widowers' Houses" strongly reflects the influence of Ibsen, but it differs essentially from "An Enemy of the People." Ibsen's play shows how a community, faced with a great crisis, may temporarily involve itself in guilt. Shaw's play shows how capitalistic society is, through its characteristic abuses, permanently guilty. Moreover, it goes beyond Ibsen in directly accusing the audience. Like Dr. Trench, we all share in the guilt of slum landlordism. Shaw's play implies that poverty must be abolished. Ibsen's does not.

"Widowers' Houses" not only horrified substantial citizens; it even shocked a socialist—chiefly, no doubt, because it deals harshly with human nature. The socialist was William Archer. In a lengthy article addressed to the author, he declares that "Widowers' Houses" is a lifeless product of pure intellect, in which corpselike characters are galvanized by sheer mental energy into a wonderful but abortive imitation of natural feeling and action. He compliments the author on an impressive intellectual effort but advises him to desist from writing plays. There is of course some justice in Archer's opinion, but only enough to prove that a sentimentalist seldom understands a satirist. For wider consumption, Shaw would have to put a little more sugar on his pills.

He was himself probably quite aware that he had written one of the most brilliant English plays since Sheridan. While in the throes of "You Never Can Tell" several years later, he wrote to Florence Farr that "Widowers' Houses" was worth fifty such, and his intimate letters of the year 1891 show an exultant, even boastful confidence in his powers.[14] Unfortunately, his success was strictly private. And in this sense his next experiment was even less satisfactory. After "Widowers' Houses," Archer had advised him to stop writing plays. After "The Philanderer," he was tempted not to speak to him on the street.

The play is Shaw's "Wild Duck," and a tiresome, inconsequential, distasteful fowl it seems. With the utmost effrontery, it challenges the ultimate sanctities of middle-class convention in the name of Ibsenism and then makes light of Ibsenism itself, so that the satire turns back on itself and seems mere desecration—the more so as the play depends on the rather tedious joke of an Ibsen Club to which only unmanly men and unwomanly women are admitted.

For a situation, Grace Tranfield, a rationalistic Ibsenite woman, and Julia Craven, a she-wolf hiding in the sheep's clothing of Victorian womanliness, are rivals for the love of Leonard Charteris, the philanderer, who is a rather tedious joke himself and also a guarantee that nothing will happen. He is of course Shaw, in his character of a typical clever young man of the nineties, much amused at himself and fascinated with the ladies so long as they do not become too fascinated with him. The union of so much interest in sex with so much caution is a little unpleasant. Charteris is an early and unpurified version of Jack Tanner. Perhaps Shaw took too seriously the ladies' word for the fascinations of this gentleman. He is amusing, to be sure, but not amusing enough to carry everything by himself, without benefit of plot, effective scene construction, or significant idea. The best thing in the play is the bitter disappointment of Dr. Paramore when he learns that the fatal disease he has discovered does not exist.

Realizing that "The Philanderer" was a failure, Shaw speedily put it aside. It was neither produced nor published until 1898.

A. B. Walkley has made Charteris the theme of a sermon on the extreme artificiality of the self-conscious, self-explanatory character so common in Shaw.[15] Such characters are certainly common in his plays and sometimes quite unnatural. Mrs. Warren, for example, is a good deal more self-analytical than one would expect a totally uneducated woman to be. The only possible defense is that she is an intelligent woman led by the stigma of her profession to reflect abnormally on the morality of her actions. On the other hand, Charteris, to whom Walkley particularly objects, seems to me perfectly probable. He is the kind of highly intelligent, well-educated sophisticate whom one would expect to be self-conscious. The same plea may be made for Jack Tanner and Louis Dubedat. In any case, Shaw's drama of ideas needs self-explanatory characters as desperately as Dostoevski's weird dramas of the soul need characters who can see into each other's inmost secrets with mutual clairvoyance. "Mrs. Warren's Profession" would be impossible without an articulate Mrs. Warren, just as "Major Barbara" would be impossible without an articulate Andrew Undershaft.

Having failed in the light and trivial, Shaw returned to grim, revolutionary social satire. About this time Janet Achurch, who had created a sensation by playing Ibsen's Nora, told Shaw, from a French novel, a story of unconventional maternity which she thought would make a good play. Shaw said, "Oh, I will work out the real truth about that mother some day."[16] A little later Mrs. Sidney Webb asked him why he didn't put a true modern lady on the stage. Shaw combined both suggestions, made the French prostitute the mother of the English lady, added to the first character some of the bold treatment of sex in "Ghosts" and to the second the courageous denial of conventional family obligations in "A Doll's House," rewrote from an early novel into terms of female prostitution the scene in which Cashel Byron explains how he became a prize fighter, perfected a dramaturgy based on a doctrine of Karl Marx—and the result was "Mrs. Warren's Profession," as unlike Miss Achurch's romantic French novel as the fourth part of *Gulliver's Travels* is unlike *Paul et Virginie*.

"Mrs. Warren's Profession," like "Widowers' Houses" and "Major Barbara," uses the member of an opprobrious profession as the basis of an elaborately constructed attack on capitalistic society. Here that familiar figure of the French problem play, the prostitute, becomes an economic and social argument. Mid-Victorians regarded her as the ultimate abomination of a society dedicated to the admiration of domesticity. Shaw tried to make late Victorians feel that in a very real sense they were all prostitutes. In short, he fashioned a satiric and dramatic device out of Marx's doctrine that virtue is impossible in capitalistic society.

> At present we not only condemn women as a sex to attach them-selves to "breadwinners," licitly or illicitly, on pain of heavy priva-tion and disadvantage; but we have great prostitute classes of men: for instance, dramatists and journalists, to whom I myself belong, not to mention the legions of lawyers, doctors, clergy-men, and platform politicians who are daily using their highest faculties to belie their real sentiments: a sin compared to which that of a woman who sells the use of her person for a few hours is too venial to be worth mentioning; for rich men without conviction are more dangerous in modern society than poor women without chastity. Hardly a pleasant subject, this!

> I must, however, warn my readers that my attacks are directed against themselves, not against my stage figures.[17]

"Mrs. Warren's Profession" allows no concilation of the emotions within the theater. The only catharsis is to go out and start a revolution—or at least to join the Fabian Society.

Shaw's satiric strategy was not new. The attack on the audience had been perfected in the early eighteenth century. "A Modest Pro-posal" and *Gulliver* are ferocious contrivances by which Swift in-sulted his readers with unsurpassable force and eloquence. The ma-neuver of introducing an opprobrious profession had also been devised about fifteen years before "Mrs. Warren." In "The Pirates of Penzance," W. S. Gilbert had used piracy precisely as Shaw used prostitution. Shaw once remarked that he had pondered the quips of W. S. Gilbert very seriously, and he told Henderson, "Most of the revolutionary ideas have come up first as jests; and Gilbert did not get deeper than this stage." [18] "Mrs. Warren" is Gilbert in deadly earnest. It represents his technique, Swift's mood, and Ibsen's realism, dedicated to the purposes of Karl Marx. It also owes a debt to Butler's *Erewhon,* from which Shaw borrowed so much later on. Like Marx, Butler declares that property is theft and that all social evil is crime in which the entire community participates.[19] This conception is obviously basic to both "Mrs. Warren" and "Widowers' Houses."

The problem of construction offered by such plays as "Mrs. Warren's Profession" is that of expressing a general attack on society in terms of a vital and interesting story of individual character. In "Widowers' Houses," Shaw had already succeeded admirably, but in "Mrs. Warren's Profession," he made his attack much more basic and general, confronted the audience much more vividly and directly with its common guilt, and at the same time created in the second act perhaps the most powerful situation in any of his plays.

The drama opens on the rural simplicity of a cottage garden. Lying in a hammock, Vivie Warren is reading and taking notes. Soon Praed, a week-end guest, arrives and enters into conversation. The scene is strongly comic, depicting the impact on the conventional and romantic artist Praed of the fantastically unconventional and unromantic Vivie Warren, who despises art, lusts after economic independence, and immensely relishes hard work, with a cigar and whisky and soda afterwards. It is not surprising that she "laid the intellect of Mr. William Archer in ruins." [20] Presently Vivie's mother arrives with Sir George Crofts. Mrs. Warren is a handsome, overblown, "fairly presentable old blackguard of a woman," and he, a "gentlemanly combination of the most brutal types of city man, sporting man, and man about town." [21] Mrs. Warren plays the conventional mother with gusto. As they go in to tea, they are joined by Vivie's young man, Frank Gardner, who suggests Puck with an Oxford education. The scene closes with a meeting between Mrs. Warren and Frank's father, a neighboring clergyman. It is clear that the two have met before.

In the second act, which develops suspense by every possibility of crisis, recognition, conflict, and peripety, Mrs. Warren divulges her profession. As the scene opens, she is superior and patronizing, complacently playing the omniscient parent. With a few incisive queries and comments, Vivie quickly reduces her to conventional tears, then drives her to anger. Mrs. Warren drops her thin pretense of elegance and reverts to the dialect of the slums. All right! If Vivie wants the truth, she'll have it. Born into great poverty, which is the Shavian version of original sin, Kitty Warren was one of two natural daughters of a fish-shop keeper. The two legitimate daughters had succumbed to the Christian respectability of honorable misery. Kitty and her sister Lizzy became prostitutes. By foresight and determination, they rose to be managers and part owners of a system of brothels extending from Brussels to Vienna. Mrs. Warren has not only succeeded—she has reasoned closely about the morality of her success. If she were not at the head of her organization, someone else would be; and her employees are better treated than the workers in a coal mine or a match factory. Moreover, nearly all women sell themselves. Marriage is simply the legal recognition of a bargain by which sexual gratification is exchanged for a consideration. Throughout the scene it is strongly implied that every member of a capitalistic society is as guilty and responsible as Mrs. Warren, who has at least shown courage and enterprise. Vivie is moved to rather sentimental admiration in spite of herself. At the close of the act, Mrs. Warren is playing once more the solicitous mother.

The third act, in which Sir George Crofts proposes to Vivie, has inevitably less suspense than the second, because a contemptuous refusal can be the only result. Nevertheless, the scene involves a sharp struggle and a dramatic reversal. At the outset, Sir George speaks with the easy, patronizing benevolence of the spider inviting the fly into his parlor. At the end, white with fury, he stabs Vivie with the sharpest weapon he knows. She and her sweetheart may be half brother and sister. The chief purpose of the act is to castigate the capitalist in the person of Sir George and to reveal the attitude of the ruling classes toward such institutions as the brothel and the sweatshop. A gentleman may with propriety derive income from these quarters, so long as he derives enough income—and is not too closely connected with the scene of degradation itself. Good society is an elegant conspiracy to ignore the hidden sources of its excessive income. The act concludes with a bit of melodrama. Refused by Vivie, Crofts seems on the point of physical violence. Frank comes out with his gun in the nick of time, and as he takes aim, Vivie, in the extremity of disgust, turns the muzzle against herself. In cold print this seems an unfortunate excess. On the stage the crude, brutal power of Sir George's part might render it convincing.

The fourth act presents the social counterpart to the evils of poverty —the vanities of wealth. It also deals with the final break between Vivie and her mother and between Vivie and Frank, thus completing the drama as a story of individuals. Appalled by the knowledge that Frank may be her half brother and that Mrs. Warren still persists in her infamous calling, Vivie turns her back on her past and flees to London lodgings. Mrs. Warren follows her there, and in a speech of wonderful self-satire, offers her all the glamorous folly, pleasure, and idleness that wealth can buy. Vivie coldly refuses, and putting aside every illusion of romance and love, gives herself up to her bourgeois thirst for work. It is true that this is a mere escape, and yet what other conclusion is possible, except that of joining the Fabian Society, which would be too little tragic and too cheaply propagandistic? Mrs. Warren ends by asserting, with coarse vulgarity, the conventional rights of a mother, and we see that Vivie has been her great romantic illusion. Through Vivie she had hoped to seize the bubble respectability.

"Mrs. Warren's Profession" was promptly hailed by the critics as a masterpiece of realism. It is certainly a masterpiece, and in comparison with many of Shaw's other plays and with the plausibly motivated daydreams of Jones and Pinero, it is also a masterpiece of realism. Yet on the whole I should say realism is not its primary merit. Some critics admire the truth and vividness with which Shaw has depicted prostitution as a social abuse.[22] As a matter of fact, he has very wisely treated this unsavory subject with much more generality than, in "Widowers' Houses," he treated slum landlordism, which as a Vestryman he probably knew a good deal better.

Again, character portraiture is superlative, but not so much psychologically as rhetorically. Frank is a convenient elf or goblin. Praed is real, but extremely insipid and conventional, in order to illustrate the economic helplessness of the mere artist. Mrs. Warren strides with magnificent confidence along the very brink of psychological credibility. She is not so much the type as the argument for her profession and is inhumanly clairvoyant for the same reasons that Gilbert's characters are baldly self-explanatory. Sir George Crofts belongs to La Fontaine. He is a character in an animal fable. Shaw's harping on his bulldog characteristics has exactly that kind of crude, powerful satiric effect. He also carries presages of Undershaft: "I don't object to Crofts," says Vivie, "more than to any other coarsely built man of his class. To tell you the truth, I rather admire him for being strong-minded enough to enjoy himself in his own way and make plenty of money instead of living the usual shooting, hunting, dining-out, tailoring, loafing life of his set merely because all the rest do it." [23] In short, the more admirable a capitalist is, the more evil he must be. Vivie herself is a victim of the somewhat undisciplined intensity with which Shaw conceives every part of a play. In the first act, she is something between a theorem in petticoats and a vigorous comic caricature of modern woman. In the second and third acts, she is modern woman facing genuine tragedy, though she recedes noticeably at times toward Victorian woman, with suggestions of sentiment, tears, fainting, and suicide. Can the total Vivie be acted as a consistent and convincing role? I think so. Her cigars and rationalism should be interpreted as youthful affectation and experiment. Her sudden delicacies and somewhat precarious consciousness are perhaps but the tribute nature paid to Victorianism in the nineties. Moreover, her untwentieth-century purity, besides being somewhat autobiographical for Shaw and very natural under the circumstances for Vivie, is dramatically necessary to give full nineteenth-century metaphysical horror to society's crime against Mrs. Warren.

Shaw had written a masterpiece. Grein had accepted it. The cast and the theater were ready. But "Mrs. Warren" was not to be produced until many years afterward. And indeed a greater outrage to the middle-class mind could hardly be imagined. It was an insult both to Philistine good and Philistine evil—to its purity and its greed. A play with a prostitute was bad enough, but to blame the prostitute on bourgeois thrift and individualism unendurable. "Mrs. Warren" was censored first by the Censor and then by Shaw himself. The Censor did not lift his ban until 1924, but already in 1897 Shaw had begun to be a little frightened by his own play, though he thought it by far his best. "It makes my blood run cold: I can hardly bear the most appalling bits of it. Ah, when I wrote that, I *had* some nerve." [24]

By 1924 he felt even less inclined to have it presented to the public. Besides, he had by then already seen it on the stage. Theaters could produce forbidden plays privately on Sunday nights, but "Mrs. Warren," with the Censor's ban on her head, made managers so nervous that they broke their promises one after another, "until at last the desperate and overworked manager of the Stage Society," who was bent on production, "could only laugh, as criminals broken on the wheel used to laugh at the second stroke." [25] But in 1902 he succeeded, and a Sunday-evening performance was given at the New Lyric Club. Shaw invited all the critics. On the stage "Mrs. Warren" proved to be so much moral dynamite and went off with a tremendous roar. The bottom dropped out of every critical conscience in the audience.

A first American performance of "Mrs. Warren" in 1905 was invaded by the police, who declared it "revolting, indecent, nauseating." [26] The Judge expressed some surprise at official severity when he had read the play, and eventually the cast was acquitted. The event is memorable for a long protest from Shaw and a shorter one from the American conservative Corbin, who concludes with a delightfully robust Americanism:

Placed as we are, to libel socialism and put it under the ban of the police, is only to redouble its power. In England, when the royal ostrich buries its head in the sand its tail feathers still make an imposing impression—many bow down before them and worship them. But the republican ostrich has no tail feathers. When it buries its head the result is an exposure of naked fatuity.[27]

Shaw had his revenge when in 1909 the Lord Chamberlain's censorship of the theater was investigated by a parliamentary committee. He was summoned to give evidence and so was able both to aid in ridding English law of an anachronism and to make an epigrammatic assault on legal dignity after the manner triumphantly inaugurated by Whistler and tragically continued by Wilde. Shaw came forth armed with a special definition of immorality for the occasion. The chairman asked whether he thought a court would forbid the playing of "Mrs. Warren."

"I think it is possible" [said Shaw]. "It is a profoundly immoral play, exceedingly so; more so than many of the people who have written about it think."

"Immoral in your own special sense?"

"In the classical use of the word in the English language. . . . The play is a conscientiously immoral play." [28]

CHAPTER TWENTY

Adventures in Success

Shaw had written three failures—and arrived at the height of his artistic achievement. "Mrs. Warren's Profession" represents the mature Shavian drama of ideas. That drama was to develop other varieties, other moods, other ideas; it was to be further complicated and refined; but it was not to be brought to a higher level. And yet "Mrs. Warren" had elicited absolutely no response from England beyond some bewildered praise from critics and perhaps a spasm of moral horror from the Censor.

But it was time to have done with brilliant failure. Shaw now began "Arms and the Man." He finished it in a hurry. Florence Farr, backed by the anonymous generosity of Miss A. E. F. Horniman, had leased the Avenue Theatre for the season. Her first production had failed, and now she proposed to revive "Widowers' Houses." Shaw offered her "Arms and the Man" instead.

Doubtless the large amount of sugar which he dumped into this concoction indicates the cynicism of some inward sourness. Certainly he neglected no obvious aid to success. Since 1870, war had become fashionable, and a rather picturesque one had recently occurred in the Balkans. Therefore Shaw wrote about war and laid his scene in Bulgaria. He added romantic love, beautiful women, handsome officers, and thrilling pursuit and concealment in the best *Prisoner of Zenda* manner. To be sure, he did not silence his own opinion on Ruritanian love and war, but he wrapped it up as innocently as possible in a Gilbertian or Swiftian device. "Arms and the Man," like "Iolanthe" or *Gulliver*, is one of those tales in which the spectator is whisked off to fairyland so that he may get a clearer view of the world of every day. But the view is Gilbert's and not Swift's. The atmosphere of Ruritania is not so harsh and clear as that of Lilliput. Shavian genius concedes to popular stupidity, as Shavian conscience to popular prejudice, as much as it can. Shaw once more attacks Victorian ideals, but this time he stops short of revolution. For the moment, he tolerates the sacredness of the pocketbook and strikes only at conventional love, honor, heroism, and war. Moreover, he expresses his views with so much gaiety and wit that the spectator can easily forget the idea in the laughter.

Shaw's attitude toward war was profoundly affected by the Ibsenite opposition between romance and reality, the ideal and the real. His reality, as I have already attempted to explain, tends to be too much Benthamite logic woven into the seamy side of illusion. Consequently, he drains so much of the heroism and romance out of war that the result, even when allowance has been made for satire and comedy, tends to be a very logical, precise, and ignoble kind of madness pursued amid blood, sweat, and dirt. What he objects to, as Chesterton says very well, is not so much war as the romantic attractiveness of war. Shaw's view receives its classical statement in "Arms and the Man." War between Balkan Ruritanias—even though set off with all the accessories of mountains by moonlight, a young lady alone in her bedchamber, a dashing cavalry officer, a rustic patriarchal estate, and a brilliant dialogue—turns out to be hopelessly prosaic. But not horrible—except from a distance. Fleeing from the enemy, Bluntschli is utterly exhausted, but his exhaustion is essentially comic. We do not see him experiencing, either physically or spiritually, the actual horrors of war. He merely mentions them:

RAINA [*passionately*] This is the doing of that friend of yours, Captain Bluntschli. It is he who is spreading this horrible story about me. [*She walks about excitedly.*]

BLUNTSCHLI. No: he's dead—burnt alive.

RAINA [*stopping, shocked*] Burnt alive!

BLUNTSCHLI. Shot in the hip in a wood-yard. Couldn't drag himself out. Your fellows' shells set the timber on fire and burnt him, with half a dozen other poor devils in the same predicament.[1]

Shaw never goes further. The horrors of war do not translate themselves into his artistic idiom.

What he really insists on is the humdrum of war. Apparently, the nineteenth century had made even war middle-class. In terms of the real and the ideal, Shaw distinguishes sharply between military efficiency and military heroism. The first is usually successful but utterly drab and glamourless. The second is rare, picturesque, impressive to the ladies, but except when backed by the big battalions, quite useless. It is symbolized by the handsome cavalryman Saranoff (drawn from the aristocratic socialist and traveler Cunninghame Graham), who wins a victory by committing an egregious blunder. Military efficiency is represented by the artilleryman Captain Bluntschli (drawn from Sidney Webb), who is matter-of-fact, Swiss, middle-class, and looks "like a commercial traveller in uniform." [2] War, as he practices it, is a prosaic business devoted to irrational ends. Not that Shaw denies courage to his Benthamite artilleryman, but Bluntschli's courage is strictly utilitarian. It does not strike the imagination and it achieves no miracles. Shaw also touches on the extravagant patriotism and ferocious pugnacity of noncombatants. But the comic idiom is not adequate to represent, nor did Shaw yet suspect, the massive dynamics of force and fanaticism which modern science and modern nationalism were to unleash on the twentieth century.

Amusingly enough, Bluntschli turns out to be a hero after all. No doubt much of the spectator's pleasure arises from the conviction that the humdrum little Swiss captain will triumph over all obstacles and win his Balkan princess in the end. He is a fairy prince whose magic sword happens to be good business methods. In many of his plays, Shaw wraps up his central thesis in a fairy tale of prosaic success and in so far is a legitimate contemporary of Horatio Alger. Bluntschli, Napoleon, Caesar, Lady Cicely Waynflete, King Magnus, even Jack Tanner—all possess, in greater or less degree, the magical powers of Shavian mind and initiative.

The courtship of Sergius and Raina is a satire of romantic love. They force themselves to worship each other, throw themselves into heroic embraces, pump out bombastic and high-flown endearments—and are bored to extinction. Meanwhile, Bluntschli tells Raina the disagreeable truth about life, war, her family, himself, herself—and finds her in love with him:

> RAINA [gasping] I! I!!! [She points to herself incredulously, meaning "I, Raina Petkoff, tell lies!" He meets her gaze unflinchingly. She suddenly sits down beside him, and adds, with a complete change of manner from the heroic to the familiar] How did you find me out?
>
> BLUNTSCHLI [promptly] Instinct, dear young lady. Instinct, and experience of the world.
>
> RAINA [wonderingly] Do you know, you are the first man I ever met who did not take me seriously?
>
> BLUNTSCHLI. You mean, don't you, that I am the first man that has ever taken you quite seriously?
>
> RAINA. Yes, I suppose I do mean that. [Cosily, quite at her ease with him] How strange it is to be talked to in such a way! [3]

Genuine and permanent love is founded on mutual knowledge. The play ends in a pleasant defeat for Bluntschli. Like Webb he abandons reason so far as to propose marriage, and Shaw preserves the integrity of his idea while gratifying public prejudice.

As an economist, Shaw is careful to emphasize that Ruritania lies hard on the borders of Philistia. The aristocratic Petkoffs are immensely proud of the bourgeois splendors of a library and an electric bell and abjectly bewildered by the silverware-and-bed-linen statistics of Bluntschli. The servant Nicola, who intends to set up a shop in Sofia, symbolizes the emergence of economic man from the dirt and romance of Balkan barbarism. He is completely given over to enlightened self-interest and readily gives up his fiancée to the eccentrically romantic Sergius in the expectation that she will be more useful as a rich customer than as a possibly industrious wife. He thus succeeds where Bluntschli fails. And indeed he is the more rational man. He feels no fascination whatever with beauty and romance. He forms his engagement with Louka—and releases her—on economic grounds. Above all, he has not made the romantic mistake of becoming a soldier. Nicola is Shaw's secret little final irony on war and romance.

If in writing "Arms and the Man" Shaw sold his soul to the devil, he got remarkably little for it. According to him, Florence Farr's company were utterly mystified by an author who regarded romance as the great heresy, gentility as ridiculous folly, chivalry as treasonable to women and stultifying to men. They rehearsed the play and on the opening night performed it in sullen and solemn bewilderment. The result was a tremendous success—the audience was wracked by spasms and agonies of laughter, for the utmost seriousness in acting was essential to the comic effect. Further bewildered by their triumph, the company now performed the play as conventional comedy—and failed disastrously. Through the generosity of Miss Horniman, "Arms and the Man" held the stage for eleven weeks and lost thousands of pounds. To be sure, the play perplexed the audience for the same reason that it perplexed the actors. People had not yet learned to laugh at the serious as well as the comic side of Shaw. Perhaps he had not sugar-coated his meaning enough. The Prince of Wales, for example, was not amused. He was not Victorian about morals, certainly. But a direct attack on the Army. . . ! Not until the end of World War I, when the Victorian Age had at length come to a close, did people fully understand the picture of war which Shaw presents in "Arms and the Man."

To fail with "Mrs. Warren" was one thing, but to fail with "Arms and the Man"—what more could he do? He was driven back again on bare faith in his own excellence. Genius had to perform anew the old miracle of creating in the welter of public mediocrity and indifference an audience educated and intelligent enough to applaud it. He set to work at once and in the same year (1894) produced "Candida," another "pleasant" masterpiece. Wisely eschewing war, property, and revolution, and touching only in the deftest manner on socialism and municipal corruption, Shaw considers the institution of marriage—and actually upholds it, at least with one hand. As "Arms and the Man" is his "pleasantest," "Candida" is his safest, play.

Essentially, it is Ibsen's "Doll's House" turned upside down. Ibsen had shown that unhappiness results when a husband treats his wife as a doll. Shaw points out that happiness may result when a wife treats her husband as a doll. His Nora sees her husband as he really is—and retains him. In fact, there is a great scene in which Nora, like the Lady from the Sea, chooses between her husband and another man. But even more than it resembles "A Doll's House" and "The Lady from the Sea," "Candida" resembles Shaw's own *Love among the Artists*. Yet more desperately unmarried and more desperately unsuccessful at thirty-eight, Shaw returns to the same double problem of marriage and genius and essentially the same triangle situation—and turns a crude juvenility into a masterpiece.

Fortunately, "Candida" has so many excellences that it does not need to be understood to be enjoyed. Acted by Janet Achurch at the Independent Theatre, it soon became a success, but it is still, next perhaps to "Major Barbara," the most widely misunderstood of all Shaw's dramas. As late as 1944, Mr. E. R. Bentley regards Candida as a kind of black-widow spider. The best that can be said is that the play is being progressively more ingeniously and acutely misunderstood. The commonest mistake is to regard Candida's choice as genuine and real. As a matter of fact, Shaw has taken pains not to present her with a choice. Eugene could have been twenty-eight; he is eighteen. He could have been Jovian and red-bearded, like Jack Tanner; he is "slight, effeminate, with a delicate childish voice." [4] His grotesque shyness and absurd cowardice are cruelly if comically insisted on to make the audience see that he could not possibly win a hardheaded woman like Candida. So far as the Morell marriage is concerned, Eugene merely precipitates the conflict between husband and wife; he is no more than a catalytic agent in the domestic rearrangement of atoms. For the real action of "Candida" is based on a very old dramatic device: a misunderstanding. In the course of the play, husband and wife come for the first time genuinely to understand each other and their actual relationship.

In the opening scenes we learn a good deal about the Reverend Morell. Toward Prossy and Lexy, he is wise and indulgent; toward Burgess, vigorous and frank. "He is a first rate clergyman, able to say what he likes to whom he likes, to lecture people without setting himself up against them, to impose his authority on them without humiliating them." [5] We learn also that he considers his wife the rock and foundation of his happiness. Meanwhile, she has been down in the country with her children for three weeks. Eugene Marchbanks, a young poet and a friend of the family, has been visiting them there. He comes back thoroughly in love with her, and she, with her mind and ideas thoroughly aired out by him. Conceiving love as a romantic ecstasy which has nothing to do with the domesticities of peeling onions and trimming lamps and little to do with the sublunary detail of physical possession, he cannot understand how a woman like Candida can have any feeling for a windbag like James Morell. He tells James so without delay, having first declared his own love. Morell meets this youthful outburst with magnificent condescension and indulgence. And yet he has apparently himself noticed in Candida's attitude toward him something disturbing, which he has always been reluctant to understand. He concludes an oratorical appeal with: "There are so many things to make us doubt, if once we let our understanding be troubled. Even at home, we sit as if in camp, encompassed by a hostile army of doubts. Will you play the traitor and let them in on me?" [6] Eugene certainly does not come to the rescue: "Is it like this for her always? . . . Do you think a woman's soul can live on your talent for preaching?" Slashing about with truths that are quite irrelevant to Candida's marriage, he cuts deep into the clergyman's self-confidence and therefore into the latter's faith in his wife's love. For James's idea of love is as romantically conventional as Eugene's is romantically poetic. It is an honest, money-down, value-received conception. He possesses Candida's love partly because as a pure woman and a good wife she owes it; and much more, because as a husband, father, and provider, he has earned it.

And what kind of woman is Candida? She is, as Shaw says, "unerring wisdom [one might almost say, Benthamite rationalism and detachment] on the domestic plane," [7] a realist placed between two romantics, whom she regards with maternal indulgence. Hard facts are her specialty, and the great facts in her life are sex and the home. Therefore she trades a little on her good looks and her good figure, and she regards the great world beyond her fireside as somewhat shadowy and unreal. Moreover, she is herself a woman of strong instincts. Shaw writes that "without brains and strength of mind she would be a wretched slattern or voluptuary." [8] It is significant that she has married a physically powerful and handsome man. The maternal instinct is particularly strong. And here both Shaw and his critics have gone too far. The stage directions and the symbolism of the play indicate that she is to be regarded primarily as the mother-woman. Her maternal indulgence toward the adult male infant is stressed to the point of objectionable omniscience. Granted that she is predominantly maternal in outward manner and psychological attitude; that the maternal manner, in a beautiful and intelligent woman, is charming to most men—and indeed it is often simply a reassuringly innocent disguise for sex—nevertheless, Candida is much more than a schematization of the mother instinct. If, for example, she were attracted to men simply for their weakness, she would be most fascinated by Lexy, who has nothing but weaknesses. Obviously, she loves Morell because he has been, in some respects at least, stronger and wiser than she. It is clearly indicated that he has formed her mind and therefore encouraged her in that freedom from convention which, he recognizes, will cause her to leave him at once if she is not held by love. Here Chesterton's comment is more accurate than the author's own. He finds in the play

> the reality of the normal wife's attitude to the normal husband, an attitude which is . . . insanely unselfish and yet quite cynically clear-sighted. . . . She regards him in some strange fashion at once as a warrior who must make his way and as an infant who is sure to lose his way. The man has emotions which exactly correspond; sometimes looking down at his wife and sometimes up at her; for marriage is like a splendid game of see-saw.[9]

But if Candida sincerely admires her husband, why, when she observes his melancholy after the skirmish with Eugene, does she attack him with such sharp and unfeeling gaiety? She assures him that his work does no good, that his parishioners do not mind him the least bit, that he positively abets them in evil by his sermons, which make them feel good without being good. And all the women are in love with him. "And you," she adds, "are in love with preaching because you do it so beautifully. And you think it's all enthusiasm for the kingdom of Heaven on earth; and so do they. You dear silly!"[10]

This is all new to James, because it is all new to Candida. She has just got it from Eugene. But why isn't she disturbed by it, both for herself and for her husband? Partly, perhaps, because she feels that a little truth will be good for James's complacency. But much more, because her rational detachment limits her sympathetic insight; she cannot understand why everybody should not relish truth as keenly as she. And finally, because the masculine world outside is not very real: whether James is winning actual or imaginary victories is not extremely important.

She is equally detached in discussing with Morell Eugene's love for her. Will Eugene forgive her for allowing him to learn what love is from a bad woman? "Forgive you for what?" exclaims her husband. For not having taught him herself, of course. Her decision has been the result of a very Benthamite calculation in moral mathematics. She explains to her husband that she is restrained not by her purity or his preaching but by the preponderant claim of her love for him.

In her too confident superiority and her present subservience to Eugene's thought, she has missed all the storm signals. She does not dream that James cannot grasp her combination of steadfast affection with clear-sighted detachment, that he has understood every word in a personal, emotional context. Morell, on the other hand, is convinced that she cannot love him, since she does not love him for his reasons. The misunderstanding is complete. When she approaches him, he waves her off, telling her with anguish in his voice that she must not touch him. From this point on, Shaw manipulates events to forestall any clarification between husband and wife, until Morell, tortured and degraded by uncertainty and suspicion, demands a "choice" between himself and Marchbanks.

This, the great scene of the play, is, as M. Hamon observes, no more than an appearance for Candida but an agonizing reality for the two men. The spectator is also on the very knife-edge of suspense, for he perceives that Candida, having in her turn been disillusioned about James's conception of their marriage, is beside herself with indignation. "And pray, my lords and masters," she cries, "what have you to offer for my choice? I am up for auction, it seems. What do you bid, James?" [11] His complacency, though badly shaken, is still monumental, and he is still wedded to his illusions. He replies with "proud humility" and magnificently restrained oratory:

> I have nothing to offer you but my strength for your defence, my honesty of purpose for your surety, my ability and industry for your livelihood, and my authority and position for your dignity. That is all it becomes a man to offer to a woman.

At length she decides superbly, "I give myself to the weaker of the two," [12] which is of course Morell. The spectacle of his bewildered suffering, now showing clearly through the polished speaker and the glossy Christian, has changed her anger to sympathy, but the sense of outrage remains. She must set him right, not with Eugene's truths but with those which are fundamental to her self-respect:

> Ask James's mother and his three sisters what it cost to save James the trouble of doing anything but be strong and clever and happy. Ask me what it costs to be James's mother and three sisters and wife and mother to his children all in one . . . . I build a castle of comfort and indulgence and love for him, and stand sentinel always to keep little vulgar cares out. I make him master here, though he does not know it.[13]

Candida has been called a prig and Shaw a preacher for this speech. Yet she must have made it, even though the curtain had fallen and the audience, preceding Eugene, had gone out into the night. It is this grave explanation which makes the play a comedy: now we know how it will be with the Morells in the future; we know also that Candida correctly evaluates her husband, for she can afford to tell him his weakness and her strength. Crushing as the outcome has been to his self-confidence, he is at least temporarily humble and grateful. Clearly, his wife believes that he will rise above his humiliating victory—and indeed men like Morell, however noble, have an automatic apparatus for manufacturing self-esteem.

"Candida" is also a study of genius in relation to worldly success and happiness. Burgess is bitter satire. He represents the very worst and shabbiest to whom the world permits the prestige of success. Morell, on the other hand, is the very best that the world admires. He has all the obvious talents and succeeds because he cannot help it. Finally, Eugene is a genius. He has all the obvious weaknesses and will eventually succeed because the world cannot prevent him. In the extremity of defeat and suffering, he rises suddenly to a realization of his destiny, and rejecting the mere happiness of Candida and her husband, goes out into the night, so that at the very close of the play the theme of the loneliness and self-sufficiency of genius surges up to dominance. Admirably effective as a dramatic instrument, Eugene is psychologically the least satisfactory character in "Candida." As a lover he is, as Chesterton observes, too turgid in his speeches and too finicky about onions. As a genius, he is perhaps too much Shelley made over to fit the definition of a Shavian realist. He "dares to love and trust" and at the same time sees facts without illusion. In so far he tends to inconsistency.

In the late nineteenth century, romantic genius divided into two species: the aesthete who retreated from the world and the superman who conquered it. In "Candida," Shaw has portrayed the first. In "The Man of Destiny," which follows, he portrays the second. Why was he interested in the superman? First, because the superman was an important contemporary phenomenon, much admired by Ibsen and Nietzsche. Second, because he is a drastic political remedy and therefore intriguing to a root-and-branch puritan like Shaw. Third, because he is a genius and a professional success man and therefore an absorbing study to an ambitious writer in a posture of spectacular failure.

In considerable degree "The Man of Destiny" returns to the subject matter of "Arms and the Man." Shaw speaks in the same language, but actually he takes a much broader view. The prolonged and epigrammatic stage direction which introduces Napoleon sets up the usual dichotomy between heroism and efficiency. Napoleon succeeds because he is a combination of Bluntschli and Saranoff. Like the first, he understands cannon, but like the second, he is ignorant of the arts of war. His ignorance leads him to perform theatrical acts of daring which inspire his own raw troops to superhuman efforts and completely bewilder the enemy, who, being highly trained, expect nothing but the routine of eighteenth-century warfare. It is implied that the victory of Lodi is as accidental as that of Saranoff's cavalry charge. Actually, of course, there is only a partial parallel. Saranoff succeeds chiefly because the enemy has no bullets. Napoleon succeeds, partly at least, because he is a hero. Grudgingly, Shaw grants courage its miracles, though he explains it as the result of fear plus rational will. Moreover, Napoleon is not ignorant. It is subtly insinuated that he understands topography, time, distances—and above all, men. In short, he is a genius. That is, he bears a startling resemblance to Shaw himself. Having a Shavian appetite for hard work, a Shavian faculty for clear-sighted observation, and a Shavian education in "poverty, ill-luck . . . impecunious shabby-gentility," and "repeated failure as a would-be author," he is

> imaginative without illusions, and creative without religion, loyalty, patriotism or any of the common ideals. Not that he is incapable of these ideals: on the contrary, he has swallowed them all in his boyhood, and now, having a keen dramatic faculty, is extremely clever at playing upon them by the arts of the actor and stage manager.[14]

He rules men because he rules their imaginations. He is a master of illusion because he is a master of reality. He is also a superman because he is not afraid of his own destiny, because he is heroically selfish, so that all the faculties of his nature are concentrated inflexibly on his great purpose.

Napoleon has a soldier's theory of life— and of war:

> There is only one universal passion: fear. Of all the thousand qualities a man may have, the only one you will find as certainly in the youngest drummer boy in my army as in me, is fear. It is fear that makes men fight: it is indifference that makes them run away: fear is the mainspring of war.[15]

Later, Shaw applied this theory to nations. Like wild animals, they are most dangerous when most terrified. Fear of attack led to general war in 1914. He was moving closer to the psychology of the twentieth century.

The difficulty with "The Man of Destiny," as Shaw says, is that it is "a commercial traveller's sample," "hardly more than a bravura piece to display the virtuosity of the two principal performers." [16] We do not see Napoleon confronted by some great soul-searching decision, by some great crisis in which he becomes, or ceases to be, Napoleon. What we get is a slice-of-life play. A slice of Napoleon's life, to be sure, but for that very reason we have a feeling of waste, of mighty forces used for trivial purposes. Napoleon is brought upon the stage simply to chase a pretty woman around an innkeeper's table. It is Napoleon in the gymnasium,

[179]

Napoleon giving an exhibition bout. Unfortunately, this is, except for "Saint Joan," the difficulty with most of Shaw's historical pieces. Nevertheless, "The Man of Destiny" is a delightful bit of closet history and a dazzling comedy of the gods, like Homer's wonderful domestic farce on Olympus.

Through the machinations of Sir Henry Irving, "The Man of Destiny" was for three years withheld from the stage, so that out of six distinguished plays, Shaw had achieved only one moderate success. "You Never Can Tell" was his "As You Like It," a final adventure in success. Soon after its completion, Mr. Cyril Maude, having heard the praises of "Candida" by one Bernard Shaw, wrote asking permission to produce that play at the Haymarket Theatre Shaw replied peremptorily that "Candida" was not suitable to the Haymarket but that he would provide a comedy which was. He then revised "You Never Can Tell" and submitted it to Maude, who accepted it.

As "Arms and the Man" is a satirical compromise with romance, "You Never Can Tell" is a satirical compromise with fashionable comedy. It has a contemporary English setting, begins excruciatingly in a dentist's operating room, is filled with love tête-à-têtes and fashionable eating and drinking amid surroundings of respectable magnificence, and contains a beautiful girl, an irate father, automatic twins, a sex duelist, an omniscient waiter, and a Dickensian lawyer out of *Great Expectations* with a Schopenhauerian philosophy. The total result suggests the Pickwick Club at the height of election excitement.

All great ideas, Shaw has said more than once, begin as jokes. In "You Never Can Tell," the Shavian theory of love very nearly ends in a joke. This plays stands midway between "The Philanderer" and "Man and Superman." Valentine is a Charteris who suffers the fate of a Jack Tanner. He is a philanderer who fears marriage but pursues women for his amusement. He meets Gloria Clandon, who is a vital woman with a rational education. Having been trained to despise sentiment, she is inaccessible to ordinary conventional love-making. Consequently, as an up-to-date sex duelist familiar with recent developments in competitive armament, he uses a more powerful gun to pierce thicker armor. Gloria will listen to nothing but logic. Therefore, he becomes fabulously self-conscious and self-critical, scientifically describing his amorous sensations as they occur and at the same time deploring them as a disgusting irrationality in a modern man.

Gloria listens with curiosity and begins to discover alarming sensations in herself. At length nature, in the words of the play, catches her by the scruff of the neck and—she allows Valentine to kiss her. The scene is intellectual love comedy at its best. The Shavian philosophy of love, with its Schopenhauerian conflict between reason and the will to mate, is complete, except that the two elements of the conflict are not yet differentiated, in the later manner, as to sex. In fact, Shavian love philosophy serves here chiefly as the dramatic design for a scene and as a plan of attack for Valentine. It is an elaborate joke in the process of becoming an elaborate dogma.

The coordinate theme of the play deals with a conventional father who, after a separation of eighteen years, is accidentally confronted by his rational family. He exudes the lukewarm steam of family sentiment, treats his children as recalcitrant infants, calls upon them with cries of agony to love, revere, and obey him—and is treated as a disagreeable curiosity. At length, rather suddenly and inexplicably, he reforms and gains the affection of his children by deserving it. The story of Crampton and the Clandons strongly suggests "Man and Superman," except that the criticism of family relationships is much more sensible.

"You Never Can Tell" is resolutely, dazzlingly, breathlessly Shavian. The sex-dueling of Valentine, like the philandering of Charteris, is in some respects unpleasant. The dialogue is occasionally forced and betrays the exhaustion of an overworked man. It is not, perhaps, so witty as that of "Man and Superman" nor so wise as that of "Arms and the Man," but the scene development is equal to anything in Shaw, and the curtains, in my opinion, better than anything in Wilde. Such a play should have been a success, but it was not—until several years later. The difficulty was that Shaw knew too much about the theater. He knew down to the last gesture and respiration exactly how he wanted the play performed, and each day he came to the Haymarket in an abominable suit of clothes and with even more abominable patience told everybody exactly what to do. Unfortunately, he was right, and therefore everybody felt obliged to do everything wrong to assert his independence. And then for the last rehearsal Shaw came resplendent in a new suit of chirping stockinet, and the cast disintegrated from the shock. The play was withdrawn at Shaw's request.

CHAPTER TWENTY-ONE

The Romance of an Invisible Man

It was at this time that Shaw achieved his most Shavian romance. He rescued a very extraordinary lady from a very abstract and complicated kind of distress. They communicated only by letter and never met until the romance was over. Undoubtedly they grew to love each other very much, though when they came to have business dealings, the knight-errant proved so sternly practical that some may wonder cynically whether he was not activated by the profit motive instead of a heart and governed by the Benthamite utility calculus instead of the chivalric code. Yet the rescue was a financial success for the lady as for himself. It was also a genuine deliverance. Unfortunately, it came too late and did not result in their living happily ever after. They knew each other's hearts but were embarrassed strangers to each other's outward, casual selves. The role of the lady was played by the most famous English actress of her time—Ellen Terry.

Of course there was an ogre, or a giant. It was Sir Henry Irving, whom Shaw as a very young man first saw in Dublin:

> . . . an actor with a tall thin figure, which, if it could not be convicted of grotesqueness was certainly indescribably peculiar, and a voice which was dependent so much on the resonance of a cavernous nose that it was, compared to the powerful and musical chest voice of Barry Sullivan, a highly cultivated neigh. . . . I instinctively felt that a new drama inhered in this man, though I had then no conscious notion that I was destined to write it.[1]

Irving had the ill taste not to fulfill Shaw's prediction. Instead of becoming a Shavian hero by interpreting Ibsen, he became a Shavian arch-villain by mutilating Shakespeare. As a great actor and the manager of the Lyceum, he was the magnificent symbol of traditional and reactionary art on the London stage. Worse, as the prince of artistic darkness, he had infernal powers of holding rival genius in thrall. His study, according to Shaw, was a graveyard of plays which he had bought so that other actors could not shine in them. Worst of all, he had long monopolized Ellen Terry as his leading lady and was thereby misusing the greatest English actress, as well as the greatest English playwright, for the base purpose of aiding Henry Irving to play Henry Irving.

The romance between Shaw and Ellen sprang up quite naturally from the man's conscientious didacticism and the woman's quick curiosity. She had written to Edmund Yates asking his advice about a young lady who sang. Yates turned the letter over to his music critic, who, probably fearing an attack on his professional honor, replied very stiffly. Nevertheless, he did go to a recital in which the young lady took part and then dissected her, in a long letter to Ellen Terry, with the utmost skill and courtesy. Moreover, he prefaced his operations with an interesting remark: "To begin with, you know that you do not hold your present position because you possess this, that, and the other personal attraction, but because you have made yourself one of the six best actresses in the fourteen thousand millions of people . . . in the world." [2]

Here was a mind as sharp and hard as steel—and that mind admired her. Miss Terry thanked the writer warmly. Unluckily she mentioned, with just a touch of satisfaction, that her protégée had earned a hundred pounds. Only one hundred pounds? queried the revolutionist with withering scorn and burst into an ironic apostrophe of all the indigent Ibsen actresses. For the moment, Ellen is one of the enemy.

There is a silence of three years. Then she reads in the newspaper a paragraph beginning, "Mr. George Bernard Shaw is always one of the most vigorous and wittiest of speakers." Now forty-seven, she has not lost her curiosity about that bright, shiny steel mind. She writes a note of friendly interest—and Shaw pours all the crimes of the British stage down on her head. "Will your tomb in Westminster Abbey have nothing but reproaches for an epitaph?" he concludes. [3] As before, he knows how to make insult flattering. But now he has more balance, more moderation. He is thirty-nine, the author of several masterly plays and the widely feared, wasp-tongued critic for *The Saturday Review*.

At once they are deep in discussion of his "Man of Destiny." Ellen writes, "If you give Napoleon and that Strange Lady (Lord, how attractively tingling it sounds!) to anyone but me I'll—write to you every day!" [4] But he is artful and skittish as a gypsy and knows how to be pursued:

It is all nonsense: you are only playing with me. I will go to that beautiful Mrs Patrick Campbell, who won my heart long ago by her pianoforte playing as Mrs Tanqueray, and make her head twirl like a chimney cowl with my blarney. *She* shall play the Strange Lady—she and the passion-worn Forbes. Yes, it shall be so. Farewell, faithless Ellen! [5]

What does he look like? The reports are strange and wonderful—especially as to garb. Now she has something new to be curious about. Her eyes are tired and strained. "They will be sent to sleep for a while and awake some day to see you in your Jaeger clothing standing beside me." [6] She is to act Imogen in Shakespeare's "Cymbeline." A wretched play! he replies. A wretched author! But he rereads it, tells her how to cut and act it, especially the part in which she awakes to find a headless corpse in her bed. During rehearsals everyone thinks the play a great success, but, keen in self-judgment, she cannot feel any joy. Then comes the opening. With a letter like a trumpet blast, Shaw summons her to renewed effort and concludes, "Hitherto, you have only *coaxed* me. Tonight you must CONQUER me. I shall fight to the last, as if you were my mortal foe, but oh, with such a longing to be conquered." [7] He sees the performance and takes her to task like a schoolgirl. "Yes, yes, yes," writes the great actress with characteristic humility, "I see what you mean about the 'headless man' bit; and the '5 bars' rest' in the Cave Scene is of course all wrong. I see it now, and will try and try at it." [8]

They discuss his *Saturday Review* articles. She is deeply touched by the one on the death of Morris. But why must he attack nice old dears like Henry Irving? Everybody says Shaw hates successful people.

> I dont hate successful people; just the contrary. But I dread success. . . . I like a state of continual *becoming*, with a goal in front and not behind. Then too, I like fighting successful people; attacking them; rousing them; trying their mettle; kicking down their sand castles so as to make them build stone ones, and so on. It develops one's muscles. Besides, one learns from it: a man never tells you anything until you contradict him. I hate failure. Only, it must be real success: real skill, real ability, real power, not mere newspaper popularity and money. [9]

She pleads to be sent "Candida." No, he must read it to her himself. But she is afraid to meet him. She looks so old and fat, now. At last he sends "Candida." She reads it. Yes, he is a very great man. But what does he look like? He sends her photographs. All her reverence for genius evaporates at once. He is none other than her Dublin cab driver: "Why, I knew you in a second! And you used to drive me wild with delight in Dublin by exciting your horse to run away." She studies the photograph. "Is that your ear? I dont like it." [10] He replies, "I am really sorry about the ears. They are a Shaw specialty. They stick straight out like the doors of a triptych; and I was born with them full size, so that on windy days my nurse had to hold me by my waistband to prevent my being blown away when the wind caught them." [11] She is completely appeased: "Give my love to every bit of you. Especially the dear old ears." [12]

No, she still does not want to meet him, but they will set up house-keeping in heaven. Besides, in his earthly epistolary form, he has become a habit with her. She takes him every morning before breakfast, "like a pill." He urges her to use him to the full, build him into the solid fabric of her life:

> All my love affairs end tragically because the women *cant* use me. They lie low and let me imagine things about them; but in the end a frightful unhappiness, an unspeakable weariness comes; and the Wandering Jew must go on in search of someone who can use him to the utmost of his capacity. [13]

He enumerates his loves, including an Irish lady with "light green eyes" and a "million of money." [14] She is a little skeptical. How many love affairs—three or thirty? And Janet Achurch really "loves" him? And the Irish millionairess, Miss Payne-Townshend, whom he actually talks of proposing to?

He hastens to assure her that he is, and always has been, as timid as a mouse. About Miss Payne-Townshend—she is not at all showy and has the good breeding always to fit perfectly and inconspicuously into her place. She is shrewd, alert, and sentimental. She has had her fill of family life, wishes to exploit her wealth and freedom, and has done so by becoming a Fabian and a supporter of the London School of Economics. For a few years she had been enjoying a broken heart, "until she happened to read The Quintessence of Ibsenism in which she found, as she thought, gospel, salvation, freedom, emancipation, self-respect and so on." [15] Since then, she has met the author and grown rather fond of him. What is Ellen's verdict? Ellen's verdict is that the lady should marry the book.

Returning to generalities, he explains that woman's lot is perpetual motherhood; man's, perpetual babyhood. He likes being a baby. So far as his relation with Ellen is concerned, there is truth in his dictum, though they each fuss a good deal over the other's health. Her eyes are very weak, and he is haunted by the fear that she may someday be blind. It is Shavian weakness that he must generalize a simple, intense feeling into an ingenious sentimentality: "Never write to me again; never speak to me ever at all; but keep your prosaic blessed eyes and dont torment me with the frightful beauty and mystery of a lovely blind woman." [16] Sometimes he sees things, like the purblindest of Ibsenite idealists, through the colored spectacles of his own humanitarian doctrine. He reproaches her with the occasion when, as Madame

Sans-Gêne, "you had that wicked, cruel, Indian-savageous, ugly, ridiculous plumage in your blessed hair to warn me that you have no heart" —and puzzles her mightily.[17] Cleverness seems to grow on him like a vice during these years. He himself complains of it: "My very love gets knit into an infernal intellectual fabric that wounds when I mean it to caress." [18]

Ellen for her part is worried that he works so hard—and not without reason, for in nearly every one of his letters he complains of extreme fatigue and intellectual exhaustion. Every minute of his day is filled. He writes his plays in little notebooks while bumping and banging about in trains, while scurrying about the city between appointments, while having his portrait painted by a young lady. Ellen is firmly convinced that the plays are much the most important things about his life; they must not be mere afterthoughts, casual sacrifices to impressive busyness.

So Mrs. Webb thinks Candida is just a sentimental prostitute. That sets Ellen wondering. She is still curious about him. She knows the "Candida" "Man of Destiny" Shaw, the *Saturday Review* Shaw, the inside-the-correspondence Shaw. Now she would like to see the Shaw other people see—so she sets them to talking and then listens and listens. "P.S. 'He is just the vainest flirt.' That is what they agreed about you yesterday. I wonder whether I know you in the least?" [19] She peeks at him through a hole in the curtain: "You *are* a boy! . . . And so that was you! How deadly delicate you look!" [20]

Both enjoy the safety of numbers in love. "Love you?" she writes. "Dont be silly. Of course I do and 'twenty such' if there *were* twenty such. If only one year back—but I never compete." [21] He replies:

> You say you do not compete: well, you need not. *I* do not compete with all the men you love (more or less—I am convinced that with you a human relation is love or nothing); there I am, not possibly to be confused with any of them, and ten times better realised because of the knowledge you have gained from them than if you knew nobody but me. Just so you are not injured by the filling-up with Emeralds (schöne grüne Augen) of that castle of my life which you left unfilled.[22]

Sometimes he becomes passionate, and then she tells him to keep his mind on Miss Payne-Townshend. He also adds a word or two about his methods: "My *impulses* are so prettily played—oh, you know: you wretch, you've done it often enough yourself." [23] And indeed she has. She can play the Shavian lover to a turn:

Off on a bit of magic carpet would I go if I could [she writes], and wave my hands over your blessed head, touch your cerise (?) hair gently with my lips, whisper to you I was there, although invisible, that I love you tho' I could not show you how much (one never does!) and then skip back again on my carpet to—this place. Tho' I'd rather go to Edy [her daughter].[24]

Meanwhile Shaw never forgets the ogre, who receives rough treatment in *The Saturday Review*. He must be changed into a harmless and virtuous Ibsenite, or the lady must be lured away from his evil power. To achieve the first of these alternatives, Shaw wrote "The Man of Destiny," in which the Strange Lady was deliberately modeled after Ellen and Napoleon admirably suited to the ogre. He offered the play to the Lyceum. Sir Henry naturally did not like the author and therefore did not like the play, but hoping to gain some immunity from the slings and arrows of outrageous criticism, pretended to show marked interest. The play remained on his shelf for some time, while slings and arrows embedded themselves in his hide about as thickly as ever.

The situation became steadily more tense and notorious, so that in the middle of Irving's first speech the opening night of "Cymbeline," a modernist called out, "What about Shaw's play?" [25] At length Irving suggested a conference—very cunningly on the morning after Shaw's review of "Cymbeline" was to appear. Nevertheless, Shaw deliberately whetted his appetite for the slaughter and performed a wonderfully dexterous double execution of Irving and the Bard. His chief compliment to Irving was that his Iachimo was better than Shakespeare's. And he made short work of the actor: "In a true republic of art Sir Henry Irving would ere this have expiated his acting versions on the scaffold. He does not merely cut plays: he disembowels them." [26] "I shall see him," Shaw exults to Ellen, "with the Saturday article . . . up to the hilt in his heart." [27] Yet the murderer is always at a disadvantage with his victim's ghost.

Ellen was nearby when Shaw came. His voice sounded "so very small," she wrote later.

> Intended coming straight into the office, but got no further than the doormat. Heard your voice and then skedaddled home again full tilt, and, oh I was laughing.

> I *couldnt* come in. All of a sudden it came to me that under the funny circumstances I should not be responsible for my impulses. When I saw you, I *might* have thrown my arms round your neck and hugged you! I *might* have been struck shy.[27]

The result of the conference was a gentleman's agreement that "The Man of Destiny" should be produced within the year. But Irving was not in earnest. Soon afterward, he came out with Sardou's "Madame Sans-Gêne," another Napoleon play. How could he possibly prefer such trash to "The Man of Destiny"? As a matter of fact, he was too self-centered really to take in Shaw's play, too much wanting in literary taste to perceive its excellence, and too prejudiced to consider it apart from "the appalling Yahoo" who was its author.

And the appalling Yahoo did nothing to mitigate himself. When Irving publicly demanded a knighthood for the acting profession, Shaw explained helpfully that Henry wanted the knighthood for himself. When Irving had to absent himself from the Lyceum during the "Olivia" run, Shaw exclaimed with a heartfelt sigh in the columns of *The Saturday Review* that it was a relief to be rid of him for a while. Then Irving played "Richard III." Shaw was, apparently with complete innocence, puzzled by the performance. He observed that Irving was not "answering his helm satisfactorily," that he was occasionally out of temper with his own nervous condition, that "he made some odd slips in the text, notably by substituting 'you' for 'I,'" and that he played his scene with Lady Anne "as if he were a Hounsditch salesman cheating a factory girl out of a pair of second-hand stockings." [28] Irving took the review as a thinly disguised accusation of drunkenness, the more unendurable because it was just. He was the kind of actor who primed himself with a dinner: "The condition in which he works is a somnambulistic one: he hypnotises himself into a sort of dreamy energy, and is intoxicated by the humming of his words in his nose" [29]—and this time by the buzzing of wine in his head. Naturally he felt that the Yahoo had violated the last decency. Through his man Stoker, he abruptly sent Shaw word that he had changed his mind about "The Man of Destiny."

Shaw's letters to Ellen begin at once to breathe fire: "Hooray! Kiss me good speed; and I'll toss them all about the stage as Cinquevalli tosses oranges and dinner plates . . . Don't bother about The Man of Destiny. . . . Leave them to me. Hahah!!!" [30] But Ellen does bother about "The Man of Destiny." She hates to see a good play thrown away on a stupid quarrel. She has her heart set on acting the Strange Lady. Irving is a donkey, to be sure, but a donkey whom she loves. Shaw's spirits are dangerously high. He urges that a good fight will be very instructive for Henry. Again he suggests that if he himself took both sides, the total result would be a fairer fight and much more agreeable for everybody, including Ellen, whom he wants above all to spare. "I should have . . . drafted him a letter to write to me which would have given him the keenest satisfaction." [31] But posterity was deprived of this document. Irving allowed himself to be soothed and petted by his leading lady, wrote Shaw asking for God's sake to be let alone, and soon relapsed into what Ellen called "his normal naughtiness. "Dont pity H.," she writes Shaw, "he thinks he has quite got the best of it. . . . The fact is he dont think the whole thing matters much." [32]

But it did, for he was soon to lose his leading lady. Under steady suggestion from Shaw, she had become more and more disgusted with the melodramatic twaddle upon which she was compelled to spend months of study and rehearsal. Meanwhile, tempting fruit was constantly being held out to her. Having created one Ellen Terry in the Strange Lady, he now created another in Lady Cicely Waynflete and placed her in a special Ellen Terry paradise provided even with a minor role for her daughter. But like a great deal of Shavian paradise, "Captain Brassbound's Conversion" had at first glance just the suggestion of a hard, brilliant, satanic glitter about it.

"I don't like the play one bit," wrote Ellen. "It's not the sort of play for me in the least. . . . The two parts, the man and woman, are right; but that *bore* Drinkwater! Mrs. Pat for Lady C! I couldnt do it." And also: "'There's not a penny in it,'—'More fitted for the closet than the stage,' occur to one when one has finished it." [33]

"Alas! dear Ellen, is it really so? Then I can do nothing for you. I honestly thought that Lady Cicely would fit you like a glove." [34]

From this point on, their story plunges from paradox to paradox, for when life becomes Shavian, it never stops at the end of the third act and seldom proves Shavian doctrine. First, neither Ellen nor her friends think she is anything like Lady Cicely. Meanwhile, her maid has been observing her with a quizzical expression. Why? Bursting with suppressed laughter she replies, "Oh, I'm very sorry. Excuse me, but Lady Cicely is *so* like you. . . . She gets her way in *everything—just like you!*" [35] Ellen is much puzzled. At the same time, she is employing exactly Lady Cicely's wiles to get around Henry Irving. Shaw shrieks with laughter. And yet there is a question whether his heroine is not Shavian idea masquerading in Ellen's temperament.

But now he makes a supreme effort. Ellen Terry's conversion must precede Captain Brassbound's, and therefore in one tremendous letter he explains the whole play to her. Lady Cicely is superior to Candida because she solves the problems of empire rather than those of the hearth, superior to Cleopatra because she does so without the aid of sex. She is the finest example of Shavian woman, and she *is* Ellen Terry. The plea succeeds. Ellen is convinced—at least her mind is, and that is what had loved Shaw first. Her heart soon follows. Even Drinkwater becomes magnificent.

She tries to coax Henry Irving into producing the play, but he is cold and distant and says, "Brassbound is like *A Comic Opera*." "Ah, I feel so certain Henry just hates me!" [36] Moreover, he offers her nothing but minor roles in antiquated melodramas. She thinks of forming her own company and asks Shaw his terms for "Captain Brassbound." Perhaps she had a little forgotten about the bright, shiny steel mind. At any rate, his next love letter bristles with statistics like a lecture on political economy. It is clear that the knight-errant believes in economic determinism even in the magic fields of romance and intends to achieve his chivalrous rescue at a handsome profit. Her friends think his terms harsh? He put in three months' hard work on the play. Besides, he is hard up, having had the misfortune to inherit an Irish estate—"all mortgages and poor relations." [37] To be sure, his egotism is benevolent, aimed at her good as well as his own. He must tie her up by a contract that will make her act quickly for the greatest good of the greatest number. Submissive as always to his mind, she tries to see the matter as he does. Nevertheless, she is obviously pained and recalls rather pathetically the many good and generous things she knows he has done. Shaw is a little horrified at himself. "I love the sordid side of business," he confesses; and bitterly, "What people call love is impossible except as a joke (and even then one of the two is sure to turn serious) between two strangers meeting accidentally at an inn or in a forest path." [38] She decides against "Captain Brassbound" as not likely to make money.

And now at last the invisible lover becomes visible and vocal. They meet by chance at a rehearsal. "They say you could not bear me, when we met, that one time, under the stage," she writes; and again at the end of her letter: "But you cant abide me! And no wonder! Can I ever abide myself!" [39]

But of course he loved her—if for no other reason, out of sheer jealousy when she made a great success in "Alice-Sit-by-the-Fire," which Sir James Barrie had written expressly for her. She had gradually been breaking with Irving, and this play was a final factor in her emancipation, so that at the somewhat legendary age of fifty-six, the lady emerged at last from the ogre's tower; though whether she was rescued by Shaw or by Barrie or whether she simply walked out remained doubtful. And then finally in 1906, when Granville-Barker was making Shaw plays profitable at the Court Theatre, life at last joined with art, and she played Cicely. Now the lovers met regularly—on business. But palpability was a disadvantage, at least to the man:

> I came to see you at the theatre because I *must* accustom myself to meet you. At present, "old as I am, for ladies' love unfit," something wild happens inside me; and I have to look on gasping for

breath whilst an artificial G.B.S. talks to an equally artificial Miss Terry, the two minuetting on the carpet while we stagger in the immensities.[40]

Nevertheless, Ellen's heart was for the moment vacant, and Shaw quite naturally thought of becoming its tenant. Then one morning, when they were talking before rehearsals at the Court Theatre, the door opened, and James Carew, a young American actor, entered.

"Who is that?" said Ellen, looking at him with quick interest. "That's the American captain," I answered. Without an instant's hesitation she sailed across the room; put Mr Carew in her pocket (so to speak); and married him.[41]

The play became, first in America and then in England, a great popular success. But success in the theater, if only it lasts long enough, becomes ridiculous tragedy for the players. Shaw wrote after seeing "Captain Brassbound" at the end of its long run:

Look at poor Rudge Harding: he is absolutely stupefied by repetition. Jim's brain is visibly half gone: he holds on to the part as if nothing but the grimmest determination could save him from going mad on the spot. Drinkwater is the only one who keeps fresh; and he only sterilizes himself by boiling furiously from time to time.[42]

Ellen felt she never played Lady Cicely to Shaw's satisfaction. He reassured her but painted a very ironic picture of her triumph:

Now you have realized that you are Lady Cicely. Her history has become your history; and instead of trying to remember somebody else's words, you simply say what is right to say in the situation (which, by the way, is mostly much better than my dialogue) and there you have the whole thing alive and perfect. It is really a very wonderful performance now; and the others are not half good enough for you.

But this involves frightful consequences for yourself and others. It puts an end to your career as an actress, because never again will you be able to play another part. The public will never stand anything now except the real Ellen and the real Cicely.[43]

He was simply taking his revenge, no doubt, for her having lingered so long in the tower with her ogre, whom she loved after all, as captive maidens in fairy tales always do—if the truth were known. Her memoirs are full of him, while to Shaw she devotes only a mysteriously casual page or two which indicate that she understood him either profoundly or not at all. He is not, she says, to be taken seriously. He has no real convictions.

But perhaps Shaw did not take their romance so *very* seriously. At least, long before the chivalrous rescue was complete—he had married.

CHAPTER TWENTY-TWO

The Dramatic Critic

From 1894 to 1899, Shaw wrote dramatic criticism for Frank Harris's *Saturday Review*. No man has ever been better qualified for his work. He was already a good stage manager, an eminent dramatist, and a brilliant critic in the field of music. Surely three volumes of dramatic commentary from such a man would be priceless! And so they are, but they are also no better than the musical volumes. The wonder is not that they are no better but that he did not kill himself writing them, for he was leading several intellectual lives all at once during these years. In 1894, for example, besides all political, critical, and miscellaneous activity, he wrote three first-rate plays.

The dramatic criticism follows much the same pattern as the musical, emphasizing performance rather than composition and aiming at immediate effect rather than ultimate justice and basic truth. It therefore says less about Shavian drama than one might expect. Shaw is endlessly copious and communicative about secondary matters but somewhat reticent and contradictory about fundamentals. Like Voltaire, he is not easily analyzed. One must compile him. He hides in a blaze of light.

Most theaters, Shaw felt, are mere opium dens where people vulgarly escape from shabby realities into melodramatic dream worlds. He wanted to transform them into gay cathedrals where people might find deeper and purer realities than they are willing to face in life itself. All great dramatists have achieved this transformation—temporarily, at least. They are all therefore didactic—some fascinatingly didactic, like Shakespeare; others austerely, like Ibsen. All win a victory of will and discipline over illusion. "Great works in fiction are the arduous victories of great minds over great imaginations." [1]

But Shaw not only wanted theaters to be gay cathedrals, but gay cathedrals of reckless heresy and carefully chaste Victorian mirth. He felt that heresy rather than orthodoxy and decorum rather than vulgarity needed protection by the state. He wanted to give theaters much greater freedom to inculcate ideas and much less freedom to titillate the senses and arouse the baser emotions. He wanted them to be more decent and less "moral." They might take almost any liberty to explain an idea, but they must tolerate no unnecessary vanity, carelessness, or vulgarity, no unnecessary brutality of humor or insinuation of sex.

The result is that he commits all his indiscretions in heaven. He snubs Shakespeare severely for the "caddishness" of Mercutio and the swaggering cruelty of Petruchio and excuses himself for what many would consider the unpardonable blasphemies of Blanco Posnet. But in spite of his restrictive views, he does not believe in a censorship of the drama, nor does strict Shavian decorum prevent him from being sometimes rather savage and cruel and often wickedly and maliciously funny.

Shaw grants that an antagonism exists between art and social discussion. "Social questions are too sectional, too topical, too temporal to move a man to the mighty effort which is needed to produce great poetry." [2] On the whole, he declares for social discussion. Shakespeare is great because he is permanently moving and admirable. Ibsen is even greater because he has become in large degree outmoded by his very success in removing the abuses against which he wrote. Shaw looks forward with equanimity to similar success and obsolescence. This attitude is not so incongruous as it seems with his view that art is a religion, and the theater, a cathedral. In declaring that art should be a religion, one may mean that beauty should be exalted either for its own sake or for the sake of such social, ethical, or religious purposes as it may serve. The only art in which Shaw seems inclined to value an abstract and useless beauty is music, and even there he admires most a composer like Wagner who brings his work into closer and more practical relation to life. Beauty is holy when joined with utility. Transient beauty with utility surpasses lasting beauty without.

In his Preface (1909) to *Three Plays by Brieux*, he draws a distinction between the literary dramatist who "tortures" his audience by adhering to truth and nature and the popular dramatist who amuses it by combining sentiment and illusion with formulas and "technique." The literary dramatist penetrates through the multifarious, confused, contradictory surface of life to what is significant and real below. He ought also to attempt more deliberatly to cure his audiences of the romantic misconceptions about love, war, and murder which they have acquired from the popular dramatist. Shaw is of course thinking of how Brieux tends to counteract Sardou but even more of how he himself tries to counteract popular authors by his own plays.

But because the public loves illusion and commercial managers love money, popular dramatists compete with each other to produce the most marketable combination of illusion and vulgarity. At its worst, the modern commercial play becomes the spectacle of "a tailor's advertisement making sentimental remarks to a milliner's advertisement in the middle of an upholsterer's and decorator's advertisement." [3] Meanwhile, masterpieces like Ibsen's must wait years to be produced, depending on the chance that some courageous and genuinely artistic actor-manager may undertake them; and if such a production succeeds, it is apt, like Miss Robins's "Little Eyolf," to be bought out by a syndicate and made "fashionable" to the point of artistic disaster. Shaw presents his solution of the problem in the 1913 edition of *The Quintessence of Ibsenism*. There must be an endowed Ibsen Theater, specializing in Ibsen but accessible to all serious modern drama.

> Performances should be in the order of academic courses, designed to take audiences over the whole ground as Ibsen and his successors took them; so that the exposition may be consecutive. Otherwise the doctrine will not be interesting, and the audiences will not come regularly. [4]

The audiences are only too likely to come, but in what spirit? Shaw ought to have remembered what Nietzsche said about Bayreuth or even what he himself had said. In his utopian mood he is apt to read his own fanatical earnestness into mankind at large. There is something of the Auld Kirk in his New Theater and of the two-hour sermon in his "academic courses."

A sketchy and incomplete but very suggestive history of the drama may be found in Shaw. On principles of development, he is quite sound though perhaps somewhat mistaken in emphasis. Since drama reflects civilization, it evolves, like civilization, complexly on various levels:

> Everything has its own rate of change. Fashions change more quickly than manners, manners more quickly than morals, morals more quickly than passions, and in general, the conscious, reasonable, intellectual life more quickly than the instinctive, willful affectionate one. The dramatist who deals with the irony and humor of the relatively durable sides of life, or with their pity and terror, is the one whose comedies and tragedies will last longest. [5]

Thus, after ten or twenty years, a play begins to date when its manners and costumes go out of fashion. Then, if it is sufficiently excellent, it comes back into repute as a modern classic, like the comedies of Sheridan. After some centuries, it will again date in ethical conception. "Yet if it deals so powerfully with the instincts and passions of humanity as to survive this also, it will again regain its place, this time as an antique classic, especially if it tells a capital story." Such is now the position of Shakespeare's best plays. They are obsolete in their fashions and manners and in their ethical ideas but "still far ahead of the public as dramatic studies of humanity." [5] Unfortunately, as will be seen, Shaw gives this eminently sensible doctrine a rather narrow application, especially in the moral sphere, so that progress tends to become a desperate and interminable battle between coarseness and propriety, in which virtue triumphs and mankind ultimately mounts the gloomy heights of Victorian reticence.

The question of origins Shaw dismisses with one tantalizing sentence, which suggests the brilliant verbal and intellectual rhythms of his own work. "The drama was born of old from the union of two desires: the desire to have a dance and the desire to hear a story." [6] But the next sentence carries him clear to Ibsen. In general, after a very fleeting age of gold, recorded history begins with an age of lead—with the Elizabethans, whose rhetorical splendors inspire him to one of his most rhetorically splendid passages of invective. Shaw hates the Elizabethans because they are windy, lewd, bloodthirsty, and contemporaneous with Shakespeare. Jonson is a "brutish pedant"; Webster, a neurotic murderer of stage victims; and Marlowe,

> the true Elizabethan blank-verse beast, itching to frighten other people with the superstitious terrors and cruelties in which he does not himself believe, and wallowing in blood, violence, muscularity of expression and strenuous animal passion as only literary men do when they become thoroughly depraved by solitary work, sedentary cowardice, and starvation of the sympathetic centres. [7]

Because Shakespeare is a giant, Bardolators assume that his age produced nothing but giants. Because he has feet of clay, they account all Elizabethan clay divine. Shaw wants nineteenth-century scholars and critics to recognize clay when they see it, and to astonish them into proper discretion, he spatters clay all over several people of whom, under other circumstances, he would probably have been more respectful.

Shaw's principal grievance against Shakespeare is that he is a celebrated author long dead. As such, he is inevitably one of the chief towers of the literary Bastile. Shaw's treatment of the Bard is almost the opposite of his treatment of Ibsen. Ibsen was a new man universally abhorred; therefore Shaw never mentions his faults. Shakespeare was a dead man indiscriminately worshiped; therefore Shaw never forgets his. But he also concedes virtues. Sometimes he admires Shakespeare freely for unorthodox reasons; sometimes he condemns him utterly or declares him hopelessly inferior to Bunyan or Ibsen; but usually he does him justice between the lines. Basically, he regards Shakespeare as an unequaled genius imprisoned within a barbarous, utilitarian, and unsympathetic age; as a keen psychological thinker whose vast powers of lyric expression lull curiosity and blunt the critical faculty; and as a writer of immense literary ability and deficient literary conscience. Shakespeare always wrote spontaneously, often carelessly, and sometimes venally and supinely, for popular success—when he injected into a play only so much of his genius as to serve as a signature. In dramatic construction, he was unsurpassed but rapid and hasty. Such plays as "Julius Caesar" and "Othello" are brilliant improvisations. Luckily, Shakespeare was a born storyteller.

There are two extraneous factors in Shaw's criticism of Shakespeare. The negative factor is that from the scholars who "explained" him to the actors who murdered him, everybody prostrated himself before the Bard as before a golden calf. The positive factor is that even while piously intoning his praises, actor-managers inveterately chopped him up to make their own particular varieties of Shakespeare-goulash. Some of Shaw's soundest criticism is a resourceful and convincing defense of complete texts as the best acting plays. True, all that is Shakespeare is not gold. His witticisms are frequently tedious and his jokes lewd; his wisdom is often platitude and his rhetoric empty bombast. All this Shaw would cut in so far as it does not change the essential dramatic situation. The result is that he would cut the great plays little and cautiously, and the lesser plays, more and intelligently. When Sir Henry Irving and Ellen Terry produced "Cymbeline," Shaw outlined in his letters to her an acting version which involved drastic cutting.[8] On the whole, I should say that he very successfully eliminated bombast and preserved poetry.

Shaw finds the key to Shakespeare in his music. It is at once his greatest beauty and the medium of his most secret meanings. Only the sensitive ear can appreciate the power of his enchantment or trace the secret play of his feeling and the hidden niceties of his character delineation, which "owes all its magic to the turn of the line." [9] Sometimes the music is articulate with a precise and intelligent meaning, as in "Hamlet"; sometimes it is marred by "miserable rhetoric and silly logical conceits," as in "Romeo and Juliet"; sometimes, as in "Othello," it has little more to say directly to the intellect than orchestral music itself —the words are but "streaming ensigns and tossing branches to make the tempest of passion visible," as in the passage where Othello compares his "bloody thoughts" to the Pontic sea.[10] Only the musician in Shakespeare never sleeps or nods, and in some plays there is little but music to be enjoyed. It follows that for him proper recitation is peculiarly important. The elocutionist who carefully chops him up into elaborate prose assassinates him. The actor who does not declaim him in the singsong way, who fails to achieve clearness of diction, "beauty of tone, expressive inflection, and the infinite variety of nuance to sustain the fascination of the infinite monotony of the chanting," deprives him of his greatest beauty.[11]

As a psychologist, Shakespeare is very brilliant but very English. Shaw insists that he delineates chiefly the idiosyncrasies of human nature. What motives then are central? Apparently, those "which have produced the philosophy, the poetry, the art, and the statecraft of the world, and not merely those which have produced its weddings, coroners' inquests, and executions." [12] Shaw is here setting forth a triple indictment. Shakespeare's characters do not feel social responsibility; they are seldom great thinkers or artists; and though usually real people, they do not live real lives. Macbeth is an overexcitable hypochondriac buccaneering through a grisly and irrelevant melodrama. Othello is a romantic poet who exhibits stage jealousy and suffocates his wife. Hamlet has the Shavian recommendation of being a realist, but only in the restricted sense of his eternal self-criticism. He is too unhealthily preoccupied with his own problem to face those of the world: "he trips over the mistake which lies on the threshold of intellectual self-consciousness: that of bringing life to utilitarian or Hedonistic tests, thus treating it as a means instead of an end." [13] Shaw does not share Shakespeare's immense gusto for stage villainy. Villainy for villainy's sake is unrealistic. And in any case, Iago, the example par excellence, is such a combination of the coarse blackguard and the recondite philosopher of evil as will require more than scholarly explication to reconcile. In general Shaw's is of course the criticism of a humdrum and socialistic century upon an adventurous and irresponsible one. Statecraft did not include murder in the nineteenth century, but in the seventeenth it did. Ironically, the most melodramatic of all centuries was at that time being born right under Shaw's nose.

If, despite much incidental and implied praise, Shaw does something less than justice to Shakespeare the delineator of men, to the thinker he is much more unjust. He allows that Shakespeare has stumbled prematurely on a few Shavianisms, that he has made some of his women pursue men after the fashion of "Man and Superman," that he has shown us examples of feminine refinement which rise immeasurably above the groveling rudeness of his age, that he has written a problem play in "Hamlet" and some genuine "natural history" in "Troilus and Cressida." Beyond this, however, he has done nothing but turn the antiquated moral commonplaces of his time into magnificent poetry.

For Shakespeare's general outlook Shaw could hardly feel much

[198]

sympathy. He himself was a puritan socialist who combined a doctrinaire creed of serving his fellow men with an instinctive moral repulsion from the dirtiness of their lives. Shakespeare was a humanist who combined a belief in balance and moderation with such a tremendous appetite for life as brought him to the verge of agnostic hedonism. His lack of any definitely formulated faith or philosophy, his love for love's sake and villainy for villainy's sake, his early pride in himself as an artist and his late respectability as a country gentleman, his passionate sensualism and eternal iteration of the theme "Out, out, brief candle!" struck Shaw as shallow, supine, sentimental, and repulsive. And at the same time that he lingered nostalgically over impractical unanswerables, Shakespeare also swallowed whole the crudest contemporary prejudices. The vulgar success story of "Henry V," with its benighted patriotism and still more benighted moral snobbery, aroused Shaw's fiercest indignation. Unhappily, he felt an indignation nearly as fierce against "Julius Caesar," which wounded his most delicate political sensibilities. Its satire of demogoguery probably irritated the Hyde Park orator; its drastic political pessimism antagonized the Fabian idealist; its neglect of Caesar offended the author of "Caesar and Cleopatra," which he was probably writing when he produced his review of "Julius Caesar" in 1898. The sincerity of his admiration for the Roman conqueror may be measured by the intensity of his resentment against Shakespeare. In any case, he would grant Shakespeare no political philosophy.

Shaw's limitations as a Shakespearian critic were that he was more interested in a jolting paradox than a rounded estimate, more interested in the future than the past, and more interested in Shaw than in Shakespeare. He was always a better Shakespearian than he admitted, but he insisted on truths and excellences rather startlingly unfamiliar to late nineteenth-century Bardolatry. And as a revolutionary he could not praise a classic too much; nor could he, as a man of faith, grant preeminence to a skeptic. The consequence is that his criticism of Shakespeare, though brilliant and knowing, tends to be provincial, requiring that the Elizabethan meet Victorian and Shavian standards.

CHAPTER TWENTY-THREE

The Dramatic Critic (continued)

When, according to Shaw, a giant like Shakespeare or Michelangelo has realized all the possibilities of a certain art form, further progress becomes impossible until a new form has been invented. Audiences are always interested in novelty and in their own age rather than any other. They are more eager to see contemporary mediocrities than antiquated masterpieces. Unfortunately, playwrights often become fascinated with the success of their predecessors. They feel that because a great man has said everything that can be said in a certain way, infinitely more can be said in the same way, and so refine his style into ever greater artificiality until at length regeneration comes, as it always does, through realism and a renewed contact with life. Thus Shakespeare has been at once the glory and the bane of English drama. He long inspired it with the vain and mistaken ambition to surpass him and at the same time so debauched it with rhetoric that it did not sober up until the late nineteenth century. Shakespearianism at its most decadent and artificial became the heroic play, which represents theater gone to its logical extreme. It is staginess, theatrical illusion pure and undefiled—in other words, life as most people like to see it. That it should ever have been superseded, Shaw feels, is a miracle that encourages the most extravagant hopes for man's rational progress. Goldsmith and Sheridan he acknowledges as modern classics but objects to "The School for Scandal" because in setting up the good-natured libertine above the ill-natured formalist, it fails to meet late nineteenth-century moral standards.

In his Preface to *Three Plays by Brieux*, Shaw offers a sociological history of European drama. Molière performed the Marxian service of deflating the professions and satirizing the bourgeoisie generally, but instead of merely indicting social institutions and so filling his audiences with a practical hope of reform, he indicted human nature itself and made them cynical and desperate. The novels continued the battle. Accusing the middle class of "hideous sexual and commercial corruption," Dickens and Thackeray broadened the attack against them; and at length Zola tried to make it scientific by the curious expedient of introducing Jack the Ripper as a psychological curiosity into the bucolic simplicity of the *Bête Humaine.* Shaw then covers the same ground for the drama, rapidly skirting the intricate desert of the well-made play and concluding with the great victory of "scientific" realism over historical romanticism.

In *The Quintessence of Ibsenism* and *Our Theatres in the Nineties,* Shaw treats this "revolution" at greater length but chiefly with reference to England. He emphasizes the predominance of romantic melodrama on the nineteenth-century English stage and minimizes the native tendencies toward realism and naturalism exemplified by Robertson's "Caste" and Pinero's "The Second Mrs. Tanqueray." England was blissfully unprepared for Ibsen. The first performance of "A Doll's House" in 1889 burst upon an astonished nation with all the moral horror of a cannibalistic orgy upon an admirer of the noble savage. It is interesting that Shaw generalizes the struggle between realism and romanticism which unfolded during these earlier years of his artistic maturity into the central conflict of human life. His articles for *The Saturday Review* show him to have been a utilitarian not only because he believed that conduct should be guided by reason and utility but because romantic melodrama had inspired him with a genuinely eighteenth-century distrust of the imagination. He was fond of reckoning up how tremendously costly to morals and sanity two or three trite and high-flown situations can be. He was suspicious of all spectacular virtue. An action must not be heroic for fear it might be theatrical and the agent too much taken up with its imaginative splendor either to calculate its full moral consequences or even to understand his own motives.

On Ibsen, the dramatic articles from *The Saturday Review* add little to *The Quintessence of Ibsenism* except detail, and that principally for acting and production. One point, however, throws light on Shaw's own dichotomy between *Plays Pleasant and Unpleasant.* It is always desirable, he says, that art should please, but the pleasing function should never interfere with the teaching. A performance of Ibsen is frequently like a visit to the dentist—painful but beneficial. In such plays as "Widowers' Houses" and "Mrs. Warren's Profession," Shaw has turned simple extraction into a major operation. They make a pedagogical virtue of unpleasantness by sharpening it with a direct attack on the audience.

Toward his own contemporaries in England, Shaw was generous but critical. Of Wilde he speaks nearly always with respect, admiring his wit and facility though reprehending his want of heart, realism, and serious purpose. Indeed, the delicate satire of "The Importance of Being Earnest" is too cruel for Shaw. The popularity of Pinero and Jones among the "intellectuals" arouse him to stern didacticism. They are not genuine Ibsen but a very English combination of superficial revolt and fundamental conventionalism. He took them less seriously as he came more and more, during the years in which he wrote for *The Saturday Review,* to tower above them as a dramatist in his own name. Of the two, he greatly preferred Jones as a close observer and a conscientious realist. Pinero's characters are as stagy as his ideas.

The articles in *The Saturday Review* express views on stage production very similar to those on musical criticism. The first duty of the manager and the actor is to carry out the intention of the author. Failure to do so not only obscures the central meaning of the play but destroys the sequence of motives so that certain roles and situations become unintelligible. Here of course the greatest sins are those committed against Shakespeare. Sir Henry Irving's "Richard III" is a crude melodrama in which Ellen Terry is condemned to imbecility and everybody else to nonentity in order that Irving may shine in his own peculiar, un-Shakespearian way.

Of setting and costume Shaw requires: first, that they be authentic to the time and nature of the play; second, that they be, in so far as possible, pleasing and beautiful in themselves; and third, that they afford every opportunity to the actor. Shakespearian costumes need not be literally Elizabethan so long as they are beautiful but should not attempt to be Elizabethan and at the same time fashionable in the 1890 sense. A mere clothes or diamond exhibit, like painted-on character, is execrable. Medieval armor should not strait-jacket the actor, though, unhappily, modern evening dress inevitably does so—and not only physically but spiritually. Shaw hails with foresight and enthusiasm the modern tendency to simplify settings for Shakespeare. The speeches of Ariel and Prospero create the magic isle—and the shouts of the boatswain, the ship and the tempest—with a vividness which formidable stage machinery can only cheapen or contradict.

Though by introducing elaborate and epigrammatic stage directions, he had invented a new and novelistic kind of closet drama, Shaw felt that a play is not complete until it has been acted. The actor unlocks the silence of the printed page, and if he is to do this effectually, he must undergo a training scarcely less arduous technically, and much broader liberally, than that of the performing musician. He must make himself over, down to his most instinctive behavior, from a human being into an artistic medium. By relentless self-discipline, he must learn how to speak, stand, sit, walk, gesture, do stage business. He must understand his part, and above all, the meaning of the dramatist in its full intellectual and artistic implications. A great actor can be made only of a man with ambition, intellect, artistic endowment, and insight into human nature. Again, the actor or actress must possess the artist's temperament. Reviewing the career of Mary Anderson, Shaw says:

> Mary Anderson is essentially a woman of principle, which the actress essentially is not: the notion that all bravery, loyalty, and self-respect depend on a lawless and fearless following of the affectionate impulses—which is the characteristic morality of the artist, especially the woman artist of the stage—is, to her, simple immorality. The actress lives only to give herself away so that she may gain the love of the whole world: Mary Anderson, asking what it shall profit her to gain the whole world if she loses her own soul, retires or rather recoils from the stage before her apprenticeship is over, because she cannot gratify her love of Shakespeare and rhetoric without giving herself away to the public nightly to be stared at.[1]

The actress must have a sense not of privacy but of publicity. Finally, she cannot be trained mechanically, from without. She must be entrusted to the guidance of her artistic sense, but that must be "cultivated to such a degree of sensitiveness that a coarse or prosaic tone, or an awkward gesture, jars instantly" upon it.[2]

Vividness of expression, according to Shaw, is the highest quality of the actor. To be lifelike is nothing. "Unless an actress can be at least ten times as interesting as a real lady, why should she leave the drawing room and go on the stage?"[3] Most actresses act a little and dream a great deal; some make half a dozen "points" with great energy; and a very few, like Duse, are continually making points and uniting them into a general conception so expressive, so unified and natural, that they seem to be making no points at all. After expressiveness, Shaw prized formal beauty. An actress must not only get all possible meaning out of her part, but she must do so with the greatest melody of diction and symmetry of movement.

> Impersonations even of ugly or deformed creatures with harsh voices have the same artistic character, and are agreeably disagreeable, just as the most extreme discords in a symphony or opera are distinctly musical, and perfectly different to the random cacophonies which arise from the tuning of the orchestra.[4]

The actor should please, but never in the vulgar, inartistic sense. Histrionic sugar stick is the curse of the modern stage. In drawing the line between expression and artistic pleasure, Shaw favors the first, as one might expect. "Playgoers naturally murmur when something that has always been pretty becomes painful; but the pain is good for them, good for the theatre, and good for the play." [5] Nevertheless, he recognizes the limits of human endurance. Of Thorpe's Oswald Alving he writes:

> Since Miss Robins's memorable exploit in Alan's Wife we have had nothing so harrowing on the stage; and it should be noted, for guidance in future experiments in audience torture, that in both instances the limit of the victim's susceptibility was reached before the end of the second act, at which exhaustion produced callousness.[6]

Though he expected the actress to be an infinitely complex and self-conscious work of art from moment to moment, Shaw would not tolerate the faults of her virtues. She must seem perfectly natural and spontaneous. She may not be in the least strained or overstudied. Even Ellen Terry, who is ordinarily teacher's pet, receives a tart lecture for being too elaborately picturesque. It follows that Shaw despised all eccentricity and broad caricature. The stage valetudinarian particularly enraged him, and Sir Henry Irving's preposterously aged soldier provokes a whole essay of malignantly exact description, executed with the gusto of a veteran assassin. On the other hand, Shaw is capable of laughing at the successful violation of his own rules:

> I always give myself away to Mr Maude by laughing under the spell of his genuine comic force and impersonative faculty, though he shocks my critical pedantry unmercifully by his naïve incapacity for distinguishing between acting and clowning. He mixes up genuine strokes of character, executed with perfect artistic dignity, with the galvanic grins and knock-kneed attitudes of a funny man at a children's party.[7]

In an essay entitled "The Old Acting and the New," he gives a number of interesting glimpses into the theatrical past. From personal memory —which, by the way, does not agree with Ellen Terry's—he demolishes the legend that the old stock-company actor, with his stage-combat and routine lines of heavy and light, old and young, was a genius whose like will not be seen again. He also gives a brief history of Shakespearian acting, from the "mad bull" performances of Macready, through the "inhuman sublimity" of Barry Sullivan, down to the Victorian, somewhat sentimental "nobility" of Sir Henry Irving, who, while reciting fragments from the texts of Shakespeare, plays himself over and over again with magnificent dignity, loftiness of style, and purity of diction.

Unhappily, the Shavian theory of stage art was an austere Platonic

[204]

heaven infinitely remote from the low and vulgar variety show of late Victorian actuality. Its curse was that the Philistines who conducted it thought they could not overestimate the vulgarity and ignorance of the Philistines who patronized it. And on the whole they were right, Shaw felt. London audiences were largely devoid of artistic taste, ignorant of stage technique, eager for illusion and escape, and preeminent only in their thirst for morality and edification. They loved to wallow in piety almost as much as in sex and blood: "Mr. Wilson Barrett has found that he can always bring down the house with a hymn." [8] Furthermore, the Education Act was pouring into the theaters more and more audience with less and less taste. Nevertheless, Shaw did not entirely despair. In fact, he found his chief hope for improvement in the British craving for edification:

> If you speak in their hearing as the great men speak (which is easy enough if you happen to be a great man), then you will find that their specialty is self-torture, and that they are always hankering, in spite of themselves, after their own boredom and bewilderment, driven, probably, by some sort of uneasy hope that Ibsen or Wagner or some other gigantic bore may exorcise the devils which rend them. [9]

That the artist and not the public determines the quality and character of contemporary art, Shaw consistently maintained.

Apparently, however, too few English artists rose above their audiences. The Independent and New Criterion Theatres presented modern dramatists to small and select audiences who combined some taste and knowledge with a craving for "boredom and bewilderment." The Lyceum performed expensive rituals of Irvingesque Shakespeare to much larger audiences, many of whom went as they might go to church. Two or three other theaters were capable of competent execution, and the rest—was noise and vulgarity. The average manager felt that he was sure to produce a successful play if only he spent enough money, hired enough people, and scrupulously avoided brains. He created a world in which it was very difficult to become a great artist. The actor could find no adequate training to replace the old apprenticeship system. He had not the incentive of wealth; for if he was competent, he could hope for only three to five pounds a week; if he was first-class, for only eighteen to twenty-five; and in any case he would have to reckon on six months' unemployment. He could not look forward to any particular prestige or standing, because his profession had not yet distinguished itself for intellect, general education, or indeed for average integrity.

Again, the actress had little opportunity to express anything but sex and little future to anticipate but that of opulent matrimony. If she was too clever and discriminating to throw herself heart and soul into silly and worthless plays, she was of course discouraged by managers, who wanted "brainless-susceptibles" capable of infinite sentimental emotion about nothing. And if at length she became brilliantly successful, she was doomed to be a clotheshorse who need never act but simply play herself in parts as tailor-made to fit as her gowns. In general, the English actress was amateurish and undertrained, lacking the smart drill of the American, the taste and artistic technique of the French, and the fine dramatic culture of the Italian, who was represented by the greatest of all—Eleonora Duse. And yet the miracles of genius are not to be prevented, even in England. A few, like Janet Achurch, Ellen Terry, and Forbes-Robertson, attained the first rank in stage art. It is interesting that, though he subjected actresses to the most rigid Victorian propriety on the stage, Shaw allowed them a good deal of sexual freedom off it. Great art requires broad experience.

Shaw the dramatic critic differs from Shaw the music critic very little except perhaps in a note of firmer authority. He can write on the drama with as much assurance as Beethoven on music. He understands his advantage perfectly and in "The Case for the Critic-Dramatist" writes a whole essay about it. The critic-dramatist, he maintains, has passed through a double experience. He has worked behind the scenes, and having endured the excruciating torture of seeing his own plays subjected to human actors and human managers, he understands acting and production far more acutely than the mere critic can. Further, he enjoys a double prestige. The actor-manager can no more help listening to him than the wedding guest could help listening to the Ancient Mariner. And the actors must listen to him—because he carries posterity around in his pocket:

> Some day they will reprint my articles; and then what will all your puffs and long runs and photographs and papered houses and cheap successes avail you, O lovely leading ladies and well-tailored actor-managers? The twentieth century, if it concerns itself about either of us, will see you as I see you.[10]

What it means to be a critic of the theater he has admirably explained. A critic must know the world and its ways as well as the stage and its technique. He must be able to take an actor apart and put him together again. He must be able to see objectively and to analyze what passes on the stage, and he must be able to describe and explain what he sees in a vivid and interesting manner. One must read Shaw's review of "Antony and Cleopatra" to see him take not an actor but a whole production apart and put it together, using paradox for forceps and epigrams

for magnifying glass.[11] He brilliantly fulfills not only his own requirements but an additional one perhaps equally important. He has the
puritan passion for perfection in others. A poor performer becomes
his personal enemy, to be pursued with malignant sarcasms until he
improves.

According to Shaw, the English theater got the kind of critics it
deserved. The majority were underpaid, undereducated, underexperi-
enced, ignorant of the fundamentals of stage technique, and capable of
little but the clever gossip which seems to say everything by saying
nothing. Nevertheless, a surprising number of critics rose to surprising
heights. William Archer was scholarly and thoughtful; Max Beerbohm
was spritely, acute, and brilliant; and Shaw himself was in my opinion
one of the greatest critics of the theater, as such, in English literature.
One must go back to Hazlitt for a comparable figure.

CHAPTER TWENTY-FOUR

Marriage

> Oh! Ellen, Ellen, did you really read You Never Can Tell? *could* anyone read it? It maddens me. I'll have my revenge in the preface.[1]

The most astonishing thing about "You Never Can Tell" is that it might be autobiographical. As the friends of Oscar Wilde recognized his dinner conversation in his comedies, so perhaps one may see in the outlines of this dazzling intellectual extravaganza the simple natural history of the Shavian animal. The scintillating sex duel of Valentine and Gloria may have transpired as the author wrote and the final victory of the heroine have been an inspired prediction of his own fate. The real Gloria would then of course be Miss Charlotte Payne-Townshend, who, though not beautiful and seductive, was at least green-eyed, Irish, and socialistic. Moreover—and what must in spite of all democratic scruples have struck the imagination of a congenital and involuntary snob—she had wealth and a quiet, aristocratic distinction of manner. Her past was not unlike Gloria's. With ladylike decorum, she had acquired several scalps from Dublin Castle and London society. At least once her heart had been touched, but in general a rational training had preserved her from the ultimate sentimentality of marriage. Finally, she renounced "society" and took the cautiously revolutionary step of associating with Fabians, so that late in the summer of 1896 she found herself, together with Charles Trevelyan, Graham Wallas, Charlotte Perkins Stetson, and Bernard Shaw, a guest of the Webbs at Stratford St. Andrew Rectory in Suffolk. Here it was customary to work furiously four hours each morning, ride bicycles furiously four hours each afternoon, watch Shaw repair bicycle tires in odd moments, and listen to him read his plays in the evenings.

> We have been joined [he wrote to Ellen Terry] by an Irish millionairess who has had cleverness and character enough to decline the station of life—"great catch for somebody"—to which it pleased God to call her, and whom we have incorporated into our Fabian

[208]

family with great success. I am going to refresh my heart by falling in love with her. I love falling in love—but, mind, only with her, not with the million; so someone else must marry her if she can stand him after me.[2]

"Millionairess" was an exaggeration. No doubt Shaw wanted to interest Ellen, and perhaps in spite of himself he had romanticized the Irish lady's money. But what happened?

The story begins rather like "You Never Can Tell" and ends rather like "Man and Superman." But even more, it is the comedy of a brilliant psychologist between two shrewd, unpretentious women, who look on with amused or exasperated omniscience while he blinds himself complexly with his own brilliance. He was always rather eager to believe what he wanted to believe, and having known very little of love in childhood, he was "a treacherous brute in matters of pure affection."[3]

Miss Payne-Townshend was very shy, very cautious, and very resolute in her freedom and independence. Probably Shaw made love according to the rational, self-analytical methods of Valentine, but apparently the fire of his heavy artillery was deflected by the natural armor of an unpretentious sincerity. After three weeks of Miss Payne-Townshend, he decides, with a sigh of relief, that she is practically impervious. Indeed he pays her the compliment of thinking her almost masculine. "The ideal woman," he explains to Ellen—and himself, "is a man; though women lie low and let that secret keep itself." She can delight in love, being finally independent of it. Hers is a "voluntary, artistic, willed (and therefore revocable) rapture."[4] Charlotte is invulnerable, and he is free to love without scruple—but not without danger, for though he does not know it, his own armor is already riddled with shot.

Back in London a week later, he announces quite lightheartedly that he has got so fond of his Irish lady that "it would be superfluous to fall in love with her."[5] Fatal words, by which so many men have unconsciously sentenced themselves to imminent matrimony. He sinks from depth to depth of fatuity—breaks off with an old love, listens gaily to the meaningful jests of his lady friends—and the wisest words he can write to Ellen are: "The truth is, she is a clever woman. She knows the value of her unencumbered independence."[6]

It is only when Charlotte has gone off on a trip to Ireland that he begins to realize his danger. For the first time in his life he feels the absence of one particular woman. For the first time he finds himself dreaming about marriage. He begins to write amusing letters to Miss Payne-Townshend and to invent desperate scruples to Ellen Terry. There are a thousand cogent reasons why he cannot marry. How could he possibly marry all that money? "Then," he complains to Ellen, "I should have ever so many hundreds a month for nothing. Would you ever in your secret soul forgive me, even though I am really fond of her and she of me? No, you wouldnt. Good." Besides, a genius is lonely. He must have the courage to be unhappy. "No, *I* shall never have a home. But do not be alarmed: Beethoven never had one either." Like Eugene, he will go fearlessly out into the night. And finally, he is terrified by the joys and comforts of conjugal bliss. In fact, he is afraid he might be accepted and afraid he might be refused. "No: I've no courage: I am, and always have been, as timid as a mouse. Really and truly."

Anyway, "she doesnt really *love* me." And yet she has fallen in love with *The Quintessence of Ibsenism*. "She got fond of me and did not coquet or pretend that she wasnt. I got fond of her, because she was a comfort to me down here. You kept my heart so warm, that I got fond of everybody; and she was nearest and best. That's the situation. What does your loving wisdom say to it?" Ellen's loving wisdom replies with some robust common sense:

> How very silly you clever people are. Fancy not knowing! Fancy not being sure! . . . One thing I am clever enough to know (TO KNOW, mind. . . .) It is this. You'd be all bad, and no good in you, if you marry anyone unless you know you love her. A woman may *not* love before marriage and really love afterwards. . . . *But a man should know.*

Poor man! He fancies the situation as intellectually complex as one of his own love scenes. The plain truth is that he is a bachelor of forty, desperately overworked and nervously exhausted. Moreover, the self-conscious method corrupts the sex duelist himself. Like John Stuart Mill searching for happiness, he evaporates love by analyzing it. Sometimes he is uncertain of the simplest facts, and sometimes he is appallingly certain of the most ingenious and complicated vagaries.

Besides, one must never forget that at this time Shaw was at the height of his epistolary passion for Ellen Terry. She was the most formidable kind of rival, competing on ground extremely favorable to herself. She was a woman whom all men admired and the acknowledged mistress of an art which Shaw loved and enjoyed. She was surrounded by all the magic of distance and unattainability and all the glamour of publicity and press suggestion. And Shaw, among other things, was an incurable romantic. In the midst of his perplexities about Charlotte Payne-Townshend, he writes to Ellen:

I hereby testify that I, G.B.S., having this day inspected a photograph of Miss E.T., have felt all my nerves spring and my heart glow with the strongest impulse to have that lady in my arms, proving that my regard for her is a complete one, spiritual, intellectual and physical, on all planes, at all times, under all circumstances, and for ever.[7]

His letters are sprinkled with such declarations, for which Ellen calmly reproves him.

The quiet, green-eyed lady returns from Ireland, and reading between the lines, one perceives that in his first delight he must have been swept off his feet, proposed, and been accepted. Then the reaction sets in: he is sick with the certainty of error. But perhaps for Charlotte's sake he should go forward. "Don't be a fool (sweet)," counsels Ellen. "Henry [Irving] married her he knew he didnt love, thought he ought to, and he had better have killed her straight off." Shaw must not break his heart in sadness, but he must "give up fooling"—and by "fooling" Ellen clearly means the habit of Valentinian philandering, of which apparently he cannot break himself even in the midst of a serious situation.

It's only because you are a boy, but it's not fair. It's horrid, and like a flirting girl who is more thoughtless, maybe, than wicked. But at 40 you ought to have felt the ache of dead-at-the-heart, the ache of it. I guess you have given it to this poor lady, and you couldnt do that if you knew the pain.[8]

Ellen counsels waiting, but overcome with remorse, he resolves to break completely. He will not linger about and starve Charlotte by sparing her and "seraphically renunciating."

And now, dear Ellen, she is a free woman, and it has not cost her half a farthing, and she has fancied herself in love, and known secretly that she was only taking a prescription, and been relieved to find the lover at last laughing at her and reading her thoughts and confessing himself a mere bottle of nerve medicine, and riding gaily off.

What else can I be to any woman except to a wise Ellen, who can cope with me in insight, and who knows how to clothe herself in that most blessed of all things—unsatisfied desire.[9]

But this apparel proves irresistibly becoming to Charlotte also. He is jubilant with having thrown himself forcibly out of her heart; he is once more uncompromised, untied, free—to throw himself forcibly back in again. He does. A week later Ellen writes with joyous and appropriate poetry:

> Oh I see you, you two, walking in the damp and lovely mist, a trail of light from your footsteps, and—I dont think it's envy, but I know my eyes are quite wet, and I long to be one of you, and I dont care which.
>
> The common usual things appearing so beautiful as you tell me. Yes, I know. It's a long time ago, but, praise be blessed, I'll never forget! Why you dear precious thing, if you are not as happy as she, you *are* wasting precious time. But you are happy, arent you? Tell me.[10]

There is still no talk of immediate marriage, but now the lovers settle down to further exploring of each other's character in a mood of secure and comfortable ownership. Being a man with a magnificent sense of publicity, he is fascinated by a woman with a deep sense of privacy:

> You wont see Miss T. unless she shews herself to you. She is, normally, a ladylike person at whom nobody would ever look twice, so perfectly does she fit into her place. . . . Perfectly placid and proper and pleasant. Does not condescend to be anything more. And takes it all off like a mask when she selects you for intimacy.[11]

All this speaks to a shy and secret sense of privacy in Shaw himself. He respects her instincts with the most delicate scrupulosity. When Ellen Terry suggests they visit her dressing room, she receives a tart little lecture on tact, which begins: "She is not cheap enough to be brought round to your room and *shewn* to you. She isnt an appendage, this green-eyed one, but an individual." [12] Though still generous and gracious, Ellen is hurt and refuses even to look through the peephole in the curtain at Miss Payne-Townshend. Shaw is not content with that, either: "If you dont look at her I will never forgive you. Oh, I cant explain; and you understand perfectly well. I want you to meet one another without any reference to me: I hate these contrived occasions." [13]

Charlotte learned to type, was initiated into the mysteries of Shavian shorthand, and became his volunteer secretary, having as her special task the translation of the plays from the tiny notebooks in which they were written to a first typewritten copy. Thus the situation continued for five months, until they foregathered with the Webbs and other Fabians for another spring holiday in the country. Living in the close intimacy under the same roof produced a second period of friction and an occasional return to the amenities of "You Never Can Tell," with sudden outbursts of savagery from the lady and a tendency to abrupt violence and affectionate insult from the gentleman. She called him a beast, a brute, and "the most self-centred man she ever met." [14] He responded by treating her as he would any other woman:

> I make it a habit when I get restless over my work to seize the nearest woman and squeeze all the breath out of her stays. She does not feel neglected under these circumstances, nor is she much scandalized after the first few shocks. And when she does anything for me I always have a stock of fantastic complaints to make of it which are much more interesting than if I insulted her with delicate acknowledgements.[15]

Nevertheless, Charlotte was vigorously preparing the sex duelist for domestication. She explained to him that he was not a man at all. He was that inhuman and unnatural monster of self-absorbed egotism—an artist. To the social idealist this truth, when it really sank in, was so wounding to his self-esteem that he could not speak of it at the time. Months later he wrote to Ellen: "That revelation of my self-centredness as a mere artistic machine was a shock; but now she says 'What a curious person you are!' or 'What an utter brute you are!' as the humour takes her; and we live an irreproachable life in the bosom of the Bo family." [16]

But the Bo family begins to conspire against him. When is he going to marry? As a Fabian he had frequently exulted in the Machiavellian skill and relentless finesse with which Sidney Webb had exerted pressure on liberal and conservative politicians. Now Shaw is himself the victim. He feels "hard and hellish" and speaks with irritation of "Miss P. T., Irish, shrewd and green eyed, finding everything 'very interesting'; myself always tired and careworn." [17] Characteristically, he seems to have been undermining marriage with Charlotte by undermining marriage in general. In a missing letter, he apparently denounces that ancient and respectable institution so scandalously that Ellen asks with some wonderment, "Is marriage such a wicked business . . . I wonder what you think could be substituted." [18] Shaw replies, "At present it is far better for two people who do not mean to devote themselves to a regular domestic, nursery career, to maintain a clandestine connection than to run the risks of marriage." [19] Ellen looks on with mixed feelings. Once she begins with some indignation, "Well, when they have all married you—" [20] but after mature reflection she declares simply, "Well, you two will marry. I've no settled opinions on such a subject, and I warn EVEN YOU not to express any, for you may chance to eat your words." [21]

But he had already uttered far more words and views than he could possibly eat: "I am at present scudding close reefed before a gale. Oh why wont women be content to leave their stars in the heavens and not want to tear them down and hang them around their necks with a gold ring!" And he continues:

> Why does their pleasure turn to pain and their love to hate without their knowing that it has happened? I will put an end to it all by marrying. Do you know a reasonably healthy woman of about sixty, accustomed to plain vegetarian cookery, and able to read and write enough to forward letters when her husband is away, but otherwise uneducated? Must be plain featured, and of an easy, unjealous temperament. No relatives, if possible. Must not be a lady. One who has never been in a theatre preferred. Separate rooms.[22]

The obvious implication is that he is suffering from Charlotte's desire to be married, from her education, and perhaps from her maddening restraint and gentility.

During the summer the houseparty periodically lost its masculine element to London. In the autumn, once more at full strength, it moved somewhat disconsolately to Wales. Ellen still inquires anxiously about "you two," and Shaw replies with the speeches of commanders dying at their posts amid clouds of shot and shell. Ellen answers with an idyllic picture: "Look now! You and Miss P. T. live in a fine house in the country and I will 'keep the Lodge'!"[23] His response is so ardent that she feels compelled to burn it at once, "for there's gas about this hotel and an explosion would detain me on my journey."[23] Charlotte was rightly concerned about Ellen, for Shaw's loyalty to the famous actress—as romantically sentimental and self-conscious in its way as Disraeli's attachment for Queen Victoria—was a very important factor in his life. Ellen herself is aware of the danger and scolds him soundly for writing improper love letters to ladies he has never met. Besides, it isn't practical:

> I dont believe you know the people you oughtnt to write to like that! And you'll get into trouble some day, and hurt some nice person very much. Why it even shakes me, just for one minute. Ah you stupid! But that's not you, I know, for you are a duck, of the best, and of the highest, and I love you. Whenever you have time to think, just throw your gratitude over Miss P.T. Make up your picture of life from material at hand, for God's sake, or you will miss it all. I see you working, working at those Plays. That's good, but dont forget to say thank you sometimes for the help and tending you are getting.[24]

Leagued together in the feminine freemasonry of the houseparty, Beatrice Webb and Charlotte Payne-Townshend doubtless theorized a good deal about G.B.S. as a lover, and being in a rather heavily Byronic mood, Shaw accepts their unfavorable views—particularly Charlotte's—

and blows them up into something portentously sentimental, which happens also to suit his own purposes:

> I am fond of women (or one in a thousand, say); but I am in earnest about quite other things. To most women one man and one lifetime make a world. I require whole populations and historical epochs to engage my interests seriously and make the writing machine (for that is what G.B.S. is) work at full speed and pressure: love is only diversion and recreation to me. Doubtless, dear Ellen, you've observed that you cant act things perfectly until you have got beyond them, and so have nothing to fear from them. That's why the women who fall in love with me worry me and torment me and make scenes (which they cant act) with me and suffer misery and destroy their health and beauty, whilst you who could do without me as easily as I do without Julia (for instance) are my blessing and refuge, and really care more for *everybody* (including myself) than Julia cared for me.[25]

Shaw's letters through the fall are missing, but he is apparently still recalcitrant, for on November 1 Ellen writes: "Do you remember what you said in your last note to me of Miss P.T.? Now you will not do anything of the sort. Oh, I'd like to PINCH you now and again. To *lard* you all over with pins, to— Nothing is devised finely cruel enough for you." [26]

But in the next couple of months he becomes much gentler and more appreciative. Perhaps the pressure on him to marry has relaxed. Charlotte herself has always been half reluctant to take the step. She also is independent and fastidious, and it is possible that something of her attitude may be seen in the Lesbia of "Getting Married" (1908). Lesbia is a conscientious objector to marriage. To enter into a contract which would not permit her a separate establishment and exclusive rights over her own person would be to violate her personal integrity: "I am an English lady, by which I mean that I have been trained to do without what I cant have on honorable terms." [27] Perhaps Charlotte felt the same way. In any case, she and her "genius" appear at this time to have come to an arrangement something short of marriage. It is clear that he shares the common weakness of stern puritan ascetics and is nearly as uxorious as Milton himself. Obviously, Charlotte has been making herself extremely agreeable. She pets him, types his manuscripts, buys tickets, runs all his errands for him, invites his Ellen as a house guest, and offers to accompany her to a banquet.

Then, perhaps with some malice aforethought, she went off with the Webbs on a tour of the world.

Whether Shaw was equal to his isolation will never be known, for in Rome Mrs. Webb received from Graham Wallas a telegram informing her that Shaw was seriously ill. Miss Payne-Townshend returned at once to London and went for the first time to the lodging in Fitzroy Square where he lived with his mother. There she found him, flat on his back, in a tiny, drafty, open-windowed bedroom-study, which hung in a crisis of disorder fully as acute as that of his own health.

Shaw was suffering the effects of what Nietzsche calls a very modern disease—the disease of overwork. For more than half a decade he had labored as coruler of the Fabian Society, drafted most of the Fabian pamphlets, given innumerable lectures, spoken and canvassed for socialist candidates in election contests, written two or three plays a year, and ground out volumes of musical and dramatic criticism. The consequence was that he had lived continually in a state of brain-pulverizing exhaustion. His whole correspondence with Ellen Terry is filled with the desperate cries of a man living habitually at the very edge of his mental endurance. And yet his appetite for life, his determination to be all that he could be, had driven him on. He would not give up his socialism or his plays, and he had needed his criticism to live. That a man so utterly worn out could write with so much freshness and sparkle is one of the miracles of inspiration.

Apparently his mind could triumph indefinitely over exhaustion, but his body could not. He had become a man of glass, whom the lightest blow might shatter. A too tightly laced shoe produced an abscess, which, when opened, revealed necrosis of the bone. In accordance with Lister's antiseptic treatment, which was then in vogue, iodoform gauze was after each dressing left in the wound, which of course did not heal. When Miss Payne-Townshend burst on the appalling domesticity of Fitzroy Square, he was tottering about, a feeble wraith on crutches, or lying in bed, as used up and neglected as one of the dusty papers on his desk. His mother, busy with her music lessons, seldom entered his room; the kitchenmaid came at intervals to lay a plate of lukewarm eggs on a pile of papers; and now and then a maternal uncle, a broken-down doctor dying of diabetes, appeared in a fantastically shabby costume to borrow the interest due to his pawnbroker and tell lengthy and irrelevant jokes.

Miss Payne-Townshend surveyed the situation. Shaw's abomination of dirt, like Bunyan's hatred of sin, proceeded from a youth of crime. The whole flat needed repapering, repainting, rebuilding; it was such a Balzacian study of chaos and ruin as only years of domestic defeat and paralysis could produce. Obviously, a man could not get well in it. She therefore at once took a house in Haslemere and proposed to carry him off to it. Shaw reflected gloomily on the consequences to Charlotte's reputation. And yet it was either the cleanly impropriety of Haslemere with her or the dirty rectitude of Fitzroy Square without her. Suddenly, he realized that for the first time in his life he thought more of someone else than of himself. They had become indispensable to each other. At the same time, her money was no longer a barrier, for the American success of "The Devil's Disciple" had netted him three thousand pounds. Therefore, putting aside with mysterious haste elaborate scruples against a ceremony and a law "somewhat less than five centuries out of date," Shaw proposed. Miss Payne-Townshend bought a ring and a license, and on June 1, 1898, they were married at the West Strand Registry Office.

At Haslemere, his wife hired a battery of nurses and began the work of restoring his health. A honeymoon might be thought a melancholy experience for a superman trapped by the machinations of the Life Force. But illness and a honeymoon together could not damp Shaw's spirits. He flirted with the nurses and tantalized his wife with exhibitions of daring on crutches. Venturing on some polished oak stairs, he came down with a clatter and broke his left arm. A little later, he mounted a bicycle, fell, and sprained the ankle of his sound foot. "I hope the dear arms and legs and things are intact," [28] wrote Ellen. But though his body remained tired and fragile, his mind regained tone and resiliency almost at once. While still breaking arms and spraining ankles, he dashed off *The Perfect Wagnerite*, and since it dealt with a Shavian divinity, proposed to his publisher that it be got up pocket-size in mother-of-pearl and Russian leather, like a book of devotion. Thereupon he plunged into "Caesar and Cleopatra," which he had been planning for a long time— and so achieved the ultimate Shavianism of writing against romantic love on his honeymoon.

Even so, he lived happily ever after.

CHAPTER TWENTY-FIVE

A New War and a New Century

"You may demand moral courage from me to any extent," said Shaw, "but when you start shooting and knocking one another about, I claim the coward's privilege and take refuge under the bed. My life is far too valuable to be machine-gunned." [1] It is extremely doubtful that Shaw ever pursued this policy—and especially during the *Blitz* of 1940. If he did, he certainly dived under the bed oftener and remained there longer than he ever expected to as a young socialist. In any case, he has done an extraordinary amount of very dangerous talking from a very dubiously safe position. What he said is important. Now it becomes doubly important—and for a double reason: the world is faced with the problem of another international settlement, and one of the principal nations concerned is dominated by a party whose policy Shaw, together with other Fabian leaders, has been largely responsible in forming.

Most people lose the real Shaw in the wit and the white whiskers. They are incredulous that a striking feature of his politics—international as well as domestic—is their cautious realism. The truth is that he is an Irishman from the wit outwards. His politics are inveterately English. In the *axiomata media* which Walter Bagehot called the peculiar ground of politics Shaw is hardheaded, shrewd, and generally consistent, as in fundamentals he is jaunty, somewhat frivolous, and effervescently logical. On the nature of God, he is quite unreliable. On the future of the British Empire, he is surprisingly sound. Altogether, he is a strange combination of Voltaire and Sir Robert Peel. We shall see that, so far as international affairs are concerned, his conception of political motive tends steadily to be Benthamite or Marxist with aristocratic qualifications. The economically powerful follow their own economic self-interest —and usually attain it. The masses are ruled sometimes by self-interest but much more frequently by illusion, through which they are victimized and manipulated. Nevertheless, Shaw's discussion continually implies the efficacy of other motives—intellectual, religious, national, and psychological. Wars are brought about not only by capitalistic imperialism but by human pugnacity—in other words, by aggressive nationalism. Yet as a rationalist and a man without a country, Shaw tends steadily to despise this motive and to underestimate its force. "Patriotism is, fundamentally, a conviction that a particular country is the best in the world because you were born in it." [2] Though keeping always in view the possibility of Marxist revolution, he tends as a Fabian socialist to emphasize continuity and evolution, tradition, and habit. Wars are not followed by millenniums of brotherly love but by situations which lead to other wars. Heterogeneous and discordant nations can no more be welded into a permanent league by a paper covenant than a democracy can be so created out of a despotism.

Shaw made his first extensive study of world affairs in 1899, when he was ordered to think about them by the Fabian Society, of which he was then literary expert. It was during the golden age of modern imperialism. For two hundred years, conquering the world had been a business with the English. Now it was becoming a modern business, with sensational press campaigns and stocks and shares on 'Change. Pursued by its Marxian dilemma of overproduction and underconsumption, led by its twin heroes of enterprise and abstinence, British capitalism was reaching out everywhere for new markets—to India, Egypt, South Africa, South America; and industrial civilization was following the pound into many a remote corner of time and space. The nineteenth century was growing up triumphantly in the midst of the fifteenth or the first or of the ages before history began. Sometimes the process was a little puzzling to the natives, but it was always exciting, and usually profitable, at home. The white man bore his burden—and clipped his coupons.

But other white men were envious. After 1870, Germany loomed ever more darkly on a previously bright Victorian horizon. The second most numerous people in Europe, the Germans seemed peculiarly fitted for the grim age which was to follow. Aggressive and energetic, yet docile, patient, and industrious, they apparently could labor more happily than the individualistic British under the close regimentation of modern industry and the strenuous, often dehumanizing discipline of modern factual research. In time of war, their scientists could be ordered to think and discover in regiments. Moreover, in superlative degree German philosophers had elaborated, and German leaders practiced, the new ethics of power. Perhaps even in the happiest ages right follows might—though at a decent interval. Nietzsche would have the two march proudly abreast, and Bismarck found the arrangement very efficient. Thirty-five years of comparative peace had taught England to think war very nearly impossible. In 1870 the abyss opened. Two of the most civilized nations in the world fought a catastrophic war in the heart of Europe. Victorian cynicism and insecurity after 1870 were not due simply to boredom and dissatisfaction with Victorian civilization. The British had awakened from a dream.

Entrusted with the task of translating Fabian opinions into effective pamphlet form, Shaw began to think internationally within the limits of the Fabian tradition—as a socialist who aspired to bring about revolutionary changes by an evolutionary and constitutional process. The immediate occasion for his services was the outbreak of that classic struggle of capitalistic imperialism—the Boer War. It was an embarrassing event for the Fabian Society. Half of them wanted to show they understood Marx by disapproving of it. The other half, headed by Shaw and Sidney Webb, wanted to follow the Society's traditional policy of ignoring all issues not directly connected with socialistic reform at home. The dispute, carried on amid the excitement of an approaching election and a war frenzy which only a developing yellow press could create in an age of innocence, was sharp and bitter in the extreme and led to several resignations from the Society, including that of Ramsay MacDonald, who was pursuing the same critical, pacifist policy which was to make him so hated in 1914. The remaining Fabians moved gradually toward a moderate position and at length decided to formulate their ideas in a pamphlet, the drafting of which was as usual entrusted to Shaw.

The task was one of terrifying delicacy. There were then eight hundred Fabians and nearly eight hundred shades of opinion about what the *Tract* should contain. How could vigor and decision be injected into anything that must satisfy such diversity? Shaw labored for three months, and then the first draft was sent to every member of the Society for comment. Though the majority approved, no less than 134 returned criticisms. Shaw achieved prodigies of verbal and logical adjustment, and at the next meeting all but fourteen voted for the pamphlet. It was published late in 1900. It pleased few besides the Fabians themselves, being too generous to the Boers for the warmongers and too imperialistic for most socialists, and particularly the I.L.P., who were following MacDonald's lead.

The Fabians were justly pleased, for under their close supervision, Shaw had produced an able and on the whole statesmanlike adaptation of Fabian ideas to imperial problems. The basis of his argument is an attack, in the name of efficiency and progress, on the principle of absolute sovereignty. A few great powers, he says, are destined more and more to rule the world, together with its trade and resources. Until a global federation is achieved, the great imperial federations are the most practical substitutes. They must govern in the interests of civilization as a whole. Isolation, especially for small states, is no longer possible. A nation has no more right to do what it pleases in its own territory than an individual on his estate. It must regard the best interests of its neighbors or submit to their interference. If China refuses to grant other nations the international rights to trade and travel within her borders, then those nations may force her to do so. This does not mean that weak countries should be steam-rollered because they are weak, any more than they should be preserved because they are romantically nationalistic. Moreover, if Englishmen have a right to trade with and travel in China, then the Chinese have a right to emigrate to Australia. Australian labor must find its protection in a minimum wage guaranteed by the state.

Superior armament does not confer moral rights on a great power, but greater efficiency and superior civilization do. Germany is a formidable rival. England will remain a great power only if she becomes calmer, more clear-sighted, more efficient and civilized. Her institutions need drastic reform. There is no genuine democracy in England because there is no rational and educated electorate, no acknowledged aristocracy of ability. The country is ruled by two plutocratic cliques—the Liberals and the Conservatives, who both represent the same restricted class. The newspapers support that class because they are owned by it. The masses vote for it because they receive wages from it.

Imperial administration must be improved, expanded, liberalized, rendered more flexible. The Consular Service needs more technical experts. It must be made less sensitive to private, and more sensitive to public, interests—especially if the causes of war are to be reduced. India should be given a greater measure of self-government. English institutions should not be imposed on her wholesale but native institutions studied and understood, so that they can be adapted to the requirements of progress. South Africa is a more complicated problem. The Boers should be granted self-government as soon as possible, but the Negroes should be placed under imperial protection. The gold fields also should not be left in the possession of a small frontier community but be made international or imperial property. The war was a terrible mistake, which the government never intended.

This *Tract* also contains, apart from "Arms and the Man," Shaw's first attack on militarism, which he satirized and vituperated for nearly fifty years. Army life hides torpor, inefficiency, and injustice under the dark cloak of brutality. The Army grossly underpays its men and suppresses any revolt with savage punishments. Officers obtain obedience not by the moral virtue of genuine leadership but by the deadening tyranny of military discipline. Hence they are obeyed everywhere except on the battlefield. They will be obeyed there only when their men are better paid and better treated. Obviously, this criticism contains much truth, for in most civilized countries army life has since become infinitely more human, its discipline infinitely more humane, and even its pay—a little higher. Shaw's criticism fails in its romantic individualism.

It discounts the military value of rigid training and habit, which, besides being necessary to the coordination of large bodies, sometimes carry a man through the extremities of peril when courage and presence of mind have failed. To be sure, Shaw appeared at the time to have the facts on his side. The Boer War seemed fought to prove regular armies unnecessary. It was a prolonged skirmish in wild country between frock-coated marksmen led by natural generals and trained regulars led by parade-ground generals whom no amount of training could have made clever and resourceful. Shaw advocated a national militia on the Boer model.

Returning to general policy, he declares that England can never hope to hold her Empire by force. Therefore, she should allow white colonies their political liberty, establish an Imperial Council, and attempt to lead not according to her own interests but those of the world. Membership should guarantee certain constitutional rights and such organization of capital and labor as to result in the highest minimum standard in the world. Exclusion from the Empire would then be regarded as a penalty. Above all, England must not, like Rome, allow capital and industry to go abroad while giving *panem et circenses* to the people at home. Free trade must be maintained, and essential industries unable to meet foreign competition must be nationalized. England must have the intelligence and generosity to become socialistic.

In its treatment of international affairs, socialism has tended to be either idyllic or cataclysmic. Shaw's contribution in "Fabianism and the Empire" is that he is cautious and practical. World peace and world order will be achieved neither by a utopian movement of universal brotherhood nor by a Marxian revolution of the international proletariat but by the continued growth and improvement of such vast political organizations as the British Empire. Moreover, mere military science will not triumph. There must be general efficiency, higher civilization, greater social justice. Thus foreign policy is largely domestic policy. The vast problems which loom at the horizon pose a very prosaic solution at our doorstep. The Empire must be fabianized.

Mr. H. G. Wells, criticizing this tract from the Olympian omniscience of 1934, condemns it as an example of that limited rule-of-thumb practicality which prevented the Fabian mind from seeing beyond the parish council in great affairs. "Fabianism and the Empire" does lip service to the conception of a world state, but it is "the contemptuous lip service of men convinced of their own superior common-sense." [3] There is undoubtedly truth in these observations. Moreover, written at the ominous close of a long period of peace, the pamphlet shows no perception of what was to follow. War is "a costly and intolerable nuisance," which nations should have the "good sense" to suppress.[4] Yet even after two terrible wars which at that time Shaw failed to foresee, our uneasy hope lies still in persuading the great powers that they have less and less to gain and more and more to lose from war, tyranny, and injustice.

To his scheme for making the Empire a Fabian utopia which small countries would be eager to join, Shaw added in 1906 a grandiose Wellsian touch. He proposed that railway and ocean transit be nationalized and made free in the interests of imperial unity. Coming in the midst of several shrewd and statesmanlike writings, *Fabian Tract No. 116,* which combines this futuristic and breath-taking proposal with a subtle and brilliant criticism of Chamberlain's tariff policy, is a clear indication of why Shaw could never aspire to a political career in the country of Sir Robert Walpole and Sir Robert Peel.

CHAPTER TWENTY-SIX

Plays for Puritans

In 1898 Shaw published his first seven plays in two volumes, as *Plays Pleasant and Unpleasant*. In 1901 he published *Plays for Puritans*, which included "The Devil's Disciple," "Caesar and Cleopatra," and "Captain Brassbound's Conversion." The *Unpleasant Plays* are chiefly realistic satires of capitalistic society. The *Pleasant Plays* are intellectual comedies attacking the romantic conceptions of war, heroism, love, and marriage, and setting up realistic conceptions in their place. *Plays for Puritans* are satiric melodramas or romances, greatly amplifying both the positive and the negative positions of the previous volume. They attack romanticism by inverting one of its most characteristic genres and imply that its evils are in large part to be traced to the theater. They exalt the Shavian puritan dedicated to work and action and ridicule the romantic hero dedicated to love and conventional heroics. They ridicule the romantic and conventional irrationalities of vengeance and legal punishment and emphasize the sudden benefits of unforeseen conversion or education. They set forth with particular clarity the central Shavian conflict between realistic vitalism and dead, unreal convention. In each play, as Mr. Bentley points out, love is introduced upon the stage only to be snubbed and ignored; in each play a vitalist hero opposes artificial system and melodrama and at the same time educates another character to vitalism. This education constitutes the inward action of the play.

In his Preface Shaw analyzes the theater and its audience at length. Managers assume that people go to plays chiefly to gratify their sex instinct. But the stage cannot represent sexual love frankly, nor can it compete with the music hall in titillating exhibitions of the female anatomy. Therefore it has developed the melodrama, or romantic play, which carefully keeps love off the stage but alleges it as the motive of every action presented to the audience. The hero makes his fantastic sacrifices and performs his impossible rescues only for love of the heroine. Yet, Shaw says, the newspapers tell us every day of lives saved and risked quite disinterestedly by total strangers, whereas what men and women do for love is recorded in the statistics of the homicide bureau.

Though continually fed romance, audiences do not really like it. Most romantic plays fail. But while no two people have the same dreams or the same preferences in sentimental heroines, everybody is interested in significant ideas, which are the proper subject of the drama. Shaw calls on the spiritual descendants of the old puritans, who rescued the theater before, "when its foolish pursuit of pleasure sunk it in 'profaneness and immorality,' "[1] to do so again by setting up a serious drama of ideas. For unlimited melodrama will eventually create a melodramatic taste and a melodramatic conception of life. He sums up with a puritan's prophecy of a melodramatic day of wrath:

> When it comes to that, the brute force of the strong-minded Bismarckian man of action, impatient of humbug, will combine with the subtlety and spiritual energy of the man of thought whom shams cannot illude or interest. That combination will be on one side; and Romanticism will be on the other. In which event, so much the worse for Romanticism, which will come down even if it has to drag Democracy down with it.[2]

The remaining two sections of the Preface deal with diabolonian ethics and with Shakespeare. Of the first Shaw says relatively little, merely observing that as Bunyan had shown that there was a way to hell from the gates of heaven, so Blake showed that from the gates of hell there was a way to heaven. The Preface to "The Shewing-Up of Blanco Posnet" explains this more fully. All morality begins as immorality and becomes solidly moral only when it already acts as a dead weight and a superstitious barrier to innovation. Therefore progress is immoral and revolt a virtue absolutely vital to man's salvation. In this cosmology, the devil may handsomely qualify as the Messiah of the Life Force. Shaw's diabolonianism is progressive and evolutionary, and his superman, as puritanical, efficient, and up-to-date as his diabolonianism.

"The Devil's Disciple" is a hair-of-the-dog cure for melodrama. It uses practically every stock trick for melodramatic suspense and "love interest" in order to drive home rational and antimelodramatic lessons about human life. And yet it is even so a moral melodrama. It is also a play both for and against puritans. In declaring moral and theological war against his mother and all she represents, Dick Dudgeon is a natural ascetic in revolt against an unnatural ascetic, a Shavian puritan in revolt against a conventional puritan, whose ethics of self-denial have turned her into a monster of envy and hatred. As a puritan Dick is impressive, but as a diabolonian he is a little tame. He does not believe in God enough to be a real devil-worshiper. He is a more active and humorous, less speculative and wrathful William Blake, who smuggles instead of writing poetry. His diabolonianism has little effect on him, except to bestow a gay cynicism on his moral views and a sinister Chesterfieldian polish on his manners.

"The Devil's Disciple" is founded on the conception that true character reveals itself in crisis. The play is genuinely melodramatic in that it contains two violent conversions. It is satirically melodramatic in that one conversion appears utterly unheroic and the other is utterly unsentimental. The chief incident is apparently based on Potts's tale to Captain Rogers in Charles Lever's *A Day's Ride*. British troops have entered the New Hampshire town of Websterbridge, and their commander decides to hang Anthony Anderson, the rebel minister. But the sergeant arrests Dudgeon by mistake. Confronted by the crisis, Dick finds himself mysteriously unable to endanger another life than his own. When Judith, the minister's pretty and romantic wife, suggests that he is motivated by a secret passion for herself, he confesses that he has not sacrificed all for love but, quite simply, all for nothing. His disinterested heroism is set off against both the sentimental ethics of romance and the disciplinary ethics of conventional religion. Dick certainly performs an act of self-denial, yet he applies no code of morals, recognizes no duty, expects no heavenly dividends, undergoes no struggle, and exercises no cramping compulsion on impulse or desire. One need look no further to see that Shaw feared formalism infinitely more than license, and suppression infinitely more than chaos. He is willing to trust to any intuition rather than interpose so much as the Ten Commandments between it and himself. He carries his puritanism to the logical extreme of sacrificing logical integrity to ethical immediacy.

Dick's action is an impressive assertion of human dignity. Yet that dignity is possible, and man is what he is, largely because of self-discipline and the corporate and inherited self-discipline which is civilization. It is not the moral thunderstorms but the steady moral climate which has made civilized human nature. In glorifying the product while deprecating its cause, Shaw is close to moral melodrama.

As Dudgeon is naturally ascetic, Anderson is naturally worldly and practical. He returns from his visit to find Dick gone and his wife in a faint. With some difficulty, he gets the truth from her. Its effect is a lightning conversion in which the mild parson is transformed into a resolute and aggressive soldier. In a whirlwind of martial wrath and efficiency, he rushes off for help. Concluding that he has run away, his wife transfers her affection to Dick. That the minister should explain nothing to his wife and that she should so quickly assume the worst of him are improbabilities which the vehemence of the conversion and the rush and hurry of the action only partially conceal. One might also question whether the most likely way to rescue a man from hanging in one's stead is to rush off, gather an army, take one town, and threaten another. But perhaps one should not look too closely into even the best melodrama, which Shaw declares is the hardest of all drama to write.

Judith, the minister's wife, is a pathetic little figure who suffers much so that Shaw may subtilize further on the futilities of duty. Seeking always to clear up the mistaken identity, she aims, like Dudgeon, at self-sacrifice, but she attempts to sacrifice herself conventionally, by acting against her personal inclination and according to her sentimental and heroic illusions—and so involves herself in one ridiculous and excruciating paradox after another. I confess I think she stands in need of a mind more than a philosophy. At the end of the play, her faith restored, she returns with tranquil, childlike trust to the protective love and care of her husband, who, by the way, in spite of Shaw's sex and marriage theories, is a kind of father-man, or male Candida.

The trial and gallows scenes are magnificently Shavian in their rapidly shifting comedy and tragedy and their complexity of tension and implication. Here we are introduced to another romantic conventionalist. Major Swindon is an Englishman who wishes to do his duty. Unhappily, his duty includes a travesty of justice involving legal murder. The central conflict is that between the Major, who wishes to make a desperate military measure solemn and dignified, and Dick Dudgeon, who wishes to show it as the murderous act of venal hirelings. Since Swindon has no brains, Dick wins an easy victory and has plenty of time for Sheridan-esque exchanges with General Burgoyne, who is visiting local headquarters. The General is an artist, a thinker, and a man of action, whose generous realism is limited only by his aristocratic prejudice and his sense of gentlemanly good taste. When Dick's attack on King George's minions becomes blunt and vulgar, Burgoyne loses sympathy—but never his temper. The play winds up to a typically melodramatic conclusion. Dick is condemned, marched to the gallows, bound, and placed on the cart with the noose round his neck, when Anderson gallops up to save him and explain he is himself by nature a soldier and Dick by nature a priest.

"The Devil's Disciple," acted as straight melodrama, became an ironic success:

> The critic who discovered a romantic motive for Dick's sacrifice was no mere literary dreamer, but a clever barrister. He pointed out that Dick Dudgeon clearly did adore Mrs. Anderson; that it was for her sake that he offered his life to save her beloved husband; and that his explicit denial of his passion was the splendid mendacity of a gentleman whose respect for a married woman, and duty to her ab-

sent husband, sealed his passion-palpitating lips. From the moment that this fatally plausible explanation was launched, my play became my critic's play, not mine. Thenceforth Dick Dudgeon every night confirmed the critic by stealing behind Judith, and mutely attesting his passion by surreptitiously imprinting a heart-broken kiss on a stray lock of her hair whilst he uttered the barren denial.[3]

In 1909 Shaw rewrote "The Devil's Disciple" in "The Shewing-Up of Blanco Posnet." Blanco Posnet revolts against the Wild West of the nineteenth century instead of the New England of the eighteenth. He is a Dick Dudgeon fifteen years further gone in disrepute and bad habits, with a mouth now only fairly resolute and eyes showing the fire of incipient delirium tremens. Developed perhaps from a hint in Butler's *Erewhon*,[4] he is a not unfamiliar combination of the diabolonian and the bad boy, defying God and goodness because they belong to pious hypocrites and Sunday-school weaklings. Blanco tries to be a bad man—hard and rough and tough. He is therefore ashamed of any involuntary display of goodness and secretly afraid that God, who is a Sly One, will trap him into an exhibition that will show everybody that he is a softy. And He does. Like Nikíta in Tolstoy's "Power of Darkness," Blanco is caught off his guard through a child. Having "taken" his brother's horse in payment for a debt, he meets a woman whose sick baby desperately needs a doctor. He gives her the horse and so allows himself to be caught as a horse thief. The trial scene is full of echoes from "The Devil's Disciple." Blanco is finally exonerated when a prostitute, who hates him, is moved by the recital of his virtuous act to give false testimony; and again like Nikíta, Blanco is converted by the spectacle of goodness in a disreputable character. He concludes the play with an impromptu sermon explaining his spiritual history, which suggests that his dissipations have left him time to imbibe a good deal of the creative evolutionism of Samuel Butler.

The play is a curious combination of Robert Service with ideas and "Caliban upon Setebos" with intelligibility. The conceptions of God, grace, and conversion are crudely and sentimentally melodramatic in the worst vein of decadent puritanism, and Shaw wrote to Tolstoy that it "might be played in a mining camp to the roughest audience."[5] As a matter of fact, it must inevitably be disagreeable to any kind of audience. It repels believers by its blasphemies and unbelievers by its theology. And Shaw's Wild West is an appalling combination of good English and bad characters. Black Bart himself would have trembled to set foot in it.

Like "Mrs. Warren" many years before, "Blanco Posnet" was forbidden the stage, and shortly after, the whole question of the Lord Chamberlain's censorship was investigated by a select committee of Parliament. Together with other eminent playwrights and actor-managers, Shaw was summoned before the committee and shook it from its monocles and top hats right down to the extremities of its boots and umbrellas by presenting it with a statement previously referred to, maintaining that immorality needs protection far more than morality. Naturally, in an inconspicuous passage he distinguished very carefully between immorality and murder, theft, and other deviations from normal behavior which could not possibly result in benefit to society. Eventually the committee proposed an elaborate reform which left everything precisely as it had been. But Shaw had the last two thousand words in the formidable Preface to "Blanco Posnet." It is episodes like this which almost make one wish that Shaw had followed other great Irishmen into Parliament and so created another legend by attacking the windmills of British dullness, with which Sheridan had jousted so brilliantly and Burke so heroically and magnificently.

"Caesar and Cleopatra" is antiromance and anti-Shakespeare. It is introduced by the section of preface entitled "Better than Shakespeare?" in which Shaw contrasts it with "Antony and Cleopatra," which, he explains, puritans cannot but despise as the acme of romantic nonsense, for there Shakespeare uses his enormous powers of language and pathos to make debauchery heroic and the derelicts of the pothouse sublime personages by whom the world seems well lost. Shakespeare could not portray a great statesman-commander because he could not get beyond the conception of the gentleman, or knight. What makes Shaw's remarks interesting is the opposition implied between the *preux chevalier,* whom the fanaticism of personal honor and the spirit of self-sacrifice drove to destruction, and the superman, whom genius and the highest intimations of the Life Force guide to the farsighted construction of history. Like most puritans, Shaw tended to be a democrat and an equalitarian, but like most puritans in a heroic or desperate mood, he was attracted to drastic remedies. The superman became inevitable when, in terms of the democratic process, socialism ceased to be so. Shaw was not altogether unwilling to sacrifice democracy to the right kind of Bismarck, and in Professor Mommsen's Caesar, though distant two thousand years backward in time, he thought he had found the right kind.

The plot is simple. Under circumstances of great poetic beauty, Caesar encounters Cleopatra; she exerts all her charm on him and—he becomes preoccupied with business and forgets about her. In so far as he thinks of her at all, he does so as a schoolmaster and a politician. And yet Shaw manages to eat his romance and have it too. Though his play bristles and bustles with prosaic realism, he manages to cast over the meeting of his principal characters something of the heroic nostalgia of two great destinies approaching each other, running side by side, and then parting—each for its own separate eternity of fame.

Like the other two *Plays for Puritans*, "Caesar and Cleopatra" contains a puritan and deals with vengeance and legal punishment. It is also the example, par excellence, of that kind of Shavian intellectual drama in which a realistic and static schoolmaster disillusions and instructs a romantic and developing pupil. Many critics have called attention to this pattern in Shaw, nor is one surprised at its frequency. It is as old as instruction itself. Mentor and disciple represent the basic conditions of the classroom as truly as narrator and chorus represent the basic conditions of early Greek drama. Plato translates didactic dialogue into comedy and irony; Shaw, into comedy and romance.

Interest centers in the character of Julius Caesar. Doctrinally, he represents a further development in the author's conception of military and political leadership. Psychologically, he is an idealized picture of Shaw in a toga. Like Napoleon, he is a walking criticism of romantic heroism. He rises to sublime moments and understands how to strike the imaginations of his followers with a magnificent gesture, but in private he is as prosaically efficient and businesslike as Henry Ford or John D. Rockefeller. He is of course very modern, and many of his ideas arrive at Alexandria of the first century through a very long subterranean passage from the London of the 1890's, so that he often seems a kind of Cecil Rhodes corrected by Shaw's exhaustive pamphlet on "Fabianism and the Empire." And yet, though a Shavian paragon, he has with great artistic skill been made sympathetic and convincing. Shaw gives us a world conqueror as his valet sees him. He has made overpowering virtues credible by uniting them with minor frailties—and a sense of humor. Caesar is frugal, rheumatic, out of humor when he is hungry, and sensitive about his age and baldness. He views himself and the world with indulgent amusement.

According to Shaw, his Caesar squares exactly with history, or at least with Mommsen. And it is true that Mommsen's Caesar is, among other things, like Shaw's, amiable and amusing; and above all, he is one of those happy politicians who have been able to grow wealthy and powerful not simply by committing crimes but by performing acts of far-sighted statesmanship. Shaw omits the crimes and seizes on the statesmanship. Whereas his Napoleon is a blind egotist, more or less unconsciously serving the beneficent interests of the French Revolution, his Caesar is that nobler kind of egotist who realizes that in pursuing his own highest good he achieves the greatest good of the greatest number.

And yet Shaw cannot resist making him at once a little too ingeniously Benthamite, a little too grandiosely Messianic. "In order to produce an impression of complete disinterestedness and magnanimity, he has only to act with entire selfishness." [6] He frees his prisoners of war to save himself the expense of feeding them and makes himself a dictator because the Roman Republic, rather conveniently and yet quite truly, has become decadent. But not only has he reconciled despotism with virtue; he has reconciled world conquest with nonviolence. He condemns revenge, legal or illegal. When Cleopatra confesses she has had her enemy Pothinus killed, Caesar says, "If one man in all the world can be found, now or forever, to know that you did wrong, that man will have either to conquer the world as I have, or be crucified by it." This leads directly to his condemnation of violence: "And so, to the end of history, murder shall breed murder, always in the name of right and honor and peace, until the gods are tired of blood and create a race that can understand." [7]

True, as a military man Caesar cannot afford to condemn all killing. He approves the useful slaughter of Ftatateeta and is of course necessarily dependent on honest killers like Rufio and dishonest ones like Lucius Septimus. A world conqueror advocating nonviolence is inevitably in an ironic—and dangerous—position. At the end of the play Shaw reminds us that Caesar is going to his own death. Is the reminder a criticism of the man or his ideas? Probably the latter. Almost two decades later, Shaw was to expose the hollowness of war to end war. [8]

Caesar's is not the kind of character which embodies a criticism of itself. His dazzling professional virtues cast no shadow of corresponding frailty. He has wrinkles and foibles but scarcely any faults. He is not meant to have them. He is a clockwork superman with a Shavian temperament softened by success, a triumphant theorem in the geometry of optimism—just such a dictator, in fact, as one would invent on a honeymoon. He is much more sentimental and much less real than Napoleon, who was invented when life was sterner and harder. And being clockwork, he is capable of a demonstration but not of a story. "Caesar and Cleopatra" is great not so much because of its Caesar as because of its wit, its comedy, its poetry, and its splendid scenes.

"The playgoer may reasonably ask," says Shaw, "to have historical events and persons presented to him in the light of his own time, even though Homer and Shakespear have already shewn them in the light of their time." [9] "Caesar and Cleopatra" is an interesting illustration of this doctrine. Shaw uses history in four ways—as history, as autobiography, as commentary on the present, and as a demonstration of Shavian theory. Cleopatra seems very convincingly first-century B.C. Egyptian, but she also proves how vividly and excitingly the Life Force was at work in that period. Britannus, the first-century B.C. British slave with a twentieth-century A.D. suburban mind, is a farcical joke aimed directly at the contemporary audience. He is a touch of Gilbert and Sullivan in the midst of high romantic comedy; and indeed, "Caesar and Cleopatra" is filled with mischievous anachronism and sly allusion to the present. Caesar himself is to a surprising degree authentic history; he is Shavian autobiography; he is a superman and a vessel of the Life Force; and he is a lively sermon on British imperial policy.

At the time Shaw was much exercised about the Egyptian Occupation, and by way of pointing out the immediate contemporary moral of his play, he prefixed, in 1913, a very condescending lecture on British imperial policy by the ancient hawk-headed god Ra. In 1882 a feelah officer, Ahmed Arabi, had taken over the government from the Khedive. The new authorities refused to pay the old debts to Great Britain. The British and French fleets appeared in the harbor of Alexandria, and after a massacre had occurred in the city, the British admiral opened fire on the forts. The London penny press railed like a gin-stricken fishwife against the heathen. "God Save the King" was sung with fervor, and a British army took over Egypt, restored order, and Lord Cromer began his statesmanlike administration of the country. In general, Shaw seems to approve of the occupation, except that he would like to see less military violence abroad and more rational calm at home. As in effect the hawk-headed god remarks, a world empire cannot be governed by a people with village minds. A great nation must rule, as Caesar ruled, with wisdom, mildness, and efficiency. Not superior might, but superior civilization, conquers the world.

"Captain Brassbound's Conversion" suggests "The Pirates of Penzance" and represents a return to the ideas of "The Devil's Disciple." It is another triumph of satirical engineering, a melodrama carefully concocted to cure people of melodrama. Shaw conjures up the glamorous adventure land of Morocco (skillfully borrowed from Cunninghame Graham) and then introduces into it the inexorable laws of political economy, the sordid realities of poverty, vice, and failure, and a wonderful engine of prosaic efficiency which dispels the great colored clouds of romantic illusion by emitting tiny jets of fact and common sense.

The plot, borrowed from proceedings in the House of Commons, chiefly concerns the vengeance of Captain Brassbound, a pirate king, who in a world of swift cruisers and Cunard liners has degenerated into a shabby combination of smuggler and guide. The one imposing fact in his life is a rather tenuous injustice done him by his uncle, Sir Howard Hallam, an English judge, who, not knowing his brother had left a son, allows the boy's Portuguese mother to drink herself into crime and then after her death acquires her estate, which, ironically, now loses one hundred fifty pounds a year. But Brassbound does not know this. He has made the estate fabulously rich, his mother a saint, Sir Howard a demon of villainy, and Sir Howard's sin of omission a black and infamous crime. Being a puritan whose life requires the stability and significance of a faith, he has dedicated himself to vengeance. Hallam and his sister-in-law, Lady Cicely Waynflete, come to Morocco and are guided to a romantic castle in the Atlas Mountains by Brassbound, who then announces that he is about to hand Sir Howard over to a fanatical sheik. But in the nick of time Lady Cicely educates him to realism and common sense, and the ferocious sheik, to amorous benevolence and a proposal to substitute her for Hallam. A superior potentate arrives full of enlightened fear of the British Empire, and from the *U.S.S. Santiago* an American war party rushes in full of ferocious understatement and solemn gallantry for Lady Cicely. It is now Sir Howard's turn to visit "justice" on Brassbound. Shaw develops between these two romantic conventionalists a close parallel in character and outlook, so that by knocking the private vengeance of the one against the official vengeance of the other, he crushes the whole conception of retributive justice at a single blow. The original impulse for this prodigy of satiric skill and strength, as well as for Shaw's long warfare against judicial punishment, probably comes like so much else from Butler, who in *Erewhon* speaks of organized revenge as one of the crimes of society.

The other important element in the play is Lady Cicely, who represents several aspects of Shavianism wrapped up in the character and temperament of Ellen Terry. She is, according to Shaw, the highest type of womanhood he has yet created—a successful and optimistic Vivie Warren, a Candida who does not take advantage of sex. Her inexhaustible vitality is expended in benevolently mothering and managing full-grown male infants and extricating them from the ceaseless follies into which they fall. Her method might be described as sentimental pragmatism. She is infinitely friendly and "dares to trust." Therefore, the most hypocritical villains are open and intimate with her at once. She is a shrewd judge of character and believes men to be neither very good nor very bad but far more susceptible to encouragement than to fear. And in this sense she is complimentary to the principal theme of punitive justice. She moves people to goodness by flattering suggestion and converts villainy not by threatening it but by overlooking it, or in extreme cases, by excusing it in such a way as to take all the grandeur and importance out of it. She is a pragmatist chiefly in that she has no fixed principles. She rescues Brassbound from his uncle and the law by taking the utmost liberties with the truth and justifies herself with the extremely Shavian exclamation, "As if anybody ever knew the whole truth about anything!" [10] As a mother-woman free from self, she has apparently never been in love and intends never to marry.

Lady Cicely is as unfailingly successful in softening villainy as Caesar is in conquering armies or Bluntschli in escaping from bedrooms. In short, she is another fairy-tale champion, whose magic weapon happens to be moral suasion. As a moral ideal, she is herself melodramatic. On the other hand, as a satiric symbol of the idea that all that men need to cure them of their miserable little follies is a little efficient mothering, she is delightful. She is of course not a human being, but she is one of the more wonderful of those amazing beings which Shaw has created by hanging the flesh of comic character on an intricate skeleton of Shavian theory.

The dialogue of the play, though not equal to that of "Arms and the Man" or "You Never Can Tell," is very brilliant, and in the part of Drinkwater, embodies a superb phonetic reproduction of Cockney dialect. Shaw's dialogue achieves the heights once more in his next play, "Man and Superman"; and as "Captain Brassbound" contains one of his most comic puritans and "Caesar and Cleopatra" one of his most impressive supermen, so "Man and Superman" contains at once his most comic superman and his most heroic puritan.

CHAPTER TWENTY-SEVEN

Man and Superman: A Step in Shavian Disillusionment

Socialism is in one sense the underlying subject of all Shaw's plays, but since it early proved a very unpopular subject, he abandoned it as an explicit theme after "Mrs. Warren's Profession" and did not return to it until "Man and Superman." But whereas "Mrs. Warren" is a savage indictment of capitalism, "Man and Superman" is a complex satire of socialism itself. Obviously, these two plays mark off successive stages in a process of disillusionment. The tides of hope and despair are not easily traced in a thinker so complexly inconsistent, so deviously auto-biographical, and so much the opportunist at once of public events and of his own inspiration. Shaw seldom admits a disappointment—perhaps not even to himself—without being ready to proclaim a new hope. Consequently, the same drama may contain both pessimism and optimism, revealing the new faith with the ghost of the old faith in its arms. Or again, it may simply take up a new set of problems.

The outward causes of his disillusionment were political events. The inward cause was what might be called his millennial temperament. Like all passionate idealists, he looked for a miraculous deliverance within his own lifetime, yet like most Victorian reformers, he was also realistic and sagacious, with a keen sense of practical possibilities. Consequently, he was trapped between his vision and the facts. As he grew older, he apparently hoped more and more desperately for less and less. He invented more and more ingenious reasons for optimism, more and more violent cures for a chronic ailment.

The first stage of his disillusionment appears in "Mrs. Warren" (1894), which is bitter satire followed by a change of subject. The second stage appears in "Man and Superman" (1903), which—somewhat in-consistently—ridicules parlor Fabianism, indicts democracy, denies social progress, asserts biological progress, proposes eugenics as a means of attaining the superman, and exalts meditation above action. A third stage appears in "Major Barbara" (1905), which impatiently sweeps away meditation and ideas as totally incapable of influencing the world of action and finds in the violent clash of materialistic egotisms themselves the promise of a Marxist millennium. A fourth and ultimate stage appears in "Heartbreak House" (1913–1919), which sees England as a declining Empire and a corrupt democracy doomed to destruction in a world plunging into the ultimate irrationality of war. After "Heartbreak House," the story repeats itself with more desperation, more extravagance, more despair, more subterfuge and evasion. Ardent reformers with a strong sense of practical reality nearly always become sadder but not always wiser: either, like Kingsley, they sacrifice their vision to common sense; or, like Shaw, common sense to their vision.

Fundamentally, then, "Man and Superman" is a pronouncement, full of desperate pessimism and even more desperate optimism, on the progress of social reform. Written one year after Shaw's famous Fabian "Manifesto" surrendering leadership of the socialistic movement to the trade-unions, it satirizes the parlor socialism of the rich intellectual in Tanner and the Bohemian radicalism of the needy intellectual in Mendoza (who, as the Devil in "The Dialogue in Hell," is the very master of illusion) and in Enry Straker rather cautiously and vaguely predicts the success of constitutional working-class socialism. Unfortunately, the working class is not made up of Enry Strakers. In "The Revolutionist's Handbook," which serves formidably as appendix to "Man and Superman," Shaw lays aside the lighthearted gaiety of the Preface and play and bursts out with the full bitterness of his despair. The formation of the Labour Party is little cause for hope. A democratic majority is simply a majority of ignorance and passion. And though his statement is troubled with more than the usual number of inconsistencies, one perceives that the author is obsessed by two dark convictions: the first Marxist, that socialism can never be achieved by constitutional means, because no great change has ever been effected without great economic pressure acting on the governed and at least the dire threat of violence acting on the governors; and the second biological, that whether bought with little or much blood, no merely social change has ever really been an improvement. Frenchmen have been no better since their Revolution than they were before it. Social progress is an illusion; real progress can only be made by evolution. We must attempt to produce a race of supermen, and we may do so in three ways: first, by a general action of the subconscious will, for Shaw maintains that "the unconscious self in mankind" sometimes breaks its way through a problem "as an elephant breaks through a jungle"; [1] second, by divorcing sex from marriage and allowing everybody to mate freely on sex attraction in a society cleared of class barriers; third, by scientific eugenics based on experiment. An improvement in human nature is absolutely essential:

Nothing can save society then except the clear head and the wide purpose: war and competition, potent instruments of selection and evolution in one epoch, become ruinous instruments of degeneration in the next. . . . A civilization in which lusty pugnacity and greed have ceased to act as selective agents and have begun to obstruct and destroy, rushes downwards and backwards with a suddenness that enables an observer to see with consternation the upward steps of many centuries retraced in a single lifetime.[2]

But what crisis brought Shaw to this prophecy? Pretty obviously the Boer War, of which, together with the conflict of 1914 to 1918, he wrote as one of the most disillusioning events of his life. But why? He upheld the Empire and approved of the British victory. I am inclined to think that the key to his disillusionment was the conduct of popular democracy at this time. The spectacle of a whole nation driven blind and mad with rage—often in direct opposition to its most obvious interests—by a gigantic spree of yellow journalism is not calculated to reassure a democratic idealist. "We must eliminate the Yahoo," says Shaw, "or his vote will wreck the commonwealth." [3]

In a graceful and generous "Epistle Dedicatory" to that snobbish and rather thickheaded critic Arthur Bingham Walkley, Shaw explains the genesis of "Man and Superman." Walkley had jestingly demanded that he write a Don Juan play. Shaw has now complied. Of course he has not written a conventional Don Juan play. That, he points out, had been rendered forever superfluous by the comedy of Molière and the opera of Mozart. To the traditional story itself he has added only, as a vision dreamed by his hero, a lengthy dialogue in hell setting forth the ultimate post-mortem views of Don Juan and the Statue. But their earthly story has lost its point. It no longer produces the old terror in the new audience. Instead of presenting a diabolonian scoffer who horrifies respectable believers by his skepticism, Shaw must present a fanatical revolutionary who horrifies respectable skeptics by his faith. Instead of depicting a libertine who pursues women, he must depict a puritan who is pursued by them. The omnipotence of woman in modern life demands no less. To be sure, love must continue basic to the theme, and its progress must be traced not as mere conventional romance which banishes real love from the stage to depict the fantastic interplay of sentimental motive but as the genuine natural history of sexual attraction.

That history is sometimes a battle and always a hunt. Man seeks nutrition and prefers freedom; woman seeks a father and provider for her children. Therefore man flees, and woman pursues. Between the ordinary man and woman the conflict is sufficiently acute, but between the genius and the mother-woman it is ruthless and total. The genius is a man "selected by Nature to carry on the work of building up an intellectual consciousness of her own instinctive purpose." [4] The mother-woman is one endowed with the lure of irresistible vitality and an instinctive divination of the mate most suitable to her for the future of the race. Both the genius and the mother-woman are completely unscrupulous because both are creative and therefore devoted to a purpose larger than themselves. Each preys upon the other sex for his own ends, flaunting every physical and personal attraction, drawing on every resource of mind and will, exercising every deceit and hypocrisy—the woman to hunt down her predestined mate, the genius to ensnare women's affections so that he may feed on them to gain knowledge and experience for his art. It is with this deadly struggle, says Shaw, that his play will deal.

The bare suggestion of his theme he probably owes to his own early sketch, "Don Giovanni Explains" (1887), in which, by a typical Shavian inversion, the great pursuer is himself pursued; but for his theory of love and marriage, he seems chiefly indebted to Schopenhauer's essay "On Women." The ideas of man's purpose, of woman's purpose, of the warfare between the sexes, of the mother-woman as a highly complicated trap baited with beauty and set with craft and deceit are all to be found there, as well as several incidental suggestions used in the play itself, such as Tanner's accusation that women throw away their beauty after they have run down their quarry. Schopenhauer's chief work, *The World as Will and Idea,* probably furnished the idea that sex attraction is a reliable guide to mating for racial improvement, and the essay "On Genius" may have afforded some miscellaneous hints, for Schopenhauer's conceptions of genius as self-consciousness and consciousness of the world and the world's will are very similar to Shaw's. The conflict between genius and domesticity is of course to be found in Ibsen's "Master Builder," in his "Rosmersholm," and elsewhere in contemporary drama.

But it is superfluous to go on tracing the ideas of an author who writes such excellent learned articles about himself. The Epistle to Walkley is a good example. Beginning with "Man and Superman," Shaw explains its relation to Mozart and Molière and his indebtedness to various sources for individual characters. Then, speaking of his work in general, he confesses to occasional pilferings from mere artists like Shakespeare and Dickens but declares that he has actually formed his mind on the great artist-philosophers like Bunyan, Ibsen, Wagner, and Schopenhauer, who rose above egotism and conventional morality to serve the Life Force in a manner more satisfactory to their own individual souls.

Even more than "Captain Brassbound" and "Caesar and Cleopatra,"

"Man and Superman" is many plays in one, a multiplex in theme and significance. It is a Don Juan play, and since Don Juan standing on his head is Bernard Shaw standing on his legs, it is a dramatic autobiography. It is a satire of the Victorian womanly woman, of socialism, and of literary genius in a world of science and action. It is the comedy of a modern Hamlet who goes on talking and philosophizing in the face of modern imperatives; a Faustian-Peer Gyntian potpourri which contains a Socratic dialogue written by a sophist and a "Marriage between Heaven and Hell" written by a Philistine. Finally, it is a philosophical and symbolic play dealing with evolution, social and biological, and offering a desperate eugenical remedy for the evils of human nature and the problems of modern democracy; for as "Caesar and Cleopatra" portrays the superman, "Man and Superman" shows how he can be achieved—and at the same time turns him into a jest.

How can a play do and be all these things and not also be a failure? "Man and Superman" is very far from a failure, but it has defects. As elaborate self-satire, it is unavoidably esoteric. As a Hamlet play, it condemns its most interesting character to relative inaction. As intellectual drama in great complication, it sometimes seems slow, abstract, unrealistic, undramatic, and even trivial—a vast amount of clever talk and fuss about a very plain case of marriage. And indeed many of the ideas, as in the sex biology and the Life Force metaphysics, now appear exaggerated and unreal to a degree only partially counteracted by the suspicion that they may be deliberate self-irony. Moreover, a very slight plot must stagger under a stupendous load of theory; and therefore the discussion often inevitably proceeds from inadequate dramatic provocation and so seems irrelevant and unnecessary. This is a fault which constantly threatens the drama of ideas—and of course, the more so as it grows more complex.

Yet "Man and Superman" is a masterpiece. The principal action, which is the struggle between Ann Whitefield and Jack Tanner, is certainly slight. It begins with an irrelevance and ends with a capitulation. Nevertheless, it is carefully constructed, elaborately motivated, brilliantly comic, and so far as the heroine is concerned, as coherent and logical as the biography of a black-widow spider. Ann persuades her father to appoint Tanner one of her guardians; she works skillfully— though unsuccessfully—to distract the young man's mind from this misfortune and to win him back to their childhood intimacy; she removes her younger sister from possible competition, jumps tigerishly at Jack's careless bravado in proposing an automobile trip to Biskra, and when at length, warned of his peril by Straker, he breaks into headlong flight, she pursues him remorselessly across Europe to the final kill at Granada. *Atē* herself is not more awfully inevitable. Unfortunately, so much inevitability makes the dramatic conflict hopelessly one-sided. There is nothing of the titanic sex struggle advertised in the Preface. Certainly Octavius, though characterized as an "artist," does not provide it; nor again does the "genius" Tanner—except in a very attenuated sense, for he is not a "child-robber" or a "blood-sucker" of women's affections. He does not prey on them "to rouse his deepest creative energies" or "steal the mother's milk and blacken it to make printer's ink to scoff at her and glorify ideal women with." [5] He is simply a very ingenious and complicated kind of tiger bait. Only as his ancestor Don Juan in Hell does he assume anything like a predatory character.

Mr. Eric Bentley identifies Tanner with H. M. Hyndman. In Mr. Bentley's opinion, "Man and Superman" is only incidentally autobiographical. Superficially, it is a brilliantly written, well-made Victorian comedy turning on the customary platitudes of money-and-love intrigue. More fundamentally, it is a fourth *Play for Puritans* in which the author attempts new variations on the perennial Shavian conflict between vitalist and conventionalist. Tanner *preaches* vitalism whereas Ann actually practices it, so that here the antagonist is the vitalist and the protagonist the representative of mere system. All this is acute and true, yet the fact remains that Tanner is very like Shaw—*echt*-Shavian in wit and conversation, super-Shavian in the stage directions (Jupiter rather than Apollo), and ironically sub-Shavian in his deeds and habits. Illustrating in his autobiography, "How Frank ought to have done it," Shaw himself writes of "Man and Superman":

> In the final act. . . , the scene in which the hero revolts from marriage and struggles against it without any hope of escape, is a poignantly sincere utterance which must have come from personal experience. . . . Tanner, with all extravagances, is first hand: Shaw would probably not deny it and would not be believed if he did.[6]

Shaw had been describing himself as an enemy of "Nineteenth Century Amorism," both because of the gorgeous amorism of his daydreams and because of his "passion" of chastity. "Man and Superman" is thus not only a scientific play about eugenics but an autobiographical play about chastity.

In causing Tanner to resemble Hyndman in outer appearance and circumstances, Shaw may simply have wished mischievously to palm off some of the wilder ideas of "The Revolutionist's Handbook" on his ancient antagonist, giving at the same time full expression to both the old Shavian optimism and the new Shavian cynicism in a dramatic dialectic which would present to the reader a secure and baffling anonymity. Inevitably, however, Tanner has suggested Shaw. His feeble parlor socialism has been taken as a bitter comment on Fabian frustration, and his fatal tendency to "go on talking," as satire not only of the philosophical socialist but of Shaw particularly and literary genius generally, which, while it may increase the self-consciousness of the Life Force, is little heeded in a scientific and utilitarian age. The uselessness of art and philosophy is emphasized by the figure of Enry Straker, a Wellsian scientist and engineer who understands machines and women far better than does Tanner but remains narrowly cockney and old-fashioned in his ethical ideas. To be sure, Tanner's own ethics do not seem to fit the facts much better. When Violet's pregnancy is discovered and he enthusiastically congratulates her on yielding to instinct in the teeth of convention, she stuns him by indignantly announcing that she is a married woman. Throughout the play Tanner triumphantly spouts all the ideas of the Preface with an unrivaled flow of eloquence and wit—and meets, like Shaw in real life, with almost universal ridicule and disapprobation. In the higher sense, Tanner is not a failure. The world is a failure. Yet, as a man of action, he does fail. His marriage undoubtedly climaxes that failure and at the same time symbolizes a new hope.

E. Strauss, whose opinion always merits consideration, finds that Shaw habitually uses his love story to illustrate his social ideas.[7] The acquisitive woman symbolizes capitalism; the rational woman, socialism. Marriage to the first indicates compromise with capitalistic society, and marriage to the second, emancipation from it. Thus Harry Trench surrenders his social scruples when he marries Blanche Sartorius, and Cashel Byron withdraws from capitalistic enterprise when he marries Lydia Carew. Certainly there is much in "Man and Superman" to suggest that Tanner's marriage represents a Shavian compromise —at least of despair—with the *status quo*. And, as E. Strauss points out, Tanner's denunciations of marriage in the last scene go beyond Shaw's usual satire of romantic love.

But the marriage of Ann and Jack also presages the coming of the superman. Only biological progress achieves really permanent gains. Social progress is an illusion. Its triumphs are satirized in Tanner's endless verbal victories over Roebuck Ramsden, who is an advanced thinker of the sixties as Tanner is an advanced thinker of the nineties. The implication is that the younger man will soon become as absurdly obsolete as the older—and the scientific workingman Straker will inherit the earth. Not being rich and idle, Straker seems likely to do something more than simply talk. Even so, being vitiated by the common scientific illusions about progress, he is interested chiefly in accumulating facts and in driving automobiles faster and faster. Soon a young man even more miraculously factual and irrelevantly swift will appear—

and Enry will be as ridiculously obsolete as Ramsden and Tanner. *Plus ça change, plus c'est la même chose.*

Only biological change is permanent and significant. Man may evolve into a higher animal, partly by the artificial selection of eugenics and partly by what one is tempted to call the sexual selection exemplified by Ann's capture of Jack Tanner—except that in his theory Shaw emphasizes not selection but instinct, or will, for like Samuel Butler he sides with Lamarck rather than with Darwin. Natural selection, as he explains in the Preface of "Back to Methuselah," is capitalistic, fatalistic, and mindless. Actually, organisms adapt themselves to environment through will and consciousness. Life began when the Life Force entered into matter and guided the molecules into organic form. The Life Force is mind plus upward-striving will. In plants and animals it is relatively unconscious, manifesting itself presumably through tropism and instinct; in man it is highly self-conscious, manifesting itself through reason as well as instinct and through an inward mystical sense to be cultivated by contemplation. Man is its contrivance for building up intelligence, and woman, its contrivance for passing on such intelligence to the next generation, for as a Lamarckian Shaw believes in the inheritance of acquired characteristics. Essentially, Shaw's religion of the Life Force is an effort to enlist the religious sense of mankind in the service of evolutionary progress. In affirming intelligent design but denying omniscience and omnipotence, in emphasizing the biological advantages of self-consciousness and implying the continuity of mind and memory from one generation to another, Shaw's evolutionary theory strongly suggests the influence of Samuel Butler, and particularly, of *Luck, or Cunning?* [8]

Again, in conceiving mind and truth as the products of will and effort, Shaw also suggests the influence of Butler. Both men are pragmatists. They look away from principles and categories toward facts and consequences. They take an instrumental rather than an absolute view of truth, seeing it not so much as conclusions which follow from premises but more as theories which yield fruitful results, whether in evolutionary biology, musical criticism, or social reform. Intelligence and its products are functional; or as Shaw says, "mind is a passion." It springs out of need and desire. In its simplest terms, truth is successful adaptation to environment and thus may be the instinctive possession of an animal as well as the self-conscious possession of a philosopher. Yet whereas Butler seems with romantic obscurantism to prefer the instinctive mind of the animal, Shaw prefers the self-conscious one of the philosopher, which in its ultimate perfection he conceives as the final goal of evolution. And again, whereas Butler is on the whole a cautious pragmatist, accepting ideas because they are fruitful, Shaw sometimes verges on mere impressionistic sophistry, accepting ideas because they are imposing, shocking, or simply individual. "In taking your side," he wrote to Ellen Terry, "dont trouble about its being the right side—north is no righter or wronger than South—but be sure that it is really yours and then back it for all you are worth." [9] In his more serious moods, as I shall attempt to point out later, Shaw is a pragmatist chiefly on religious and social grounds. The general tendency of this strain in his thinking is of course to impose his subjectivity too much on his picture of objective reality.

According to Shavian theory, the higher operation of the Life Force requires first, ideas, and then their execution by the will. For the former purpose, the philosopher is of course immensely important. A genius like Tanner creates new brains for the Life Force simply by thinking and new zeal and fanaticism for mankind by thinking new ideas, which, as Don Juan explains in Hell, transform men from cowards into heroes. Thus, in spite of Shaw's denial of social (and therefore of intellectual) progress, Tanner's marriage may symbolize the propagation not only of the capacity for thought but of thought itself. His ideas may inspire humanity when it is sufficiently improved to appreciate them.

Shaw describes "The Dialogue in Hell" as a philosophic comedy, in which the sainted Statue, "after paying several reconnoitring visits to hell under colour of urging Don Juan to repent, determines to settle there permanently"; and Juan, bored to extinction amid infernal pleasures, resolves to take Don Gonzalo's place in Heaven.[10] But except for occasional touches, the "Dialogue" is anything but a comedy. It begins like a kind of cosmic "Mrs. Warren's Profession" and ends like the "Phaedrus." Hell is another satirical stratagem, of which, incidentally, the earliest suggestions date back to the musical criticism. Hell is this world, only more so. It is the world as it exists in the minds of ordinary people—conventional illusion purified of reality. Hence the dialogue is a very bitter and illuminating way of saying that most of us are in hell already or at least very anxious to be there.

The Devil himself is something between respectable and fashionable. He is a democrat and a gentleman, believes in the will of the majority, is apprehensive of what people think, and talks very much like an above-the-average Member of Parliament, orating platitudinously when dullness is expected of him, and when cleverness is expected, breaking into sententious epigram. He is in fact a kind of second-rate Disraeli —clever, cynical, and witty, yet shallow and for all his wit a little solemn and deficient in humor, with the heart of a Philistine, the imagination of a vulgar romantic, and the attitudes of a melodramatic actor.

Conscious of his own respectability, Shaw's Devil feels piously superior to mankind, in whom he can see his own faults with great realism when he needs to strengthen his illusions. He retains, therefore, his traditional role of accuser, and forced to assume it toward the end of the "Dialogue," acquires for the first time genuine stature and impressiveness, becoming the spokesman of Shaw's pessimism as Don Juan is of his optimism. With an epic sweep of idea and loftiness of diction, the battle protracts itself through the rather awful leisure of eternity. Juan asserts the indomitable will of the Life Force and the high and fruitful protestantism of the human mind. Satan replies with an appalling indictment of man's rationality, cataloguing all the crimes of the nineteenth century and predicting all those of the twentieth. For more than a hundred years, he declares, man has devised machines of wealth and plenty, by which, out of petty greed, he has ground most of his fellows into hideous poverty and suffering. Now he is devising machines of destruction, with which, out of fear and hatred, he will murder his fellows for another hundred years. Juan answers—rather optimistically, some of us may think nowadays—by declaring that the Devil takes man too seriously. The discussion turns to love, woman, and the superman; and having very eloquently adapted to his own purposes a good deal of Shavian autobiography, in which he recounts how he pursued the illusions of love and happiness on earth and in Hell, Don Juan resolves to enter Heaven and spend the rest of his eons in contemplation.

Undoubtedly, this decision symbolizes a strong change of attitude in Shaw. Disillusioned with contemporary politics, he now turned to an inward world of meditation. One can only guess, but in general Shaw's "otherworldliness" seems to have consisted in a speculative plunge into the future. Its course may be roughly traced in succeeding plays from Don Juan through Peter Keegan to Cusins and Major Barbara. Judging from these characters, one may surmise that as Don Juan, Shaw looked forward with confidence to what ideas—and eugenics —might ultimately achieve and exercised his new optimism with a savage fling at his old illusions and the follies of the early twentieth century in general; that as Peter Keegan, he began to lose faith in eugenical deliverance, saw his world of ideas threatening to turn into a world of dreams, took bare consolation in art and nature, and felt his sharp social criticism sink into a pessimistic hatred of facts; that as Barbara, he experienced a final sharp disillusionment with the life of the spirit, and as Cusins, found in the capitalistic facts themselves a Marxist hope of ultimate communistic redemption.

The interval from "Man and Superman" to "Major Barbara" represents a complete cycle. In "Man and Superman," Shaw escapes from contemporary facts by asserting that, in the long run, thought governs history. In "Major Barbara," he exorcises contemporary facts by asserting that they evolve necessarily into a Marxist utopia. The end of the process is apparently implicit in the beginning. "Man and Superman" has at least two planes of significance. On earth the bandit Mendoza seems to explain ideas in terms of economic status, while in Hell Don Juan explains economic status—and everything else—in terms of ideas.

The play itself requires little further discussion. Of the minor characters, Hector Malone, Jr., is interesting as perhaps Shaw's best satire of an American; Hector Malone, Sr., as a rather sorry first in a long series of great capitalists; and Octavius Robinson, as a somewhat mysterious vestigial remains of the traditional Don Juan legend. But after Tanner the most interesting character in the play is of course Ann Whitefield. Shaw sketched her after seeing a performance of "Everyman." She is meant to be Everywoman, in the sense that she is generic female instinct translated into the didacticism of highly rational self-consciousness. Incidentally, she is also a satire of the Victorian womanly woman, for female instinct, as Shaw conceives it, is the deadly tendency to use a pose of brainless innocence as protective coloring in which to stalk the male. Ann is full of sweet sentiments, pious professions, and conventional morality. She faints in the presence of young men, and in the presence of old men she is daintily coy and appealingly feeble-minded. Her gentle hypocrisies are but the meshes of a web within which she lurks as a ferocious egotist and an unrelenting huntress of a father for her children. Ann is not a human being but a walking idea. She is not alive, but she strides about the stage with tremendous energy, as though she were absolutely determined to be alive.

"Maxims for Revolutionists," which concludes "The Revolutionist's Handbook," reveals Shaw to be antidiscipline, antimarriage, antidemocracy, antiroyalty, antiaristocracy, antipunishment, and pro very little—chiefly proequality and prosuperman. In general, his ethical position is that of emotional anarchism rather illogically crossed with utilitarian rationalism. There are epigrams in the best tradition of John Stuart Mill:

> Economy is the art of making the most of life.
> The love of economy is the root of all virtue.[11]

But his attitude is for the most part gloomily anarchistic. The "Maxims" are barbed with bitterness even more than wit. Extreme disillusionment seems to make him more of a romantic than ever. Not Blake nor Shelley himself could have been harder on kings, laws, capitals, or governments:

Kings are not born: they are made by artificial hallucination. When the process is interrupted by adversity at a critical age, as in the case of Charles II, the subject becomes sane and never completely recovers his kingliness.

The imagination cannot conceive a viler criminal than he who should build another London like the present one, nor a greater benefactor than he who should destroy it.

Civilization is a disease produced by the practice of building societies with rotten material.[12]

In his disillusionment he is hard even on human nature. And here we come to an ancient impasse in Shaw. To improve human nature, people must build up mental muscle for the Life Force, conjure up the superman by eugenics, think humbly of their own faults, be self-reliant, pity others or scorn them—in short, do very nearly anything except exert self-control. That, Shaw's romantic fear of suppression and insistence on inward unity will not permit:

Self-denial is not a virtue: it is only the effect of prudence on rascality.

The golden rule is that there are no golden rules.[13]

Of course, being a Victorian, he wants the effects of control even though he fears the cause. In the section on virtue he demands that people desire good spontaneously, and in the section on marriage he complains, in effect, that what most people spontaneously prefer is evil.

I need hardly add that the religion of the Life Force does not conduce to sound ethics. To tell a man that he is the highest embodiment of divinity does not encourage him in humble self-criticism; to tell him that his instincts and impulses are divine intimations does not encourage him in consistency, moderation, or justice. In fact, the Schopenhauerian tendency to lump instinct and impulse together with will makes it very difficult to distinguish between morality and animality or between rational free will and the mechanistic fatalism from which Shaw probably thought he was escaping. If natural selection condemns man to blind fatalism, Lamarckian functionalism does not necessarily free him from it, for man's "will," like that of plants and animals, remains that of the Life Force, as Tanner found to his cost when he tried to escape from Ann. Of course Shaw argues that though the individual does not entirely develop his own course, the race—or rather Life itself, past and present—does. Nevertheless, to make self-conscious mind the distinguishing characteristic of man is to remove some of the blindness, but by no means all of the fatalism, from evolution. In "Back to

Methuselah," Shaw becomes more deeply and explicitly involved in this confusion.

In form and to some degree in content, the "Maxims" suggest Nietzsche and also Blake's "Marriage of Heaven and Hell." Shaw has several times acknowledged a debt to Blake, whose diabolonianism, romantic ethics, hatred of poverty, and fierce indignation against social injustice were inevitably sympathetic. Such sayings as the following probably owe something to Blake's influence:

Never resist temptation: prove all things: hold fast that which is good.

Imprisonment is as irrevocable as death.

Beware of the man whose god is in the skies.[14]

It is also possible that Juan's famous remark, "Hell is the home of honor, duty, justice, and the rest of the seven deadly virtues," [15] may have been suggested by a passage in Blake's "Everlasting Gospel."

> The Heathen Deities wrote them all,
> These Moral Virtues, great and small.
> What is the Accusation of Sin
> But Moral Virtue's deadly Gin?
> The Moral Virtues in their Pride
> Did o'er the World triumphant ride
> In Wars and Sacrifice for Sin,
> And Souls to Hell ran trooping in.[16]

In 1896, Shaw had devoted part of a weekly *Saturday Review* dramatic criticism to Nietzsche, with whose writing, he explains, he first became acquainted some time in 1891, when he was asked whether *The Quintessence of Ibsenism* had not been inspired by *Beyond Good and Evil*. The 1896 essay contains a brief outline of Nietzsche's ideas together with Shaw's reactions to them. He admires Nietzsche's paradoxes and his criticism of established values—including, apparently, that of truth—but utterly abhors his idealization of certain periods of history such as the Renaissance, his preference of Bizet to Wagner, and above all, his condemnation of modern democracy, socialism, and Pauline Christianity as conspiracies of the weak against the strong. In "Man and Superman," Nietzsche is again referred to several times— usually as a German-Polish madman but always with indulgence. Perhaps Shaw had recently discovered that Nietzsche was a Lamarckian. At any rate, the "Maxims," and particularly the section entitled "Stray Sayings," contain a number of more or less Nietzschean ideas. Shaw insists on the importance of masks and idols in government, observes that the noble succeed in a period of ascending life and the weak in a period of declining life, ironically explains nature as a struggle for the survival of rascality, praises the educational virtues of action, and counsels the reader to hit the other cheek as hard as possible. The following particularly suggest Nietzsche:

Compassion is the fellow-feeling of the unsound.

If you injure your neighbor, better not do it by halves.[17]

But Nietzsche's influence is never great, either in "Man and Superman" or elsewhere. Shaw's Life Force theory owes much more to Ibsen, Schopenhauer, and Butler; and his superman more to Wagner—and most of all, one is tempted to say, to Jeremy Bentham. Critics sometimes mistake Marx for Nietzsche in Shaw's writings. Both philosophers tend to teach the cunning and violent pursuit of self-interest: the one, as part of a modern and scientific value theory; the other, as the fulfillment of an economic predestination. Thus in "Major Barbara," the supercapitalist Undershaft is frequently interpreted as a Nietzschean figure. He is much more Marxist. He preaches struggle because he believes in class struggle, and when he foresees his own *Untergang*, the implication is not so much that he will be followed by the superman as by a classless society.

"Man and Superman" is perhaps not Shaw's greatest play. It lacks the concentrated satire of "Mrs. Warren's Profession," the elaborate irony of "Major Barbara," the realism and deep feeling of "Saint Joan," and the dramatic complication and varied character portrayal of "Candida," yet it does combine all Shaw's most characteristic brilliance with all his most characteristic ideas. Taken with its utopian dialogue in Hell and its hellish handbook about utopia, it is something between a Shavian epic and a Shavian encyclopedia.

CHAPTER TWENTY-EIGHT

Plays for Capitalists

Disraeli had proved that failure, if only it is big enough and lasts long enough, can become extremely profitable. Shaw had now begun to fail all over Europe and America.

> There is a Shaw boom on in Germany [he writes Forbes-Robertson], because four of my plays have been produced in Vienna, Leipzig, Dresden and Frankfurt; and they have all failed so violently, and been hounded from the stage with such furious execrations, that the advanced critics proclaim me the choice and master spirit of the age; and no manager respects himself until he has lost at least 200 marks by me.[1]

The German managers paid him advance royalties, so that he made a commercial success of unsuccessful genius. Having become a capitalist, he naturally began to take an interest in his species. The plays from "Man and Superman" to "The Dark Lady of the Sonnets" contain a formidable series of capitalists, indicating a tendency, largely hostile, to explore that unregenerate economic animal both as a living creature and as a satiric device.

About this time Shaw also began to be a modest dramatic success in England. On May 21, 1905, "Man and Superman" was produced by the Stage Society with Granville-Barker, as Jack Tanner, made up like a youthful G.B.S. Two days later it opened at the Court Theatre, where Shaw was at last creating the artistic utopia of which he had dreamed so wittily and precisely in his dramatic essays. Early in 1904, Vedrenne, the manager of the Court, asked Barker to supervise a revival of "Two Gentlemen of Verona." Barker, who served art as coldly and shrewdly as Vedrenne served money, agreed to do so on condition that the Court Theatre would give half a dozen matinees of "Candida." The venture was moderately profitable, and Shaw received about thirty pounds. As a consequence, Vedrenne and Barker formed a partnership—at first for the production of matinees and later for evening performances also.

The Vedrenne-Barker-Shaw combination lasted only from 1904 to 1907, but it created a whole dramatic literature and a whole theatrical tradition. Vedrenne performed the major miracle of making genius pay, and Shaw and Barker, the minor miracle of providing the genius, which is perhaps the only quality they had in common—and even there they differed. Barker was elegant and restrained. "He expected his actors to understand and underplay their parts," whereas Shaw liked them to have energy and style, and indeed his plays, "with their carefully built-up speeches, required flamboyant acting." [2]

> I truckle to Granville Barker in order to conciliate him when he is forty [writes Shaw in 1902]. He regards me as a vulgar old buffer who did my best in my day to play up for better things—his things, for example. In revenge I call him "serious relief," etc. But he is always useful when a touch of poetry and refinement is needed. . . . He rebukes me feelingly for wanting my parts to be "caricatured." [2]

Shaw calls him "a cold-hearted Italian devil, but a noble soul all the same." [2] And yet with his cold-hearted Italian passion, Barker seems to have loved art too well. He fell victim to his own sense of the sublime, and like Otto Ludwig, devoted a lifetime which gave promise of much excellent creative art to the study of Shakespeare.

Shaw's works were the mainstay of the partnership, though Maeterlinck, Schnitzler, Hauptmann, Yeats, Hankin, Masefield, Galsworthy, Barker, and Gilbert Murray were also presented. Shaw not only provided the combination with most of their plays but with probably the most finished and beautiful young actress on the stage at that time. The story might be described as "Pygmalion" written by Sir James Barrie. Like all romances, it began "long ago"—when Shaw was dramatic critic for *The Saturday Review*. The young lady, then very young, was about to play Lady Macbeth. Someone came in to whisper that the great Shaw was down in front. Good! She would freeze him with horror, melt him with pity. Perhaps she did, but the extremities of temperature did not seem to affect his critical apparatus. *The Saturday Review* began with one of its most grisly dissections: she spoke wrong, walked wrong, did everything wrong. In a rage she burned the paper before she finished the article. Then her brother burst in, waving *The Saturday Review*. There it all was! At the end of the article, the implacable Shaw had been placated. She was "rich" and "born to act"—only, she "ought to go into the country for ten years and learn [her] . . . business." [3] She did, and having learned how to breathe, speak, move, and act, presented herself at the doorstep of the dramatic critic who had since become a famous playwright.

"Why," he exclaimed, "here's Ann Whitefield." [4]

As a matter of fact, it was Lillah McCarthy. Shaw himself has drawn her portrait:

> It is an actress's profession to be extraordinary; but Lillah was extraordinary even among actresses. The first natural qualification of an actress who is not a mere puppet, impotent without a producer, is imagination. Lillah had a great deal too much of it: she was of imagination all compact. It was difficult to get her feet down to the ground, and almost impossible to keep them there. Her life was rich in wonderful experiences that had never happened, and in friendships with wonderful people (including myself) who never existed. All her geese were swans, flying about in an enchanted world. When, as inevitably occurred from time to time, real life and hard objectivity brought her down with a stunning collision, she could be tragically disappointed or murderously enraged; but she could not be disillusioned: the picture changed; but it remained a picture. On the stage she gave superb performances with a force and sureness of stroke and a regal authority that made her front rank position unassailable; but if by chance her imagination started a fresh hare before she went on the stage she would forget all about the play and her part in it, and, whilst mechanically uttering its words and moving through its business, revel in the feelings of some quite different character. . . . You could not say that she had the faults of her qualities. Her faults *were* her qualities.[5]

Shaw knew how to challenge such a woman. A few days after their first meeting, he wrote her a letter:

DEAR MISS MCCARTHY,

I want to ask you two questions "without prejudice."

1. If the Stage Society were to ask you to play for them on Sunday evening the 8th April, and on the afternoon of the 10th and 11th in an exceedingly difficult and possibly shockingly unpopular leading part, by which you gain nothing but three guineas to pay for your cabs, and enough trouble and worry to take quite 50 guineas' worth of energy and temper out of you, would you say Yes or No?

2. Did you ever read a play by me called "Man and Superman," and if so, can you imagine any woman playing the part of Ann Whitefield?

If not, I will send you a copy.

Yours faithfully,

G. BERNARD SHAW [6]

She took up the task and for years forfeited money and fame in order that she might become the greatest of Shaw heroines. Her first part was not that of Ann Whitefield but of Nora in "John Bull's Other Island." Later she played Ann, as well as nearly every other leading feminine role in Shaw up to that of Elly Dunne in "Heartbreak House." Inevitably, she also became a Shaw-worshiper and even propitiated her idol with rites of vegetarianism, enthusiastically sharing his fruit-and-milk luncheons despite the eloquent inward protest of a vigorous appetite.

Though Granville-Barker directed all the others, Shaw directed his own plays. Pearson describes him as an ideal director—courteous, encouraging, skillful, and knowing. His first action was to read his play to the cast, sharply differentiating each character and striking despair into the hearts of the minor actors by the excellence of his performance. Then for a week he conducted a leisurely reading of the play on the stage, explaining and directing the business, which had been carefully planned beforehand. When the company were capable of going forward by themselves, he retired to the auditorium and there made voluminous notes, which he went through on the stage at the end of each act, giving copious illustrations and always with exaggerated inflections and gestures, to prevent the actor from simply mimicking him without grasping his meaning. Mr. Pearson concludes:

> His manner was genial and sympathetic, and he never uttered a harsh or hurtful word, laughing over his own lines, which he could never repeat accurately. His high spirits were as infectious as his Irish speech; he was clown, conjurer, acrobat, actor, all in one; and he got his own way in everything without the smallest friction.[7]

In spite of some testimony to the contrary, like that of the actor Maurice Colbourne, there is no doubt that Shaw was an excellent director, combining courtesy and self-possession with the utmost frankness in a way that was sometimes inspiring and sometimes infuriating. The letters to Iden Payne, who managed and directed the Gaiety Theatre in Manchester, indicate that he was often peremptory and always critical. Misacting or misproduction of his plays was a torture to him. After seeing Payne's "Widowers' Houses," he begins, "It was a most conscientious and most infamous performance"; remarks a little further on, "Bibby [in the part of Cokane] is an appalling miscast. . . . I cannot imagine what induced you to cast him for such a part"; blandly concludes, "So buy a new wig, wash your face, talk frank Lancashire, watch, pray, fast; and then perhaps I will come again and give you all some more encouragement."[8] The correspondence contains a rejected draft of Mrs. Payne's reply. She is obviously cooking with rage, and several times she saves herself from furious outbreak only by crossing out what she has written.

In 1904 Shaw cometed into the orbit of the Celtic Movement. With astonishing intrepidity, the Abbey Theatre asked him for an Irish play. It was romantic Ireland asking realistic and comic Ireland to conjure up mist and twilight. As a matter of fact, "John Bull's Other Island" contains some genuine Celtic twilight and mist as well as some very acceptable Celtic daylight. The exposure of the drunken stage Irishman and the spectacle of "the absurd Anglo-Saxon in a ring of ironical Paddies" would undoubtedly please the Abbey audience, but the triumph of an Englishman in Ireland they could not be expected to endure. "John Bull" was at bottom too international, too common sense. Like all Shaw's plays, it was aimed directly at some of the dearest beliefs of its destined spectators. Very gently, very politely, the play was rejected—and lived to win an ironical popularity in England.

"John Bull's Other Island" is a definition of English and Irish national character, an explanation and a solution of the Irish problem, a satire on democratic politics, and above all, a confession of what Ireland and England meant to Shaw. As objective definition of national character, the play is suggestive and illuminating but dangerously paradoxical. Shaw will allow Englishmen no common sense and Irishmen no sentiment, not even the sentiment of hating Englishmen. But no one could hate Broadbent. He is in part admittedly modeled on that irreproachable Saxon and theatrical critic A. B. Walkley, who, on seeing a performance of the Abbey Players in 1903, fell in love with them, as Broadbent with Nora, because of their Irish accent. Broadbent himself could not be more absurdly and sentimentally wrong than Walkley in his review, which appeared shortly before "John Bull" was written:

> First and foremost [he explains] there is the pleasure of the ear.
> . . . You are listening to English spoken with watchful care and slightly timorous hesitation, as though it were a learned language. That at once ennobles our mother-tongue, brings it into relief, gives it a daintiness and distinction of which, in the rough workaday use of it, one had never dreamed. . . . No doubt there is a touch of affectation in their methods; they have something of the self-importance of children surpliced for service at the altar. . . . A style "deliberately adopted" is the harmless little boast of their prospectus.[9]

Here is Broadbent writing his own lines. Surely Shaw must have drawn ammunition from this very review.

From a wider view, Broadbent is both more and less than fact. Interpreting the play as another struggle between system and vitalism, Mr. Bentley sees him as a unique instance of a triumph of the former. Actually, in the scale of Shavian evolution, Broadbent belongs somewhere between Roebuck Ramsden and Andrew Undershaft. Like Ramsden he is a liberal idealist and a sentimentalist; like Undershaft he is a capitalist and successful man of action. His peculiarity is that he is almost entirely brainless. He confuses politics with civilization, melodrama with life, personal advantage with moral idealism. He fancies that Irish melancholy is due to the recent death of Gladstone. As a human being, he is a little hard to credit. As a mythological monster in the folklore of nationalism, he is wonderfully piquant and illuminating. His business success may be accepted as something magically belonging to his nature, like Jack's ability to kill giants. On the other hand, his success in Irish politics stretches even the license of fairy tales, for the most mythically rational Irishmen would scarcely vote for a hereditary enemy in whom they could see nothing but a little money and a great deal of folly. But Shaw felt they ought to vote for him—or at least for union with England, on which the prosperity and safety of both countries depended. In fairy tales a wild and extravagant plot often contains a sound and cautious moral. It is not surprising that Arthur Balfour, the Conservative-Unionist Prime Minister, went to see the play four times and took with him the Opposition leaders, Asquith and Campbell-Bannerman.

But on the stage Broadbent does not need to be real; he is so uproariously funny. For farce, quite as much as melodrama, can hurry away the critical sense with a rush of action and excitement. Shaw selected for the part a well-known Shakespearian actor, Louis Calvert, of whom, as Antony, he had written several years before:

> Mr. Calvert is a comedian—brimming over with genuine humane comedy. . . . As a lover, he leaves his Cleopatra far behind. His features are so pleasant, his manner so easy, his humor so genial and tolerant, and his portliness so frank and unashamed, that no good-natured woman could resist him.[10]

Broadbent is difficult because he must himself remain very solemn: only the audience can laugh. Calvert did not at first get the hang of the part, and at his request Shaw "fed" him the lines.

> "What is this that you are asking me to do?" [Calvert asked Shaw.] You want me to pick out all the insignificant words and hand them out syllable by syllable as if they were the last words of God's wisdom."

[254]

"Exactly," said G.B.S. "That is the secret of British political oratory. Broadbent must be never so impressive as when he is talking nonsense and making the bloodiest fool of himself."

Calvert . . . seized the idea; and there was no more trouble: his Broadbent became perfect.[11]

But by the time it reached the stage, the play was too funny. Its lesson was lost in a gale of laughter. When it was revived in 1913, Shaw had distributed to the audience a leaflet in which he asked them not to take part in the play "by shouts of applause and laughter. . . . Have you considered that in all good plays tears and laughter lie very close together? . . . Do you not know that an act of a play is intended just like a piece of music, to be heard without interruption?" [12] It was perhaps because "John Bull" failed of serious effect that in creating his next capitalist Shaw simply extracted from Broadbent the rib of hilarity and out of the rib made he a woman, Lady Britomart. He then performed an operation on the head of the capitalist and injected a rich mixture of brains and Marxism. The result was Andrew Undershaft.

It is ironical that when people finally learned to laugh at Shaw he had sunk into deep pessimism. In "John Bull" he has some very grim things to say, not only about Ireland but about the universe in general. On the first subject his spokesman is Larry Doyle; on the second, Peter Keegan. These two, even more than Morell and Marchbanks in "Candida," represent aspects or fragments of Shaw himself, but of a Shaw much more cynical and hard and more sharply in division against himself. Keegan is a romantic visionary closely related to Marchbanks. "Every dream," he says, "is a prophecy: every jest is an earnest in the womb of Time." [13] But he is a Marchbanks gone mad with the bitterness of earthly realities, a Marchbanks who has lost all his illusions though he has preserved all his dreams. He walks in Don Juan's Hell and longs for Don Juan's Heaven. He is endowed with special economic knowledge of Hell, so that he can confront Doyle and Broadbent with their capitalistic sins. His Heaven, too, is a place which an economist would understand—such as might be achieved in time by a far-off divine event:

In my dreams it is a country where the State is the Church and the Church the people: three in one and one in three. It is a commonwealth in which work is play and play is life: three in one and one in three. It is a temple in which the priest is the worshipper and the worshipper the worshipped: three in one and one in three. It is a godhead in which all life is human and all humanity divine: three in one and one in three. It is, in short, the dream of a madman.[14]

This is certainly Morrisite socialism. It also sounds like Comteism, though in this respect no doubt it is simply Ibsenism and creative evolution adapted to the idea of a church. What is striking is that Keegan's mysticism, with all its poetical madness and rhythmic incantation, is a very secular and rational mysticism. One might almost say that, like Comte himself, Shaw thinks nineteenth-century thoughts with an eighteenth-century mind, for even his boldest meditations in romantic organicism form themselves into the precise, geometric, secular patterns of Voltaire, Hume, and Bentham. His mystic vision of Heaven resolves itself into perfectibility, socialism, cooperation, enlightened egotism, romantic spontaneity, and the religion of humanity.

Larry Doyle, Broadbent's partner, is that part of Shaw which went to England and became a business and professional success. One suspects there is a good deal of the private, personal Shaw in the moody, impatient, clairvoyant, talkative young Irishman, who accepts the brutality of facts because he fears the opiate unreality of dreams. The inconsistency encountered in the Preface, of Shaw's fact-facing Irishman who lives on dreams, is at least partly reconciled by Larry's impressionistic speech on the effects of Irish climate and scenery—to which might be added the much more tangible effects, also explained by Larry later on, of Irish poverty and English oppression. The Irishman can recognize facts, but he has been able to do so little about them that he has come to prefer dreams or the narrow treadmill of industry, parsimony, vice, and brutal laughter in which Barney Doran and Mat Haffigan live. Nevertheless, England has taught Larry that Ireland's future can only be created with resolution and intelligence out of Ireland's present, however grim that present may be. His program, explained at length in the Preface, is broadly rational and unsentimental. He is for Home Rule, because without autonomy all Ireland's strength goes into nationalism; it can bear no fruit, it can only grow more twisted and starved and shut off from the light of the world. And yet some form of union with England is essential to prosperity: "I want Ireland to be the brains and imagination of a big Commonwealth, not a Robinson Crusoe island." [15] In 1917 Shaw was still maintaining the same view, though with less faith in Irish logic: "Sancta simplicitas! The beggar refuses to pool with the millionaire; and the millionaire, terrified, calls for horse, foot, and artillery to force the beggar to rifle his pockets." [16]

Again, Larry Doyle is for an established Catholic, though non-Roman, Church, partly because he can't "bear to see her begging her bread from the ignorance and superstition of men" and partly because "a disestablished Church is the worst tyranny a nation can groan under." Father Dempsey "has nothing to hope or fear from the State; and the result is that he's the most powerful man in Rosscullen." [17] Finally, Doyle is for solving the agrarian problem by calling every landlord to strict account and for guaranteeing the agricultural laborer a minimum wage which will prevent the risks of cutthroat competition with England. Nevertheless, Larry prefers the indifference and absenteeism of the great landlords to the jealousy and parsimony of the small, for the first at least have capital, and they are largely indifferent to the laborer, whereas the second wring out of him the very last drop of strength and self-respect.

Ireland was undoubtedly a very congenial subject for Shaw, not only because it permitted him to indulge his taste for autobiography but because it practically compelled him to preach a sermon on his favorite theme—the cardinal sin of poverty, of which the Irish were deeply guilty. In this respect "John Bull" is closely related to "Major Barbara," for as in one the question is whether to be Christian or capitalistic, in the other it is whether to be Irish or industrialized. The debate develops in the last act, with the Doyle-Broadbent partnership defending capitalism and industrialization, and Keegan half defending, half mourning the Ireland that is passing away. As the argument proceeds, the jovial English muddler, preaching efficiency and prosperity, gives sudden, almost incredible signs of intelligence and sinister significance. It becomes clear that Doolan and Haffigan are his gulls on a far vaster scale than he is theirs. And yet he is blissfully unaware of the fact, for as Keegan explains, the right side of his brain does not know what the left side does. He is a more dangerous, because a more innocent, Undershaft. But the dialectic of the fourth act turns Larry Doyle into an Undershaft also, and a much more authentic one because he recognizes that he is the servant of an economic predestination. As Shaw once wrote of Marx, "he has discovered the law of social development, and knows what must come. The thread of history is in his hand." [18] And like Marx he believes that, though the process must be dire, the end will be good:

> Our syndicate has no conscience: it has no more regard for your Haffigans and Doolans and Dorans than it has for a gang of Chinese coolies. It will use your patriotic blatherskite and balderdash to get parliamentary powers over you as cynically as it would bait a mousetrap with toasted cheese. It will plan, and organize, and find capital while you slave like bees for it and revenge yourselves by paying politicians and penny newspapers out of your small wages to write articles and report speeches against its wickedness and tyranny, and to crack up your own Irish heroism, just as Haffigan once paid a witch a penny to put a spell on Billy Byrne's cow. In the end it will grind the nonsense out of you, and grind strength and sense into you.[19]

But though the syndicate has no conscience, Larry Doyle has. The awful miracle which Shaw performed in Undershaft is that he fitted a syndicate into a man's hide. Keegan predicts him in one vivid and inspired sentence—which is aimed at Broadbent: "He is efficient in the service of Mammon, mighty in mischief, skilful in ruin, heroic in destruction." [20]

The debate itself is nip and tuck. Keegan overwhelms the two capitalists by foretelling their future machinations with an accuracy that makes them stare, but again Larry is allowed some blows against Keegan and his "dreaming":

> KEEGAN. In the accounts kept in heaven, Mr Doyle, a heart purified of hatred may be worth more even than a Land Development Syndicate of Anglicized Irishmen and Gladstonized Englishmen.

> LARRY. Oh, in heaven, no doubt! I have never been there. Can you tell me where it is?

> KEEGAN. Could you have told me this morning where hell is? Yet you know now that it is here. Do not despair of finding heaven: it may be no farther off.

> LARRY [ironically]. On this holy ground, as you call it, eh? [21]

On the whole, it seems clear that Shaw is moving from the visionary socialism of Juan and Keegan to the Marxist realism of Doyle and Undershaft.

The Preface of "John Bull's Other Island," written in 1907, is significant for two reasons. A discussion of the Irish question, it reveals Shaw, in so far as he is affected by national feeling at all, as an Irish rather than an English patriot. Again, it marks a less optimistic attitude toward the Empire. It lashes at imperial injustice everywhere and culminates in a ferociously satirical narrative of the Denshawai Incident in Egypt. In this essay Shaw touches also on the British fear of Germany. As in 1898 he began to think beyond the limits of Fabian England, so now he begins to think beyond the limits of Fabian Empire. Evidently, the British world is threatened with problems which cannot be solved exclusively in terms of the British world. The next time Shaw writes on international affairs, he proposes a league of the Western European nations.

Shaw was proud of the speed and efficiency with which he could turn out a play at request. In 1905, he wrote a brief one-acter for the American manager Arnold Daly, who was playing "The Man of Destiny" and needed something to fill out his program. Combining a minimum of subject matter with a maximum of technical mastery, "How He

Lied to Her Husband" is as convincing a demonstration of professional competence in its way as the sonnets of Shakespeare are in theirs. It is graceful, vivid, and compact, full of good business and opportunity for the actor. In theme, it is another of Shaw's "Wild Ducks." It satirizes Ibsen's "Doll's House" and Shaw's own "Candida" and manages to convict both of melodrama. The young hero, who tries to play Marchbanks in the midst of a suburban marriage, is astounded to discover that the gross, commercial husband not only has considerable taste in literature but is actually very proud of his wife's prowess as a heartbreaker. His wife is a very reckoning Candida, who values nothing so much as her respectability, and Candida herself is under continual fire from an invisible sister-in-law, who apparently shares Beatrice Webb's opinion that Shaw's heroine is a sentimental prostitute.

"Major Barbara," like "Hamlet," is peculiarly characteristic of its author and its century. As the clarifications of critics accumulate, it threatens to become equally perplexing. William Archer discovers in the play two largely contradictory themes: the Shavian doctrine that poverty is a cardinal sin and the Nietszchean doctrine that everything must be blown up to make way for the superman.[22] Socialistic reviewers, like Thompson in the London *Clarion*, see the threat of revolution by force.[23] Mr. E. R. Bentley considers Cusins, not Undershaft, the hero and briefly points out the influence of Marx.[24] A. B. Walkley resolutely discerns nothing but a brilliant confusion about which it is impossible to generalize.[25]

Shaw himself, anticipating bewilderment, extended elaborate "First Aid to Critics," which critics have regarded as distrustfully as though it camouflaged one of Undershaft's bombs. Actually, this Preface is quite straightforward and illuminating. It informs us that the play is founded on Butler's dictum that poverty is a crime against society. Tainted money is far better than no money at all, and therefore Undershaft, with all his munitions on his head, is good because he is rich, and Peter Shirley, the superannuated workman, is evil because he is poor. In so far "Major Barbara" is an attack on all romantic liberals and socialists who sentimentalize about the "poor but honest" common man languishing supinely in his filth, disease, and ignorance. And this attack is pointed the more directly, as E. Strauss observes, by the satiric sketch of Snobby Price, who talks like a socialist and acts like a rascal.

"First Aid" also makes clear that the play deals with "our mercanto-Christian morality" at its best.[26] Undershaft, representing capitalism, solves the problem of poverty—or material evil—at least for the individual; and Major Barbara, representing Christianity, solves the problem of moral evil. Her solution is not very convincing, however. The episode of Bill Walker is at best a triumph of plausibility. On the surface, all is vigorous realism; below the surface, it is a rigid and didactic geometry of ideas—a kind of morality play inculcating the Christian virtue of contrition with much of the contrition and all the humility left out. Barbara has more than a touch of Shavian snobbery, and Bill Walker, sodden ruffian though he is, possesses a Shavian pride that prevents him from owing anyone a moral halfpenny. In general, this episode teaches that if we all refused to punish or to pardon, we should, after courteously ushering a few impossibles into the lethal chamber, release the full sensitivity of the human conscience.

But though Barbara can—at least to Shaw's satisfaction—cure men's souls, she cannot cure their poverty, which indeed Christianity serves to perpetuate. Essentially, Shaw told Henderson, the play represents a conflict between the Salvation Army morality of Major Barbara and the gunpowder morality of her father.[27] According to the common pattern of Shavian drama, Barbara's morality is what modern civilization professes; Undershaft's, what it practices. When the crisis comes, the real triumphs as usual over the ideal—or in Marxist terms, the economic over the ideological. Ruthless *laissez faire* is victorious over otherworldly Christianity. Sardonically flaunting the blood upon it, Undershaft offers his money to General Baines, and before Barbara's eyes she accepts. True, she does not compromise the Salvation Army, but as Undershaft explains later, Christianity serves his purpose. It tends to make poverty acquiescent and antirevolutionary.[28] The play concludes with an apotheosis of the munitions manufacturer, whom Shaw designates as the hero.

Does "Major Barbara" indicate, then, as E. Strauss suggests, that Shaw was tending to compromise with capitalism?[29] His dramas of this period contain several impressive capitalists and several more or less ridiculous socialists. He appears also to have been searching for a new approach to reform through religion. Undoubtedly, he was making a deliberate effort fairly to evaluate the forces which form the *status quo*, but he does not seem to have carried compromise much beyond praising capitalists in order to infuriate socialists. To be sure, he hugely enjoys Undershaft as a kind of antichrist to Philistine respectability, and after the fashion of proud and rebellious puritan artists, he has made his Lucifer the hero of his play—though without for an instant forgetting his theology, which is Marxist.

But for variety, Shaw told Archibald Henderson, "Major Barbara" might have been called "Andrew Undershaft's Profession."[30] His munitions manufacturing, like Mrs. Warren's prostitution, is an accusation against society. If his explosives slay thousands, industry in general, including yours and mine, starves, maims, and destroys millions. If his business promotes war, so does all capitalistic enterprise. If he exercises a sinister influence on government, if he sits ferociously on the lid of society with a machine gun on his arm, so do all plutocrats. Asked what are the two things necessary to salvation, Undershaft answers, "Money and gunpowder."

> Cusins [*surprised, but interested*] That is the general opinion of our governing classes. The novelty is in hearing any man confess it.[31]

As a human being, Undershaft is infinitely less convincing than Mrs. Warren, but as an engine of rhetorical destruction, he is infinitely more deadly. He is Everymillionaire, a Benthamite abstraction of a millionaire, with all his middle-class illusions removed and all his interests consciously rationalized and inarticulate. The result is, as Mr. Bentley observes, an exquisite irony. Undershaft is a millionaire who takes a Marxist view of religion and the state, of himself and history—except that he remains in the capitalistic phase and on the capitalistic side of the class struggle. Shaw uses him as a weapon against all elements of British political life. His efficiency and moral courage are a shattering reproach to wishy-washy Labourite socialists. His clarity of vision demolishes purblind and righteous "idealists," who are symbolized in his son Stephen. But if his virtues are poisonous to socialist politicians and moral deadheads, his vices are equally, though more subtly, poisonous to capitalists. To them Shaw seems to be saying, "Here is your favorite hero, a great captain of industry. I have given him every advantage, endowed him with every virtue proper to his nature. I have shown him shrewd, efficient, dominating, triumphant. I have even granted him some insight into the central truth that poverty is the basis of all evil. I have made him intelligent enough to see what he stands for, honest enough to proclaim it 'unashamed'—a man who makes a religion out of being a millionaire, that is, of course, out of being a ruthless exploiter and warmonger." From this point of view, "Major Barbara," even more than "Widowers' Houses" and "Mrs. Warren's Profession," is a carefully concocted irritant. There is no reconciliation within the theater. The only catharsis is to go out and start a revolution.

But as Shaw remarks in the Preface, Undershaft is not only a millionaire but a mystic.[32] He has an ideal as well as a satiric significance. He serves not only to indict the present but to foreshadow the future. His profession accuses capitalism of fomenting war, and it threatens capitalism with revolution by force. In both cases it functions according to Marxist doctrine.

Shaw's attitude toward war was condemnatory but ·realistic. In his Tract "Fabianism and the Empire," he had declared that not military power but civilization makes a nation great. In "Arms and the Man" and

"The Man of Destiny," he had ridiculed the romance and irrationality of war. Nevertheless, he always recognized it as an inescapable reality in human life. He was always skeptical of disarmament programs and maintained that in the absence of any effective international police system, a nation which has acquired great wealth and sound institutions must stand ready to defend its own by force of arms. In the cynical idiom of Undershaft, money and gunpowder are the keys to modern life.

To be sure, "Major Barbara" expresses an unusual friendliness toward war. In a country where monstrous poverty and injustice exist, law and government become a mockery. Violence must be the ultimate reality. "First Aid to Critics" contains a passage of insight rare even in so self-conscious a genius:

> Here am I, for instance, by class a respectable man, by common sense a hater of waste and disorder, by intellectual constitution legally minded to the verge of pedantry, and by temperament apprehensive and economically disposed to the limit of old-maidishness; yet I am, and have always been, and shall now always be, a revolutionary writer, because our laws make law impossible; our liberties destroy all freedom; our property is organized robbery; our morality is an impudent hypocrisy; our wisdom is administered by inexperienced or malexperienced dupes, our power wielded by cowards and weaklings, and our honor false in all its points. I am an enemy of the existing order for good reasons; but that does not make my attacks any less encouraging or helpful to people who are its enemies for bad reasons. The existing order may shriek that if I tell the truth about it, some foolish person may drive it to become still worse by trying to assassinate it. I cannot help that, even if I could see what worse it could do than it is already doing.[33]

Never, before or since, has Shaw explained so precisely why he was usually a Fabian but often a Marxist. In writing "Major Barbara," obviously he was inclined to be the second:

> UNDERSHAFT. Vote! Bah! When you vote, you only change the names of the cabinet. When you shoot, you pull down governments, inaugurate new epochs, abolish old orders and set up new. Is that historically true, Mr. Learned Man, or is it not?
>
> CUSINS. It is historically true. I loathe having to admit it. I repudiate your sentiments. I abhor your nature. I defy you in every possible way. Still, it is true. But it ought not to be true.[34]

Indeed, both "Major Barbara" and its Preface imply the theory of class war in its most drastic form. Shaw tells us that Undershaft is prepared to defend his wealth at the risk of his life and that "it is for the poor to repudiate poverty when they have had enough of it." [35] The ultimate and distant result of such antagonism must be the Marxist ideal of a classless society. And therefore Undershaft's profession is glorious because he can blow up the past and throw the future into the melting pot, or as he puts it, "Whatever can blow men up can blow society up." [36] His bombs act on tradition as his logic acts on illusion. He is a Benthamite who mixes his empiricism with dynamite. Such a man is in considerable danger of being blown up himself. And the destruction of capitalists to make way for communists is good Marxism, as the destruction of heroes to make way for superheroes is good Nietzscheanism. For once, Zarathustra might speak for Marx as well as for his creator: *"Ich liebe Den, welcher die Zukünftigen rechtfertigt und die Vergangenen erlöst: denn er wird an den Gegenwärtigen zu Grunde gehen."* [37]

The destruction of Undershaft seems likely to be hastened by Barbara's fiancé, Cusins, whom Mr. Bentley regards as the hero of the play. It is clear that in considerable degree he represents the viewpoint of the author. He is a young man of demonic temper. His love for Barbara is rationally irrational. He imbibes Undershaft's gospel together with a great deal of sherry, undergoes a kind of Dionysian conversion, and then, as Mr. Bentley feels, overcomes his master, accepting the future directorship of the factory only upon his own terms. He will use his power to equalize the professional and the working classes by putting arms in the hands of the latter. "All power is spiritual," because it determines what is spiritual.[38] Cusins is undoubtedly important to the drama, but not so important as to be considered the hero—and indeed we have Shaw's own word to the contrary.[39] The major theme of the play is the drastic political criticism embodied in the character of Undershaft. The story of Barbara and Cusins forms a secondary theme of hope. In fact, Barbara herself seems to represent not so much religion as faith and confidence in life itself, so that in accepting Cusins and resolving to fight for the salvation of the laborers in her father's factory, she not only illustrates Shaw's doctrine that people cannot be developed spiritually until they are freed from the debasement of poverty, but she symbolizes a general renewal of faith and hope.

But this renewal is undeniably vague and faint. It involves a compromise with capitalism, and both Cusins and Barbara agree that they will be in the power of forces beyond their control. It is very easy to sell arms to national governments and very hard to sell them to poor people. On the whole, Cusins himself is an irony.

Having temporarily lost faith, then, in democratic constitutionalism, Shaw takes refuge in the Marxian dialectic of force. Perhaps the last Victorian optimism is the belief that force can be the rule of progress.

Marx seems trying to build a Victorian dream of universal comfort out of twentieth-century explosives. In a world of atomic energy, the result may well be universal poverty and a period of Christian abnegation. In Shaw the optimism of force is at once desperate and halfhearted.

CHAPTER TWENTY-NINE

The Decline of the Fabians and the Fall of Mr. H. G. Wells

Through the first decade of the twentieth century, the Fabians continued to grow in fame as they declined in vital influence on the labor movement. There might have been no limit to their respectability, had they not fallen briefly under the influence of an extraordinary personality. The impact of Mr. H. G. Wells on the Fabian Society was no less violent than that of the Boer War itself. Having as an obscure student long observed the Fabians, he came to them in 1906 full of theories of what they ought to be. After some preliminary threats, he set off in a shy, courteous monotone a tremendous bomb entitled "The Faults of the Fabian," in which he blasted the Society mercilessly for a lack of "imaginative megalomania." It was still half a drawing-room coterie trying to carry out a revolution over its teacups. The Fabians were attempting

> nothing less than the alteration of the economic basis of society. Measure with your eye this little meeting, this little hall: look at that little stall of not very powerful tracts: think of the scattered members, one here, one there. . . . Then go out into the Strand. Note the size of the buildings and business places, note the glare of the advertisements, note the abundance of traffic and the multitude of people. . . . That is the world whose very foundations you are attempting to change. How does this little dribble of activities look then? [1]

The unfilterable viruses which caused this sleeping sickness were the Old Gang, who as the Executive Committee had long molded Fabian destiny. Wells demanded expansion not only of the Committee but of income, expenditure, staff, propaganda, and membership. A socialist millennium would never be achieved by permeation and secret diplomacy. It must be brought about by brute votes. There was much point in this criticism. Webb had formed the Society in his own image. The struggle was to decide whether it would continue to fit his conception of a select group of highly educated wirepullers or expand toward Wells's conception of a large political organization. If it was to survive Webb, it might well have to transcend his influence.

The bomb was not only shyly tossed but meekly received. In the spirit of Wells's criticism, the Executive Committee voted to turn the proposal over to a larger committee composed equally of the Executive and of nonofficial members. But apparently Mr. Wells expected nothing less than immediate acceptance. Patience and shyness were suddenly both at an end. He flew into a pet, contemptuously refused to allow the Old Gang any voice in deciding their fate, and indignantly accused them of exhibiting the vanity and duplicity of aging favorites threatened with eclipse. The ferocious veterans of numberless polemical massacres responded once more with saintly patience. Wells might appoint his own committee to consider his own reforms. He did so but delayed the millennium for a trip to the United States, from which he returned several months later determined to transform the wizened-up little Fabian Society into a Samurai Order after the manner of his own *Modern Utopia*.

The meetings of the larger committee were resumed. In an essay that is one breathless tirade of gay fury, Shaw has indicated their general tenor. Wells, he explains, had been received among the Fabians

> with a distinguished consideration never accorded by that irreverent body to any mortal before or since. He insulted it freely and proceeded to rearrange it according to his own taste. No pen can describe his conduct during this process. Take all the sins he ascribes to his colleagues: the touchiness of Hyndman, the dogmatism of Quelch, Blatchford's preoccupation with his own methods, Grayson's irresponsibility; add every other petulance of which a spoiled child or a successful operatic tenor is capable; multiply the total by ten; square the result; cube it; raise it to the millionth power and square it again; and you will still fall short of the truth about Wells. Yet, the worse he behaved the more he was indulged; and the more he was indulged the worse he behaved.[2]

This vicious circle of patience and effrontery was prolonged by a miraculous event. Keir Hardie had been chosen leader of the new Labour Party. The minuscule I.L.P. had captured the great voting power and financial strength of the trade-unions. The Fabians were dazzled by the truth of their ancient prophecy. But Wells had made the same prophecy more recently and pronounced it for the Fabians themselves. That society of cynical Machiavellians was fascinated. Never has prudence fallen an easier victim to temerity. Shaw indulged a favorite illusion and dreamed of a socialist party of middle-class intellectuals. He decided that in the south of England there were county constituencies where independent middle-class socialists might win though laborite candidates could not. These *ultimae Thulae* of bourgeois intellectualism were never found, but meanwhile the clash of so much temperamental genius had made Fabian socialism a fashionable sensation, and the funds of the Society mounted to unprecedented figures.

The meetings of the large committee were said to have been brilliant and contentious, but its report was dull and unanimous. Wells's most daring proposals had somehow filtered down into the appendix. The rest was administrative detail, which hardly seemed to promise a millennium. The one constructive proposal was that the Fabians should participate as a political organization in Parliamentary elections. This, Wells declared later, was to be regarded as a "secondary and subordinate" part of the report. Representing the Old Gang on the committee, Shaw presented "A Reply," in which he argued brilliantly against the unanimous report and then agreed with it by proposing the formation of a middle-class socialist party.

Puzzled by so much difference and so much harmony, members of the committee, including Mrs. Shaw herself, signed the documents. On December 6, 1906, the report of the committee was to be submitted to the Society as a whole. Since the two sides differed little on essentials, the real issue would be whether the new emperor or the Old Gang should rule. The debate would of course be sharp, and the Old Gang, now at length fully aroused, was savagely aware that Wells was a poor debater. Webb and Bland, upon whom he had heaped particular insult, were crying for blood, but Shaw, not wishing the Society to lose its gifted recruit, once more intervened in the role of diplomatist and insisted on representing the Executive Committee. Before a tense and crowded meeting heralded by sensational publicity in the newspapers, he performed the execution—apparently with exemplary benevolence and detachment. It was a splendid achievement in the euthanasia which he has so often recommended for dangerous criminals. The meeting rejected Wells's report but softened the blow by offering to accept any part of it after full discussion.

Quite unconsciously, Wells took a terrible vengeance. He had been thinking about free love and had decided that as communism in wealth must produce social ease, so communism in love must produce sexual ease. Economic socialism inevitably involves sexual socialism. These incredible views he unfolded very earnestly to the reddening and horrified middle-class ears of the Executive Committee. Exactly what Mr. Wells proposed to do, says Edward Pease dryly, was not clear. With less courtesy than before, the Committee contented itself with putting women's suffrage into the Fabian Basis.

Wells was twice elected to the Executive Committee, each time ranking fourth on the pole, but he attended very few meetings and in 1908 resigned from the Society.

His swift and fiery trajectory across the Fabian heavens is chiefly significant in illustrating how conservative, practical, empirical, and English the Society was. Wells himself managed to apply a very English mentality to the rather un-English field of utopian speculation. For more than seventy years, according to changing circumstances of knowledge and experience, he shuffled off old worlds for new and muddled through innumerable utopias, plunging with every fresh glimmer of light into the remotest spheres of time and space. Like most Englishmen, he had a historical sense, but it worked in reverse. His present, ballooned up by all sorts of perfectionistic speculations, rose uncontrollably into the future. The past was a tiny sandbag dangling impotently on a rope in midair. The history of Wells's political opinions is simply a chain of bright, iridescent, soap-bubble worlds, which he tossed off and allowed to explode with remarkable spontaneity and gusto.

From this exhilarating activity, he returned to the petty issues of the present only with the utmost impatience. What attracted him to Fabianism were Fabian brains, Fabian science and efficiency. The rest was uncongenial, as practical politics were uncongenial. In his autobiography he observes with infinite disgust:

> A paragraph from *Tract 70* published in 1896, dealing with the "Mission of the Fabians" is probably unequalled in all literature for self-complacent stupidity. "The Fabian Society . . . has no distinctive opinions on the Marriage Question, Religion, Art, abstract Economics, historic Evolution, Currency, or any other subject than its own special business of practical Democracy and Socialism." As one reads one can almost hear a flat voice, with a very very sarcastic stress on the capitals, reciting this fatuous declaration.[3]

And not only the speculative caution but the harsh utilitarianism of the Fabians was uncongenial to Wells. He approached, perhaps more nearly than any other modern writer, the aesthetic socialism of Morris and Ruskin. He approached them also in the directness and naïveté of his tactics. To believe in an idea was to urge it, to try to make others believe in it. To conceal an idea so as to avoid friction or to carry it into effect—as Webb did—by finesse and secrecy, to lure those who opposed it into unwitting support, seemed to him, from intellectual vanity if for no other reason, at once stupid and dangerously hypocritical. It was inevitable that he should leave the Society. It was unfortunate that he discovered his distaste so early, for he was immensely valuable. The Fabian dilemma had always been how to unite practical caution in solving immediate problems with idealistic enthusiasm in envisaging distant goals. A man like Shaw, with his critic's grip on the past and his controversialist's grip on the present, could solve problems, but despite his immense poetic gifts, he could not so easily create faith. Wells could. And that, one suspects, explains more than anything else the miraculous patience of the Old Gang.

Wells's color and enthusiasm served to more than double Fabian membership, and several attempts were made to form a political party. By 1911 there were thirteen Fabian Members of Parliament, but they did not in any sense constitute a bloc. Wells also occasioned a veritable stampede of genius into the Society, so that it threatened to lose all political character and transform itself into the Athenaeum of the twentieth century. Arnold Bennett, G. M. Trevelyan, Edward Garnett all became members, and Granville-Barker was for a while extremely active. Yet this influx of irrelevant mind was but a passing phase—another example of the Fabian magnetism toward success and respectability. It may have in part contributed to one interesting event: in 1907 Shaw founded the Fabian Arts Group, which was to study the relations between the arts and to illustrate the principle, laid down by Morris, that socialism and beauty can be joined. The group did not last long, for Mrs. Sidney Webb was then quietly turning the Society into an instrument of propaganda for her new Poor Law.

Both nature and marriage had made Mrs. Webb a Fabian. Moreover, as a resolute and imperious woman who had carved a fairy-tale happiness out of the solid granite of blue books and labor history, she very naturally took over control after the voluntary exile of Wells. Under her guidance, the Society became more Fabian than ever, in spite of the waves of syndicalism that beat down from Oxford. Its chief work was a steady and tactful agitation for the "Minority Poor Law Report," which proposed to reduce destitution by a comprehensive scheme of education and pensions. This document, drawn up by the Webbs, is generally regarded as the most characteristic of all Fabian writings. It is obviously significant that in the later as well as the earlier part of Shaw's life, the Society remained firmly Fabian, strengthening in him the tendency toward cautious compromise and weakening that toward bold and romantic speculation.

Of course, now that the Executive Committee had become a kind of Praetorian Guard and the scepter passed swiftly from emperor to emperor—or empress—it must not be supposed that the grave senatorial influence of the Old Gang remained untroubled and unchallenged. A younger generation, threatening utopias, clamored loudly for power. Shaw, together with several others, decided to give them their chance and in 1911 resigned from the Executive. The result was paradoxical. No utopias transpired, and Shaw's power was greater than ever. The Executive could no longer draw up a plan with any assurance of having it carried out, for he might at any time rise from the floor and persuade a business meeting to vote for something entirely different.

In conclusion, the question might be asked: What did Shaw owe to Fabianism, and what did Fabianism owe to Shaw? Perhaps the greatest achievement of the Fabians is that they made socialism English; they combined, or attempted to combine, irreconcilables—revolutionary change with evolutionary caution, distant theoretical ends with immediate practical compromise. In this mode of thought and action, introduced into socialism chiefly by Webb, Shaw began his political development, and so became an English politician before he became an Irish playwright. To be sure, he has himself said that all really distinguished people grow more revolutionary as they grow older, and Shaw grew both very old and very revolutionary—but in an obstinately English manner.

What did Shaw give the Fabians? Primarily, a gay, resilient temperament and an eloquent and epigrammatic idiom. He allowed them to remain English yet prevented them from being dull. How far he is responsible for the basic structure of Fabian economics is of course a question. That structure seems to have arisen directly out of the discussions of the seven essayists in the Hampstead Historical Society. But which of the seven contributed most? Probably Shaw more than Webb. Webb was apparently the first to see the state socialism latent in the law of rent, but Shaw discovered Jevons and refuted Marx. Moreover, he seems to have possessed, if the more unstable, also the more speculative mind. Fabianism owed its dash and brilliance to Shaw, its gradualism and its statistical method to Webb, and its basic doctrines to both.

CHAPTER THIRTY

Doctors, Women and Children

Late in the summer of 1906 Shaw and his wife were staying at Meva-gissey on the Cornish Coast, where he plunged alternately into the surf and into blue books and Karl Pearson's *Biometrika*. Suddenly Granville-Barker appeared demanding a play. For once, Shaw was quite idea-less. Then his wife reminded him how, while talking once with Sir Almroth Wright at St. Mary's Hospital, an assistant had come in to inquire whether the noted physician would accept one more tuberculous patient for his new opsonic treatment. "Is he worth it?" asked Wright. Shaw had perceived that here was a play.

"Why not use the idea now?" Mrs. Shaw wanted to know.

A play about doctors, about science! Shaw's mouth watered. He called for his tablet at once, and the play went down on paper with astonishing swiftness. His enthusiasm requires some explanation, which concerns not only medicine in general but the universe in particular, for in those days a schoolmaster could not whip a child nor a doctor vaccinate a patient, Pavlov could not cut a dog's throat nor Michaelson and Morley measure the speed of light, without listening to a lecture from Shaw on the subject. History happened in its volumes, and Shaw explained how it should have happened in his tens of volumes. Or rather, he argued, for as always he regarded life as a controversy and truth as an argument. Voltaire at Fernay was an uncontentious drone compared to Shaw at 10 Adelphi Terrace.

For him, "*Ecrasez l'infame!*" meant science. What he really thought about science is not altogether clear. Probably, with negative common sense, he flatly disbelieved in its methodical skepticism and elaborate objectiveness. He could not ignore all its achievements, but he ignored a good many. He opposed it because he feared its mechanism, its cruelty to experimental victims, its priestly assumption of authority, and the superstitious awe which it inspired in laymen. He could not forget that scientists were human beings. Here Samuel Butler had been illuminating, and indeed Shaw's attitude toward science probably derived in large degree from that philosopher, who opposed the abolition of the church, for fear "a blatant, bastard science would at once step into its place." [1]

> There is nothing [wrote Shaw in later years] that people will not
> believe nowadays if only it be presented to them as science, and
> nothing they will not disbelieve if it be presented to them as religion.
> I myself began like that; and I am ending by receiving every scien-
> tific statement with dour suspicion whilst giving very respectful
> consideration to the inspirations and revelations of the prophets and
> poets. [2]

If the world were a committee table and nature as political as sewer-
age, he would undoubtedly have driven every experimenter cowering
and trembling behind the bolted doors of his laboratory. As it was, he
seems to have won most of the battles and lost the campaign. He made a
great many scientists feel very angry and very helpless, but despite the
avalanche of Shavianisms, science still moved, or rather—for it was the
age of Einstein and relativity—reeled from discovery to discovery; and
the public, together with most experts, continued to regard Shaw as a
madman and science as absolute. But then, he did not expect to alter the
course of modern civilization in a moment.

Of all scientists, doctors were his favorite antagonists. They represented science to the general public, and they were central to the great
social problem of health, which is nearly as important as those of marriage and education, so that as time went on he became almost as interested in doctors as in women. An early trophy of this interest is of course
the discoverer of Dr. Paramore's disease. His attitude was strongly hostile, partly because doctors were perhaps the most priestly, and the least
scientific, of scientists; partly because their human responsibility was
the greatest and the most direct; and partly because they had proved all
too fallible in his personal experience, having killed one of his early
friends by a blundering operation, very nearly cost him a foot by the
Lister method of dressing a wound, and failed by any method to cure
him of severe monthly headaches from which he suffered for years. He
was fond not only of using doctors to try to cure his headaches but of
using his headaches to investigate doctors. His attack on inoculation,
perhaps legitimate enough when "The Doctor's Dilemma" was written
in 1906, was continued long after it has ceased to be so. It is characteristic of the dramatic tension which marked so many of his friendships that
despite his opinions about physicians, Shaw was intimate for half a
lifetime with Sir Almroth Wright, of whom he always speaks with admiration.

But the evils of medicine were not sufficient to fill a whole play. He
was never content to kill a single bird. Fortunately, William Archer had
provided him with another. At Ibsen's death Shaw had written a gener-

ous appreciation, in which, however, he had objected as usual that the great Scandinavian was unrealistically murderous at the end of his plays. Fired with indignation for his hero, Archer had retorted that Shaw was merely rationalizing his own weakness: he could not keep a straight face long enough to get at the profounder aspects of character involved in a great tragic scene. A few weeks later, when "The Doctor's Dilemma" was nearly completed, *The Tribune* contained a letter from Shaw, part of which read:

> Mr. William Archer . . . denied that Mr. Shaw could claim the highest rank as a dramatist until he had faced the King of Terrors on the stage. Stung by this reproach from his old friend, Mr. Shaw is writing a play all about death, which he declares will be the most amusing play he has ever written.

What price tragedy now?
Yah! [3]

The play was ready in record time, and in 1907, with Granville-Barker as Dubedat and Lillah McCarthy as Jennifer, it had a triumphant run of six weeks at the Court. Of course Archer declared himself unsatisfied with the death scene, and of course he was right—but for the wrong reason. If anything, Shaw was too much in earnest—too much in earnest, perhaps, to take his play seriously as a work of art; too much, certainly, to take his medical characters seriously. The heavy, relentless, joyless satire of the first act destroys all our faith in the doctors. Consequently, when Ridgeon is faced with his dilemma—whether to save his friend Blenkinsop or the artist Dubedat—we do not quite believe either in the surgeon or in his dilemma. But he is not faced with a genuine choice between art and friendship. He simply falls in love with Jennifer Dubedat and as he confesses, makes his decision with a view not so much to saving Blenkinsop as actually to killing Dubedat by entrusting him to the even more homicidal ignorance of Sir Ralph Bloomfield Bonington. A much sounder course, one is tempted to think after five acts of that doting lady, would have been to murder Mrs. Dubedat herself. At any rate, the revelation, with characteristic Shavian anticlimax in the last act, of Ridgeon's true motive makes the play a broad satire, rather than a comic study, of medical ethics. Finally, the dilemma is not in any significant way linked with the co-theme propounded in the Preface with regard to Dubedat: that a man seldom has more than one or two points of honor. Certainly Dubedat (modeled after Edward Aveling, who seduced one of Karl Marx's daughters) had only one or two.

In brief, Shaw allowed his grim earnest about doctors to outweigh every other consideration. The result is a rather poor play about rather disagreeable characters; and the climax, which in accord with Shaw's promise to Archer kills off one of them, is not much better. It is not, as Archer declares, too comic. In fact, it has definitely the exaltation and the poetry that Archer ordered. It also succeeds in making Dubedat, in spite of his faults, for the moment a sympathetic and impressive figure and in making the play itself, despite its many elements of comedy and satire, something of the "tragedy" which the title promises. "The most tragic thing in the world," Ridgeon explains immediately after Dubedat's death, "is a man of genius who is not also a man of honor." [4]

But the spectator is not made to feel this very deeply. Meanwhile, the death scene is too long, too full of Sir Patrick's medical moralizing, and too stagy. The immediate reappearance of the widow, magnificently attired, seems to me deplorably melodramatic—the more so in the actual production of the play, as Shaw and Lillah McCarthy contrived a bizarre and tremendous headdress, totally irrelevant to contemporary fashion. That Shaw should have chosen to follow up Dubedat's death with a bit of broad comedy in which Sir Ralph attempts to quote Shakespeare need worry no one but Archer. One might just as well object to the Porter's scene in "Macbeth." A significant feature of the death scene is the satire on the daily press in the person of an incredibly prying, vulgar, ignorant, slovenly, and imbecile reporter. In the early nineties, Shaw had been proud of being a journalist. After the Boer War, he hated journalists for what they could do to the public mind. Perhaps the real strength of his love for democracy can be measured by the depth of his hatred for yellow journalism.

The Preface, which was published with the play in 1911, is a kind of reader's dilemma about doctors. Shaw uses all his brilliance to defend nearly all his prejudices—or, more accurately, he exerts all his powers of argument to urge a quarter-truth. That medical associations are conspiracies to conceal medical incompetence, that doctors defer to public taste by diagnosing fashionable diseases and prescribing fashionable cures, that they get into the habit of cutting off legs and arms because operations are profitable and impressive, that in short the profession represents a vested interest in ill health—all this undoubtedly contains some truth, but a great deal more prejudice and eccentricity. Shaw feels that the sins of English doctors are largely due to their poverty, and of course he recommends socialized medicine as a cure. Discussing his favorite crime of vivisection, he predicts that since modern philosophy recognizes no distinction between man and beast, the modern state may presently permit vivisectors to progress from the use of beasts to that of men. It is ironic that this prediction seemed so extravagant such a short time ago.

"The Doctor's Dilemma" was a strong financial success. In fact, Shaw was now looked on as uniformly profitable, and large commercial managers began to ask him for plays. Barker and Vedrenne began to ask themselves why they worked so hard and risked so much simply to earn a modest income by filling the Court Theatre. Accordingly, they hired three large West-End houses, playing a Shaw repertory at one, Shaw's new play "Getting Married" at the second, and a Laurence Housman play at the third. But it was too much rent—and perhaps too much Shaw. "Vedrenne got out with nothing but a reputation," Shaw told Hesketh Pearson; "Barker had to pawn his clothes; and I disgorged most of my royalties; but the creditors were paid in full." [5]

Shaw's next play is as sunny and amiable as "The Doctor's Dilemma" is acid and sharp. It is so little offensive to anybody that instead of setting up the usual informative shrieks and yells of pain, critics dismissed it patronizingly as plotless and pointless, no play but a mere conversation. To be sure, all Shaw's plays are discussion plays. All his characters are extremely articulate. But "Getting Married" is more of a discussion play than any of the preceding, and its characters subordinate every other phase of their existence and reality to their articulateness. They are the psychologically motivated spokesmen of intellectual points of view. Its very considerable plot, kept off the stage in the interests of discussion, involves an unsuccessful attempt at writing an ideal marriage code. As comedy should, it begins in folly and ends in common sense—or its best Shavian substitute.

At the outset, everyone wants to marry, and no one can. After a little conversation, it emerges that no one wants to marry unless the law will guarantee that in any difference of opinion both partners shall have their own way. Conventional marriage seems hardly so flexible, even though, as Alderman Collins (a variant on William, the waiter in "You Never Can Tell") points out, there are as many kinds of marriages as there are kinds of people. Thereupon the Bishop, who believes in giving the devil plenty of play, suavely suggests a civil contract especially adapted to the situation. Without troubling to discover what the situation is, they set about drawing up an agreement in which everybody insists on securing his own peculiar conditions for everybody else. The result is that Edith, who wants to live comfortably with Cecil, must have her own separate quarters; Lesbia, who wants no husband at all, gets two; and Leo, who wants two always on tap, must have none at all for two years after the birth of each child.

Somewhat less hopefully, they take up the question of health. Edith wants to be guaranteed the right to follow medical authority; Reggie, the right to ignore it; and Lesbia, the right to make all medical decisions herself. Under the weight of this and half a dozen other problems, the legal contract collapses. Everybody—in a manner so characteristic of Shaw as to indicate some self-satire—has minded everybody else's business to a complete standstill. Conventional marriage is upheld as the only workable arrangement. Everyone gets married who really wants to, and everyone else lapses into comparative respectability, including "Sinjon" Hotchkiss, "the celebrated coward," who heroically becomes the Platonic lover of Mrs. George.

Each character is of a wedge of the marriage-problem pie: Reggie is the man who marries late; Boxer, the sentimental, rejected lover; Hotchkiss, the philanderer; Soames, the celibate. Mrs. Collins stews her family remorselessly in sentimental love; Leo wants masculine friends after marriage. The Bishop and his wife are happily married in a conventional way; Mr. and Mrs. George, in an unconventional way, with the wife instead of the husband as free lance. Boxer, Leo, Reggie, Cecil, and Edith are concerned with marriage as such; Mrs. George and Lesbia, with what Shaw makes clear in the Preface should be an entirely separate thing: "No political constitution will ever succeed or deserve to succeed unless it includes the recognition of an absolute right to sexual experience, and is untainted by the Pauline or romantic view of such experience as sinful in itself." [6] For Lesbia, sex means children; for Mrs. George it represents the peaks of emotional intensity and inspiration. Both insist that marriage has nothing to do with either experience. But the Preface puts their case much better than the play does, for a theory about human beings is nearly always more convincing when the human beings are left out. Lesbia objects to marriage in the name of independence, refinement, and self-respect; but she talks far too much about the evils of pipe smoking. One gathers that she loathes tobacco more than she longs for motherhood. In fact, she is a little too real for the point of view she represents.

But if Lesbia is too real to be good rhetoric, Mrs. George is too rhetorical to be quite real. Here Shaw dares to look his own doctrine in the face and follow it to its awful and un-Victorian conclusions. Candida is not a voluptuary because she is intelligent; Mrs. Warren, because she is a business woman; Cleopatra, because she is Caesar's protégée. But Mrs. George is a voluptuary whose only condition is that her emotion and her lover's be deep and sincere. Shaw himself is slightly appalled at the result:

> Her beauty is wrecked, like an ageless landscape ravaged by long and fierce war. . . . Her cheeks are wasted and lined, her mouth writhen and piteous. The whole face is a battle-field of the passions, quite deplorable until she speaks.[7]

While he has faced the physical results like a man, the spiritual results he is inclined, like a Victorian and a romantic, to whitewash with poetry which raises Mrs. George from the genial profligate she seems to a generalized symbol of sexual ecstasy. She falls into a trance and delivers herself of one of the principal ideas of the Preface: that the priceless boon of sexual elation should not be joined to the domestic drudgery and humdrum prostitution of ordinary marriage.

> When all the stars sang in your ears and all the winds swept you into the heart of heaven, were you deaf? were you dull? was I no more to you than a bone to a dog? Was it not enough? We spent eternity together; and you ask me for a little lifetime more. We possessed all the universe together; and you ask me to give you my scanty wages as well. I have given you the greatest of all things; and you ask me to give you little things. I gave you your own soul: you ask me for my body as a plaything. Was it not enough? Was it not enough? [8]

She is sex not for sex's, but for inspiration's sake. In short, she is a bit of psychologized rhetoric, or idea.

Mrs. George rather remotely suggests Ellen Terry. She has some of the practical wisdom and robust common sense which one observes in the Terry correspondence, but Shaw has rather incongruously joined with these qualities his own fastidious aestheticism, which sanctioned sexual experience for inspirational and reproductive purposes only. The real Ellen was more conventional, more charitable, more human, even more animal than that. Her letters show that she was also humble at heart and did not think of herself as a very good woman. Altogether, one is glad to have her letters to Shaw rather than Mrs. George's to the Bishop.

In "Getting Married," Shaw observes the classical unities of time and place, making no division into acts. In this experiment he was influenced particularly by Euripides, whom in Gilbert Murray's translations he very much admired and had introduced into "Major Barbara" through his Murrayesque professor of Greek, Cusins. In an interesting essay, Gilbert Norwood has pointed out a striking parallel between Euripides and Shaw.[9] Both are the products of an age of criticism following an age of political expansion and boisterous optimism. Both attack traditional values, champion women and the underprivileged classes, and are antiheroic, naturalistic, satiric, and brilliantly rhetorical.

A few words about the Preface to "Getting Married." It begins with a grisly denunciation of the Victorian family; proceeds to a cool and statistical discussion of monogamy, polygyny, polyandry, and other terrifying "-andries" and "-gamies"; calls on Prime Ministers to undertake, on pain of permitting the direst racial degeneration, the most drastic of reforms according to the vaguest of plans; then settles down to a vigorous and common-sense argument for easier divorce; and concludes with a proposal that unless marriages meet certain standards, they should be interfered with by the state. It is amusing that Shaw, who hates schools, should frequently want to turn life itself into a school with rules, inspections, and examinations, all complete.

This Preface is not one of Shaw's strongest. On the ills and weaknesses of matrimony he cannot be bettered, but on the virtues and advantages he is harshly and narrowly rationalistic. His attitude can be summed up in a single sentence: there is no magic in marriage. Though many marriages are sordid and most are prosiac, one is inclined to maintain that there is some magic in them all. Undoubtedly the solemnity of the vow, the dignity of the institution, and the enchantments of sex itself have power to strike the imagination and at least in some degree to raise up a long companionship above the human dangers with which it is all too thickly beset. Certainly it would be most unwise to cut sex loose from its natural moorings and set adrift its immense potentialities for good and evil as an anarchic force in human relations. As usual, Shaw is generalizing from his own temperament and situation, as well as from certain books which had impressed him very deeply—above all, from *The Way of All Flesh*. With vivid and compelling realism, this book says precisely what Shaw wanted to believe about marriage, the family, and education. And yet Shaw's father was not at all like Theobald. If Butler hated Victorianism because his father was Victorian, perhaps Shaw hated fathers because, in his experience, most of them were necessarily Victorian.

The Preface to "Misalliance" continues the same discussion, proceeding from marriage to children and education. Shaw also employs the same strategy, beginning with the most reckless generalizations and ending cautiously with the Bible and comparative common sense. How successful this technique is—whether it startles the torpid into ideas more than it repels the logical to complete distrust—is a question. At any rate, Shaw is fond of drawing rather safe or ambiguous conclusions from terrifying premises, and as this cannot be accomplished without some expense to consistency, he is continually shifting fundamentals to suit the temporary convenience of his argument. All schoolmasters are sadistic monsters for the sake of a little relaxation of academic discipline; and for the sake of explaining the benevolent dullness of his own early education, they are merely good fellows marooned in their profession by poverty.

Of course his basic ideas amount to a total condemnation of education in the ordinary sense: children should be taught nothing which might interfere with the fresh and spontaneous intimations of the Life Force; schools are prisons where children are incarcerated chiefly so that they will not annoy their parents; schoolmasters are fiends who have been attracted to their posts by the lascivious desire to beat their fellow beings. These views are wittily and eloquently put in the Preface to "Misalliance" and savagely put in his Preface to the Workers' Educational Association *Yearbook* for 1918. It would be an interesting geological study to uncover their precise history. They have no relation to contemporary reality, for by the early twentieth century the English school had long since ceased to be cruel and morbid. They may have been effected by Shaw's own early experience, for apparently his teachers were guilty of all the Victorian dullness of instruction though without the Victorian liveliness of punishment. But much more, one suspects, he got his ideas out of Dickens. Squeers, to whom he refers several times, seems to stand in his mind as the great, eternal Platonic idea of a schoolmaster. As a reformer, of course, he wanted to believe in the infinite fiendishness of schoolmasters in order that he could believe in the infinite perfectibility of children under a better system. Where he was wiser, he was less original. Nearly all his more moderate ideas, which comprise his proposals of specific reform, are to be found in Butler's *Erewhon.*

However, it is not to be expected that where major premises bark so loud, conclusions will not bite a little. At one point or another Shaw suggests that family bonds should be loosened, that compulsory education should be abolished, that children should be supported by the state and permitted to wander wherever they wish. They should receive only indirect discipline—through the necessity, first, of getting along with their fellows, and, second, of learning an irreducible minimum of mathematics and socialism in order to qualify for traveling privileges. These ideas, baldly stated, sound extreme, but actually Shaw speaks of "organizing the liberty of the child," makes voluntary education sound rather compulsory, has a good word to say for the family and many good words for discipline and moral law. He yells anarchy from the footlights and intermittently whispers self-control from the wings; but he never brings the two together in a working arrangement. We find him dancing anxiously—and gaily—on the horns of his old dilemma:

> What corrupts civilization, religion, law and convention (and they are at present pretty nearly as corrupt as they dare) is the constant attempts made by the wills of individuals and classes to thwart the wills and enslave the powers of other individuals and classes. The powers of the parent and the schoolmaster, and of their public

analogues the lawgiver and the judge, become instruments of tyranny in the hands of those who are too narrow-minded to understand law and exercise judgment.[10]

Since he cannot have everything perfect, Shaw is determined at least to have it natural. He is all for liberty and instinct because reason and civilization are subject to error. He will not undertake character building because schoolmasters are sometimes tyrannous. He is reluctant to embark on his educational program because he does not want to turn innocent children out on streets unimproved by socialism. He rejects the teachings of experience lest the future be no better than the past: "The present must not attempt to schoolmaster the future by pretending to know good from evil in tendency." [11]

Like "Getting Married," "Misalliance" emphasizes discussion but combines with it much more interest in plot and character. It is a powerful, but not a pleasant, play. Intentionally, it is a satire of marriage, the family, contemporary education, and capitalism. Unintentionally, it is a refutation of its own Preface, for the heroine is all too easily identified as a very sinister example of the kind of education Shaw recommends. Of course she is intended to illustrate the ill effects of parental indulgence and favoritism, which, however, simply create the same anarchy in another institution. "Never treated as a child"— and therefore full of a child's brutality and trickery; undisciplined—and therefore bored and restless, with nothing cultivated but her sensations; Hypatia, in order to drive away the dullness of a long afternoon, rides sadistically roughshod over the delicacy of an older gentleman who has placed himself in her power; chases, catches, and purchases a suitable mate who providentially drops from the skies; and then, after some coarse jokes at the feebleness and garrulity of age, gives a fillip to her fun by quite gratuitously working herself into a cool rage of insolence and her father into a fury of impotent horror. One regrets that she is not after all to marry Bentley and have him kicking and screaming among her bride's *décor*, but perhaps no marriage would be successful if everyone got the mate he deserved. At any rate, Percival himself has perhaps had enough good fortune in his model education, and it will take a young man reared by three philosophers to remain impervious to such a wife.

Any drama with Hypatia for heroine is properly entitled "Misalliance." However, the misalliance to which Shaw refers is that between man and woman and between parents and children. Marriage is a mere matter of purchase: Hypatia buys Percival; Lucy Titmus, paid for by Tarleton, bought herself a husband and set him up in business; and

Lina, the Shavian female acrobat, though good-humoredly tolerant of the improper advances of Lord Summerhays, Tarleton, and Bentley, ·is outraged to the soul at Johnny's honorable proposal of marriage:

> And this Englishman! this linendraper! he dares to ask me to come and live with him in this rrrrrrabbit hutch, and take my bread from his hand, and ask him for pocket money, and wear soft clothes, and be his woman! his wife! . . . You may tell your Johnny to buy an Englishwoman: he shall not buy Lina Szczepanowska; and I will not stay in the house where such dishonor is offered me.[12]

Lina is the woman of the future because she stands above the contaminating influences of modern marriage, education, and capitalism. She has received the kind of artistic education which Shaw advocates; she is not flabby and weak, physically or morally, because her profession subjects her to the severest discipline; and being able as an artist to do something supremely well, she actually earns the income she receives from society and so may live without buying or selling herself as other women must in the world of capitalism and Dolls' Houses. Her descent from the empyrean and her return to that element, carrying young Bentley with her, are pure allegory. Bentley is by nature an artist, destined like Shaw to succeed at fifty.[13] Incidentally, Lina herself is by nature a schoolmistress, worthy of all the fiery execrations heaped on that tribe in the Preface. But then, schoolmasters are nearly as often the heroes of Shaw's plays as the villains of his prefaces.

Shaw's treatment of the family, both in the Preface and in the play, is a curious mixture of Benthamism, Marxism, and protestantism. He reckons up a mother's blessings and a widow's sorrows in the calculus of pains and pleasures and speaks of the conflict between parents and children in a way that reminds one a little of Marx's class struggle and a little of Milton's warfare between the good and bad angels. Youth wants freedom and independence; age wants service and obedience. Youth covets power; age clings to it. Youth is robust, vulgar, and vigorous; age is delicate, refined, and contemplative. And even when old and young, like Tarleton and Bentley Summerhays, find common ground, parent and child cannot: the natural incompatibility frays into torture with continual association. Furthermore, as Tarleton says, "The relation between the young and the old should be an innocent relation. It should be something they could talk about." [14] But the facts of begetting are not innocent; they establish an insurmountable barrier of shyness between father and child. "Once the little animal has got . . . what you might call a sense of decency, it's all up with the relation between parent and child. You cant get over the fearful shyness." [15]

The central idea of the play is expressed at the climax of a tragicomic scene in which Tarleton, having purchased Percival, the handsome brute with a faultless education, for his daughter, is goaded by her impudence beyond all endurance and bursts out, "No man should know his own child. No child should know its own father. Let the family be rooted out of civilization! Let the human race be brought up in institutions!" [16] This scene, together with the matchmaking preliminaries, in which Hypatia clamors for Percival and then gloats over him with "Oh, you beauty! you beauty!" reminds one of the scene in "The Importance of Being Earnest" in which Ernest and Lady Bracknell discuss the eligibility of Cecily. Shaw's scene is far more searching and ferocious as satire—but it goes too far. Wilde attacks late-Victorian marriage. Shaw attacks marriage itself. Wilde's chief character is an amusing puppet. Shaw's is an incredible monster of pampered female savagery. It is difficult to think that the Tarletons deserved Hypatia. It is difficult to think that she can represent anything typical or general, even a general failure of the family as an educational institution. Consequently, one is repelled by this scene, despite its wit and comedy, and only after some reflection does one feel the force of its accusation.

"Misalliance" is also a satire of class education under capitalism. Gunner, a white-collar proletarian with a tendency to melodrama, attempts to assassinate Tarleton, an idealistic capitalist with tendencies to polygamy and the endowment of public libraries. Over the barrel of the pistol, Tarleton learns that Gunner has acquired his melodramatic view of life from reading novels in the public library, and Gunner learns that his mother's affair with Tarleton, far from being her ruin, has actually been her salvation. Gunner is also the means of satirizing the good form of the public schools. While secreted in the Turkish bath, he has overheard with lower-class indignation Hypatia's improper advances to Percival. When an explanation is needed, he tells the truth —and is bullied with admirable correctness by Percival into a retraction completely vindicating the young lady's good name. Then Mrs. Tarleton spoils everything by bluntly announcing her unbelief. Finding that the gentlemanly fiction no longer serves his purpose, Percival desperately appeals to Lord Summerhays. "Youve done your best, Mr Percival," says Lord Summerhays, who represents aristocracy grown skeptical of its own function of ruling over empire for capitalism. "But the correct thing depends for its success on everybody playing the game very strictly. As a single-handed game, it's impossible." [17]

The play is filled with roles to make an actor's mouth water—and particularly that of Tarleton, with his injunctions to "Read Shakespear!" "Read Chesterton!" Seldom has so bitter a pill as "Misalliance" been covered with such wonderful sugar-coating.

[282]

CHAPTER THIRTY-ONE

Shakespeare, the Middle Classes, a Saint's Legend, and a Fairy Tale

The Preface to "The Dark Lady of the Sonnets," published in 1914, is chiefly significant as revealing Shaw's later attitude toward Shakespeare, which, with respect to politics at least, is the exact opposite of his earlier. He continues to stigmatize the Bard as snobbish, vulgar, melodramatic, immoral, and irreligious, but for the rest claims him, along with Shelley, Wagner, Ibsen, and Jesus, as a Shavian. The mature Shakespeare, freed from popular tyranny by the superb acting of Burbage, was a republican, a democrat, and a ruthless satirist of monarchy and privilege. His castigation of municipal corruption was "quite in the vein of the Fabian Society." He saw the world, "if not exactly as Ibsen did (for it was not quite the same world), at least with much of Ibsen's power of penetrating its illusions and idolatries, and with all Swift's horror of its cruelty and uncleanliness." [1] Unfortunately, this portrait suffers from ambiguity: Shaw cannot make up his mind whether the poet was a cavalier or a puritan.

The Preface also contains some shrewd biographical observations. Shaw cites telling evidence to indicate that Shakespeare was neither a homosexual nor a sycophant and that he did not break his heart over the "Dark Lady of the Sonnets," whether she was Mary Fitton or the mother of Davenant, for he possessed "the irrepressible gaiety of genius which enables it to bear the whole weight of the world's misery without blenching." [2] Apparently he was pessimistic for the most part out of sheer Shavian perversity and privately rejoiced in his genius and in the world spread out for it to portray. This view embodies an overstatement of the truth that art, especially when joined with greatness, has like science or religion its own solace, its own detachment, and its own triumphant joy of achievement. One is reminded of Wells's remark to Vincent Sheean that Shaw is primarily an artist, for obviously he sees himself in Shakespeare. [3]

The play itself is a brilliant little tour de force in which Shakespeare, stealing into the grounds of Whitehall for an assignation with Mary

Fitton, discovers so many of his best lines in the casual conversation of the beefeater on guard that in scribbling them down he quite forgets his purpose, until Queen Elizabeth comes out, walking in her sleep like Lady Macbeth and muttering her remorse over the execution of Mary Queen of Scots. Shakespeare mistakes her for Mary Fitton, makes love, proves that he is not a sycophant by being both very bold and very adroit, and finally winds up to a lengthy plea for a national theater. "The Dark Lady" is a delightfully comic admonition to Bardolators that Shakespeare was a human being and an artist who worked as other artists do.

"Fanny's First Play" (1911) is also little more than an occasional piece. It is in the nature of an exhilarating workout on a favorite punching bag. The author attacks first the dramatic critics and then the middle class in general. His performance is somewhat routine, of course, yet full of the verve and power one expects in a skilled pugilist.

Shaw had always managed to remain friendly with his critics. He had long been intimate with Archer. He had gracefully dedicated *Man and Superman* to Walkley. He had taken good-naturedly Clement Scott's abuse of Ibsen. Nevertheless, he must often have been irritated at the patronizing superiority with which these gentlemen, and Walkley in particular, dismissed his own work as monstrous ingenuities and cynical extravaganzas. Occasionally, he had struck back. In 1894, he had written in *The New Review* that the London dramatic critic, for all practical purposes, had never been out of a theater:

> Consequently to a man who derives all his knowledge of life from witnessing plays, nothing appears more unreal than objective life . . . and the more exactly I reproduce objective life for him on the stage, the more certain he is to call my play an extravaganza.[4]

"Fanny's First Play" is set in a frame, which permits the author to represent the critics as commenting on what is presented. Walkley, Baughan, and Cannan are satirized good-humoredly as Trotter, Vaughan, and Gunn, while the dramatic critic as a species is crucified in a composite individual named Flawner Bannal.

The inner play portrays two middle-class families who are protected from both good and evil by the petrifying habits of respectability. Once the outer crust is broken, as the puritanical and omniscient Mrs. Knox explains, such people are lost. Their religion is no longer genuine illumination, nor their conscience, inward strength.

The play had a great London success. Nevertheless, discriminating friends of the author felt that, like "Getting Married," "Blanco Posnet," and other recent productions, it was not up to his highest level. Beatrice

Webb wrote to Lillah McCarthy, who had played Margaret Knox and also produced the play, "I wish you could persuade G.B.S. to do a piece of serious work, and not pursue this somewhat barren tilting at the family." [5] For once Shaw looked grave. He had a deep respect for Beatrice Webb's opinion.

"Androcles and the Lion" deals with the ancient story of the little Greek tailor who is saved from Christian martyrdom in the Colosseum by his friendship with the king of beasts. Actually, the play is a *ragoût fin* of the choicest pantry leavings from "The Devil's Disciple" and "Major Barbara," with not a little horse meat—or rather horse-play—thrown in. It is a highly spiced, exotic dish but a masterpiece. The chief delicacy is the supreme moment of "The Devil's Disciple," prolonged and complicated with wonderful dramatic skill. As martyrdom draws nearer, Lavinia's Christianity drops from her bit by bit until in the final crisis she no longer believes, but though she might easily save herself and marry her young pagan captain, she realizes like Dick Dudgeon that she must die for no reason at all, simply to satisfy her pride and sense of integrity. She ceases to be a Christian but remains a puritan. This passage reminds one of the crushing anticlimax in Hebbel's "Judith," except that Shaw's Lavinia is the optimism, rather than the pessimism, of negation. Again, Ferrovius is a combination of the preacher Anthony Anderson, who discovers in the instant of crisis that he is a warrior rather than a man of peace, and of the Salvation Army wrestler Todger Fairmile, who makes converts by the sweet reasonableness of physical intimidation. But Ferrovius is subtler and deeper than either of these—a morbid, self-righteous, self-deceived man of gloomy conscience, gloomy strength, and precarious self-control. Finally, the young Roman captain is the pagan, as General Burgoyne is the Christian, gentleman. There is the same elegant restraint and classical common sense, the same code of honor and absence of religious enthusiasm.

But "Androcles" looks forward as well as backward. In its simple, matter-of-fact treatment of Christian miracle, it presages "Saint Joan," though Androcles's friendship with the lion is broad farce, whereas Joan's causing of the hens to lay and the breeze to change is thrillingly serious drama. In its essential situation, "Androcles" is also like the later play. The Christian martyrs are a whole company of Saint Joans, who like her might easily have saved themselves by a formal recantation before a public official. But their problem is of course less profound and tragic than hers, partly because the Roman Emperor is so much less worthy an embodiment of constituted authority than the Grand Inquisitor. The difference between the two plays in this respect is that "Androcles" is frankly satirical. The Emperor cannot be noble and generous, because he is a travesty of modern imperialism.

"Androcles" is also meant to be a religious play establishing the doctrine that though men band together in sects for political purposes, nevertheless in the crucial moment each man discovers he has his own fairly particular creed. Thus: "Androcles is a humanitarian naturalist, whose views surprise everybody. Lavinia, a clever and fearless freethinker, shocks the Pauline Ferrovius, who is comparatively stupid and conscience ridden." [6] But if Lavinia is a freethinker, the play is religious, in the ordinary sense of that word, only as a satire which makes fun of modern sentimentality about the primitive Christians. They are not wailing and reluctant victims but enthusiasts joyous in their faith, who march to their doom with unseemly laughter and lugubrious horseplay. In this aspect "Androcles" may owe something to the *Thaïs* and *L'Île des Penguins* of Anatole France, with whom Shaw had become friendly.

E. Strauss regards "Androcles" as the significant link between "Major Barbara" and "Saint Joan." Religion, according to this critic, is the means by which Shaw escapes from the cul-de-sac of Barbara's surrender to capitalism and ascends to a more abstract but also more satisfying moral attitude. Heaven then becomes a thinly disguised symbol for a contemplative and idealized socialism. Thus, Father Anthony in "Getting Married" declares that he is a Christian—therefore a communist; and after her religious fit Margaret, in "Fanny's First Play," has an irresistible impulse to go out and mingle with the people. In "Androcles," Lavinia is confronted with Barbara's problem in the guise of Christian martyrdom. Barbara had been corrupted by a family predilection for the use of force. She feels like Lavinia but acts like Ferrovius, availing herself first of the muscles of Fairmile and then of the millions of Undershaft. Lavinia proves stronger and nobler. She too is disillusioned with Christianity, but still she cannot sacrifice to the heathen gods any more than Shaw can bow down before the hideous idol of capitalism. Lavinia is, however, saved from the final consequences of her heroism. Shaw still needed a Barbara who would face the full tragedy of not choosing Undershaft. He found her in Joan.

This explanation is admirable, except that it seems to imply Shaw had no genuine interest outside of socialism. Even here E. Strauss would be very nearly right. Shaw understood religion largely in terms of socialism, as he understood Jesus largely in terms of Ibsen and Shaw. But he was also obviously interested in religion for its own sake. He was curiously sensitive to outside influences yet curiously resistant to drastic change. He could approve of nothing without Shavianizing it, as he could criticize nothing, or almost nothing, without declaring war

[286]

against it. But what, then, is the original entity "Shaw" or the developmental principle "Shavianizing"? Undoubtedly socialism is basic, but so are rationalism, romanticism, and puritanism. In terms of these principles, Shaw was constantly adopting new ideas, changing them, and being changed by them.

"Androcles" was backed by Lord Henry de Walden and directed by Shaw and Granville-Barker. Artistically, it was an immense success. As Lavinia, Lillah McCarthy elicited a poem from John Masefield, and a veteran and accomplished animal impersonator roared magnificently as the lion. Yet "Androcles" held the stage but a few weeks. It could arouse only horror and bewilderment in audiences which, as Pearson observes, had formed their ideas of religious plays on "The Sign of the Cross." Shaw relished the bewilderment, which he explained in various writings at great length, but he was offended by the horror and wrote to Lillah McCarthy, "I see no prospect of anyone (except myself) kicking the British public into good manners. I shall peg away until the theatre is as silent as the grave." [7]

When he published the play in 1915, Shaw prefixed a gigantic Preface on Jesus and the Gospels. It may well reflect some animus against the public, both for their reception of his play and for their disapproval of his stand on the war. At any rate, the Preface to "Androcles" is a masterpiece of satiric maneuver, executed with rare Shavian perversity. It begins by observing that the world has followed Barabbas, who was a thief and therefore a capitalist, rather than Jesus, who of course was a Christian and therefore a socialist. Pursuing this opposition, Shaw ingeniously exploits Christian prejudice against capitalistic, then by a sudden turn refines Jesus' socialism into Fabianism, and at length piously announces that for his part he sees nothing for it but to return to the wholesome truths of the Gospels.

But he is far too skillful not, at all times, both to have his cake and eat it too. Abruptly, he attacks the whole question of religion from a starkly naturalistic point of view. Basically religion is a means of propitiating God for one's own sins by sacrificing a scapegoat. To be sure, only the rich could at first afford scapegoats, but finally the poor began to clamor for the luxury of a clean conscience. Their demand was answered by the conception of a mythical redeemer, who died again and again at a moderate charge for the expiation of everybody's sins. As a defender of the poor, Jesus was naturally identified with this conception, but as his Church grew in wealth and power, its ministrations became more costly, until, at the dawn of commercial capitalism, Luther met the demands of a numerous proletariat by declaring that salvation required faith alone. It is interesting that at this time Shaw was explaining Christian peace, as well as modern war, by Marxism.

[287]

On the life of Jesus, Shaw is suavely irritating and plausible. The founder of Christianity was a middle-class intellectual, who in the earlier part of his career combined an advanced social and ethical doctrine with the habits and tastes of a Bohemian. From the moment when Peter hailed him as "the Christ, the son of the living God," he became "obsessed with a conviction of his divinity" and deliberately brought about his own destruction in conformity with the primitive conception of a redeemer.[8] The crucifixion was a great political success —in fact, too great, for it distracted attention from the teachings of Jesus and so allowed them easily to be debased by the apostles and particularly by Paul, who made Christianity what it now is by adding the dogmas of original sin, the fall, the warfare between conscience and passion within man's nature, and the forgiveness of sins through vicarious atonement.

The most eloquent part of the Preface is of course devoted to an exposition of what Shaw asserts to be Jesus' true doctrine. To be sure, Jesus could hardly have anticipated Ibsen, Butler, and the Fabian program in its full complication, yet in declaring that the kingdom of God is within, he obviously taught the divinity of man, and in asserting that we should give up private property and that we are members of one another, he clearly implied the necessity of socialism. Jesus modernized turns out to be a combination of creative evolution and constitutional socialism.

All this is so eloquently and forcefully argued that it is difficult to believe Shaw is not in earnest. And if he is in earnest here, why not in many of the more aggravating parts of the Preface—where, for example, he asserts that belief is a mere matter of fashion, so that medieval man believed what was presented to him in threes and sevens as modern man believes what is presented in millions and billions? His extreme pragmatism banishes the problem of sincerity for Shaw himself and throws it, in tortuous and exasperated form, into the lap of his critic. The Preface to "Androcles" may be at the same time both fun and earnest. It is certainly intended to tease and irritate conventional opinion. It may also be a quite serious expression of serious convictions.

"Overruled," also produced in 1912, is one of those delightful little plays, so common with Shaw, which would receive much more attention had they been written by a lesser dramatist. The author attempts to prove that the theoretical libertine is too busy defending his ideas against public indignation to carry them out, whereas the practical libertine sins unnoticed because he is so loudly and conventionally indignant about other people's sins. According to the Preface, only farces are licensed to deal with delicate subjects, and therefore "Overruled" is a farce. It is chiefly remarkable for witty dialogue and a very ingenious and effective, though too lengthy, development of a very slight situation.

"What is the difference between a modern and an old-fashioned play?" Archibald Henderson once asked Shaw, who replied, "A play with a discussion is a modern play. A play with only an emotional situation is an old-fashioned play." [9] Shortly afterward, the great modernist achieved his own damnation. "Pygmalion" is indisputably an old-fashioned play. Of course Shaw was nervously aware of the fact, and of course he tried to throw dust in people's eyes. He writes ostentatiously in the Preface:

> I wish to boast that Pygmalion has been an extremely successful play all over Europe and North America as well as at home. It is so intensely and deliberately didactic, and its subject is esteemed so dry, that I delight in throwing it at the heads of the wiseacres who repeat the parrot cry that art should never be didactic. It goes to prove my contention that art should never be anything else.[10]

But the truth cannot be concealed. "Pygmalion" is shameless art for art's sake, a fairy tale told with relentless logic and realism. Professor Higgins, a phonetician with magical powers (who is really a little boy in disguise) transforms an ugly flower girl into a beautiful duchess —chiefly by improving her accent. Of course the story has special Shavian significances. The professor, as Mr. Bentley explains, is a Pygmalion in reverse. He changes, or attempts to change, a live flower girl into a marble formality. The climax of the play and the scène à faire is not the court performance of the marble formality but her rebellious insistence on coming to life again. For she sees only too clearly that Higgins has not quite realized she was ever alive. Besides, he is an insufferable bully, and he has a mother fixation. And so they do not marry and live happily ever after.

The nearest approach to *Tendenz* in the play is Alfred Doolittle, who illustrates the vanities of philanthropy. Together with a natural talent for oratory, Doolittle possesses a genius for Nietzschean morality which enables him to distill the quintessence of happiness from a wretched existence as a member of the "undeserving poor." His felicity depends on the studied neglect of organized charity. But the long and brainless arm of American philanthropic wealth reaches out and plunges him into a lifelong hell of respectability by endowing him as lecturer on ethics to the world-wide Wannafeller societies.

Shaw was perfectly aware that in "Pygmalion" he had a gold mine.

It was born to be produced, but it very nearly had to be produced over the dead bodies of Shaw, Mrs. Patrick Campbell, and Sir Herbert Beerbohm Tree.

"Pygmalion" offers many parallels to Shaw's correspondence with Florence Farr, but according to his own story, Eliza Doolittle and her transformation were suggested to him by Mrs. Patrick Campbell, whom he once described to Pearson as a mixture of the "suburban persifleuse" and "the noble and beautiful Italian patrician." [11] Naturally, he wanted the fictitious Eliza played by the real one, but since the romantic Mrs. Campbell was very far from regarding herself as a guttersnipe-aristocrat in latent metamorphosis, he perceived that his task was delicate. Without a hint as to his intention, he read her the play in his most skillful and dramatic manner. She began by objecting superciliously to the impossible noises of the flower girl. Then gradually the double truth dawned on her. Shaw somehow associated *her* with that horrible creature, and that horrible creature was a great part. Indignation flared up and then gave way to enthusiasm. The actress overcame the snob.

Then, just as Shaw was about to enmesh her in his usual cold-blooded business arrangements, he fell ecstatically in love with her. One suspects that many years before, when as a dramatic critic he had recorded with fascinated contempt her triumph as the second Mrs. Tanqueray, she had been one of the many women he loved at a distance. In any case, the result was that Shaw became putty and Mrs. Campbell became impossible. Shaw wanted Loraine for Professor Higgins. Loraine was unsuitable to Mrs. Campbell, and as it later proved, unavailable. Shaw suggested Tree. Tree had personally insulted Mrs. Campbell. Then Lord Curzon came forward with the kind offer of the Prince of Wales Theatre. Mrs. Campbell told him to keep out of her private affairs. She wanted to produce the play herself, but while Shaw would not give it to anyone else, he would not give it to her entirely. As Pearson neatly observes, he had lost his heart but not his head. Finally, however, he did lose interest: a newer play absorbed him. He was angered, too, by the reception London critics always gave his plays, which damaged his reputation not only in England but abroad, and the delay with the London production facilitated his resolve to give London a lesson: before the first English performance of "Pygmalion," the play had been performed in six foreign countries and translated into five foreign languages.

But Mrs. Campbell's purse was alarmingly empty. With the air of having a fresh and happy thought, she asked Shaw, "What about Tree?" And so Tree became Higgins—or Higgins became Tree, for like Mrs. Pat, Sir Herbert looked on plays as empty vessels for his personality. Neither of the two was a technically trained actor such as Lillah Mc-

Carthy, whose classic stage mastery had been at Shaw's disposal since "Man and Superman." Of Tree, Shaw writes:

> What Tree could do was always entertaining in some way or other. But, for better for worse, it was hardly ever what the author meant him to do. His parts were his avatars; and the play had to stand the descent of the deity into it as best it could. Sometimes, as in my case, the author understood the situation and made the best of it.[12]

Elsewhere Shaw translates "making the best of it" as "the conflict which raged between him and me at the rehearsals." [12] Twice Shaw washed his hands of the business, but

> on both occasions Tree took leave of me as if it had been very kind of me to look in as I was passing to see his rehearsals, and received me on my return as if it were still more friendly of me to come back and see how he was getting on. I tried once or twice to believe that he was only pulling my leg: but that was incredible: his sincerity and insensibility were only too obvious.[13]

A charming and whimsical Higgins Shaw endured with grinding teeth. An enamored Higgins, however, he would not endure. Nor would the play itself, until Tree "lit on the happy thought of throwing flowers to Eliza in the very brief interval between the end of the play and the fall of the curtain." [14] But of course Shaw had the last word. After "Pygmalion à la Tree" had enjoyed an immense popular success, he published the play together with a closely reasoned psychological narrative. About Higgins and Eliza he is relentlessly austere. For Higgins he concedes nothing; for Eliza, at the very most, that sometimes, in the deep secrecy of her private thoughts, she transports herself and Higgins in a daydream to a desert island where middle-class responsibilities do not exist. Meanwhile, realizing that Higgins will never respect his creation, she prudently marries the more tractable Freddy and waits rather polyandrously for the professor to grow old and harmless and dependent upon her. Hans Christian Andersen ends like Arnold Bennett.

One of the enduring marks of Shaw's early shyness is the tendency to cover up, to show that he is not hurt. There is a hint of this in the letter to Lillah McCarthy in which he announces his belated infatuation with Mrs. Patrick Campbell:

> Though I entered on the business with the most insolent confidence in my superiority to a dozen such Delilahs, I fell head over ears in love with her—violently and exquisitely in love—before I knew that I was thinking about anything but business. . . . There

has never been anything so ridiculous, or so delightful, in the history of the world. . . . I was in love for very nearly 36 hours; and for that be all her sins forgiven her! [15]

He was in love for rather more than thirty-six hours. Mrs. Campbell's attraction was mainly physical. His letters, though moderated by humor, definitely belong to the fleshly school of poetry. On September 28, 1912, he writes:

> When I saw you last you were ill in bed, but you had the energy of ten tigresses; and your remarkably fine neck would have carried the pediment of the Parthenon like a feather if you had been snatched from between the sheets and set up as a caryatid.[16]

In November, writing of himself in the third person, he warns her, with words that recall many an earlier love letter, against his defects as a lover:

> He cares for nothing really but his mission, as he calls it, and his work. He is treacherous as only an Irishman can be; he adores you with one eye and sees you with the other as a calculated utility.[17]

Did Mrs. Campbell recall one of Don Juan's speeches in "Man and Superman?" Probably not, for she was obviously charmed.

These letters reveal, like few others, the swift, strange succession of Shavian moods and masks. Once he watched while a splinter was drawn from under her nail. The veins of her neck swelled with the pain. "By Jove! what a throat, 'Michael Angelo'!" he exclaimed with fine, disinterested enthusiasm. And then later:.

> I think all that was good for my soul because it tore everything that was selfish and imaginary right out of me, and made you a real fellow creature in real pain. (O Lord, my fibres all twist and my heart and bowels torment me when I think of it): and the more real you become the more I discover that I have a real, real, real kindness for you, and that I am not a mere connoisseur in beauty or a sensualist or a philanderer but a—but a—a—I dont know what; but something that has deep roots in it that you pluck at. Only why should you have to be hurt to cure me of selfishness and of little fits of acting? Why should it not be an ecstasy of happiness for you, that would move me too, perhaps still more deeply? [18]

Perhaps the most revealing of all—in the sense of revealing a weakness—is the garrulous, rhetorical little letter which he wrote when her son was killed in the war. It concludes with nine "damns" and six "dears." Why did he write it? At the time he was probably too excited, too talkative, too much in a hurry to feel. And he did not want to feel.

CHAPTER THIRTY-TWO

World War I

War in the eighteenth century was still but the most extravagant and dangerous of feudal sports. Though played for very high stakes, it was confined to small armies made up chiefly of the aristocratic and (according to the Duke of Wellington) the criminal classes, and might be protracted for years without disrupting a nation's economy. After 1870, war and the preparation for war became more and more a major industry and a major expense, as well as a way of life and a habit of thought, for the whole population of Europe. The result was that European civilization became epileptic, falling into periodic fits of internecine fury which left her more and more shattered and pathological. The Continent itself became as dangerous as a small island overshadowed by a smoking volcano. Yet Europeans continued to make merry. They took no steps either to secure their lives or to prepare themselves for death. In fact, danger rather added a zest to life. Naturally, so much frivolity moved thoughtful men to indignation. Shaw was one of these thoughtful men, and "Heartbreak House," largely written in 1913 but not published till 1919, represents his indignation.

In a general way, he had long been aware of the danger. In "Man and Superman," he had eloquently propounded what might be called the basic problem of the twentieth century—how to bring man's moral and political character to a level with his military weapons. In "Major Barbara," he had called attention to the international threat of the arms industry. In the Preface to "John Bull's Other Island," he had indicated the dark abyss of terror and violence into which all Europe was slipping and had shown that, having expanded his Fabianism to cope with imperial questions, he could expand it still more to cope with international ones. "Heartbreak House" deals not so much with the danger as with people's indifference to it. Shaw expresses the satiric fury of a puritan at the spectacle of Englishmen fiddling while Europe smolders.

He wrote "Heartbreak House" after seeing a number of Chekhov's plays—particularly "The Cherry Orchard" and "Uncle Vanya." He describes his work as a "Fantasia in the Russian manner on English Themes." [1] Certainly "The Cherry Orchard" and "Heartbreak House" present a close parallel in dominant idea and mood: both symbolize the demoralization of a whole society in the demoralization of a group of people at a country house; and both combine comedy with a tragic sense of impending doom. Otherwise, the two plays are very different. Shaw's characters are ethical abstractions, though partially psychologized; Chekhov's are human beings, though afflicted with deep moral disease. Shaw's are allegorical; Chekhov's are typical. His characters confess their inmost secrets by the inward compulsion of a wonderful spontaneity and naturalness; Shaw's expound their significance, social or moral, by the outward compulsion of a complex logical necessity. "The Cherry Orchard" is prophetic as a slide beneath a microscope is prophetic; "Heartbreak House," as the interpretation of a formula or the demonstration of a theorem.

This comparison seems much to Shaw's disadvantage—but not necessarily. His play has immensely the greater amplitude and complexity of idea. Its strength is not in psychological realism but in general meaning, in satiric conception, in comedy and wit. It might be described as a medieval morality with a modern discussion, or again, as spectacular surgery disguised as rollicking farce. In artistic conception it is poignantly dramatic: gradually the farcical mask grows transparent, and the lurid skull and crossbones of allegorical significance show through clearer and clearer. Then, by a series of anticlimaxes, the skull and crossbones are shown to be papier-mâché. Only the anticlimaxes are not sufficiently massive.

The first act begins like innocent comedy. We are introduced to a delightfully incredible and Bohemian family, who, with the utmost good humor, treat their house like a hotel and their relations like intrusive strangers. But as the play continues, we perceive, especially if we have read the Preface, that Captain Shotover, the patriarch of the family, is not simply a comic old sailor who drinks three bottles of rum a day and attempts to achieve the seventh degree of concentration. We see that the ironhearted consistency with which he fastens his own identities on other people is meant to indicate not only farcical eccentricity but the useful English habit of seeing what one chooses in exterior reality. His house, built like a ship, somehow symbolizes the sea trading out of which English wealth and commerce grew. The selling of his soul to the devil in youth and his marriage with a black witch in Zanzibar signify the ruthless colonial exploitation and the savage insistence on prestige inseparable from imperial power. Captain Shotover is English heroism, English genius, English intellectual and moral leadership. When he looks into the past he is Sir Francis Drake—and Bernard Shaw when he looks into the future. He is noticeably Bernard Shaw, for he is fond of macaroni and generally regarded as mad.

At the very end of the first act, the conversational pattern of prose dialogue suddenly mounts to operatic rhythm and symmetry, and in elaborate trios and duets the inmates of Heartbreak House speak not in their literal but their allegorical characters. We see that of the Captain's two daughters, Lady Utterword symbolizes empire, or England abroad, and Hesione Hushabye, England at home, or woman's love and domesticity. Hector Hushabye is what she has domesticated—English romantic heroism turned into a magnificent lap dog full of melodramatic daydreams and irrelevant courage.

The other characters are symbolic as types. Mazzini Dunn is a nineteenth-century liberal whose illusions and sentimentality prevent him from making his intelligence effective. His daughter Ellie, who represents modern English young womanhood, is at first filled with the sentimental conventionalities of her father; then after a romantic encounter with Hector Hushabye, becomes hard and disillusioned; very nearly marries a capitalist for his money; is disillusioned by him and at the same time advised by the Captain, contrary to the doctrine of "Major Barbara," that money will not save her soul; and finally enters into a spiritual marriage with the Captain himself, thus symbolizing probably with ironic optimism a union between English youth and English genius. The capitalist in question is Boss Mangan, who is a capitalist for the edification of capitalists as Undershaft is a capitalist for the edification of socialists. Mangan is an overbearing, vindictive, insecure, snobbish little man, who has a heart but very little head and is driven almost to madness when realities are stripped of the shabby decencies among which he lives. By a series of anticlimaxes, he is revealed as a capitalist without either industries or the power of command. At best, he is a species of financial buzzard who devours with borrowed funds the courageous failures of abler men.

Not until almost the end of the play is the key to its meaning explicitly given. Then Lady Utterword remarks, "There are only two classes in good society in England: the equestrian classes and the neurotic classes," [2] and she connects the neurotic with her father's house. As the Preface explains, the nation is ruled by Horseback Hall, or sporting England, and Heartbreak House, or cultured England. The Captain then declares that their country is a ship that is driving "on the rocks." Shortly after, enemy bombs fall and kill Boss Mangan. A great war is to break out in which capitalism will perish.

Impressive as it is, both in conception and execution, "Heartbreak

House" seems to me nevertheless inadequate to its theme. Its weakness lies partly in the amorphous and essentially undramatic structure of the last two acts but chiefly in a conflict of mood resulting from the use of comic characters to symbolize a tragic significance. Especially on a first reading of the play, we are struck with astonishment that these thin caricatures are meant to typify the moral degeneration of Europe, that they are meant to explain a gigantic disaster. The Captain is certainly adequate, and perhaps Boss Mangan, particularly if he could be kept formidable a little longer. But the others—one might as well try to explain the Crimean War by the failings of the Pickwick Club. Again, the long discussion of the last two acts, brilliant and searching as it is, robs the splendid first act of its momentum, so that the bombs fall not merely as an ironically relevant irrelevancy, as Shaw intends, but as an artistic irrelevancy as well.

It is certainly prophetic that Shaw should have written much of this play before World War I. Of course he does not in any precise sense diagnose either the event or its causes. There is some talk of propaganda and the irresponsible manufacture of munitions but no talk of alliances and naval rivalries. At one point, Captain Shotover declares that England is shriveling up with age inside the shell of empire. This remark was also prophetic, though perhaps a little premature. Assigned by the postwar General Staff the problem of analyzing Germany's defeat, General von Rundstedt decided that the primary cause was the economic power of England.

Shaw says that he was fully aroused to the dangers of the European situation only when Count Harry Kessler attempted to promote an *entente cordiale* between England and Germany by the interchange of a manifesto of friendship signed by famous people. Shaw was invited to draft the London document. He consented. Yet as an austere rationalist with a code of studied impoliteness, he could not make a purely superfluous gesture of courtesy. Therefore, between complimentary references to Shakespeare and Goethe, Leibnitz and Newton, he inserted an experimental sentence "to the effect that England, far from being jealous of the possession of a fleet by Germany, could regard it only as an additional guarantee of civilization." [3] He had put his finger precisely on the sore point. Nobody would sign the document. The offending sentence was removed—and everybody signed but Shaw.

It is interesting that Shaw was the notable asked by Kessler to draw up the English testimonial. Clearly, he was felt to be sympathetic to Germany. As a thinker, he had been receptive to the philosophical ideas of Wagner, Nietzsche, and Schopenhauer. [4] As a music critic, he had been perhaps more responsible than anyone else for the early success of Wagner's music in England. As an admirer of organization and efficiency, he had formed a high estimate of German municipal government. To intelligent and highly educated German audiences and to the state-supported national theater, he owed an extremely favorable reception of his plays.[5]

Perceiving the increasing gravity of the situation, Shaw published in March, 1913, and in January, 1914, letters in which, after attacking the melodramatic secrecy of European diplomacy, he proposed a security pact between England, France, and Germany. If any one of these nations attacked another, the third should side with the defender. Shaw had invented the Locarno Pact twelve years in advance. He had come to see, as Mr. Thomas Dickinson points out, that only a frank understanding among the great powers could dissipate the labyrinth of deceit and disbelief, hatred, fear, and bluff which was leading Europe, as though fascinated, down to war.[6] Unfortunately, every foreign minister in Europe, including Sir Edward Grey, was working not so much to prevent war as to guarantee victory. War was "inevitable." Shaw did not point out that, in order to make his plan practical and effective, some solution was needed to the fundamental differences between Germany on one side and France and England on the other. What he thought about Alsace-Lorraine, he did not say. He did say, however, that Germany had as much right as England to a large navy. Both countries had colonies, and both were vitally dependent on imports. German naval policy was perhaps ill-advised but not immoral, for no nation has the right to dominate the seas. Apparently, his proposal would have been an international police force under the joint control of the most powerful and civilized nations.

In August of the same year war broke out and with it an unparalleled spasm of mass hatred. In Belgium and northern France, modern science and industry speedily created a hell whose terrible secrets had to be carefully guarded from all but the sufferers themselves. Yet there, brutalized, humiliated, agonized though they were, men contrived to be heroes and even to be men. It was at home that they became less. Behind elegant club windows, in the grave council chamber, in the quiet library, an appalling atavism sprang up. To utter less than ferocious hatred of the enemy was a crime against society. Shaw quickly became guilty of that crime. He collected all possible documents, retired to Torquay, sunned himself on a hotel roof for two months, and then published in the November supplement of Sidney Webb's *New Statesman* his lengthy pamphlet "Common Sense about the War." Most Englishmen—like most Germans and Frenchmen—were hysterically self-righteous. Therefore Shaw was coolly judicial—noticeably generous to Germany and sharply critical of England. Then, and for many years afterward, his alert, witty detachment was regarded as, at best, criminally frivolous perversity in the face of appalling tragedy. He seemed more than ever a monstrous enigma.

As a matter of fact, he had never been more frankly himself. In "The Man of Destiny" he had recognized that the sword could be a constructive force in history. In "Caesar and Cleopatra" he had, somewhat ambiguously, exalted it to the level of the cross. But now these ideas, whether relevant or not, were completely forgotten. Faced with the overwhelming reality itself, he was revolted not only by the tremendous waste but by the spiritual degradation of war. In the crisis he reverted to what was fundamental in his character—to the puritan and the rationalist. He sought above all clarity of vision and of conscience. Only by coldly telling the truth could he maintain his integrity and declare his independence of the pandemonium of furious lies that screamed around him. And what joy to explode a few facts under his old enemy— the complacent Philistine who looked forward with civilian gusto to war news in the papers as to a blood-and-thunder drama in the movies!

Writing a year later, Shaw himself explained his cold detachment and therefore his absolute rightness by his Irish background. When, taking as usual the opposite side, G. K. Chesterton wrote him that "there was in Prussia an evil will," he replied, with reference to "Common Sense":

> It is perfectly useless for you to try to differ with me about the war. NOBODY can differ with me about the war: you might as well differ from the Almighty about the orbit of the sun. I have got the war right; and to that complexion, you too must come at last, your nature not being a fundamentally erroneous one.
>
> At the same time, it is a great pity you were not born in Ireland. You would have had the advantage of hearing the burning patriotism of your native land expressing itself by saying exactly the same things about England that English patriotism now says about Prussia, and of recognizing that though they were entirely true, they were also a very great nuisance, as they prevented people from building the future by conscientious thought. . . . In fact you would have learned a devil of a lot of things for lack of which you often drive me to exclaim "Gilbert, Gilbert, why persecutest thou me." [7]

Knowing his power as a propagandist, Shaw was clearly resolved to propagandize truth and sanity. "I was fiercely determined, like Ramsay MacDonald," he said afterward, "that the diplomatists and militarists who brought about the war should not get the credit for having saved the world from the peril which they had in fact created." [8] Otherwise, fifty years of reactionary government might have ensued instead of five. Moreover, he was determined that at least one man should see at least one war, if for the first time in history, in terms of common sense rather than of romance. He addressed his words to a rational minority in England, to the United States—which was peacefully inheriting the future while Europe fought over the past—and above all, perhaps, to the American President, whose international views, he early foresaw, were to be more important than those of any other living man. Actually, except perhaps in America, the hour was too late for truth, or near-truth, so undiplomatically stated.

In writing "Common Sense," Shaw apparently did not, as so often before, have the advice of Webb, who maintained a prudent reserve. To him war was an awful irrelevancy interrupting the orderly course of socialistic reform. Without Webb, Shaw was more outspoken, more uncompromising. He tended to be Marxist in his analysis of the problems but Fabian in his solution of them. He advocated a powerful league of nations, and in this course the Fabians and the Labour Party in general, following him and Ramsay MacDonald, came more and more to concur.

Applying Marxist doctrine, Shaw regards the war as a horrible accusation against capitalistic leadership. If it must be fought, let it be fought with a minimum of illusion. If the common man must die, he owes it to himself to know how uselessly he is dying, to understand that English capitalists contribute to war by competing with German capitalists, that they profit from war because war raises the rate of interest. Indeed Shaw uses the big guns as a kettledrum to summon the world to a lesson in basic realities. The horror is not so much that Rheims has been destroyed as that in the hands of a private firm, it would have been torn down long since, the statues sold to American collectors, and the ground rented out for building sites. What the world needs, he declares, is not a war but a revolution, which would indeed occur if the common soldier of all nations understood his true interests. Mere victory will bring no millennium but simply, after infinite suffering and destruction, a French or a Russian instead of a German danger. The war might have been avoided entirely, had not international politics been in the secret and almost exclusive charge of *Junker*, not only German but English and Russian.

This introduces the question of war guilt, and here Shaw was dependent chiefly on the newspapers and the English "White Paper." He maintains that though the German *Junker* were more militaristic, the English *Junker* were more quarrelsome and that they began to talk about war first. He then cites such articles as that by Lord Roberts in *The Hibbert Journal*, in which the author speaks of "the White Man's

Burden" and "our fitness as an Imperial race." [9] Moreover, the English are the true masters of *Realpolitik*. Instead of being isolated by Germany, they have isolated her—with an air of the most innocent self-righteousness, for England is the Pecksniff of nations. She has a genius for finding her duty in her advantage; like all genuinely successful deceivers, she is best at deceiving herself. Measured by his own intentions and by English opinion, Sir Edward Grey is a gentle and virtuous statesman. Measured by his actions, he is an incompetent Machiavelli whose very shortsightedness has enabled him to carry out the purposes of such militarists as Winston Churchill better than they themselves could have done. Being a Liberal, Sir Edward could not promise certainly to fight—and the end of the militarists was achieved: Germany attacked. When Sir Edward declared war, he was astonished to find the nation applauded him frantically. Yet had he published the secret military agreement with France and Russia, he might have prevented war. Shaw rightly discounts as common practice the violation of Belgian neutrality. Among the underlying causes of the war, he lists the sensational press, secret diplomacy, the armament race, and above all, plutocratic government, which fattens on war.

Shaw reiterates the proposals which he had made in 1899 for the reform of military life. The soldier should have a union, elected representatives in the War Office, the union wage of a skilled worker in a dangerous profession, and proper compensation for his wife and children. Military discipline might then be relaxed.

In part at least, the test of a historical critic, as in greater degree of an experimental scientist, consists in his ability to predict the future. In writing of the war, Shaw met this test brilliantly. In fact, his predictions may have contributed to their own fulfillment, for "Common Sense" probably exerted considerable influence on Woodrow Wilson, though a lesser or negative one on America in general, partly because it was divided unstrategically into two installments when printed by *The New York Times*.

Shaw predicts the ultimate defeat of Germany and proposes a generous peace. For Germany can only be destroyed as a nation by the mass slaughter of German women, and that is unthinkable. She cannot be permanently disunited. In fact, the disappearance of the Hohenzollerns and Hapsburgs will probably lead to union with Austria. The best solution is to democratize the German constitution. All nations should pay reparations to Belgium, but unlimited reparations from Germany would be silly. Poland should become independent. Shaw deplores the alliance with Czarist Russia and sees little hope for democracy there. Indeed, the war is really a conflict between the barbarous East and the civilized West. The English people are really fighting for English investments in Russia. England, France, and Germany should form a league of peace, and if Germany were democratic, the United States might enter. The greatest hope for world peace is in a federation of states organized against war on the basis of international socialism. Armaments should not be reduced but pooled. Shaw concludes by attacking the Hun-haters, particularly those who were also Christian clergymen. England's war guilt is as great as Germany's. Peace will not be possible until everyone fights militarism at home.

Despite some superficial caprice and some fundamental misjudgment, "Common Sense" is one of the sanest documents that came out of the war. Its great virtue is its practical, farsighted statesmanship. Like President Roosevelt many years later, Shaw wanted to "quarantine" war, to keep sane as many people as possible—in England as well as in the one great nation that remained at peace. He also fought against the conception of total war. A world mobilized for its own destruction might achieve its purpose. Above all, he wanted to temper public fury with a rational plan for peace.

Nevertheless, his interpretation of causes is frequently too narrowly Marxist. The war becomes too exclusively a struggle between plutocratic imperialisms. It is of course also urged that he minimizes German guilt. Actually, he accuses England more than he excuses Germany. He vigorously attacks Prussian militarism. Perhaps the worst that can be said against him is that he fails to analyze the connection between German character and German destiny. The connection was not so clear in 1914 as it is now. One might almost say that Germany suffered catastrophe in 1914 because of the foibles of German character; in 1939, because of the mortal sins. The pamphlet is also marred by some typical inconsistencies, as when Shaw declares that England was and was not prepared for war.

"Common Sense" is frequently said to reflect a perverse frivolity. Nobody writes an eighty-page pamphlet on a dangerous subject out of sheer frivolity. But though definitely in earnest, Shaw is undoubtedly carried away by his talent for didactic comedy. He does not make history too frivolous, but he does make it too clever, too superficially lucid and self-conscious. In order to heap ashes on the heads of his countrymen, for example, he makes Sir Edward Grey sometimes too mischievously clairvoyant and sometimes too ludicrously the purblind Englishman who muddles through. Again, he grossly exaggerates the vision of Sazanov, the Russian foreign minister, who "faced the facts" and saw that England could have prevented war by promptly declaring her adherence to the Entente. The chief fact which Sazanov faced was Russia's advantage. The British were afraid to take too strong a stand, as Sir Francis Bertie declares, partly so as to meditate and partly so as to prevent Russia from becoming too exacting with Austria.[10] But Shaw was a pragmatist. He was attempting not so much to put truth on paper as to produce sanity in the English public mind by magnifying English guilt.

When it first appeared, "Common Sense" had met with a largely unfavorable but nevertheless mixed reception. Like Ramsay MacDonald, Shaw was always enthusiastically welcomed at mass meetings of the working classes. Poor people liked "Common Sense" because it advocated higher wages for soldiers and more compensation for their wives and widows. Most people-in-the-street thought it either traitorous and fiendish or merely Shavian and ridiculous. Intelligent people thought it extravagant, inept, untimely, and a dangerous weapon in the hands of German propagandists in the United States. As war fury mounted, those who thought it fiendish naturally prevailed. Shaw was attacked in the newspapers, expelled from the Dramatists' Club, and dropped by many of his friends. Red-blooded Englishmen like Herbert Asquith declared that he ought to be shot. He hid his feelings under a cloak of hilarious and jocular rationality and yet never, one suspects, even as a struggling and obscure young socialist in a triumphantly capitalistic world, had he known moral isolation so complete and painful. He defended individual liberty during the war, but he defended popular democracy very little after it.

His tendency to simplify and enliven history is evident again in the brilliant letter which he addressed to *The New Statesman* on December 12, 1914, after going through the French "Yellow Book." That prosaic collection of documents, according to Shaw, imparts a delightful fable about an Old Lion, who, though he maintained himself ruthlessly as king of the jungle, insisted on going about piously in the lamb's wool of pacifism. At length his reign was challenged by another beast, who won a great fight over the Lion's old enemy. The Lion watched jealously but purred and bleated so convincingly that the other beast, who was rather gullible, decided that the Lion actually was a lamb. Meanwhile, the Lion had formed a league with his old enemies, and when just the right moment came, he suddenly stopped purring and leaped on his new rival. Shaw admires the Lion even while condemning him—chiefly for not being a better socialist. The letter is a curious mixture of covert patriotism and the detached gusto of the born comic writer in stripping his victim "morally naked." [11]

For some time after the outbreak of hostilities, Shaw continued to make various excellent proposals which neither side dreamed of accepting. The British should feel less pious horror about the violation of Belgian neutrality and do something about getting the Germans out of the country. He himself proposed that both sides withdraw and fight elsewhere. At length he perceived that once the forces of destruction had been put in motion, they must obey their awful logic until the end. In any case, events moved so fast that his suggestions were nearly always out of date by the time he got them on paper.

Shaw early became interested in British propaganda to the United States—and particularly to German-Americans. In May, 1916, he published in *The New Age* his own "Case against Germany." Here he calls attention to the dangers of the German monarchy and the German officer class, who not only behave like dangerous paranoiacs in a civilized society but, being *Junker* who until lately enjoyed medieval privileges, treat their soldiers like serfs.[12] So far as it goes, the indictment is just, but Shaw is too much afraid of falling into the ferocious partisanship of his countrymen to see the full possibilities of the case against Germany. He sees nothing new or sinister in the Prussian state. It is simply the French or English state arrested in the eighteenth century or earlier, the *Roi Soleil* system as yet unmodified by democratic revolution. Again, Prussian militarism is but another example of the bullying tendencies of an officer class. There is no special influence of the German officer on German society or of the German General Staff— which in its irresponsible anonymity and priestlike devotion to war and country Liddell Hart compares to the Society of Jesus—on German policy.[13] Indeed Shaw denies, and with some justice,[14] that the Germans were as well prepared for war in 1914 as the French and English. That the ethical romanticism of Nietzsche or the *Volk* mysticism of Wagner and Houston Chamberlain constitutes a force in German civilization Shaw decries as utter nonsense. His indictment of the enemy always verges on defense. He is in his skeptical mood and views the question with a kind of Voltairian common sense. Of Cecil Chesterton's *Perils of Peace* he says, "It starts from the monstrous assumption that any sixty millions of modern white Europeans can differ from any other sixty millions of them."[15] Though in other contexts he often speaks of English, Irish, French, or German character, so far as war guilt is concerned, Shaw is as incredulous that nations have a distinctive character as Voltaire that the fossils of sea shells had been found on the summits of the Alps.

In his letters on conscription, Shaw offers the interesting spectacle of a state socialist championing the cause of individual liberty. Though favoring conscription as a necessary general measure, he sympathizes entirely with the conscientious objector. His letters imply a much more thoroughgoing conception of liberty than that, for example, of *The Intelligent Woman's Guide to Socialism and Capitalism,* in which he identifies liberty with leisure. Unlike nearly all of Shaw's other writings, these

[303]

letters also imply some faith in public intelligence. In fact, on one occasion he maintains that the many who read newspapers are more sane and coolheaded than the few who write them. But perhaps he is merely flattering with a purpose.

At this time Shaw wrote a number of "Playlets about the War." "O'Flaherty, V.C." is, according to its author, designed to promote recruiting among the Irish. It is remarkable for bitter satire of female pugnacity, representing trench warfare as a pleasant relief from domestic bickering. "The Inca of Perusalem" is a gay and indulgent sketch of the Kaiser. "Augustus Does His Bit" crucifies the brainless patriot in high place. "Annajanska, The Bolshevik Empress" is an early Shavian vision of Slavic Communism. All of these plays, trifles though they are, show the dramatist at the height of his powers—witty, skillful, and full of dramatic resource. Yet, though "O'Flaherty" and "The Inca" were given at the front, only "Augustus" and "Annajanska" reached the stage at home. Filled with a breezy, disturbing tendency to see both sides of the question, the "Playlets" were unsuited to the hot, close atmosphere of war hatred.

Early in 1917, Shaw was invited by Sir Douglas Haig to visit the front and "say his say about it." His report is vivid, sane, and inconsistent. In part he sees what he has imagined about war in such plays as "Arms and the Man." But he learns a good deal also. Modern war is humdrum, but it is also exciting. It is unromantic, but it is frequently heroic. It is methodical but inefficient. Nothing happens according to plan. Shells don't go where they are aimed and never kill nearly enough soldiers. Nevertheless, danger makes even the most monotonous and impersonal combat fascinating. It throws Shaw into such a state of high spirits that even his horror descriptions are jaunty and facetious. He is convinced that war gratifies many instincts which civilian life leaves unsatisfied. This is an argument "not for the perpetuation of war but for the purification of peace." [16]

CHAPTER THIRTY-THREE

The Russian Revolution and the Peace

In 1918 came the Russian Revolution. To Shaw the collapse of the Eastern front seemed trivial by comparison. Here it becomes sharply clear how much more he was a socialist than a patriot. He predicted direly that now the real war would begin. Now the battle between competing capitalisms would become the battle between rulers and ruled, between capitalists and proletariat. Upon the Russian Revolution itself he cautiously refused to pronounce. Successful Communism weaned him only gradually from his early contempt, shared by many Labourites, for Slavic ignorance and barbarism.

In 1918, soon after the failure of Ludendorff's offensive, the Germans collapsed, though having clung to capitalistic methods they were, in Shaw's opinion, at the beginning rather than the end of their resources. "Capitalistic bookkeeping is useless for vital as distinguished from commercial balance sheets." [1] It is characteristic that while the socialist criticized publicly, the patriot secretly exulted. "The British Empire," he wrote Frank Harris with boyish disregard for the facts, "has smashed the German Empire: that is the point to be seized. That she did it with French troops, with Russian troops, . . . and finally with American troops only enhances the demonstration of her amazing instinctive statecraft." [2]

Now the mind of a generation suddenly found itself faced with the problems of centuries. It seemed such a moment as utopian idealists dream of. The past was in the melting pot. The victors were omnipotent. All they seemed to need were ideas.

These ideas were ready. Essentially, they were an attempt to eliminate the causes of the last war in terms of nineteenth-century liberalism. There were also idealists ready to believe in them. The Union of Democratic Control, headed by C. P. Trevelyan and Ramsay MacDonald, had in September, 1914, declared for no territorial transfers without plebiscites, democratic control of foreign policy, a European organization, and reduction of armaments. In April, 1915, the pacifist Independent

Labour Party voiced similar principles. In the same year, L. S. Woolf, acting for the Fabian Research Department, drew up somewhat more elaborate aims, including that of establishing a league and a court, with power to carry out decisions by economic sanctions and even by force. These proposals were eventually published in a book, for which Shaw wrote the Preface. Violently nationalistic at the beginning of the war, Labour moved steadily to the left and in 1917 advocated a negotiated peace, to which they got the assent of all Allied labor except that of Russia and the United States.

Undoubtedly Shaw played a principal part in formulating and propagating the ideas which animated this trend. In the American President, he thought he saw the man to carry them out. "I had to stand up for Wilson," he wrote Frank Harris, "not as an American, but as a great man of whom his country is utterly unworthy." [3] "Common Sense" had been published prominently in *The New York Times,* where it could scarcely have escaped Woodrow Wilson's notice. A little later Shaw had addressed an open letter on Belgium to the President. He had seen that statesman's attitude develop from splendid isolation to his own democratic internationalism.[4] The outlook was favorable, but Shaw was not optimistic. His newspaper interviews up to this time do indeed indicate an enthusiastic approval of Wilson's moves and pronouncements, but his next lengthy pamphlet, "Peace Conference Hints," issued shortly before the gathering of the victors at Versailles, is a realistic warning of the dangers ahead. Clearly, Shaw felt the idealism of that hour too ecstatic to be sustained. Perhaps he already perceived with what irony the cold rationalism of "Common Sense"—and of similar European literature on the peace—had by Wilson's magnificent catchwords been transformed into a fiery symbolism with which to stir up unprecedented war enthusiasm and vague Messianic zeal.[5]

"Peace Conference Hints" is a seventeenth-century puritan sermon on twentieth-century politics. Except for much Swiftian irony and some Voltairian wit, it might have been written by the ghost of an enlightened Covenanter. Shaw begins with his usual dichotomy between illusion and reality. He gravely observes that when war is in progress, the common soldier cannot be told what he is really fighting for. The struggle must be represented "as a crude melodrama in which his country is the hero and the enemy the villain." [6] But now the war is over. It is time for truth.

Accordingly, the first part of the pamphlet, which reviews events leading up to the war, is a stern admonition to England not to be self-righteous at the peace table. Self-deception is her great vice. She must realize her heavy responsibility in bringing about the war. Moreover, four years of unexampled slaughter will not automatically result in a millennium of brotherly love. New rivalries, which Shaw treats rather melodramatically, already exist—as for instance, those between the navies of England and the United States. The rest of the pamphlet is obviously directed at Wilson again. It is at once criticism, counsel, and solemn adjuration. The President will need all his mystic force for the coming ordeal. He has already suffered the fate of a prophet, for though he has a wide following in Europe, that in the United States is small. The complicated situation may easily turn into a chaos of greed and opportunism. Genuine success will depend on the presence of a true leader— a man of principle, energy, and courage—and for this Europe looks to Wilson. Turning to the problems of the peace settlement, Shaw warns against too extreme an application of the principles of democracy and nationalism, lest the great states be surrounded by small buffer states which they may later absorb. The Austrian Empire should not be Balkanized but federated.

Shaw is most interesting and original on the league. For a loose, heterogeneous, sentimentally splendid league of all countries, he shows no enthusiasm whatever. The problem will be not how to bring nations in but how to keep them out. Those involved should have similar forms of government, common ideas, traditions, civilizations, and if possible, a common language. They should be capable of sustained unity and ultimate fusion. The ideal combination would be England, France, Germany, and the Scandinavian states. The south Latin states ought probably to be excluded. Clearly, despite some grievances against the British Empire, Shaw has not departed greatly from his imperialistic thinking of 1899. The best guarantee of peace lies in a world dominated by superstates, which have everything to lose and very little to gain from war. "Peace Conference Hints" is "Fabianism and the Empire" applied to a more complicated problem in a graver crisis. Shaw's league could scarcely have been realized in 1919, but it must be realized eventually, unless Europe is to become a hyphen between Russia and the United States. Shaw ends on a Fabian note. Balance-of-power wars lead inevitably to class war. It is dangerous to give people the idea that they can get liberty by fighting for it.

Shaw's conception of the settlement was only in part Wilson's. They agreed on the freedom of the seas, open diplomacy, the independence of Poland, self-determination of peoples, and a league of nations. They differed in that Wilson more or less necessarily wanted a loose and all-inclusive league, was much more inclined to be severe with Germany, and was less inclined to temper his principles by practical considerations of power politics.

Shaw had hoped for a prosaic success achieved by Fabian common sense. What occurred was a Greek tragedy enacted in a madhouse. Wilson achieved with antique fatality the classic failure of democratic statesmanship. Intelligent, determined, idealistic, and passionately devoted to the interests of the "people," he fell victim nevertheless to the excess of one talent—eloquence, which is perhaps most typical of the popular leader. "The people" became in his mind an abstract verbal symbol. Their will he came with Calvinistic pride more and more to identify with his own and so lost touch with the actual trends of public opinion. Relying on his eloquence and his sincerity he appealed again and again to a people over the heads of their representatives and convinced himself that he was making millions of friends far off when he was only making a few more enemies at the conference table. To be sure, his eloquence won him great momentary popularity—particularly in Europe, where he was greeted as a savior. The Old World seemed waiting to be remade at his touch.

Actually, it had been considerably remade already. The British and French had sold the peace to win the war—and paid much too high a price. They had bought weak allies with extravagant promises. Moreover, the French quite understandably wanted security, though it meant perpetuating the military superiority of forty million people over sixty. Idealism had therefore to begin with bribes, and wisdom, with injustice and unreality. But wisdom had little opportunity in the pandemonium of Versailles. Ironically, it was the atmosphere of a great democratic election many times magnified. The principal leaders infuriated themselves with newspaper denunciation of the enemy, exhausted themselves with crowds of assistants and delegates, irritated themselves with noise and confusion, and stupefied themselves with facts and overwork. In this inferno, Wilson strove heroically, achieved much, and ultimately failed. The treaty left Germany still strong enough to attack and at the same time vaccinated her against peace and democracy by dooming her to failure in them. It also created a league which, though it achieved much good, lacked the cohesive force to survive the follies and venalities on which it was founded.

Shaw's disappointment was extreme. Later he pronounced Versailles "the greatest disaster of the war for all the belligerents." [7] At the time, however, he made no comment but watched with growing bitterness the gradual liquidation, in a strange atmosphere of idealism and fear, of the international machinery which Wilson had painfully constructed. Why was Shaw so sharply disillusioned? In "Peace Conference Hints" he had told everyone not to hope too much. Apparently he suffered more from a romantic conflict between head and heart than the shrewd sobriety of his prose would lead one to suspect. After all, he had hoped desperately.

Versailles marks the end of an era in Shaw's development. He felt that capitalism had caused the war and that democracy had lost the peace. He had always been hostile to capitalism. Now he was growing hostile to democracy, which had been his one common bond of faith with the Anglo-Saxon world he lived in. As he lost sympathy with that world, he lost influence, and as he lost influence, he lost the sense of responsibility. Moreover, the logical opposite of capitalism and democracy is communism and dictatorship. Apparently Marx's prophecies were all coming true. Private enterprise seemed ever more bankrupt; depressions were becoming more acute and disastrous. The class struggle was becoming more violent; capitalistic imperialism, more brutal and rapacious. Force alone seemed able to achieve anything, and in Russia force was apparently building up something very like the utopia Shaw had always worked for. Sometimes when he was particularly disgusted with democracy, it seemed exactly the utopia he had always worked for. Yet the Fabian never quite died within him. *The Intelligent Woman's Guide to Socialism and Capitalism* and *Everybody's Political What's What?* are both attempts to solve the old problems in the old way.

CHAPTER THIRTY-FOUR

Biology and Metabiology

Versailles had legislated at last "the far-off divine event" toward which the whole nineteenth century had been moving. The millennium now actually existed—on paper. The old despotisms had become democracies. Self-determination, universal suffrage, freedom of speech and action prevailed officially throughout nearly the whole of Europe. A World Court had been established to reduce national ambition to legality and logic, and there was a League of Nations which had officially voted oppression, secret diplomacy, war, and political wickedness out of existence.

But if the Peace Conference had restored an ideal nineteenth century, war itself had created a very real twentieth. The Pacts of Paris and Washington were the last pious hypocrisies of a century in which the contrast between the ideal and the real had always been acute, for while those great capitals declared universal peace and happiness, most of the world was plunged in conflict and misery. War had apparently reduced capitalism to an absurdity by raising an incredible and paralyzing labyrinth of international debt. It had precipitated something very like Marxism in Russia, yet in the rest of the world it seemed to have undermined Marxism by inflicting all of its miseries without fulfilling any of its promises. For while war had once again taught stubborn rationalists like Shaw that socialism was right, it had taught others that socialism was impotent. On the day World War I was declared, Mussolini ceased to be a Marxist. War on an unprecedented scale had released on a precariously rational world a new and more terrible atavism. It had greatly advanced technological progress, and it had greatly weakened men's hope of ever attaining the economic freedom and equality in which that progress was to eventuate. Life was becoming more mechanistic, more intricate, and less logical. Faith in law was giving way to faith in force. The paper millennium of Versailles could not long stave off despair.

While politicians and economists were still trying to cram man's soul and destiny into his pocketbook, thinkers were apparently freeing his mind and will from the laws of classical logic and classical physics. Philosophers had turned logic into a convenience, and truth, into an exciting and pragmatic adventure with the unknown. Physicists had abandoned the law of gravitation for the law of relativity and had discovered the law of chance in the infinitesimal subleties and precisions of electronics. Man was learning more and more and believing less and less.

In the Preface to "Heartbreak House," which was finally published in 1919 and produced in 1920, Shaw reckons up the moral and social costs of war. He declares that war makes bestiality permissible to everybody and highly profitable to the journalist. It debases the theater into the brainless escape of variety entertainment and perverts youthful genius to abandon art and take pride in efficient destruction. What particularly infuriates Shaw, here as earlier, is the complete inability of ordinary people to conceive of the vast horror of war except as a boyish game or a crude melodrama. War, he feels, is, like poverty, too awful a reality for average human nature. Perhaps he is a little too sure of this. The powerful puritan indignation of this Preface is marred by a want of charity and a vein of aesthetic snobbishness characteristic of Shaw. Fulminating against the lust for killing Germans, he exclaims, "Imagine exulting in the death of Beethoven because Bill Sykes dealt him his death blow!" [1] Some may think him a little too exclusively preoccupied with stray bullets hitting Bachs and Beethovens.

During the next few years he watched with bitterness, in a strange atmosphere of idealism and hate, the gradual liquidation of the international machinery which Wilson had so painfully constructed. Shaw had predicted a return to the politics of fear. He was nevertheless much exasperated at the French for their harping on security. And when Lloyd George set up the same cry against the American threat of naval supremacy, he burst out in a paroxysm of epistolary scorn. [2] Nobody, he declares, can walk even in a quiet country road with perfect security. The exaggerated demand for security leads to war. Mr. Lloyd George will not be content until the American and French fleets are both at the bottom of the sea. Shaw seriously predicted war between Britain and the United States and reiterated his belief ten years later. His letter is sensational and melodramatic. Perhaps he saw British and American relations too much from an Irishman's point of view. In any case, he overestimated British naval power, not perceiving—as many did not—that her immense industrial production gave the United States virtual supremacy at almost any time she chose to assume it.

Shaw wrote three letters on the Washington Conference for Naval Disarmament. Invited to attend as a journalist, he refused on the grounds, as he explains in his first letter, that all the important agreements would be secret and that even these, so far as England is concerned, would have no significance because the English are not sufficiently intellectual to pursue distant purposes. They become passionately pacifistic, as they become passionately warlike, when it suits their immediate advantage.

Shaw has never seen any guarantee of peace in disarmament. "The notion that disarmament can put a stop to war," he argues in his second letter, "is contradicted by the nearest dog fight." [3] Besides, human nature is not efficient enough to make really valuable military preparations. In the last conflict both armies did great damage, but neither one achieved a premeditated objective. One feels nowadays that such argument is Voltairian skepticism at its most superficial.

His third letter reveals the depths, and in part the causes, of Shaw's postwar pessimism. In his opinion, the experience of 1914–1918 proves that war can only be carried on by telling the civilian population lies on a tremendous scale, can only be won by starving or bombing that population out, and can only create a situation in which that population, whether defeated or victorious, lives more miserably and precariously than before. Can war be prevented? Only if men become wiser than their rulers and refuse to be deluded into hatred and fear. Will they? Shaw thinks not. Perhaps never before had he concluded on a note so close to complete despair.

And indeed he never recovered his earlier optimism, nor did the wars, inflations, repudiations, depressions, and doles which added their irony to the pious idealism of the international conferences restore his confidence. In 1922 Mussolini became Italian Premier and shortly after assumed dictatorial powers. With quick insight, Shaw perceived that democracy itself was on trial. Nevertheless, when hysterical shrieks of terror arose from the London press, he felt only contempt. What had English journalists to set up against the cold rationalism of Mussolini? The sentimental liberalism of the post-Gladstonians? All over again, it was realism *vs.* romanticism, Andrew Undershaft *vs.* General Baines of the Salvation Army. He stupefied the gentlemen who write letters to *The Times* by defending Mussolini:

> Are we to give him [he says] credit for his work and admit its necessity and the hopeless failure of our *soi-disant* Socialists, Syndicalists, Communists, Anarchists, &c., to achieve it or even to understand it, or are we to go on shrieking that the murderer of liberty and Matteotti is trampling Italy underfoot? [4]

Anyway, Shaw had always found irresistible the temptation to give the devil his due. The Duce's scathing attacks on democracy caused him to rejoice not as a Fascist but as a socialist who wished to see parliamentary government put on its mettle. In his opinion, British politicians would have to inject more intelligence and decision into democracy, or democracy might cease to exist.

As "Heartbreak House" is a vision of disaster, "Back to Methuselah" (1921) is a prescription for cure. It is, in fact, nothing less than "a Metabiological Pentateuch," a new bible setting forth a new religion, with an explanatory Preface by the prophet himself. The Preface, which one is tempted to prefer to the bible, is brilliantly written, with delightful anecdote and a magnificent sweep of idea, tracing the intellectual history of the nineteenth century to its final disaster in World War I and forming from the salvage of nineteenth-century ideas themselves a religion for the future. The underlying cause of the war was "neo-Darwinism in politics"; [5] the means of imposing it on the people, "the cinema-fed romanticism" of the popular mind; the basic problem, how to make the human animal equal to the perils and horrors of the civilization which he has himself created. Though shrewd and penetrating so far as it goes, Shaw's diagnosis is weakened by too much Marxism. It sees the disease too much in terms of class struggle and bread and butter. Man is a helpless atom lost amid endless complexities—exploited by an economic system which he cannot understand, misled by a political system of which he is the pathetic gull, threatened and bewildered by an industrial and technological system which has become hardly less dangerous and far more unhealthy than the primitive jungle.

Shaw's remedy is twofold: first, that man must have an intelligent creed, for without faith he will continue a moral coward, unable to do more than hide his head in a pile of machinery; second, that he must learn to live longer, for without the sobering prospect of a longer future, he will continue a frivolous idler, unable to acquire the sound knowledge and serious habits necessary to life in a complex civilization. If he chooses the right religion, he may soon acquire the necessary longevity. The right religion is of course creative evolution, and of course Shaw's discussion of it owes a great deal to Butler—in facts, ideas, and even in phrasing.

Having distinguished between evolution and theories of how it occurs and between Darwinism and Lamarckianism, Shaw argues for Butler's version of Lamarck, drawing chiefly from *Life and Habit*. All organisms have a degree of consciousness, memory, and will. If they try long and hard enough to develop an eye, a nose, a digestive tract, or the innate ability to ride a bicycle, they will eventually succeed, one generation passing on to another not all that it has learned and achieved but a tiny residue of organic modification or unconscious memory which gradually accumulates until it suddenly produces the organ or instinct required. Butler and Shaw differ as to the rate of change: the first taking the nineteenth-century view that evolution proceeds by imperceptible degrees;

[313]

and the second, the more modern view that it proceeds by abrupt mutation.

In fact, this Preface affords an unusual opportunity to compare the two men as creative evolutionists. Whereas Shaw is mainly a mystic and a social reformer, Butler is mainly a scientist. He wants to turn Lamarckianism into a scientific fact. Essentially, he is an armchair investigator, deriving his data from books, introspection, and literary analysis. He might also be called a vicarious, or parasitic, experimenter, for he preys on the experiments of others, subjecting them to an acute, practical, almost forensic criticism which sucks out the results he needs. Though by no means afraid to disagree with Butler—particularly about the nature of variations and the function of sex—Shaw largely accepts his results, in order to turn them into a religion and a political program. He wants to enlist at once the moral, religious, and biological forces of human nature in the cause of social progress, with the immediate objective of enabling men to live longer and so to become wiser and more mature. Consequently, he is interested in Butler's theories rather than in his proofs. Shaw is skeptical whether science can prove anything beyond reasonable doubt. He demands of ideas chiefly that they satisfy his moral or religious sense, and having decided what to believe, attempts to infuse that belief in others by skillful argument. He scorns experimentation as cruel and senseless and exalts the thinking cap:

> The laboratory workers worked very hard indeed to find out what would happen to a dog if they tied up its bile ducts, or to a monkey if half its brains were burnt out by a man with no brains at all, much as a child will pull off a fly's legs to see what will happen to the fly. Lorenz Oken *thought* very hard to find out what was happening to the Holy Ghost, and thereby made a contribution of extraordinary importance to our understanding of creatures having nothing wrong with their bile ducts or brains. The man who was scientific enough to see that the Holy Ghost is the most interesting of all the hard facts of life got easily in front of the blockheads who could only sin against it.[6]

In one respect Shaw is Butler much intensified. He is inclined to regard the acquisition of truth as a controversy rather than an inquiry. Perhaps this tendency is inherent in pragmatism.

According to Butler, Darwin knocked the brains out of the universe. Yet why should people have welcomed this atrocity with so much gladness? Partly, Shaw thinks, because they understood it so readily. Darwin was wonderfully obvious: though "his patience, his perseverance, his conscientiousness reached the human limit . . . , he never got deeper beneath or higher above his facts than an ordinary man could follow him." [7] But according to Shaw, the principal reason why people welcomed Darwin was that, at the time, they preferred the universe without brains, for the only brains it had were those of Blake's Nobodaddy and Shelley's Arch Fiend—of a maniac and a tyrant, who enforced by terror a savage code of morals and an impossible theory of creation. Such a deity could only hang as a dead weight of discouragement on nineteenth-century moral and physical science. His demise was an immense relief. Moreover, the conception of evolution offered a substantial hope of infinite material progress, and Darwin's theory of natural selection, or cosmic accident, permitted humanitarians to regard evil as a matter of chance rather than as divine malignance.

But in the course of time, mechanistic fatalism has proved even more vicious than old Nobodaddy. The survival of the fittest, applied to the human sphere, leaves no room for morality, and—what is an unusual criticism from Shaw—the neo-Darwinians do not believe in the cardinal virtue of self-control. Statesmen who do not feel the will of God do not serve the people. Nations dedicated to a ruthless struggle for survival are likely very soon to survive their civilization, which cannot stand many world wars. Politically and morally, Europe is bankrupt. It needs a religion equal to its culture and credible to its skepticism. That religion, Shaw believes, can only be creative evolution.

On the whole, Shaw's diagnosis is sound and shrewd, though many will not see so much virtue in creative evolution nor so much evil in Darwinism. Certainly Darwin is basic to nineteenth-century materialism. Yet because he has proved vicious in politics and international relations, he need not therefore necessarily be eradicated from biology. On the other hand, Shaw is right that men were losing faith in the far-off divine event in political time and space toward which both Darwinistic competition and Marxist class struggle were supposed to move. Shaw wanted to create a new faith by a metabiological miracle. He also wanted to inject new biological significance into the old legends and religious symbols of Western culture. At the same time, he warned that legend and symbol must never be substituted for doctrine and principle. In actual practice, as Dean Inge has pointed out, the separation between symbol and meaning is not so easily made. [8]

Shaw is also weak in his treatment of Christianity, from Nobodaddy to the churches. For Protestantism he has a few good words, but for Catholicism, nothing but ridicule. The nineteenth-century Church that, at one time or another, included Newman, Lamennais, and Döllinger is so much antiquated and irrational superstition. "Saint Joan" embodies a strange reversal of this opinion. Shaw the artist rose to magnanimity of which Shaw the controversialist was apparently incapable.

The play "Back to Methuselah" itself traces the history of longevity from the time when Adam, bored at the prospect of eternal life, vows himself to mortality, until the time far in the future when the Shavian ancients, having freed themselves of every temporal limitation except that of death by physical accident, are willing themselves into whirlpools of pure thought. In her *Samuel Butler*, Mrs. Stillman [9] suggests that Shaw got his central idea from a passage in Butler's *Alps and Sanctuaries,* but Henderson explains that he began rather with Weismann's observation that death is not a necessity but a device by which nature has provided the advantages of renewal and experiment without the danger of overcrowding.[10] Shaw felt that man might gladly forfeit these advantages in exchange for longer life and greater maturity. As a creative evolutionist, he could will himself what he desired. "Back to Methuselah" is, first, the story of this great resolve and, second, a political extravaganza of the sort to which Shaw later devoted himself more and more.

As a modern Pentateuch, "Back to Methuselah" is a lengthy disappointment. Shaw succeeds even less than Milton. Metabiology in the Garden of Eden is even duller than theology in heaven, and pure thought among the tertiaries is more tenuously vague and didactically unpleasant than aesthetics in the lecture room of a minor German philosopher. Apparently, thought does improve with age, for the ancients, who constitute a further development of the tertiaries, are a little more agreeable and impressive. Yet no part of "Back to Methuselah" bears any comparison with "The Dialogue in Hell." As political extravaganza, the play is not much better. It is true that satire had to remain subordinate to longevity, but Shaw's attitude had always been, the more subjects the merrier.

This time he was too angry to be merry. Like "Major Barbara" and "Man and Superman," "Back to Methuselah" is a battlefield of hope and despair. As a Metabiological Pentateuch, it expresses a desperate faith in the future. As a political satire, it tragically reveals the depths of rage and disillusionment which Shaw felt against mankind for the monstrous folly of the war. The best of it is "The Gospel of the Brothers Barnabas," in which he satirizes Lloyd George and Henry Asquith as Burge and Lubin. But even here he is too furiously eager to attack these men to represent them as really worthy of attack or to construct a satiric situation in which they can be effectively attacked. He cannot forgive them for having been the wartime leaders of British democracy; nor British democracy, for having owned such wartime leaders. He cannot forgive anybody for either the war or the peace. Above all, he cannot forgive democratic government. Here his bitterness knows no bounds. He can grant his foe no dignity whatever. In "The Thing Happens" Confucius, a twenty-second century bureaucrat, remarks of a successful candidate for the House of Commons: "He was released from the County Lunatic Asylum a fortnight ago. Not mad enough for the lethal chamber: not sane enough for any place but the division lobby. A very popular speaker." [11]

Ominously, Shaw seems throughout the play obsessed with the idea of execution, more or less benevolent. One feels that the artist Martellus speaks the author's own sentiments when, having been ordered to kill two murderous human beings whom he had created, he confesses, "With fierce joy I turned a temperature of a million degrees on those two things I had modelled, and saw them vanish in an instant into inoffensive dust." [12] The consequence of so much anger is that bad manners must often serve for smart repartee, insult for witticism, and endless wrangling hung on a slender thread of dramatic construction for such masterly satiric scenes as those in which Sartorius reveals his business to Harry Trench, or Mrs. Warren, her profession to Vivie.

But the weaknesses of "Back to Methuselah" cannot be entirely explained by Shaw's war fury. He seems to have written from conviction rather than inspiration. I suppose no one approaches the task of composing a bible with lighthearted enthusiasm, and probably Shaw was feeling at the time a reaction from the moral and mental strain of the war years. Probably he felt old and written out. At the end of his Preface he says:

> I am not, I hope, under more illusion than is humanly inevitable as to the crudity of this my beginning of a Bible for Creative Evolution. I am doing the best I can at my age. My powers are waning; but so much the better for those who found me unbearably brilliant when I was in my prime. [13]

Shaw's metaphysics require some comment. In general, "Man and Superman" explains the process of creative evolution. "Back to Methuselah" clarifies its total history and ultimate direction. In his essay on "Shaw's Philosophy," Mr. C. E. M. Joad has dealt very ably with this whole subject. [14] Shaw's universe, he points out, is made up of two elements: life and matter. Life can mold, even create matter but is limited and obstructed by it, so that—though Shaw is ambiguous here—individuality must always be linked with death and immortality await the somewhat cheerless universality of pure thought. Evolution upward is instinctive and conscious. Conscious evolution occurs in two stages. First, a genius enunciates some new idea in art, politics, ethics, or religion. Being a precocious sport and therefore maladjusted to his environment, he is of course misunderstood and persecuted by his contemporaries. At length, however, the second stage sets in. The masses adopt his idea and thereafter persecute later geniuses who attempt to go beyond it. Art, then, is properly "a device, one of the most important, for refining and enlarging the awareness of men and women and so

[317]

lifting Life itself to a higher level of consciousness." [15] Mere romantic art viciously distracts attention from the high purpose of evolution to the glorification of women and sex.

At this point Mr. Joad makes a comparison between Shaw and Plato. The latter began by condemning art as hostile to reality and then in later years tended to approve of it as offering, in beautiful fable and parable, the only vivid reflection of reality. Shaw seems to reverse this process. In the last play of "Back to Methuselah," art has become the amusement of children. Mr. Joad concludes with the complaint that Shaw is not at all clear about his final end. If life evolves toward ever greater awareness, of what does it become aware? If of itself, then it reverses its earlier tendency to subordinate itself to an evolutionary purpose. But of course the difficulty is inherent in any system which exalts process. And perhaps it is not surprising that a metaphysic built upon ethical romanticism should embody a contradiction, so characteristic of romantic theory and practice, between extreme egotism and extreme altruism.

The truth is of course that Shaw's metaphysics were conceived not in the anxious quiet of the study but in the din and fury of the intellectual battlefield. Consequently, like peace terms laid down in the midst of war, they are full of the logic of enmity and struggle and overwhelming temporary crisis, subordinating every kind of fact and truth to the cause of immediate victory. The whole tendency of Shaw's thought is to merge biology, economics, history, art, ethics, and theology in a great battle to make the universe safe for Shavianism. As a biologist, he is a Lamarckian because he is against the cosmic capitalism of Darwin. As an artist, he is a puritan and a utilitarian because he is against the social aridity of art for art's sake. As an economist, he is a Ruskinite because he is against the aesthetic aridity of Benthamism. As a theologian, he is a creative evolutionist because he despises superstitious slavery to the Old Testament God of Wrath. As a moralist, he advocates freedom of instinct and impulse because he despises the timid and benighted conventionality of middle-class conscience. As a historian, he exalts evolution and vilifies progress, because as a socialist, he has lost faith in the efficacy of mere political reform. But having rejected social progress, he tries to make biological progress as much like it as possible. He merges will with instinct, habit with organic function, mind with unconscious adaptation to environment, so that mind, will, and habit may take over evolution and dedicate it to rational, moral, and social ends. Then, by means of eugenics and longevity, he speeds it up until it looks like a more startling kind of Victorian progress.

In fact, "Back to Methuselah" confronted him with his old inconsistencies in embarrassingly acute form. He could no longer define happiness, freedom, work, and contemplation in terms of devotion to a process, because the process was by assumption over. Yet the problems remained, and the old traditional answers must have stared him in the face. Why didn't he accept them? They were part of a Victorianism which he had fought to the death, but now he had annihilated Victorianism by poetic license. Why would he not recognize that if human excellence is to mean anything, it must always be an end in itself; that if human freedom is to mean anything, it must mean conscious, rational choice based on self-control? Unfortunately, Shaw was himself too much of a Victorian to see the permanent truth in the cultural inheritance of his own age. Having also like a good Victorian postponed his most important problems to the remote future, he had possessed the courage to journey to the end of the future to face them, and of course he solved them, but mostly with poetry and eloquence. The concluding scene of "Back to Methuselah," so suggestively similar in structure to the Epilogue of "Saint Joan," is disappointingly vague. As his supermen are incessantly talking of the future, so his Lilith talks of the past; and the great problems which always face us in the present, then as now, remain unanswered.

In "Saint Joan," Shaw was to return characteristically to a heroic delineation of process, though, significantly enough, he was to see its spiritual aspects, and particularly those which were conservative and traditional, more profoundly than ever before.

The fate of Shaw's plays in the theater has always been paradoxical. Despite its five-drama length, "Back to Methuselah" occasioned a triumph both for the author and for Sir Barry Jackson, who since 1913 had been producing Shaw's plays with great success at the Birmingham Repertory Theatre. Granting that he had achieved for "Back to Methuselah" a miracle of staging and direction, one must find some other cause than the merits of the cycle itself for the unprecedented enthusiasm with which the audience called for Shaw at the end of the last night's performance. The truth is that the aged revolutionist had, quite naturally and yet quite magically, become a British tradition. He had become the official gadfly of the British state, as almost a hundred years before, the Duke of Wellington had become the official defender of the eighteenth-century constitution. Like Ramsay MacDonald, Shaw had descended to the depths of public opprobrium during the war to mount the pinnacles of popularity immediately thereafter. Shavianolatry was one of the symptoms of general reaction from war enthusiasms.

CHAPTER THIRTY-FIVE

"Saint Joan"

In 1923 Shaw succeeded as an artist where he had failed as a philosopher. In "Saint Joan" he achieved the detachment and serenity he had not achieved in "Back to Methuselah." How he came to do so is a long and somewhat ironic story. Mrs. Shaw is commonly credited with having suggested Joan as a dramatic theme. The subject, together with that of Mohammed, had lain in his mind for years. From the Preface of "Getting Married" onward, he refers frequently to Joan and to the idea of a saint in conflict with her Church or a prophet trapped by the conventions of his age. In fact, it was a subject which he had treated comically and romantically several times, notably in "Caesar and Cleopatra" and in "Man and Superman." As a socialist and a puritanical hero-worshiper, Shaw has two basic themes: that of "Widowers' Houses," in which an individual convicts himself of robbing society; and that of "Saint Joan," in which society is convicted of martyring an individual. Nearly all of Shaw's plays can be regarded as variations or complications of these two themes.

The great merit of Joan's story was that here, apparently, history had worked out his heroic theme for him better than he had ever done himself. It was simpler, nobler, more complete, more tragic, and in better taste. Formerly he had treated history too much as something between a spiritual autobiography and a racy parable of contemporary politics. Mommsen's Caesar had inspired him to write a magnificent romance, but somehow the newspaper and the looking glass had got between him and his object of vision. But now, opening Quicherat's records of Joan's trial, he found—in the stark yet poetic authenticity of verbatim report—a woman, a tragedy, and a principle so profoundly expressive of his own deepest experience and conviction that he felt he could change nothing. Of course he did change everything a little, but remarkably little. Before, he had Shavianized history. Here, in a very deep sense, history had realized Shaw. He rose to the challenge, and in depicting the conflict between Joan and the Church, achieved, symbolically and temporarily at least, a magnanimous detachment toward his own conflict with democratic society. It is significant that he compares the Church with modern democracy in the Preface.[1]

By revealing the weaknesses of modern materialism, the war had softened Shaw toward traditional religion. He was ready to understand even Roman Catholicism. The churchmen who tried Joan had been as guiltless according to their code as she according to hers. Ibsenite-Shavian tragedy is paved with good intentions, because good intentions are the only kind that test moralities. Like "Major Barbara," "Saint Joan" represents a clash between moralities—in this case between the advanced morality of a genius and the established morality of a contemporary institution. A genius is an instrument singled out by the Life Force to achieve progress, warring not against the evil of his time but against its good, which from his higher view appears evil. It follows that all geniuses or prophets are protestants, as Joan, Jesus, and Mohammed were protestants.

But is Shaw's play, then, accurately historical? According to the records of the trial itself, on which he depended almost solely—yes, remarkably so. Events are of course telescoped and characters made unnaturally articulate concerning their roles in history. Certainly Peter Cauchon never anticipated the twentieth-century view of himself half so prophetically as Shaw represents. On the other hand, no one can read Quicherat's records without perceiving that the churchmen of the court were acutely and rather clairvoyantly uncomfortable about their positions. It is all there, and more than Shaw had space to show: the reluctance to assume responsibility, the seeking of further opinion, the continued consultations, the patient explanation to Joan of why she must deny her voices, the offer to bring in clergy of "her own party" to instruct her if she would, the decision once again urgently to exhort her —and once again, and again. All this, to save a girl whom every power in Europe, including one of the focal centers of Church power, was frantically eager to destroy.

Ironically, Shaw's one magnanimous gesture toward conservatism was repudiated, so to speak in advance, by the Catholic Church itself, when twenty years after Joan's death, the court was itself tried and convicted, Peter Cauchon posthumously excommunicated, disinterred, and his bones cast into the common sewer. Naturally, most Catholic historians agree in condemning the court which condemned the future saint and regard Cauchon, its leading spirit, as able and intelligent but a partisan of Burgundy and England and probably moved by hatred and ambition. Nevertheless, the court is not condemned by its record, nor Cauchon, by such of his letters as I have read. Both might have been as Shaw has represented. That they felt Joan's innocence, tried to rescue it, and were continually defeated by the plainest and most obdurate heresy from her own lips is as apparent in the records as in the play. At times they even proceeded on the assumption that her visions might be authentic. But why then did she insist on wearing man's attire? What priest today would see divine inspiration in the admonition that a young girl attend church in a two-piece bathing suit?

> After the said lawyers had exhorted her by all the goodness and piety which she seemed to have, to wear a dress fitting to her sex, the said Jeanne answered that it was not in her to do it; and if it were it would soon be done.
>
> Then she was told to speak with her voices to discover if she could once more wear woman's dress to receive the Eucharist at Easter. To which Jeanne replied that as far as in her lay she would not receive the Eucharist by changing her costume for a woman's; she asked to be permitted to hear Mass in her male attire, adding that this attire did not burden her soul and that the wearing of it was not against the Church.[2]

If Joan were not a saint—and her apparent lewdness hardly warranted such a conclusion—then she was certainly a heretic; and so her judges decided. But Shaw is not content with this. As a moral and religious genius, she must stand in even more drastic opposition to her time. She must be a protestant and a Shavian, exhibiting all the impatience, pertness, arrogance, and *hubris* that accompany an excessive sense of personal rectitude. Referring to her voices, she is made to say, "Even if they are only the echoes of my own commonsense, are they not always right?"[3] Shaw was in the habit of asserting, just as baldly, that he had always been right about the war.

Actually, Joan was very far from thinking herself always right. She begged earnestly that she might receive confession, for "one cannot cleanse one's conscience too much."[4] On another occasion, she gravely corrected the record of her testimony, "Where it is written 'All that she has done is at God's bidding' should read 'All the good I have done.'"[5] She attempted in every way to comply with the churchmen who tried her. Her refusal to swear the oath or to reveal certain information was the result of scruples, not of pertness and pride. "What I have permission to [from her saints], that I will gladly answer," she says.[6] Moreover, there are only the most tenuous grounds for regarding her as a protestant. She was ardent to receive the sacraments, eager to submit to Church doctrine and clerical authority in all save the single particular of rejecting her visions, which were as real and physical as the judges who sat before her. A bishop might as well convince her that she had not fought at the battle of Orléans as that she did not speak with St. Margaret and St. Catherine. The deadlock between her and her judges was simply this: what she *knew* to be a fact they were convinced was at best illusion or imagination. Hers was a tragedy which began and ended within the framework of Catholic doctrine.

> In your play [a Catholic priest wrote Shaw] I see the dramatic presentation of the conflict of the Regal, sacerdotal, and Prophetical powers, in which Joan was crushed. To me it is not the victory of any one of them over the others that will bring peace and the Reign of the Saints in the Kingdom of God, but their fruitful inter-action in a costly but noble state of tension.[7]

Joan may have been a heretic, but she was not a protestant.

Yet, though perhaps one may suspect in his characterization of Joan a mischievous desire to bait English protestant audiences with an enhanced picture of Catholic justice, Shaw sincerely believed his portrait entirely faithful. "I have done nothing but arrange her for the stage," he told Archibald Henderson. "There really was such a woman. She did and said all those things." [8]

Apparently he could not imagine anybody being as right as Joan without being as cocksure as he. He could not conceive of a saint ex-cept as a kind of genius, and his conception of a genius was inveterately Bohemian and rationalistic. Her "mysticism" amounts to the bare fact that she is a "visualizer"; that, as she is quite distinctly aware, her natural common sense and clear-sightedness express themselves in visions and voices. But the thoughtful spectator may well feel that she could scarcely have been canonized by virtue of the saintliness with which Shaw has endowed her. Indeed, she is hardly equal to her enemies—to the magnanimous Ladvenu, the scrupulous Cauchon, the coldly judicious Inquisitor, the magnificently satanic Warwick. To many, Shaw's Joan will seem brash and hard; and indeed her tragedy, far more than the real Joan's, is a tragedy of precocious youth, full of fierce energy, of hard innocence, and of audacious simplicity.

The play may be described as Shaw translated into tragedy or tragedy translated into Shaw. In other words, it is far from being totally serious. Warwick and John de Stogumber are sharp satire, the Dauphin and Robert de Baudricourt are comedy, more or less gay and delightful. What makes the play tragic are Joan, Peter Cauchon, and a noble simplicity of tone and treatment. There is of course less wit, less in-tellectual brilliance than in Shaw's earlier masterpieces, but there is a severe and lofty eloquence which is not surpassed even by the "Dia-logue in Hell." Many prefer "Saint Joan" to the rest of Shaw because it does not try to be six plays at once but treats a single theme on a single plane of significance with sustained power and unbroken illusion.

The construction is masterly. Three swift, bright scenes, climaxed by miracles, illustrate Joan's rise. A slow, sinister scene of discussion shows feudalism and clericalism plotting against her. A fifth reveals her triumphant yet already isolated and doomed; a sixth represents her trial and martyrdom. The miracles are convincingly simple, sudden, untheatrical. There is no preparation. In each case a straightforward, highly secular scene, with no element more mysterious than that of an unusual personality, concludes with a miracle impressing itself mesmerically on Baudricourt, on Dunois: the Maid goes, the hens lay, Baudricourt crosses himself; the Maid comes, the wind changes, Dunois falls on his knees.

Scene Five is constructed like a piece of music. It is logical as counterpoint, emotional as harmony, balanced as rhythm. Joan is depressed; the affectionate, rational Dunois explains her enemies in terms of their jealousy, and her miracles, in terms of the big battalions. Her spirits sink lower at the entrance of the King, Bluebeard, and the Archbishop; their disapproval is cold and vocal, Joan's defense, a fresh attack on their follies. "The old Greek tragedy is rising among us," warns the Archbishop. "It is the chastisement of hubris." [9] Dunois predicts her capture, explains that once the enemy discovers she is not invincible, she will be worth nothing to the Army, and he cannot risk one soldier's life to save her. Joan appeals in turn to the King and the Archbishop and is repudiated by each, in the name of State and Church. Her allies oppose her for little reasons, as her enemies, for big. Then, deserted, denied, and doomed in the midst of her triumph, she rises abruptly from despair to the full height of her lonely pride and inspiration. She will follow God and her voices to the end. The trial scene is a magnificent and beautiful irony on human politics. Never were reasons of state more eloquent, more lofty, more imperious, yet never did they lead to greater catastrophe.

"Saint Joan" represents a victory, rare in Shaw, of the dramatist over the satirist and the socialist, of the objective artist over the interested propagandist. Could the rest be silence? "I could hardly be expected to stultify myself," says Shaw in the Preface, "by implying that Joan's history in the world ended unhappily with her execution, instead of beginning there." [10] He had shown angels weeping at the murder; now the gods must laugh at the murderers. He had made thoughtful spectators feel that nobler men than they had condemned an innocent woman; now in his usual fashion he had to put the audience itself in the dock. And so we have heroic tragedy with a detachable problem-play appliance.

The gravest fault of the Epilogue is that it is unnecessary. It is beautifully written and beautifully constructed—in the elaborately rhythmic manner of the scene in Rheims Cathedral. Each character, kneeling before Saint Joan, praises her for the special liberation she has brought to the class he symbolizes. After all have spoken, she offers to return to the world of the living; and then in turn each one repudiates her for the very reason he has praised her. The Inquisitor, symbol of the judge, worships her for freeing men's souls from the bondage of law and denies her because "under existing circumstances," that bondage cannot be dispensed with. Cauchon, who represents all that is noblest in conservatism and in institutionalized morality, worships her because she has shown the girls in the field "that there is nothing between them and heaven" but denies her because "mortal eyes cannot distinguish the saint from the heretic." [11]

Even de Stogumber is treated with surprising gentleness and magnaminity. He is one of Shaw's many John Bulls. The difference between him and Britannus is Shaw's bitter experience in World War I. His story is a parable on contemporary history. He is cruel only through lack of imagination and in the fury of patriotism. The spectacle of Joan's burning arouses in him a mania of guilt which leaves him finally a gentle, broken, slightly crazed old man. He worships Joan because she has changed his cruelty into kindness. But he is as terribly unprepared for her return as England, having emerged from the madness and cruelty of war, was unprepared for anything but peace. His reply to Joan is prophetic: "You must not come back. I must die in peace. Give us peace in our time, O Lord!" [12]

Toward Warwick, the politician and the gentleman, Shaw is merciless. "The cunning counsellors praise thee, because thou hast cut the knots in which they have tied their own souls." [13] But it is clear that he cares nothing either for the knots or his soul, for when Joan offers to return, he hastily excuses himself in political generalities. In fact, the redoubtable Earl has no soul. When pricked, he collapses into nothing, with a little noise of unctious, polysyllabic clichés. This may be a good joke, but it is poor realism. Great evil cannot proceed from a vacuum, nor can the satanic statesman of the play be turned into the don't-quote-me newspaper politician of the Epilogue. Joan also loses stature. In fact, she becomes nothing less than exasperating. She can be humble to add a cubit to her moral stature, but only if everybody else will take her at her own highest valuation. "I shall owe nothing to any man," she snaps at Warwick. "I owe everything to the spirit of God that was within me." A moment later she remarks with great self-satisfaction: "But fancy me a saint! What would St. Catherine and St. Margaret say if the farm girl was cocked up beside them!" [14] With regard to the play itself, the Epilogue is an anticlimax, a vulgarization, and a lengthy elucidation of the obvious. Even so, it is too irresistible to lose its place on the stage.

In the year following "Saint Joan," Shaw was given the Nobel Prize. "He supposed it was awarded to him because he wrote nothing in 1925." [15] Of course, Shaw liked Nobel's prizes even less than his dynamite and accepted only on condition that he might immediately transfer the seven thousand pounds sterling to a society expressly created to promote closer relations between Sweden and Great Britain in art and literature.

Having worked himself into a breakdown at forty, Shaw proved that he had the energy to do so again at seventy. "When I rose to leave the platform after your speech at King's College," he wrote Forbes-Robertson, "I found myself thunderstruck with some appalling illness which had turned my spine into a bar of rusty iron grating horribly on the base of my skull." [16] A little later, he speaks of his health as definitely broken. Nevertheless, he hardly allowed himself a respite from the gigantic task of writing *The Intelligent Woman's Guide to Socialism and Capitalism*, which occupied him from 1925 to 1928.

CHAPTER THIRTY-SIX

Behind the Mask

It is customary to call Shaw a puritan and to define puritanism as an instinctive repulsion from life in the world. And yet Shaw has lived with infinite gusto in half a dozen worlds at once. Moreover, he has insisted on being a citizen of each one, with an easy, colloquial command of its idiom, an inside knowledge of its affairs, a direct hand in its business, and a vital hope for its future. In fact, he has worked tirelessly for the salvation of each—and therein lies his puritanism. He has carried his passionate love of life to the extreme of rejecting, in the name of purity, a good deal of it that other people thoroughly enjoy.

In the golden age of the restaurant and the café, for example, he was the contemptuous enemy of elaborate and ceremonious conviviality. Dining—and particularly wining—accomplished no business, and it could do considerable damage to the insides. Shaw's sense of personal integrity extended sternly to his insides. After a hasty survey, he quickly abandoned the literary set because they did so little and dined so much. "I might," he exclaims, "have spent my life sitting watching these fellows taking in each other's washing and learning no more of the world than a tic in a typewriter if I had been fool enough." [1]

Shocked at such open heresy to his own personal religion, Frank Harris dragged him to some of the *Saturday Review* luncheons at the Cafe Royal, but having carefully observed the guests, noted the atmosphere of the place, studied its prices, calculated its expenses and profits, and warned Harris that he ate too much meat, Shaw announced he would come no more, feeling he could not continue to accept an expensive dish of macaroni which might be got elsewhere for twopence. Years later, lured by Maurice Baring to such a bachelor dinner as Chesterton has immortalized in his *Autobiography*, Shaw observed the proceedings with increasing disgust and finally addressed the company as follows, "Gentlemen, we shall enjoy ourselves very much if only you will not try to be convivial." [2] Shaw would not have been at home in the *Iliad*.

But dining has in any case the excuse of being moderately essential to sustain life. Most sport Shaw regarded as absolutely irrational. Games were the last resort of desperate boredom, and hunting combined a pathological escape into action with a bloody lust for slaughter—or at least a barbarian callousness to animal suffering. For an honest country squire to broach the day's shooting in Shaw's presence was about as safe as for a medical scientist to attempt his conversion to vivisection. "In point of giving pain to many worthy people," he confesses, "I can hold my own with most dentists and beat a skillful sportsman all hollow." [3] In fact, Shaw's tireless incapacity for sport and idleness often made him dangerous at a country house.

> You invite him down to your place because you think he will en-
> tertain your guests with his brilliant conversation [a hostess ex-
> plained to Frank Harris]; and before you know where you are
> he has chosen a school for your son, made your will for you, regu-
> lated your diet, and assumed all the privileges of your family
> solicitor, your housekeeper, your clergyman, your doctor, your dress-
> maker, your hairdresser, and your estate agent. When he has
> finished with everybody else, he incites the children to rebellion.
> And when he can find nothing more to do, he goes away and forgets
> all about you. [4]

Shaw was safest at a Fabian house party, where people knew how to keep him busy. To cycling, swimming, and even boxing he was for many years enthusiastically devoted, both as performer and as spectator. They met Shavian standards of rationality, utility, or art.

Though formidably respectable, the Shaws made little concession to the amenities of "society," as such. They gave luncheons, which were much appreciated both for G.B.S.'s conversation and for the dead ani-mals Charlotte, as a nonvegetarian, kept bounteously in the house for herself and her guests. Shaw himself practiced old-fashioned courtesy according to his new-fashioned code of utility. He was ready to do a friend almost any kind of service but a useless one. He never paid social calls until late in life, when, with obvious relish and congeniality of temperament, he embarked on the career of a twentieth-century celebrity in the crasser sense. It was then that he made friends with Lady Astor and Gene Tunney, hobnobbed with American movie ac-tresses, did Shavian things in famous places, and said Shavian things on solemn occasions. For he did not twinkle quite like any other star, and on the whole he twinkled with an ulterior purpose, using his position in capitalistic society conscientiously to work for the destruction of capitalism.

Apparently Shaw's marriage was all Ellen Terry could wish. It was a typically Shavian relationship—very rational, very undemonstrative, yet founded on deep loyalty and understanding. He came to meals on time, and Mrs. Shaw eliminated petty friction from his life. He respected her privacy, her decorous cannibalism, the unobtrusive efficiency of her household, as well as the many interests and tastes of a marked individuality, and she worked with quiet and tactful industry to make the noisy and flamboyant adventure of his career as successful in the present and as famous in the future as it could be. She was liberal about his friendships with beautiful young actresses and invited them frequently to Ayot-St. Lawrence, but in real life Queen Jemima herself regulated King Magnus's "mistresses." They must be a diversion and an inspiration, not a strain and an interference. When Lillah McCarthy did not receive an invitation in many months, Mrs. Shaw wrote in explanation:

> Do not be uneasy. . . . You have noticed that I have not asked you for week-ends. . . . G.B.S. has been really badly overworked this winter, so that I have to keep the week-ends as quiet as possible. . . . You are such a wonderful and unsettling apparition that you upset the whole establishment when you descend upon it! So I have to indulge in you sparingly until we are all used to you, or until you are older and plainer.[5]

If Shaw has not been taken seriously by the world, he was taken very seriously by his wife, though what she began with tact she sometimes overdid with gusto and enthusiasm. In her quiet zeal to perpetuate her husband in marble, she started a process which engaged the efforts successively of Rodin, Troubetzkoy, Davidson, Strobl, and Epstein, and as H. G. Wells complained, blocked the traffic of Europe and America with Shaw effigies. But Mrs. Shaw did not allow life with a genius to atrophy her critical sense, nor was she above regulating her husband. Once, while writing *The Intelligent Woman's Guide to Socialism and Capitalism*, Shaw was asked to say something about socialism after dinner. "Of course I will," said Shaw, but after dinner he changed his mind. "G.B.S.!" said Mrs. Shaw very gently, "You promised to talk to us about socialism and you must." [6] He did.

Of course her difficulty was usually the other way. Arnold Bennett, after a dinner at Wells's, wrote in his *Journal*, "Shaw talked practically the whole time, which is the same thing as saying that he talked a damned sight too much." [7] With this opinion Charlotte frequently agreed, but when she urged Shaw to give others a chance, he complained he would be glad to eat his lunch in peace but people came simply to be entertained and so compelled an endless repetition of the same jokes and lectures.

Renewed contact with his relatives never failed to evoke the weird

Dostoevskian comedy in which his life began. In 1913 his mother died. With the thoughtful surprise of an older man, he realized that, having lived with her for many years in complete harmony and comparative indifference, he really knew very little about her. Shaw had a horror of the clammy contamination of earth burial, and therefore Mrs. Carr Shaw was cremated. Taking only Granville-Barker with him, Shaw sat through a rather "macabre" Church of England funeral service, but "when he went behind the scenes and saw the coffin pushed into what seemed a chamber radiant with sunshine, and bursting into twirling ribbons of soaring garnet-coloured flame, he was transported by the wonderful aesthetic effect." [8] Pearson tells the story:

> When the furnace closed he went for a walk with Granville-Barker. Before they returned the cremation was finished. They found the calcined remains of Mrs. Carr Shaw strewn on a stone table at which two men in white caps and overalls, looking exactly like cooks, were busily picking out and separating the scraps of molten metal and wood ash, so as to leave nothing on the table but the authentic relics of the deceased lady. Shaw's sense of humour at once extinguished his sense of propriety. He felt that his mother was looking over his shoulder and sharing his amusement. He was recalled to the decencies of the occasion by Granville-Barker's amazed comment: "You certainly are a merry soul, Shaw." [8]

The cremation of his sister Lucy was no less bizarre and merry. The will of the deceased forbade any religious service, but the chapel was filled with a crowd of Lucy's friends, who clearly expected something to happen. Shaw rose to the proprieties: "I could not let her be thrown on the fire without a word, like a scuttleful of coals. So I had to mount the pulpit and deliver a full dress elegy, concluding with the dirge from *Cymbeline*. Coal was very scarce then; and Lucy burnt with a steady white light like that of a wax candle." [9]

Most great men are great only for rather brief and very public intervals. Their casual "moments" are seldom impressive. Shaw's casual moments were perhaps the most formidable thing about him. He spent them in the committee room. There the irrepressible mountebank became the suavest and gravest of diplomatists. Bores that he would not have endured an instant in the drawing room or the debating hall he flattered and propitiated over the committee table. Hesketh Pearson has described how as a negotiator he became modest, prudent, cautious, sly, indefatigably busy—taking notes, transcribing documents, giving information, yet conscientiously effacing himself, and in a quarrel trading the disputants their self-esteem for the point he wished to secure.

And though he spent a lifetime in committee, he never luxuriated in rules of order nor negotiated for negotiation's sake. He accused S. G. Hobson of being a villainously unceremonious chairman and then invited him to preside at the next meeting of the Authors' Society.

Shaw prided himself on always striking the right note and speaking the authentic idiom. One can observe the results in his correspondence. Writing to politicians, he was brisk, serious, impersonal, and full of facts. To actors and stage folk, he wrote like this:

DEAR LEE MATHEWS,

I will see the Stage Society brimstoned first. Why should I? I asts you, Lee Mathews, as man to man, why should I? Why the devil should I? Why the ——— ——— ——— ——— ——— should I? [10]

To William Archer, he wrote—with perfect truth—like this:

Why, you stupendous ass, you draw a line through my plays which represents your own limitations in your most fatuously lazy mood; and you then proceed to explain that everything outside that line is mere Shawism (which doesn't in the least account for it), and everything inside it is heaven-born genius . . . everything that is not a stagily sentimental *coup de théâtre* makes you simply petulant. [11]

It is not surprising that Archer believed Shaw to be conspicuously undiplomatic—chiefly because he miscalculated his audience. "The paradox of his career," Archer maintained, "is the extraordinary disproportion between his fame and his influence." [12] There is some point in this. For Shaw, an audience was a temptation as well as a fact. He enjoyed "bowling people over" far more than convincing them. Nevertheless, the most reliable testimony seems to indicate that where he tried particularly to be tactful, he usually succeeded. Archer's pronouncement lumps Shaw's various personalities rather indiscriminately together.

Though unwilling to idle and gossip with his fellow authors, Shaw was always ready to work with them. He sedulously joined their clubs and societies, laboring incessantly to bind them to his own purposes. Like a good Fabian and a good Victorian, he strove tirelessly to achieve the ideal by the practical and to reach utopia by cautiously creeping toward it. He tried to interest the reading public in literature, publishers in genius, and established authors in their unestablished rivals. In the class struggle between publishers and authors, he felt as a socialist that authors could get a much fairer share of the profits if they organized. And again in the complex warfare between young and old and between compromising mediocrity and uncompromising excellence, he urged that if proved ability got prompt recognition, unproved ability would have a better chance. To bring about this dark purpose, he attempted a one-man infiltration of the Dramatists' Club.

That organization was not unlike the junta in Max Beerbohm's *Zuleika Dobson*. It did not narrow down to the ultimate exclusiveness of a single member, but for years it was composed only of Pinero, Jones, Carton, and Grundy, who could think of no one worthy of adding to their company. Finally, they invited Shaw to join, fondly certain he would refuse. To their horror, he accepted. The situation was difficult, for the dictator of the club had always been Pinero, who very sincerely signed his letters to Shaw "with admiration and detestation." Nearly everybody hated the new member—on Ibsen's account as well as on his own—and blackballed every candidate he proposed. Nevertheless, he continued to scheme, always pushing talent in preference to mere monetary success.

Shaw was variously active in the Shelley, Browning, Stage, and Authors' societies. He was continually urging inexperienced authors to make use of the last to bargain with publishers and persisted especially with G. K. Chesterton, who was selling some of his best work for a song at a time when he needed money very badly. Shaw wrote to him in the tone of an enterprising insurance salesman:

> Remember: you pay Thring [the barrister employed by the Society of Authors] only £500, for which you get integrity, incorruptibility, implacability, and a disposition greatly to find quarrel in a straw on your behalf. . . . Your obligations to us wretched committee men are simply incalculable. We get nothing but abuse and denigration: authors weep with indignation when we put our foot on some blood-sucking, widow-cheating, orphan-starving scoundrel and ruthlessly force him to keep his mite of obligation under an agreement which would have revolted Shylock: unless the best men, the Good Professionals, help us, we are lost. We get nothing and spend our time like water for you.[13]

When the occasion warranted, Shaw did not shirk the much more ungrateful task of investigating and aiding complete unknowns. One of his discoveries was the poetical tramp W. H. Davies, who in 1905 sent him a thin volume of verse, privately printed, to be retained if satisfactory on the payment of a half crown. So much sound business instinct coupled with so much virgin business innocence awakened the sociologist in Shaw at once. He began to read and discovered, in the man's verse as in his life, the same conjunction of ability and innocence, "that pleasant combination of childish freshness with scrupulous literary conscientiousness only possible to people for whom speech, spoken or written, but especially written, is still a feat to be admired and shewn off for its own sake." [14]

Shaw bought eight copies of the book and instructed Davies to send them to critics and reviewers. This purchase, Shaw explains, "moved him to offer me the privilege (for such I quite sincerely deem it) of reading his autobiography in manuscript." [15] That work was another eye opener. In a simple, elegant, Jane Austen style Davies relates with classical restraint how he begged, stole, received stripes at the hands of the police, drifted and vagabonded up and down the United States, casually lost a leg jumping off a railway car, and did many other astonishing things painful to the contemplation of a middle-class mind. Shaw helped the *Autobiography* along with a Preface, in which he observes rather wistfully:

> When I think of the way I worked tamely for my living during all those years when Mr. Davies, a free knight of the highway, lived like a pet bird on titbits, I feel that I have been duped out of my natural liberty.[16]

On another occasion, a workman named William Margrie, having had his play rejected by nearly every manager in London, indignantly sent it to Shaw for a Preface. Looking it through, Shaw noted that it was rather pedantically subtitled "a romance of low life." He responded tartly that "it is not a picture of life, low or high: it is a navvies' paradise put on the stage." [17] Thereupon ensued a spirited epistolary altercation. "How could you possibly suppose," expostulates Shaw, "that a West End audience would tolerate such romance? Those are not their dreams. . . . Does any atheist keep clamouring to be allowed to preach in Westminster Abbey, and complaining because he is refused?" He concludes with some home truths on success in art:

> You have some talent; but talent is so common in this world that it is much more important not to be a damned fool than to have much talent; for with good sense and industry a little talent will go a long way, whereas you may have more talent than some famous men have had and spoil it all by being a damned fool. Are you quite sure you are not the least little bit in the world a damned fool? There must be something standing in your light. What do you think it is? [18]

Some men become friends by working together, some by playing together, some by eating together, and a few by having ideas together. Chesterton's friendships were basically eating friendships. Nearly all Shaw's were thinking friendships, being fundamentally connected with a cause or a theory—Webb's, with socialism; Archer's with Ibsenism; Salt's with Shelley and vegetarianism; and Thomas Tyler's, with the Mary Fitton theory in Shakespearian biography—so that Shaw's anecdotes of old times, though always delightfully bright and comic, are laid not in jolly inns and taverns but in rather gloomy and inhuman places, like committee chambers, debating halls, and the British Museum Reading Room. Ideas are a strong but cold bond; they make for loyalty but hardly for warmth and affection. And perhaps there is some truth in the much repeated quip of Oscar Wilde: "Shaw has no enemies, but none of his friends like him." Kind and generous as he was, there seems to have been a reserve of rationality in a great many of his friendships; and indeed a man who passes his most casual and intimate moments under pressure of the rules of order is perhaps not likely to have a genius for intimacy.

If Shaw's friendships show less than ordinary warmth, they also show less than ordinary perversity and flightiness. He could be inhumanly patient and good-natured. The furious and inspired insults of Wells failed to ruffle him, as the envious detractions and malicious libels of Frank Harris failed to destroy his cheerful sympathy and ready helpfulness. Harris was preeminently one of the friends who never really liked him. Harris represents the anti-Victorian principle in Shaw's friendships and preferences and is in fact so indicative a phenomenon in Shaw's life that I must say a few words about him, though very few, for the relation between the two men has already been excellently treated by Hesketh Pearson and Hugh Kingsmill.

Frank Harris was the desperate victim of a big voice and a little body. The result was an aggressive egotism so vast as to leave no room whatever for conscience and very little for sanity. Once, when writing a book on Jesus, he said to Hugh Kingsmill, after a long silence, "Christ goes deeper than I do, but I have had a wider experience." [19] Incapable of thinking anybody his equal, he patronized both Jesus and Shakespeare, but he could on occasion write of them with a jealous and accurate eye to the facts of their achievements. He also had those moments of illusionless lucidity characteristic of a man who has spent a lifetime deceiving himself and everybody else. But criticism was only an avocation. His occupation was swindling and his amusement seduction, which gratified his vanity even more than his senses.

Harris regarded Shaw as an inferior who by some vindictive caprice of the British public was acquiring the fame that should have belonged to himself. For a time Shaw was a little inclined to the same opinion. As a man who had overcompensated for his own shyness and sensitivity, Shaw admired noise and arrogance in themselves, and, to do him justice, Frank Harris grew to be an artist whose rich, deep-voiced profanities sometimes rose to cadenced and unprintable sentences of insight and judgment. As he had been a little overawed by Henry Irving the pontiff of Victorian artistic respectability, so Shaw was ill at ease with Frank Harris the pontiff of Georgian disreputability. It was useless to be brilliant in the face of that brass-armored arrogance because it was impervious to everything but itself. Wherever doors were ajar, it stalked through the ruins of late-Victorian England, putting the proprieties to terrified flight. Shaw rejoiced in the spectacle, and with a taut brilliance which shows how much he was impressed, explains Harris to Harris:

> Somebody in London society who likes interesting people meets you and invites you to dinner. He asks you to take in a bishop's wife. You entertain her with deep-voiced outpourings of your scorn for the hypocrisy and snobbery of the Church, finishing up with a touch of poetry about Mary Magdalene and her relations with Jesus. When the poor lady escapes to the drawing-room and you find yourself between the bishop and Edmund Gosse, you turn the conversation on to the genius of Rops, and probably produce a specimen of his work, broadening your language at the same time into that of the forecastle of a pirate sloop.[20]

Always grateful for the freedom Harris had given him as dramatic critic on *The Saturday Review,* Shaw at first regarded the editor's recklessness as courage and his vulgarity as iconoclasm. But the reality was unmistakable. When Harris was imprisoned, Shaw wrote, "You got two weeks where Wilde got two years. You deserved hanging. What had a man like you to do with the dregs of bucketshop finance and journalism?" Harris's *My Life and Loves* evoked even stronger language. "You had better burn this letter," Shaw concluded.[21] Later Charlotte read and burned the book and refused ever to receive its author. Nevertheless, Shaw's belief in Harris the writer persisted as a prejudice, as irrationally detached from fact or personal interest as his belief in the menace of vivisection or the turpitude of meat eating.

An interesting illustration of his attitude toward Harris appears in the Preface to "The Dark Lady of the Sonnets," which was played in 1910 to aid the campaign for a national Shakespeare theater. Harris had written a book on *The Man Shakespeare,* in which he had, as Kingsmill explains, oscillated between worshiping Shakespeare as Frank Harris and pitying him as Oscar Wilde. Having praised Harris as being "everything except a humorist, not, apparently, from stupidity, but because scorn overcomes humor in him," [22] Shaw pronounces *The Man Shakespeare* sentimental and melodramatic but real and alive and therefore infinitely more valuable than the infinitely labored abortions of the professors, who are unable to regard Shakespeare as a living man.

CHAPTER THIRTY-SEVEN

Shaw and Chesterton

Every eminent man with any sense of drama or feeling for his biographer should have a great friend and a great enemy. If he must choose one or the other, he should prefer the enemy. Gladstone's moral earnestness gains immensely from the contrast with the oriental subtlety of Disraeli, and Disraeli's wit and insight gain perhaps even more from their target in the tortuous and interested scrupulosity of Gladstone. If Shaw was somewhat austere and prudent about his friends, surely no man was more fortunate in his enemies. At any rate, he fulfills magnificently the needs of the biographer. He chose for himself a great friend in Sidney Webb, and in G. K. Chesterton, the most gallant and friendly of enemies.

Perhaps, even in literature, every force arouses its counterforce; but it is seldom that they meet on the same debating platform; it is seldom also that the dialectic of history speaks in epigram. As Maisie Ward observes, Shaw and Chesterton put the same questions to the dying Victorian world in which they lived.[1] Both demanded a religious certainty, a moral anchor, a virtuous and intelligent democracy, and a just and satisfying national economic life. To these demands they found answers which differed increasingly as Chesterton moved from Christian socialism to Catholic distributism. They agreed only about science, of which both were critical—Chesterton, chiefly because it tried to be a genuine religion, and Shaw, chiefly because it failed to be a genuine religion. In general, Shaw tended to be right about new things; Chesterton, about old things. Against Shaw's eugenics and rationalistic separation of sex and marriage, Chesterton stood for the traditional solidarity of the family. To Shaw's creative evolution and romantic emotionalism, he opposed Christian theology and Christian ethics. To the complex Fabian ideal of representative democracy, hedged about by all manner of educational qualifications, he opposed a romantic ideal of direct democracy with no qualifications whatever. To Fabian state socialism, he opposed peasant proprietorship and small ownership aiming at individual liberty and responsibility.

On ethics and religion, Chesterton was certainly sounder than Shaw. On economics and government, he was probably less sound, for though it is wise to safeguard individual liberty and initiative, it is less wise to attempt to do so by turning the clock back. He saw that a nation must have a soul to be great, but he did not see that it must have a pocketbook to survive, that in a world where war and industry are so nearly the same, to reduce the industrial potential of a great state is to invite its destruction. Like Churchill, he sometimes assumed romantic attitudes for conservative reasons. As he idealized childhood because it loves limits and definiteness, so he idealized "the people" because they are the repositories of tradition and legend. Despite many doubts and misgivings, especially as the press became more sensational, he felt that the people knew far better than the politicians what was best for them, and the more directly they could express their will, the wiser government would be. Chesterton wanted to make men freer, braver, more self-reliant by returning to an old world of faith and peasant economy. Shaw wanted to make men freer, more intelligent, more artistic by creating a new world of greater wealth, larger comfort, and more abundant leisure. Shaw had a rationalist's faith in machinery, and Chesterton, a fundamentalist's faith in human will and fortitude.

> I cannot remember when I first met Chesterton [wrote Shaw many years later]. I was so much struck by a review of Scott's *Ivanhoe* which he wrote for the *Daily News* in the course of his earliest notable job as feuilletonist to that paper that I wrote to him asking who he was and where he came from, as he was evidently a new star in literature. He was either too shy or too lazy to answer. The next thing I remember is his lunching with us on quite intimate terms, accompanied by Belloc.[2]

The two men probably met about 1900, when Shaw was forty-four and Chesterton twenty-six. It is only a moderate exaggeration to say that they debated with each other for the rest of their lives. By far the best part of that long polemic was waged in books and newspapers. The results were chiefly dramatic. Shaw's international fame added luster and compass to the rapidly growing reputation of Chesterton, and the latter's delightful amiability removed some of the ice from the cold glitter of Shavian intellectuality. In fact, the more they argued, the friendlier they grew, and as the equal brilliance of their wit made them sound very much alike, many people assumed that they really had the same ideas and disagreed simply in order to call attention to themselves.

The great irony of their relationship is that though they might have learned so very much, they actually learned so little, from each other. They could not make themselves understood across the spiritual distance which separated them, so that, like the public at large, they came more and more to admire each other as writers and to discount each other as thinkers. Chesterton had probably learned most of what he could learn from Shaw before they met. Shaw was perhaps too old and too proud to learn. He was also too busy talking and teaching, for as Lillah McCarthy discovered very early in their friendship, "Shaw is not a listener at all." [3]

"I began arguing with Mr. Bernard Shaw in print, "says Chesterton in his *Autobiography*, "almost as early as I began doing anything. It was about my Pro-Boer sympathies in the South African War." [4] In two wars Shaw and Chesterton managed to be both for and against England but always against each other. As far as war itself was concerned, the contrast was that between Bluntschli and Saranoff. More broadly, Shaw was a benevolent imperialist, while Chesterton was a Little Englander, believing that nationalism is better than internationalism, and fair play, better than any *pax Britannica*. In 1899, Chesterton denounced England as an imperialistic bully and supported her in 1914 as a heroic defender of Christian civilization against Prussianism. Shaw supported her in 1899 as taking a necessary step toward world peace and of course criticized her in 1914.

As Shaw very early perceived, Chesterton was realistic but impractical. He could read character at a glance but had far too little coolness and far too much good nature to profit by his insight. One result was that he was notoriously victimized by publishers. Shaw was soon writing him gargantuan letters, containing enough material to fill half a dozen manuals on the practical economics of writing and publishing. Finally Chesterton solved his problem by going to an agent. But Shaw had got in the habit of assuming a paternal attitude, and having early decided that Chesterton had "colossal genius," [5] was soon urging him to turn his wit and narrative skill to account in producing a comedy. He greatly admired the younger man's biographies, and particularly the *Dickens*, which had elicited from him a letter of penetrating comment on the novelist.[6] Determined to win Chesterton for the theater, he actually wrote him a scenario and began to dangle seemingly shrewd but actually generous proposals, bristling with figures and provisos.

Chesterton had become interested not in the drama but in Shaw. In 1905 he devoted an essay in *Heretics* to Shaw, and in 1909, a whole book. The essay is only fair, and rather more Chesterton than Shaw; but the book remains still the soundest and most brilliant contribution to Shaw criticism.

Chesterton understood his subject much better than his subject ever understood him. The difference between the two here is chiefly the difference between humility and pride. Chesterton was violently impulsive

and humbly felt the need of control. In many obvious though superficial ways the flesh was weak, and he had a great deal of it. Moreover,
he had none of Shaw's efficiency and shrewdness as a businessman, his
tact and astuteness as a politician, his clearheadedness and pugnacity as
a man of action. On the contrary, he was incredibly absent-minded and
so helpless that he could not meet an appointment nor make himself a
cup of tea without aid. He could not possibly have survived in his own
self-reliant, peasant utopia. But worldly incompetence had opened his
eyes. Not having Shaw's sense of magnificent adequacy to all the crises
of life, he could enter more humbly into another's character and understand more fully another's strength and greatness.

George Bernard Shaw is a triumph of historical intuition. Chesterton
finds in Shaw the virginity and violence of the Irishman; the hardness,
realism, and homelessness of the Protestant Garrison; the joylessness,
pride, and logical dogmatism of the puritan; the impersonal sympathy
of the austere humanitarian; the enthusiasm of the reformer; and the
narrowness and rigidity of the Swiftian rationalist who cannot accept
the contradictions of life and who hates, rather than loves, the absurdities
of human nature. He has used not so much the facts of Shaw's life as the
whole history of civilization to explain George Bernard Shaw.

The latter did not appreciate the compliment. He granted that the
book was a brilliant and gallant performance, but he took refuge in
being horrified at its inaccuracies. Reviewing it in *The Nation* he called
it

> the best work of literary art I have yet provoked. . . . Everything
> about me which Mr. Chesterton had to divine he has divined mi-
> raculously. But everything that he could have ascertained easily by
> reading my own plain directions on the bottle, as it were, remains
> for him a muddled and painful problem.[7]

How far did he allow the defects of the book to blind him to its keen
yet sympathetic criticism? Chesterton had presented him with a very
special mirror. Probably he was not able to see himself in it.

The two met several times on the debating platform. The results were
disappointing. Apparently Shaw set the tone, and from the way he refers
to "this silly debate of ours," [8] one suspects that he did not take either distributism or Catholicism very seriously. Moreover, Chesterton was not at
his best in these encounters. A huge man with a small voice, an erratic
speaker incapable of careful preparation, he must have felt some restraint in facing one of the most brilliant debaters of the age, who,
though always easy and conversational, put as much energy and skill
into a speech as a prima donna puts into an aria. Chesterton seems to
have shone in repartee and rebuttal, but in any case, both men were so

busy being clever that they had little time to be constructive. Simple truth and verbal cleverness are most soundly wed in the quiet and leisure of the study. In the rough and tumble of the platform, the one or the other must be sacrificed. When paradox and witticism flew thick and fast, truth suffered more than either combatant. They never knocked that inconvenient goddess quite off the platform, but they seldom left her as they had found her. At their worst, they were brutal and bloody. Chesterton kicked the poor woman in the stomach and laughed at her contortions, while Shaw sawed her into halves and quarters and made epigrams over the bleeding corpse.

The two most publicized debates occurred in 1911 and 1928. On both occasions Hilaire Belloc presided. Shaw was at once the Nestor and the Achilles of these conflicts. Before the first he wrote Chesterton a prodigious letter in which he made complex proposals of procedure, illustrating from bygone battles with Hyndman and Foote, incited Belloc to forget his chairmanship and join the fray against him, and concluded,

> Did you see my letter in Tuesday's *Times?* Magnificent!
>
> My love to Mrs. Chesterton, and my most distinguished consideration to Winkle [the Chestertons' dog]. To hell with the Pope!
>
> Ever
>
> G.B.S.[9]

This debate was apparently not recorded, but that of 1928 was taken down in shorthand and published under its title, *Do We Agree?* It is remarkable chiefly for Belloc's introduction, which ends, "They are about to debate. You are about to listen. I am about to sneer," [10] and for Shaw's first speech, which is not so much an argument as a scintillating conversation with himself about himself.

More revealing is a fortuitous drawing-room encounter of 1923, which is reported in full by Hesketh Pearson. On the point of leaving when Chesterton came in, Shaw attacked at once, "Have you any adequate excuse to make us for not being drunk?" And when, somewhat startled, Chesterton had parried this thrust, Shaw promptly broadened his offensive by explaining Chesterton in terms of a very crass Shavianism:

> You suddenly realized with a shock that there was no room for a second Shaw among the modern intellectuals. Were you daunted? Not you! You instantly proclaimed to the whole world that you had examined Socialism and found it wanting. Actually you had examined nothing except the state of the book-market. . . . Your slogan became: Back to the land, back to the priest, back to the bottle! [11]

From this point, quarter was neither asked nor given. Chesterton seems to have been the more constructive and finished more strongly. What the encounter reveals is how much both men owe their personalities and conversation to the nineties. Their common ground was *fin de siècle* effrontery and witty insult, so that when they came together, they became less than themselves and rather like Oscar Wilde. Chesterton hardly attempted serious combat; and in so far as he did, Shaw pummeled an imaginary Chesterton. In 1919 the real Chesterton told Maurice Baring:

> Bernard Shaw has written an article which is supposed to be about his view of me and Socialism; but which may be said more truly to be about his blindness to Hilary and his Servile State. It is quite startling to me to find how wholly he misses Hilary's point; and how wildly he falls back on a sort of elderly impatience with our juvenile paradox and fantasticality.[12]

In 1922 Chesterton became more incomprehensible to Shaw than ever. Long an Anglo-Catholic, he was now received into the Roman Catholic Church. Soon afterward Shaw wrote to him:

> I am an Irishman, and know how far the official Catholic Church can go. Your ideal Church does not exist and never can exist within the official organization, in which Father Dempsey will always be efficient and Father Keegan futile if not actually silenced; and I know that an officially Catholic Chesterton is an impossibility. . . . I believe that you would not have become a professed official Catholic if you did not believe that you believe in transubstantiation; but I find it quite impossible to believe that you believe in transubstantiation any more than, say, Dr. Saleeby does. You will have to go to Confession next Easter; and I find the spectacle—the box, your portly kneeling figure, the poor devil inside wishing you had become a Fireworshipper instead of coming there to shake his soul with a sense of his ridiculousness and yours—all incredible, monstrous, comic, though of course I can put a perfect literary complexion on it in a brace of shakes.
>
> Now, however, I am becoming personal (how else can I be sincere?) [13]

Shaw felt that as an Irishman he knew all about the Catholic Church, and as the creator of Father Dempsey and Father Keegan, he had expressed about it very nearly all there was to express. He made no further effort to understand Catholicism until the subject was thrust upon him by "Saint Joan." Whether that play represents in any sense a continuation of the debate with Chesterton or whether Chesterton contributed in any way to Shaw's understanding of the world of medieval faith is very dubious. Questioned by Hesketh Pearson about the play, Shaw replied, "I distinctly remember writing *Saint Joan,* or working on it, at Parknasilla on the Kenmare Estuary in Co. Kerry, where two friendly priests discussed the trial scene with me." [14]

In any argument with an ordinary mortal, Methuselah was certain to have the last word. "A Glimpse into the Domesticity of Franklyn Barnabas," published in 1933 [15] but written earlier, introduces Chesterton as Immenso Champernoon into a hornets' nest of Shavian vitalists. This dialogue is a wonderful little reproduction of his generous outer husk in violent and comic motion. Champernoon transforms himself into a Highland chief with a traveling rug, does medieval battle with a golf stick, drums out "The Campbells Are Coming" with a dinner gong, and delivers himself into the hands of a Shavian sybil with speeches that set ablaze elaborate filaments of Chestertonian wit, paradox, and wordplay in an almost complete vacuum of sense. With devastating brilliance, Shaw proves that the style is not the man. But the dialogue goes beyond travesty. It is a patronizing puritan's indictment of a cavalier. The Shavian sybil is good-natured, indulgent, and often sound. In fact, she does everything but take Champernoon seriously and grants him everything but a point of view.

It is not surprising that so little came of the witty and pleasant enmity of these two men. Dangerously clever, exuberantly high-spirited, wildly impulsive, they were nevertheless basically very different. Chesterton had a genius for enjoyment and friendship; Shaw, for work and action. Belloc has said that Chesterton possessed "the royal virtues" of humility and charity.[16] They are almost the only virtues Shaw did not possess. Sanely romantic, Chesterton filled his leisure with games and dreams and playthings. Rather insanely serious, Shaw hated leisure, games, dreams, and playthings. Completely, though innocently, undisciplined, Chesterton founded his system upon law. Naturally disciplined, Shaw founded his upon a rather complicated and logical kind of anarchy. Confronted by the acute dilemma of disintegrating Victorianism, Chesterton decided for the old world of faith and order, and Shaw, for the new world of chaos and development.

CHAPTER THIRTY-EIGHT

Labour Inflated and Exploded

The General Elections of 1923 returned 258 Conservatives, 191 Labourites, and 158 Liberals. The Liberals supported the Labour Party in an amendment to the speech from the throne. Stanley Baldwin, the Conservative Prime Minister, resigned. White-whiskered Tories froze with terror behind their club windows and prepared to look on while Britannia met a fate worse than death. Ramsay MacDonald was summoned by the King to form the first socialist government in English history. But of course the Liberals held the balance of power. The Labourites were able to do just enough to hearten their friends and frighten their opponents. They passed a reassuringly unsocialistic budget, made a good impression abroad, and attempted to establish better political and economic relations with Russia. But their Russian policy alarmed the Liberals, who withdrew their support. MacDonald dissolved Parliament. On election eve a police raid brought to light the famous Zinoviev Letter, which seemed to indicate a communist conspiracy to undermine morale in the military forces. While the Labour vote actually increased, the Conservatives absorbed most of the Liberal strength and so obtained an overwhelming majority.

The first Labour government had lasted but a few months, but it had been impressive and respectable. MacDonald had proved a host in himself. Five years before, as an opponent of British war policy, he had been as execrated as Shaw; now he was perhaps the most popular man in England. He was tall, handsome, and picturesque, with a deep, vibrant Scottish voice, a faculty for friendly, condescending exposition, and a wonderful and eloquent command of the vague, cautious idiom of the House of Commons. He also had the ability to shed an aura of lonely idealism, very piquant to the sentimentally cynical twenties, upon the hurly-burly of politics. His later career was curiously like Wilson's, without the heroic finale. He was a figure very useful to labor in its march to power but a paradox very dangerous to himself. He was a sincere democrat with aristocratic tastes, a thoughtful idealist with a flair for phrases, a skillful politician with a weakness for world conferences. Before his career was over, conferences had undermined his thinking, and his friendships with aristocrats had undermined his popularity among workingmen. More and more, he degenerated into a magnificent ornament. He and Shaw had often been brought into close association, particularly during the war, but they were never intimate. Though Shaw was always cordial, MacDonald regarded him as vain, frivolous, and irreligious.

But Shaw was never dampened by disapproval, tacit or expressed, and in 1923 MacDonald, like everything else, probably looked rather good. So did the period which followed, in spite of abortive world conferences and a Conservative ministry. The General Strike of 1926 was a fiasco, but it was rich with suggestions of peaceful and orderly revolution. The Labour Party had become the official opposition, and everybody expected it to return to power. Under these conditions, Shaw, at the age of seventy-two, undertook the most ambitious stratagem of his long career as a propagandist.

The Intelligent Woman's Guide to Socialism and Capitalism represents Fabian pamphleteering on a grandiose scale. It is an attempt to "permeate" the whole female sex. Shaw had long felt the political importance of women. They had so little political past; surely they must have a great political future. As early as 1883, in *An Unsocial Socialist,* Sidney Trefusis-Shaw declares, "We Socialists need to study the romantic side of our movement to interest women." [1] Shaw had been more practical; he had also studied women. But they have always been a surprising study. In 1919, they obtained the vote and very nearly hanged the Kaiser with it. Thereafter politicians were a little timid about experimenting with the female electorate, so that a vast expanse of political mind remained long unexploited. Shaw determined to fabianize it by a complex and tremendous display of the talents of the author, lecturer, and tea-table lion.

The Intelligent Woman's Guide is a triumph of tactics. The author keeps statistics to a minimum, sometimes to the great convenience of his argument. He avoids technical terms and is always ready with an illustration. He purposefully lays aside his fireworks. He is seldom epigrammatic, eloquent, or poetic, but he is always friendly, personal, confiding, and so wonderfully interesting and clear that the reader is apt to form the exhilarating conviction that political is as simple as domestic economy. A social revolution begins to sound as easy and pleasant as a game of bridge—and far more idealistic. And Shaw is so reassuring: "If this, or any of the other plans," he purrs, "happens to startle and scandalize you, please do not blame me or throw my book into the fire. I am only telling you the different plans that have been proposed and to some extent actually tried." [2] Some of his boldest ideas he puts into the mouths of interlocutors, whom he then reproves and cautions. And when he finally comes out with downright revolution, it seems hardly to involve any change at all. Who could state the principle of equal income more innocuously? "The only novelty proposed is that the postmen should get as much as the postmasters, and the postmasters no less than anybody else." [3]

He is full of understanding for feminine problems, quick to take advantage of feminine sympathy and prejudice. Poverty is often translated into undernourished children, plutocracy into Mrs. Mammon's irritating snobbery. Sometimes again, he is extremely frank, and sometimes he cannot resist ironies which must infuriate many "intelligent women." He insinuates, for example, that socialism is "the latest thing" and therefore the fashionable doctrine. On another occasion, he innocently observes, "If I have not convinced you by this time that there are overwhelming reasons of State against inequality of income, I shall begin to think that you dislike me." [4]

Shaw devotes the first part of his work to a doctrine which has come to distinguish Shavian from Fabian and other kinds of socialism. That doctrine is equality of income. Shaw had argued for it as early as 1913 in a speech delivered before the National Liberal Club. In *The Intelligent Woman's Guide,* he expands it into an ethical and biological, as well as a social, philosophy. Equality of income would greatly strengthen the national economy, because it would create a market encouraging the production of necessities rather than luxuries. It would not weaken economic incentive, and in any case, mass production forces its own pace on idle and industrious alike. Equality of income would tend to improve the race because it would widen to the maximum the field of sexual selection. It would promote the greatest happiness of the greatest number because it would free the poor from misery and the rich from boredom. It would promote truth, justice, and honesty, because it would remove plutocratic power over the press, the law courts, the schools, and the church. It would secure the recognition of talent, because it would establish genuine equality of opportunity. Finally, it would create a maximum distribution of leisure or liberty in the community, because an equality of return would naturally involve an equality of useful labor. And if everybody does some work, nobody will have to do very much.

Since 1918, British economy had undoubtedly been moving in Shaw's direction. Higher taxation was equalizing income. A higher minimum wage was strengthening the domestic market. Subsidies were being used to stimulate agriculture and other essential production. Technological advances were raising the productivity of the individual worker. Moreover, Shaw's proposal of nationalization was in many respects superior to the system of doles and subsidies by which several declining industries, like coal mining, were kept painfully alive. Nevertheless, he was violently optimistic as to what socialism and equal income might achieve. "Let us pretend," he suggests enticingly, "that if we all worked four hours a day for thirtyfive years each of us could live as well as persons with at least a thousand a year do now." [5] Such pretending was very far from the facts. In 1928, the per-capita income of the United Kingdom was four hundred eleven dollars, or less than one hundred pounds. Utopia cannot be bought with such a bank balance. To realize Shaw's suggestion, a socialist government would have to expand British production and purchasing power by ten times. Even when fighting for her life, England had not produced so much, nor had she limited herself to anything like a four-hour day. Obviously, despite the despair of two wars and four decades of thwarted socialism, Shaw had not lost the capacity to dream.

He was no doubt also a little in love with his "case." For the inveterate controversialist, reality lies not in a heaven of ideas nor in a world of vulgar facts but in the beauty of an argument and the clarity of an exposition. In "Too True to Be Good" (1933), Aubrey Bagot declares:

> Lucidity is one of the most precious of gifts: the gift of the teacher: the gift of explanation. I can explain anything to anybody; and I love doing it. I feel I must do it if only the doctrine is beautiful and subtle and exquisitely put together. I may feel instinctively that it is the rottenest nonsense. Still, if I can get a moving dramatic effect out of it, and preach a really splendid sermon about it, my gift takes possession of me and obliges me to sail in and do it.[6]

To be sure, Shaw was not himself the *reductio ad absurdum* of a controversialist. He was too realistic to adopt views which he believed "the rottenest nonsense."

The Intelligent Woman's Guide is also a lengthy exposition of the stock exchange, the money market, banking, rent, profit, supply and demand—a primer of political economy, in fact. It is an elaborate indictment of capitalism and a handy blueprint for the creation of the Fabian state, with all the old Fabian and Jevonian doctrines adapted to new propaganda stratagems and applied to new problems and situations. An approximate equalization of incomes by taxation is not socialism. All the waste of strikes, lockouts, doles, subsidies, and unnecessary competition must be eliminated. A planned, largely nationalized economy must be substituted which will eliminate profit and place prices below the maximum cost of production, compensating for losses on submarginal locations by gains on those which are particularly rich or favorable.

[346]

Finally, *The Intelligent Woman's Guide* is a stern criticism of contemporary democracy. The party system disenfranchises all but the undecided, and universal suffrage leads simply to a tyranny of demagogues. In Shaw's opinion, the House of Commons has been decadent since the Boer War, and now in 1928 it seems on the point of breaking into such fragments as forced Cromwell to intervene with the Long Parliament. Shaw speaks of the Labour Party with respect but without much faith in its efficacy. The trade-unions, he feels, are less likely to work for socialism than to combine with big business in a raid on investors' dividends. Democracy talks endlessly, but it seldom acts until too late. I do not mean Shaw is pessimistic. No one plans the future so elaborately without having a great deal of faith in it. He is convinced that the future will be socialistic and equalitarian, but he is less convinced that it will be democratic.

Shaw obviously admires the strong men of history—and even more of course the strong women, particularly Queen Elizabeth, whose government he seems to consider far superior to the democracy developed thereafter. For the immediate future he clearly envisages the possibility of dictatorship, but in the last analysis he does not welcome it. Dictatorship is often swift and efficient, but it leads to megalomania and usually dies disastrously with the dictator. For a man already seventy-two, he is amazingly fluid in his conceptions and receptive of fresh facts. Keeping a sharp eye on the Continent, where democracy is being overthrown by dictatorships both of the left and the right, he makes several emendations to Marxist doctrine. The class war between capital and labor is not a war between the few and the many but between "the parasitic proletariat and the Socialist proletariat." [7] The army of capital would be made up not only of the professional and military classes but of domestic servants, luxury tradesmen, and all the other hangers-on of plutocracy. Especially if a scientific test for political capacity can be found, constitutional democracy remains the best way to achieve socialism.

In August, 1929, Sir Barry Jackson realized the ambition of many years and translated his hero, without any preliminary ceremony of death, into the company of Wagner and Shakespeare by creating the Malvern Festival, perpetually dedicated to Shaw and devoted chiefly to the performance of his plays. Of course no one enjoyed these rites so much as the genial, white-bearded deity himself. They combined, in a cheerful way, the pleasures of a mourner at one's own funeral and an animated statue in one's own pantheon. For several years Shaw basked and frolicked enthusiastically in the worship of admirers and other pilgrims. But by 1938 he had tired of this and stayed during the

Festival at Droitwich instead of Malvern, driving over for the plays he wanted to see.

Shaw was a very gay septuagenarian. He told George Bishop that between fifty and sixty, life was at its worst. He was continually reflecting on his mortality and making wills. Afterward, he forgot all about mortality and hardly kept his will reasonably up-to-date.

The Conservatives lost their majority in the General Election of 1929, and MacDonald found himself at the head of a new Labour government, in which Sidney Webb, as Lord Passfield, was Colonial Secretary. Of course Shaw had suggestions for the Honours List. "What about yourself?" asked MacDonald, when he had noted the names. "Not on your life. How would you like to be Sir Ramsay MacDonald?" demanded Shaw.[8] It was also suggested that he might be useful in the House of Lords, but he declared that he could not afford to keep up a dukedom, which would be his only appropriate reward. Very properly, Shaw refused to spend the rest of his life incognito.

Meanwhile, however, his old friends were departing. William Archer died in 1924. Just before the operation which proved fatal, he had written Shaw:

> Accidents will happen, and this episode gives me an excuse for saying, what I hope you don't doubt—namely, that though I may sometimes have played the part of all-too candid mentor, I have never wavered in my admiration and affection for you, or ceased to feel that the Fates had treated me kindly in making me your contemporary and friend. I thank you from my heart for forty years of good comradeship.[9]

When he returned to "an Archerless London," Shaw felt for the first time the loneliness and superfluousness of age. The long friendship had been deeper and warmer than its tensions and irrationalities, to which indeed Shaw had paid little attention. Archer had wanted to be a great dramatist. To find that not he but the man beside him had been chosen must have been a humiliating experience, which perhaps he revenged unconsciously—as honest, simple men will—by persistently overestimating Shaw's capabilities and underestimating his performance. He was one of those always in a state of excited disappointment about Shaw, having just discovered the half-realized greatness of his last play but one.

A few years later, Shaw found himself following in the footsteps of the Duke of Wellington up the aisles of a crowded Westminster on a great ceremonial occasion. He was a pallbearer at Thomas Hardy's funeral.

Fortunately, some of the long and splendid afternoon of his genius survived into this period of earthly immortality. Early in 1929, he completed in six weeks the best of his political extravaganzas, "The Apple Cart," which was played for the first time in England at the new Malvern Festival and probably written in mischievous anticipation of a new Labour government. Being very well timed, the play created an immense sensation and was of course widely misunderstood. Extreme Tories rejoiced, and Labourites fumed at the exaltation of monarchy and the attack on socialistic democracy. As a matter of fact, monarchy, like munitions manufacturing in "Major Barbara," is simply a satiric expedient. "The comedic paradox of the situation," as Shaw himself explained, "is that the King wins, not by exercising his royal authority, but by threatening to resign it and go to the democratic poll." [10] Shaw does not attack either democracy or socialism as such. He simply challenges them with their problem. The real enemy is big business behind the scenes.

Like "Back to Methuselah," "The Apple Cart" looks into the future, but much less myopically and mistily. Ignoring Mussolini and the possibility of another war and assuming the permanence of Versailles and the League, Shaw transports us to an instructive, rather old-fashioned utopia of the 1960's. It is a world in which democracy has survived without succeeding, labor has triumphed without becoming socialistic, and industrial capitalism has decayed without ceasing to accumulate profits and foreign investments. England is dominated by big business, symbolized by Breakages, Ltd., which, as the name implies, suppresses invention and excellence and encourages waste and perishable production, so that there will always be plenty of work to be done and profits to be made. Breakages, Ltd. has invested heavily in essential industries abroad, where labor and raw materials are cheap, and built up at home a parasitic economy producing Christmas crackers, chocolate creams, and golf clubs. It exploits the press, pays high wages, and offers all sorts of social benefits. Therefore it can permit a carefully controlled Labour Party to remain permanently in power. Politics are entirely political, having descended to such ineffectual noise and vulgarity that no able man will take part in them—except the King, who alone stands above "the tyranny of popular ignorance." [11] Possessing great personal prestige with the masses, immense social prestige among the plutocracy, and a theoretical veto on legislation, King Magnus has been able to moderate the influence of big business and maneuver the government into something like constructive action.

At the opening of the play, the Cabinet has revolted and presents Magnus with an ultimatum designed to strip him of all power. The Cabinet (headed by Proteus, a wicked satire of MacDonald) is represented as a gang of crafty demagogues, who exploit their clamorous

[349]

vulgarity to gain temporary advantages as the diplomats of a more aristocratic age exploited tact and decorum. The King is a Shavian philosopher on the throne, such a man of expert knowledge and broad experience as severe competitive examination might admit to a panel of prime-ministerial candidates. Naturally, he triumphs—by threatening to abdicate and stand for Parliament. But his victory promises in fact to be a mere episode in the tragi-comic fate which England's economic and political weaknesses have brought upon her, for the American Ambassador has announced shortly before that the United States is willing to reverse the Declaration of Independence and rejoin the Empire—in other words, add England as a forty-ninth star to the flag. Since British capital is heavily invested in American industry and therefore at the mercy of American political power, the offer will be hard to refuse.

Superficially puzzling, the play is actually a very clear and witty dramatization of some of Shaw's favorite theories about how England can go wrong or right. "The Apple Cart" implies that unless England is to lose her position in the Anglo-Saxon community of nations, she must solve two problems: she must escape such a utopia of big business as Shaw depicts, and she must secure a series of prime ministers as able as King Magnus—in other words, she must secure social justice and the right rulers. Since a solution of the second problem would go far toward a solution of the first, Shaw devotes himself in his Preface chiefly to the second, developing some of the ideas in *The Intelligent Woman's Guide*. He recognizes the world-wide threats of dictatorship and revolution and condemns both: dictatorship, because it leads to megalomania; and revolution, because it is a last resort which too frequently achieves only an impoverished and chaotic inversion of the *status quo*. Democracy is the only reliable means of peaceful progress. Its great merit is that it enables the governed, when dissatisfied, to remove the governors, but as at present practiced, it offers very little guarantee that the new governors will be any better than the last. Shaw proposes that excellence be insured, as in the Civil Service, by competitive examination, which could provide a panel of candidates for all elective offices, from the lowest up to that of prime minister. He also prefers the nonpartisan committee system of English municipal government to the two-party parliamentary system of the House of Commons. Above all, he feels that democratic officials must be made more independent of the passing whims of the electorate. King Magnus represents more truly than his Cabinet the permanent interests of his people, precisely because he is not so precariously subject to their momentary approval.

In "The Apple Cart," as in so many of the later works, Shaw applies his old ideas to the world's new problems. His forecast of the future is shrewd but somewhat narrow, drawing out a few tendencies in the contemporary situation to their logical extreme. One suspects that Aldous Huxley's *Brave New World* has more of the future in it. And yet, though perhaps unintentionally, "The Apple Cart" is wiser than its Preface, in which Shaw attempts to solve a moral problem simply by accumulating ingenious apparatus. Competitive examination is an excellent tool, but it will improve democracy only so long as examiners and examinees want it to. King Magnus is a good ruler not because he has passed an examination but because he represents a high aristocratic tradition of political leadership. Apparently Shaw regards him as one of his Lamarckian supermen, who, in the practical sense, represent nothing more spiritual than an ingenious device for ringing up fortuitous moral and intellectual effort as realized earnings on the cash register of solid matter. If he cannot have the superman, Shaw falls back on panels, examinations, and as a last resort perhaps, on contemporary dictators, of whom he took somewhat too jaunty a view. The only test which a Mussolini passes is the test of strength, and when he does so, it is the constitution which is flunked out.

Structurally, "The Apple Cart" is a prolonged Cabinet crisis, interrupted by a puritanical roll on the carpet. The Cabinet crisis has fine dramatic moments, like the King's long, eloquent speech on the state of English democracy, but is also somewhat static and too prolonged to justify its completely negative result. The roll on the carpet is autobiographical and therefore only indirectly relevant to the rest of the play. Yet it is such witty, concentrated autobiography, illuminating and suggestive on so many planes of significance, that no one could wish it away. Having received the ultimatum from his Cabinet, Magnus retires to the apartment of his mistress, Orinthia, who, instead of comforting him, imperiously demands that he divorce his wife and marry her. "You are worse than blind," she complains, "you have low tastes. Heaven is offering you a rose; and you cling to a cabbage." [12] When the king replies that cabbages are more useful than roses, Orinthia makes a powerful attack on the ugliness and insignificance of all mere utility. Plain people labor at vulgar tasks simply in order that she may reign in her beauty:

> ORINTHIA. Am I not worth it? [*She sits, fascinating him*]. Look into my eyes and tell the truth. Am I worth it or not?
>
> MAGNUS. To me, who love beauty, yes. But you should hear the speeches Balbus makes about your pension. [13]

The symbolism is clear. Orinthia is romance, beauty, art, art for art's sake. The episode defines her place in the world, her place in Shaw's life. She herself declares:

[351]

There is more of you in me than of any other man within my reach. There is more of me in you than of any other woman within y o u r reach. We are meant for oneanother: it is written across the sky that you and I are queen and king.[14]

She dares him to resist her. He replies in words reminiscent of Lord Henry Wotton's epigram: "I never resist temptation, because I have found that things that are bad for me do not tempt me." [15] Much as he cares for beauty and art, Shaw is not tempted to make them dominant in his life. Society—and therefore socialism—comes first.

Of course, as I have already explained, Orinthia is also Mrs. Patrick Campbell, who in 1912 had suddenly flushed Shaw's prosaically busy existence with a swift sunset of romantic love. And if Orinthia is Mrs. Campbell, Queen Jemima is obviously in several characteristics Mrs. Shaw. In this light, Magnus's summing up is interesting:

Jemima has her limitations, as you have observed. And I have mine. Now if our limitations exactly corresponded I should never want to talk to anyone else; and neither would she. But as that never happens, we are like all other married couples: that is, there are subjects which can never be discussed between us because they are sore subjects. There are people we avoid mentioning to oneanother because one of us likes them and the other doesnt. Not only individuals, but whole sorts of people. For instance, your sort. My wife doesnt like your sort, doesnt understand it, mistrusts and dreads it. Not without reason; for women like you are dangerous to wives. But I dont dislike your sort; I understand it, being a little in that line myself. At all events I am not afraid of it, though the least allusion to it brings a cloud over my wife's face. So when I want to talk freely about it I come and talk to you. And I take it she talks to friends of hers about people of whom she never talks to me. She has men friends from whom she can get some things that she cannot get from me. If she didnt do so she would be limited by my limitations, which would end in her hating me. So I always do my best to make her men friends feel at home with us.[16]

Meanwhile, the most scientific and the least rational of centuries had fresh surprises and new trials in store for this resilient and miraculous old man.

CHAPTER THIRTY-NINE

Utopia in the East

In 1929 the world depression began with a metaphysical tragedy on the New York Stock Exchange. Following just before its nose the golden path of high profits, American capital had built up an industrial machine which, while providing adequately for the United States, had flooded Europe first with munitions to blow itself into decrepitude and then with materials to put itself back together again. Meanwhile the fabulous machine, growing like a genie larger and larger, poured consumers' goods upon the American market, but through combination, prices did not fall with the increase in supply; nor did wages rise, because workers competed with the machines they operated. For a while purchasing power was maintained by an unprecedented extension of installment buying. But bankers began to worry. Europe had paid for its swords and its plowshares with credit. Americans paid for their automobiles with credit or grew wonderfully rich on paper wealth in a wildly inflated Stock Exchange. Finally, having greatly curtailed European trade through a refusal of further loans, the bankers applied the pinprick which caused the pop heard round the world. They reduced brokers' loans—and stocks collapsed. Financiers found themselves the masters of ever so many idle factories and mountainous stock piles— and bankrupt on paper.

As innocently as Ibsen's Oswald, MacDonald and his new Labour Cabinet had inherited the sins of capitalism. Indeed, having lost many of its markets to the mechanized production of the United States, English economy had never quite recovered from the war. Unemployment was never below one million, and an adverse trade balance was compensated only by the "invisible imports" of interest on a four-billion-pound foreign investment. With a Victorian idealism characteristic of British socialists, MacDonald and his colleagues made Herculean efforts to maintain the gold standard and, incidentally, to prevent value shrinkage in the four billion invested abroad. But the high price of pounds further discouraged foreign trade, and the adverse balance became more acute. Then the sudden contraction of American credit paralyzed world economy. The number of England's unemployed passed two million. Her budget would not balance, and Snowden, the Chancellor of the Exchequer, spoke of grave financial peril. Foreign capital, taking fright, began to leave the Bank of England, which maintained its funds by loans from France and the United States. Finally in 1931, MacDonald, desperately determined on solvency, proposed to cut unemployment insurance. The great majority of his colleagues refused to approve. Thereupon, sacrificing party to currency and country, he placed himself at the head of a National government composed of a few Labourites and a great many Tories. By the most rigid economies the budget was balanced and the pound saved—for less than a month. Then England went off the gold standard. Apparently, the socialist leaders had split their party and sold their socialism for a capitalistic illusion.

For Europe, the great depression was a watershed of effects and causes between two great wars and between a declining liberalism and an advancing totalitarianism. For Shaw, it was to a somewhat less degree a watershed between English Fabianism and Russian Communism. Henceforth, he kept one eye on the Fabian future and the other on the Russian present. What he thought of the former is pretty clearly indicated by his 1931 Preface to the *Fabian Essays*, which is as gloomy and ominous as the 1908 Preface is gay and optimistic. One staggering blow after another had been dealt constitutionalism. Four years of socialistic government had not, essentially, brought socialism one inch nearer. Meanwhile, force was performing elsewhere all sorts of utilitarian miracles. After half a century of failure with speeches and votes, the Irish had gained their freedom in a few months with bayonets and knives. By the same kind of persuasion, Russia had got Communism, and Mussolini, having cleared away the "putrefying corpse" of Italian liberty, had electrified a moribund nation.

Shaw spoke his mind about MacDonald and his National government in "On the Rocks" (1933), one of the more vigorous and unified of his later plays. MacDonald, transformed into the aristocratic Liberal Sir Arthur Chavender, becomes a vain, attitudinizing phrasemaker at the head of a coalition of Tories, Liberals, and Labourites, who fumble helplessly with the problems of depression. On the verge of a breakdown, Sir Arthur consults a mystical woman doctor, who finds him suffering from an acute want of mental exercise. With a box of Marxist books, he packs off to her sanitarium in Wales, and having learned how to think, returns to attempt a Leninist coup with a view to curing the depression by force and a totalitarian economy. He is blocked at the

[354]

last moment by the Labourite socialists, who would die rather than give up the right to strike.

Such "trade-union capitalism" reminds one of *The Intelligent Woman's Guide,* which, in fact, contributed a number of ideas to "On the Rocks." This play marks Shaw's most extreme stand against democracy. One is not surprised, for in the period from Versailles to the depression, democracy had fallen from the height of its legend to the depths of ridicule, impotency, and fear, whereas dictatorship still had all its most spectacular crimes to commit. Accordingly, Shaw declares that what people want in time of great distress is not discussion but action. In short, they want orders to obey. A dictator who senses this need is more democratic than a prime minister who sentences all his measures to death by debate in the House of Commons. Moreover, only a dictator will be able to achieve a genuine socialist revolution in Great Britain. And yet at the end of the play, Chavender says to his wife, "I'm not the man for the job, darling. . . . And I shall hate the man who will carry it through for his cruelty and the desolation he will bring on us and our like." [1] Clearly, Shaw feels that force is necessary—but unpleasant.

"In Praise of Guy Fawkes," an essay which Shaw wrote at this time, recapitulates all his objections to democracy and suggests as a partial remedy that there should be two cabinets—one to administer and one to think. The author praises Mussolini for harnessing Italian water power, despairs of MacDonald, and obviously regards war as a certainty.

By this time his attitude toward Russia had undergone a complete change. In 1914, he had regarded her as the very symbol of a benighted nation, dominated by a cruel and Machiavellian despotism at the top and weighed down by oriental barbarism and ignorance at the bottom. In 1918, he was wary and noncommittal, but in 1921, when the Bolsheviks had replaced the Boches as the enemies of mankind, he sent Lenin an autographed copy of his latest book. Thereafter, except for a protest against Russian political executions, he became steadily more favorable, until by 1930 he defended the Russians—with some humorous exaggeration to be sure—as a miracle of spontaneous idealism led by middle-class intellectuals who emerged from the café, the study, and the classroom to astound capitalistic politicians with prodigies of practical statesmanship. World War I, despite the millions who died, was a benefit to humanity because it brought about the Russian Revolution.

In the late twenties, it had become fashionable to visit Russia. Labourites went to prove their piety, and Tories, to prove their open-mindedness. Most of them stayed only a few days and knew nothing of the country or the language, so that what they saw was chiefly the tint of their own political spectacles and the radiant images evoked by Russian propaganda. Nevertheless, a pilgrimage conferred honor and prestige even on the greatest—particularly among socialists and advanced thinkers, who might as well not have opened Karl Marx as not have set foot in Russia. Shaw had read Marx. Naturally, he visited Russia. Yet how seriously he took his visit, how much he saw, whether he tried to see anything at all, what he thought about what he saw, and what he meant by what he said have aroused nearly as much argument as the meaning of Andrew Undershaft's character or the historicity of "Saint Joan."

He could not have expected to learn much, for he stayed only nine days. It is also significant that he set the stage for himself very carefully, traveling with Lady Astor and other well-known Tories and arriving in time to celebrate his seventy-fifth birthday in Moscow. Russian officials had awaited him with trepidation, for the country was in the darkest throes of its first Five Year Plan, and many a skeleton was grinning awfully and unmistakably from its closet door. Trotskyites were still being liquidated. Corrupt officials were being shot by the dozens. Obscure people were disappearing every day for obscure reasons. The Army was decimating the peasants, who persistently refused to be collectivized. Food was rationed, and everybody was very tired and very hungry. Much of this Shaw must have known, not only from his own close attention to current events but from his association with the Webbs, who were probably by now at work on their exhaustive study of Soviet society. But there are two ways of regarding the official Russian severities. They may be reckoned as needless and unmitigated cruelties or as acts necessary to achieving the classless society. Communistic theory enjoins the sacrifice of the present to the future, and to the determined zealot, present suffering, even though unnecessary, can give reality to future promises as nothing else can. Shaw could sympathize with such faith. Moreover, the ruthless daring of Stalin may well have been electrifying after the pompous fumbling of MacDonald. Both blundered, of course, but it is more heroic to blunder in blood than to blunder in red tape and to aim for a goal than to aim simply for the spotlight.

Shaw arrived in immense high spirits, intent on playing G.B.S. against a Soviet background. He smiled his friendliest greeting to large crowds at the Moscow station, saw sights indefatigably, belittled Russian revolutionaries for being less red bloodedly destructive than the English Puritans, tested the acoustics of the great hall of the Soviets by throwing up his white beard and yodeling melodiously from the high tribunal, baited Lady Astor with Russian virtues, and allowed himself to be mothered and spoiled by her. Visiting a model prison for young thieves, he was asked to make a speech to the inmates. He delighted the boys and horrified their sinister guards, the O.G.P.U., by delivering himself as follows:

> When I was a child I used to steal too, but I stole so cleverly no one caught me. A thief is not the one who steals, but the one who gets caught. All of you must have been very poor thieves. Outside of the borders of Russia thousands of criminals are going about in freedom, having committed and still committing many different kinds of crimes. For the time being they are not caught, only because they commit their crimes very cleverly; but a time will come when they too will get caught.[2]

But ordinary citizens who had lived among the grim realities of the Five Year Plan were apparently not pleased by Shaw's behavior. Eugene Lyons, the shrewdest of the journalists who covered his visit, writes dourly:

> Deftly Shaw skimmed the surface, careful not to break through the lacquer of appearances; if Lady Astor asked too many questions he neatly slapped her wrist. He judged food conditions by the Metropole menu, collectivization by the model farm, the G.P.U. by the model colony at Bolshevo, socialism by the twittering of attendant sycophants. His performance was not amusing to the Russians, I happen to know. It was macabre. The lengthening obscenity of ignorant or indifferent tourists, disporting themselves cheerily on the aching body of Russia, seemed summed up in this cavorting old man, in his blanket endorsement of what he would not understand. He was so taken up with demonstrating how youthful and agile he was that he had no attention to spare for the revolution in practice.[3]

Shaw's speech at the old Noble's Club on the occasion of his seventy-fifth birthday Mr. Lyons terms "the apex of cynicism." In his eyes, the scene was as double-edged as the charity of Undershaft or the madness of Father Keegan. Shaw knew that food rations were short, that he faced a hungry audience; yet he dwelt mercilessly on the plenty of the Hotel Metropole:

> "When my friends learned that I was going to Russia," he said, "they loaded me with tinned food of all sorts. They thought Russia was starving. But I threw all their food out of the window in Poland before I reached the Soviet frontier." He laughed like a mischievous schoolboy. . . .

Shaw's listeners gasped. One felt the convulsive reaction in their bellies.[4]

The effect of disillusionment on wit is cynicism, and in a Jonathan Swift or a Bernard Shaw it can be extremely cruel. Perhaps he had to revenge England's comfortable despair on Russia's starving yet confident hope. Moreover, his instinctive reaction to any social environment was critical and iconoclastic. Attempting to smooth over a rather unsatisfactorily Shavian interview with Russian publishers, an official said, "Well, Mr. Shaw, anyway you are a friend of the Russian people." "No," he cried, "I am not the friend of any people as a whole. I reserve the right to criticize every people—including the Russians." [5]

What really moved Shaw was the tomb of Lenin. Immediately after his arrival in Moscow, he went to the immense mausoleum in Red Square where the embalmed body of the great man may be seen in a glassed sarcophagus. Shaw lingered for a long time. What he felt he expressed in a talking movie which he allowed to be made a few days later:

> I do not know whether there will ever be a man to whom so much significance will be given as the future will give to Lenin. If the experiment which Lenin started succeeds, it will be the opening of a new world era. If the experiment fails, then I shall have to take leave of you when I die with something of melancholy; but if the future is the future as Lenin saw it, then we may smile and look forward to the future without fear.[6]

Here, in his own time and his own faith, was a new hero for the passionate admirer of Caesar, Cromwell, and Napoleon.

Probably the extreme rational idealist tends always to oscillate between anarchism and despotism. In periods of antiquated legalism, he dreams of the popular mind freed from the unreason of law and prejudice to express its native rationalism in corporate action. In periods of license and chaos, he dreams of a master-mind imposing its individual logic despotically on the unreason of the masses. Shaw nourished both dreams, though with typical English caution he never quite gave himself up to either one. But dictatorship may have had another attraction. Perhaps, after all his bitter disappointments, he may have felt that mankind deserved the rationalist rigors of a despot, as Luther felt that they deserved the vengeance of an omnipotent God. But if the Marxist tradition attracted him for a protestant reason, it repelled him for a catholic. He never forgot that the Communist Party was a church.

At the conclusion of their stay in Moscow, Shaw's party had the honor of a two-hour-and-a-half interview with Stalin. Pearson reports the conversation at length, but it conveys little beyond the impression of a polite chat with a leviathan. Dana, in his article on Shaw's visit to Russia, says that Stalin was much interested in Winston Churchill and refused to accept Shaw's assurance that he was an overrated man.

Returning to England with his diploma of personal knowledge, Shaw characteristically announced to a London audience that the U.S.S.R. was really a union of Fabian republics. And apparently Sidney Webb agreed with him. The aged apostle of gradualism, having shaken the dust of two Labour Cabinets from his feet, had himself become impatient, and with a curiously English inconsistency, was in 1938 to admire dictatorship for carrying through an industrial democracy which he declared had always existed in Soviet Russia.

In singing the praises of Bolshevism, Shaw addressed himself with sure dramatic instinct less to England than to the United States, where the depression had struck first and seemed likely to linger longest. Without ever having troubled himself to visit that country, he was always ready to explain it. In fact, after his trip to Russia, he commonly began his American radio addresses with a very succinct explanation in the vocative. "Hello boobs!" he cried in clipped and cheerful English. Of course it was just G.B.S., and yet, between gasps and laughs, Americans wondered why he was so hard on them. Some of them remembered that he owed his political awakening to Henry George and his earliest dramatic success to New York and Chicago. What they did not remember is that gratitude is not an epigrammatic emotion, and praise, not exactly a scarcity in the American moral diet. Since "Captain Brassbound" and "Man and Superman," Shaw had made fun of Americans for their antiquated ideas and their oratorical manners. On the other hand, he had sometimes held up American virtues to British conscience. He admired the practical courage of American utopian experiments, including that of the Mormons; and in the twenties he dilated on the wisdom of Prohibition, which he usually represented as an unqualified success. But as Russia became in his mind the symbol of socialistic idealism, so America became the symbol of middle-class capitalism at its most colossally complacent. Depression had transformed that complacency into a grotesque and appalling absurdity. As time went on, Communism endowed Russia with every virtue, and capitalism blackened America with every vice.

In two interviews reported by *The New York Times*, he elaborates on this dichotomy with his usual skill in special pleading.[7] The profit motive is not a "realistic" incentive. Capitalism says, "Without the incentive of becoming parasites men will not produce. . . . Parasitism is therefore one of the inevitable costs of production." But Russian experience proves that parasites are not necessary. There is "no use in protesting all this cannot be done because human nature is greedy and selfish.

It is being done. It works." Furthermore, he declares, it works without any party politics and votes-for-everybody nonsense. Whereas America ridicules and vilifies her natural leaders, Russia, having allowed nature to select them, gives them every educational and political advantage.

But of course he argues that depression is the *reductio ad absurdum* of the capitalistic system, and here he does not scruple to do great violence to the realities of the situation. At a time when famine still existed in Russia and agriculture was still deep in the chaos of hasty and premature collectivization, he boasts of a trebling of Russian harvests and contrasts the want and unemployment which had brought England and the United States to the brink of revolution. "Our statesmen on both sides," he declares, "can do nothing but break the heads of starving men or buy them off with doles and appeals to charity." Russia has learned how to get rid of legal and illegal robbery. In America "they kill you for committing murder and praise you for making money. In Russia they have abolished capital punishment for murder" but shoot you for making money.

CHAPTER FORTY

Disaster in the West

The last arguments of the humanitarian idealist are the sword and the pistol; and for these arguments, after nearly half a century of fruitless talk, Shaw evinced an increasing and sanguinary fondness. In fact, he always had the puritan's appetite for violence, more or less sublimated. His literary style bristles with metaphoric illustrations from the wheel, the rack, the boot, and the executioner's scaffold. It is not altogether surprising, therefore, that he should see logic and wisdom in the Russian practice of liquidation. The Preface (1935) to "The Simpleton of the Unexpected Isles" demands that every day should be a judgment day and that the citizen who takes more from the community than he contributes should be summarily shot by some kindly Tcheka devoted to efficiency.

Perhaps the ablest of his later political tracts, the Preface (1933) to "On the Rocks" is a neat and skillful defense of the mass executions carried out by the O.G.P.U. With an adroitness now become instinctive, Shaw takes the strongest moral position possible. He defines property as a legal power over the persons of others. In early nineteenth-century England, private property amounted to a private right to kill, which petty capitalists exercised with the utmost ruthlessness out of mere greed and money lust. How much better that such a right be exercised by a great Communistic state in its own highest interests! I need hardly say, whatever the particulars of either case, that the practice of beating dead criminals in order to excuse live ones is extremely dubious. Shaw winds up his defense of benevolent execution by turning the tables and attacking law itself because it means "limited liability in morals." Almost any crime can be committed within the law. And law is noxious not simply because it often protects rascals in their rascality but because it protects fools in their folly and idlers in their idleness. Apparently Shaw is afraid of everything but a government firing squad.

As a matter of fact, he is attempting to translate his intellectual pragmatism into politics. He wishes to construct a society which will combine great fluidity in fundamental principles with great efficiency in action. Religion, not law, must provide cohesive force, because religion can be more fluid and at the same time achieve a closer identification of letter and spirit. To be sure, the religion must be one which, like his own creative evolution, can remain credible and effective by keeping up to date with scientific and social discovery. Even so, alterations can be wisely made only if authority listens tolerantly to criticism. Reviewing the persecution of Socrates, Jesus, Galileo, and other great teachers, Shaw decides that none of them attempted a real defense of his case. None of them maintained that, though not free to *act* against the government, he should always be free to *criticize* it. On the other hand, the government should also be free to criticize the individual—and without any restraint on action—with a view either to curing his moral ailments or to removing him if those ailments prove incurable. Thus, unlimited power is to be corrected by unlimited thought and discussion. Probably Shaw has in mind the Russian Communist Party under Lenin.

On the whole, one is inclined to think that the government would have the better of the argument. In fact, many years before, Shaw had himself said that nothing ideal can exist long in the presence of absolute power. But we should not expect formal consistency from such a writer. As Mr. Barzun points out, his thinking, like Rousseau's, maintains both freedom and authority, anarchism and collectivism, in a state of dialectical tension.[1] "Maxims for Revolutionists" is his *Discours sur l'Inégalité*, as the Preface to "On the Rocks" is his *Contrat Social*. But how does he expect to achieve a synthesis? Clearly, through eugenics, education, thought, and the steady exertion of the creative will, which constitutes at least a more hopeful resolution of political and economic antitheses than Marx's.

Incidentally, the Preface to "On the Rocks" effectively undermines the interviews in which Shaw had insisted on the prosperity of Russia. Having whitewashed the secret police, he settles down to a shrewd and businesslike history of Soviet economic policy from the Revolution to the latter days of the Five Year Plan. Here he shows himself fully aware that there had been widespread hunger, economic confusion, and agrarian war.

In the Preface for "Too True to Be Good," also published in 1933, Shaw draws an elaborate parallel between the Russian state and the Catholic Church. The Communist Party is like the Roman clergy. It is not chosen by the hackneyed methods of Western democracy but is self-elected, bound by oath, tested by conduct, and supervised from above. Shaw finds this system—when devoted to the humanitarian ends of socialism—the most practicable that has been evolved in an imperfect world. He had previously called for an improvement of democratic leadership through panels of candidates qualified by competitive examination. In the meantime, he gave his approval to Karl Marx's visible Church; yet he never ceased to criticize Marx, nor did he ever join the Communist Party.

In December, 1932, Shaw had set off on a trip around the world, packing up Russia and a whole workshop of projects in his suitcase. He was naturally anything but a globe-trotter. His universe was twentieth-century London, as Voltaire's was eighteenth-century Paris. He carried around with him a head too full of strictly mundane and contemporary business to be very deeply interested in the ruins of antiquity or the shrines of the East. But Mrs. Shaw was nomadic, and her husband, being fond of driving automobiles and writing on steamers, tamely followed her. They stopped first at Cape Town, where he informed South Africans they still lived in the seventeenth century, made a speech on Russia and contributed handsomely to the local Fabian Society. Afterward, they took an automobile trip inland, but because, after a masterly negotiation of precipitous mountains, Shaw mistook the accelerator for the brakes and mesmerically persisted in his error, they had an accident, in which Charlotte was badly battered. While she was convalescing through a hot African winter, he wrote *The Adventures of the Black Girl in Her Search for God*, in which he relates, in the form of a Voltairian *conte*, the history of God from Noah and Moses to Shaw and Bergson. Of course, like King Charles's head, Russia creeps into the Appendix.

After Charlotte's illness, the Shaws returned to England, but in the following year set out afresh on their world tour, spending much time in India and the Middle East. Undoubtedly the voyage stimulated his interest in religion. Though he would not perhaps have gone to the Near or Far East just to see temples and monuments, he was quite willing to look at them and think about them when he got there. From the Indian Ocean he wrote a remarkable letter—full of penetrating secularities in the spirit of Voltaire and Bentham—which he addressed to a Methodist minister, the Reverend Ensor Walters, an old friend and ex-fellow Vestryman. Shaw finds that people nearly always make God a magician, often a fiend, and very seldom an ennobled and bodiless Presence. Everywhere he finds protestants and catholics, but particularly catholics, whom he regards as essentially idol-worshipers. Because of their tolerance and flexibility, the Hindus are particularly interesting catholics:

> The main difference between the opposition of Islam to Hinduism and the opposition between Protestant and Catholic is that the Catholic persecutes as fiercely as the Protestant when he has the

power; but Hinduism cannot persecute, because all the Gods—and what goes deeper, the no Gods—are to be found in its Temples. There is actually a great Hindu sect, the Jains, with Temples of amazing magnificence, which excludes God, not on materialist atheist considerations, but as unspeakable and unknowable, transcending all human comprehension. So far, it is all simple enough for anyone with religious sense. When you are face to face with the Temples and the worshippers, you find that before Mahomet and the founder of the Jains were cold in their graves, the institutions and rituals they founded began to revert to the more popular types, and all the Gods and no Gods became hopelessly mixed up, exactly as the Apostles backslid when Jesus was killed. In the Jain Temple you find shrines and images, and baths where you must wash all over before you may enter the shrine and adore the image. If you can find an intelligent Priest who is a real Jain theologian, you say "How's this? A God in the Jain Temple!" He explains to you that the image is not a God but a portrait of one of their great Saints; and that the man just out of the bath prostrating himself is not worshipping but expressing his respect for the memory of the late eminent Ensoramji Waltershagpat. But it is like Dean Inge trying to explain away St Paul. It is perfectly plain that the image is a super refined Buddha, and that Jainism and Buddhism have got hopelessly mixed. Jain Buddha is attended by sculptured elephants. You ask what they mean, and are told that they are purely ornamental works of art. Then your eye lights on an image of Ganesh, the Hindu God with the head and trunk of an elephant. On the point of exclaiming '*Que diable fait-il dans cette galère?*' you remember that you must not put your courteous host in a corner, and politely hold your tongue, but think furiously.[2]

Since on his way home he could not conveniently avoid the Western Hemisphere, Shaw landed in 1933 at San Francisco for his first visit to the United States. Presently a private airplane came to whisk him away to the palaces of William Randolph Hearst, but of the marvels he saw there and of that magnificent American Tiberius himself, the dramatist has published no literary record. Eventually he reached New York, and there, speaking in the Opera House, he delivered his most lengthy comments on American civilization.[3] His criticism is sensible and reasonably just but not particularly brilliant nor well informed.

In Shaw's mind America represents a museum of sociological antiquities, and Shaw is not an enthusiastic antiquarian. He characterizes the Constitution as a "permanent charter of anarchism," which carefully guards Americans from an official dictator and imposes on them hundreds of unofficial dictators in their ward bosses, employers, and financiers, who convert too much freedom into many petty tyrannies. In fact, the real ruler of modern capitalistic society is the financier, who is the very opposite of the statesman, because he thinks in terms of money rather than of men. He was mainly responsible for the depression, and unless he comes to see that the greatness of his country does not depend on its foreign investments, he will involve it in hazardous imperialistic rivalries, and if no other catastrophe occurs, turn it finally into a kind of gigantic night club of idle rich living on tribute which may at any time be repudiated. Ignoring the facts, Shaw simply assigns to the United States the future of economic parasitism which he had long foreseen for Great Britain.

He demolishes American national character without a trace of malice. Beginning as a secondhand European, the American became first rhetorical and then simply noisy. Yet, despite his ridiculous sentimentality and eighteenth-century mental furniture, he has a capacity for political action, as his Mormon experiment amply proves. In any case, having always liked noisy people and long practiced self-advertisement, Shaw confesses that he is fond of Americans, and the facts of his life bear out the statement handsomely.

Home once more, Shaw settled down to observing, with the detachment of age and long disillusionment, the rise of Hitler and the genesis of World War II. In the "Preface on Bosses" (1935), prefixed to "The Millionairess," he writes in twenty-odd pages an epitaph for the nineteenth century, an explanation of the twentieth, and a policy for the twenty-first. In the nineteenth, says Shaw, citizens had the pleasant delusion that more votes would solve any political problem, and rulers, the useful delusion that public opinion would punish any act of unprincipled ambition. But more votes simply betrayed the magnitude of public ignorance and stupidity, with which the public itself became so heartily disgusted that when Mussolini trod on the "putrefying corpse" of Liberty, the whole Italian people rejoiced. Hitler (whom Shaw correctly guesses to have been influenced by Houston Chamberlain) delighted the German people no less, but in persecuting Albert Einstein, he warned the world of the awful peril which lies in the unlimited power of a born political boss over an unthinking populace. Apparently, the much greater sufferings of many million other Jews seem less significant to Shaw. In any case, dictators can be restrained only by a citizenry as politically wise as themselves, though their political wisdom, one suspects, must be of a different sort from Hitler's. In this Preface, more clearly than in his other writings, Shaw recognizes the importance of nationalism in contemporary history. He also recognizes that socialism without high political honesty would be the form of socialistic justice without the substance.

In *Everybody's Political What's What?* (1944), Shaw wins a final victory over pessimism. His renewed confidence does not spring from new facts or new ideas. Rather, it seems to be a reassertion of basic attitude toward problems of which he was now, after a lifetime struggle, taking final leave. Ironically, the facts themselves were never so black. The most destructive war in history had been raging for nearly five years, strewing desolation literally around the globe and leaving civilization so battered and shellshocked that hardly even the false dawn of another Versailles rose to hearten the idealist. Nevertheless, Shaw puts the issue as squarely—and evades it as skillfully—as ever. "Is human nature incurably depraved?" he asks, and answers at once, "No." History is the record not of a confirmed criminal but of a mental patient who can be restored to sanity. Man's disease is a persistent time lag of ideas behind events. Once he attempted to guide early nineteenth-century economy according to the ideas of William the Conqueror. Now he attempts to guide twentieth-century economy according to the ideas of Adam Smith. That this unhappy retardation has never been cured in the past does not daunt Shaw.

Unfortunately, he suffers a little from it himself, particularly in his attitude toward Fascism and World War II. He interprets twentieth-century Fascism in terms of nineteenth-century Marxism. It is simply state capitalism, and the war itself mainly a struggle between state capitalism and state socialism, in which England and America rather illogically range themselves with the latter. Shaw's eighteenth-century contempt for nationalism purblinds him to much in the twentieth century. One of the most unreasonable of all ages is not to be unlocked with the skeleton key of reason.

Though his ideas are old, Shaw urges them with new discretion and common sense. More than ever before, he sees both sides of a question. Consequently, though he does not change his position, he does sometimes shift his weight. The war has shocked him into a graver and more critical attitude toward dictatorship. He finds Hitler's government swift and efficient in action and wonderfully effective in marshaling popular enthusiasm behind official policy, but its complete absolutism leads to insanity and at the same time renders insanity appallingly efficacious. Ideal government must lie somewhere between Nazi dictatorship, which sets no limit whatever on power, and British constitutional democracy, which sets so many limits that nothing is ever accomplished except in times of direst crisis. The golden mean which Shaw has in view turns out of course to be Russian Communism. But now there is a change of emphasis. He continues to insist—and here one sees how little of a gradualist and how much of a Hegelian dialectician he is—that in any transition to socialism, there must be less democracy at first in order that there may be more later on. Yet in general he dwells not, as in the middle thirties, on the grim actualities of the Russian dictatorship and the secret police but on the complex theoretical democracy of the Russian paper constitution, which in 1936 the Webbs had explained so elaborately. In the English system, Mr. Everyman casts a blanket vote for one of two parties, neither of which may correspond very closely to any of his own ideas. In the Russian system, he may express himself directly in local assemblies, and he may also cast as many as a dozen votes, which—because they correspond to his various affiliations, political, economic, and social—are likely to be a fairly precise indication of opinion.

But Russian democracy is not perfect. It is excellent in giving strong temporary power to the executive and in removing the systematic obstruction of an opposition party, but apparently it could be more scientific in its choice of leaders. In fact, throughout this discussion Shaw emphasizes the problem of leadership rather than that of justice. Communities must learn more fully to marshal their latent mental resources. Political genius always exists. It needs only to be made available by careful intelligence testing and by abundant practical opportunity. Everybody must enjoy sufficient equality of income to fraternize, intermarry, and above all, to acquire all the education that his abilities warrant. Every candidate must qualify for panels by competitive examination.

These proposals are of course not new. What is new is the considered moderation with which they are stated. Shaw does not insist on strict equality of income. He recognizes that though the potentialities of mechanized industry are great indeed, they are not unlimited, and that if a handsome provision cannot be made for all, at least professional men must have the means of living an intellectual life.

This question is of course bound up with that of individual liberty, to which again he gives unusually full and careful treatment. He does not, as in *The Intelligent Woman's Guide*, tend to stop with the remark that tolerance will grow naturally with the equalization of leisure and wealth. The question is obviously much more complicated. As usual, his attitude is pragmatic. There are no inalienable liberties, no perennial moral laws. Yet every political system assumes a moral system and must educate and—in greater or less degree—persecute according to that moral system. The wrong kind of nonconformity can be prevented, particularly in early life, by teaching children salutary fables, of which with sufficient maturity they may be disillusioned. But one would hardly look for genuine freedom in a state where law is so much minimized to prevent formalism, and force so much concentrated to guarantee efficiency. As in the Preface to "On the Rocks," Shaw is willing to do almost everything for liberty but give it a solid legal basis. He would safeguard it partly by strengthening instruments of mercy like the jury and partly by keeping ethical and scientific questions open to discussion, particularly in the several parliaments which his multiform ideal requires. He sees that large numbers of people will not be free until they have something to be free about, until their liberty has a positive content. This content must be conveyed by art, which alone can strike the imagination and convert ideas into objectives.

As a criticism of democracy, *Everybody's Political What's What?* is of course in considerable degree invalidated by its biased and ambiguous picture of Russian Communism, which Shaw idealizes at least partly to put England and America on their mettle. It is also not free from the weaknesses of age: Shaw sometimes rambles, digresses, and repeats himself, but he is always cogent and vivid. He usually keeps his eye on the facts. If in some respects he has become too old and Victorian for the contemporary reader, in others he remains still too youthful and futuristic. Moreover, it is no little thing to exhibit fresh signs of maturity at eighty-eight and to lead a vigorous intellectual life at an age when most men lose the appetite for life itself.

To many, Shaw's later political record may seem to consist chiefly in a bitter and impatient theoretical marching up and down before the daily facts of history. Indeed, one of the chief defects of his political thinking is that he profits too much from experience. He takes so much to heart the latest lesson that he forgets all the earlier ones and so is constantly revising his fundamental principles to fit the sensation of the hour. War is efficient and inefficient; journalism, a boon and a menace within the space of a decade or two. The general development of his international opinions is curiously circular. Versailles awakened his cynicism and deepened his early suspicions of democracy. Mussolini strengthened his admiration of the strong man. The Russian Revolution made him an almost unqualified advocate of Communist dictatorship. World War II was ideologically too ambiguous an event to produce any sharp reversal of opinion, yet the wild, criminal fiasco of Fascism aroused him to such renewed distrust of force and despotism as to revive his interest in democracy and somewhat dampen his enthusiasm for Russia, though she emerged triumphant from the conflict. And so fifty years of political experience and political thinking have brought him back almost to his starting point. But the value of his exploration must not be judged by its goal, nor the worth of his political writings, by any resultant accumulation of a program or system. Their inner logic is historical and their real meaning to be found in a long satirical dialectic between political events and a somewhat refractory yet deeply serious critical intelligence. Shaw is in fact a weather vane, sensitive to every breeze that blows through the morning headlines, but the method of his turning is complex and obstinately individual.

CHAPTER FORTY-ONE

The Later Plays

Coming from an unknown dramatist the later plays might seem significant and interesting, but coming from Shaw they indicate chiefly that he has no more to say and is saying it with less and less brilliance and power. The artist is slowly declining. The Shavian virtues begin to disappear, and the Shavian vices, to accentuate themselves. The old unity and the old complexity disintegrate. Frequently scenes, and sometimes whole plays, become mere conversations without theme, climax, or events. Old ideas, old characters, and the fragments of old situations recur again and again, sometimes set in an elaborate symbolism which throws light on earlier plays and sometimes drifting in a chaos of perky chat that doesn't throw light on anything.

Ostensibly, "Too True to Be Good" demonstrates the cruelty of capitalism to the rich. In the company of a clerical burglar and his Sweetie, the heroine escapes from wealth, snobbery, artificially induced illness, and a madly indulgent mother, having yielded to a parable of Fabian dialectic in which the preacher explains that by peacefully sharing her riches (a necklace), the three can realize full value, whereas by quarreling, the owner will get nothing and the robbers at best only a thieves'-market valuation. Once freed from the stifling hothouse in which she has languished, the Patient becomes a majestic, naked-minded Amazon, who exhausts the pleasures of nature, discovers that without work she is no more than an inefficient fertilizer factory, converting "good food into bad manure," and resolves to go off to Russia and form a sisterhood "to clean up this filthy world and keep it clean." [1]

Presented in summary, "Too True" sounds like a fairly well-knit play. Actually it is a curiously desultory conversation about the universe, particularly the twentieth-century universe. The characters are too withdrawn in their philosophical subjectivity to take any great interest in the action, which suffers accordingly. There are some good speeches, some wit, bits of comedy, but little drama and no carefully built-up scenes. The tragedy of the magnified microbe is appalling bathos which only a very great man in a very uninspired moment would dare to set down on paper.

"Too True" is as currently omnitopical as the Sunday supplement. The Nazis, the League, Einstein, Mussolini, all come in for a comment. The League is twitted for its impotency, and the Nazis are rebuked, with a double-edged irony, for baiting the Jews. Commenting on the Old Testament, the Sergeant exclaims:

> All this . . . thinking you can do what you like to other people because youre the chosen people of God. . . . No: damn it, we're civilized men; and though it may have gone down with those old Jews it isn't religion.[2]

There is also the only half-successful comedy of the disillusioned atheist, who, having discovered Einstein and nuclear physics, sees his solid, brainless, deterministic mechanism of a universe dissolve into the awful uncertainties of the second law of thermodynamics. The original for this character is said to be Dean Inge, whose intellect Shaw admired and whose education he deplored. Apparently he extracted the Cambridge University Inge for the part:

> It is the oddest experience [he writes in a review of Inge's _Outspoken Essays II_] to find the real Inge . . . smashing this heathenish nonsense with one contemptuous punch of his pen, and then suddenly relapsing into the Cambridge classroom and assuring us that there is nothing for us to do but to wait as best we can until our extinction is completed by the cooling of the sun.[3]

But the chief topics of this cosmic conversation are war and the younger generation. Europe is again drifting toward war; Berlin, London, Paris, and Rome will be destroyed from the air, for modern war is a slaughter of innocents in which everybody is as guilty of murder as if he had committed it in civil life. Private Meek is interesting as an intended portrait of T. E. Lawrence, but he resembles the fabulous author of _Revolt in the Desert_ only superficially. Taking a closer look, one perceives that Meek is really none other than Bluntschli, as alert and efficient as ever though somewhat less witty. And Colonel Tallboys is surprisingly like Major Saranoff, sunk into a routine officer with thirty years of service, military and marital. More than ever, Shaw is optimistic about women—even about Sweetie, though she has no conscience and is dominated entirely by her "lower centers." At least her frankness challenges our domestic institutions. At least, like Mrs. George, she knows the difference between curiosity and love, and represents the reality of sex, which, as the Sergeant explains, is "one of the facts that religion has to make room for."[4] The Patient, on the other

[371]

hand, is dominated by her higher centers and like Lesbia, the Bishop's sister-in-law, regards sex mainly as a complication. She is of course the closest approximation to Shaw's own point of view.

Aubrey Bagot is to be understood in terms of his double profession. He is a thief because he is an idle consumer. He is a preacher because, like the younger generation in literature, he combines a facility for words with no capacity for faith or action. He also represents youth, or perhaps middle age, demoralized by war. Sometimes, however, he becomes all at once fantastically old, and like Lord Summerhays in "Misalliance," shrinks with elderly exhaustion and Victorian sensitivity before the crude energy, the unveiled minds, and the "shouted" indecencies of the young. Aubrey is by no means, as several critics have remarked, Shaw's last desperate view of Shaw, but he is inevitably an exaggeration of that part of Shaw which stood as spiritual forefather to the twenties. Seldom has an author had the opportunity, at such long range, to criticize a phase of his own tradition.

But now the master's hand was failing fast. What he does feebly and chaotically in "Too True," he had already done powerfully and dramatically in "Misalliance." Sweetie, the Patient, and Aubrey are, with variations, the pale loquacious ghosts of Hypatia, Lina, and Bentley Summerhays.

"Village Wooing" (1933), though very slight, reveals that its aged author has not lost his gift for sprightly and eloquent dialogue. A forthright, twentieth-century Ann Whitefield of village life, having squandered her prize money on an ocean cruise, infuriates with her advances a rather desiccated intellectual whom she meets on shipboard. He is afterward drawn as by a magnet to her native village, becomes the proprietor of the shop where she works, and after a feeble resistance, surrenders to matrimony and a useful life. The point of the play is twofold: it illustrates the Shaw-Schopenhauerian doctrine that two people of very different character and background can be united by the unconscious wisdom of sex attraction, and it expounds the very romantic doctrine that copulation affords not so much a gratification of the senses as a mystical insight into the poetic beauties of the universe.

"The Simpleton of the Unexpected Isles" (1934) shoots off some very heavy artillery at some very old targets. The lunacy of patriotism, the narrowness of conventional morals, the spirituality and cleanliness of vegetarianism are illustrated by a bewildering and sanguinary combination of suicide, multiple marriage, threatened civil war, and a full-dress last judgment, complete with thunder, trumpet blast, and an angel with a flaming sword. The play is violent, chaotic, and feebly spendthrift of good artistic ideas. In the Prologue a young man blows his brains out to get his name in the papers, thereby demonstrating at once the modern thirst for notoriety and the perennial folly of rejecting life. His antithesis, a vigorous young woman not unlike the heroine of "Village Wooing," masterfully gets her way and preaches the doctrine of "letting life come to you," which proves, however, to be only the subjunctive of the suicide's negation. Her activity, like that of most modern vulgarians, is supine, directionless, and accidental.

Pra and Prola, the native priest and priestess, represent the true Shavian elect. Entering a sexual alliance with two English couples, they determine to produce a eugenic race combining the virtues of the East and West. The results, full of vague mockery both of the author and of his adopted country, are four lively phantasms who symbolize Love, Pride, Heroism, and Empire, "the artistic, romantic, and military ideals of our cultured suburbs." [5] Significantly, the only suitable mate who can be found for the girls is the impotent Simpleton, "a man fed on air from his childhood." [6] On the Day of Judgment they not only cease to exist, but it becomes apparent that they never did exist.

Shaw's last judgment is a fine cosmic conception. British politics encounter a divine event and react with speeches, bills of Parliament, proposals of compromises, and a mounting patriotic enmity against heaven. Unfortunately, the details are not particularly amusing, and the angel is in no way worthy of the devil whom he had created long ago for "The Dialogue in Hell." In fact, Shaw rolls his thunders, summons his angels, and puts a stop to time for rather slight cause, artistic or practical. His divine justice consists pretty much in getting out his little list, and it is no surprise to find that most of the medical profession disappears in short order.

The play concludes with an interesting conversation between Pra and Prola, who on one plane of significance turn out to be a version of Mr. and Mrs. Shaw.

> PROLA. Pra: I always knew from the very beginning that you were an extraordinarily clever fool.
>
> PRA. Good. That is exactly what I am.
>
> PROLA. But I knew also that nobody but a fool would be frivolous enough to join me in doing all the mad things I wanted to do. And no ordinary fool would have been subtle enough to understand me, nor clever enough to keep off the rocks of social ruin. Ive grown fond enough of you for all practical purposes. [7]

"The Six of Calais" (1934), a brief one-acter, has no particular importance except that it exhibits, undiminished, Shaw's powers of developing a comic situation, so that one is tempted to think that if his later plays are less comic than his earlier, it is because he chose to make them so. In subject matter, "The Six" is a Shavian epigram on history. The sex struggle and the class struggle are everlasting. Woman dominated over man, snobbery dominated over good manners, in the fourteenth as in the nineteenth century.

"The Millionairess" (1936) is also brilliantly comic in dialogue and situation. Essentially, it is *Cashel Byron's Profession* reconstructed to prove a new moral. Cashel is transformed into an amiable nonentity, and the insufferable Lydia, into Beatrice Webb, who becomes a comic heroine worthy of Shaw's finest achievements. Beatrice-Epifania is one of nature's bosses, an acquisitive Woman of Destiny born to own and rule. Her story is a fairy tale translated into modern finance. A millionaire father has laid down the condition that she can be won only by the man who turns one hundred fifty pounds into fifty thousand. The first act of the play demonstrates the fallacy of this arrangement. A stroke of luck awards her to a brainless boxer who appeals only to her con-cupiscence and can hold his own with her only in physical combat. Separated from this husband, she falls in love with an Egyptian doctor, whose mother had required that his bride prove *herself* by earning her living for six months. Beginning like Beatrice Webb among the sweaters, Epifania makes a fortune in six months. Now the doctor tries to escape, but as a votive of the Life Force, he falls in love with her wonderful pulse beat. Epifania wisely overlooks his failure to pass her father's test. The chief weakness of the play is that the Egyptian doctor is worthy neither of Epifania nor of the prominence he must enjoy in the closing act. He is like one of Disraeli's Jews, whose distinction consists chiefly in being mysteriously and inscrutably Jewish.

"Geneva" (1939) is one of Shaw's weakest plays. It is nebulously in-coherent, interminably talky, and wildly improbable. A German Jew, working through the International Committee on Intellectual Coopera-tion, complains of Nazi persecution to the World Court at The Hague. Incidentally, his case, coupled with two others, provokes a world eco-nomic war and the dissolution of the British Empire, but these events seem quite unimportant to the rulers they concern and so disappear from view. The summons of the Court is answered by the three dictators—Battler, Bombardone, and Flanco—and the English and Russian Foreign Ministers attend as observers; whereupon everybody talks about every-thing but the business in hand, until a scientific last judgment is an-nounced in the form of a stellar catastrophe and a new Ice Age.

E. Strauss finds in "Geneva" a satire of Fascist dictators and an approximation of average English public opinion. Shaw is certainly sympathetic to the Newcomer, who represents the typical English small tradesman, but he puts some of his most eloquent abuse of democracy into the mouth of Signor Bombardone, the Italian dictator, whom apparently he much prefers to the Nazi Battler. Characteristically, the real victim of his satire is Sir Orpheus Midlander, the English Foreign Minister, who is a Sir Edward Grey straight out of "Common Sense about the War."

"In Good King Charles's Golden Days" (1939), Shaw places King Magnus in the past instead of the future. Charles II is less hopeful of improving the British Constitution than is Magnus. He has less evolutionary appetite and is more content simply to keep his head on his shoulders. In fact, he is a compromise between Shaw and history—or rather, perhaps, an adaptation of history to Shaw's later pessimism. Posthumously chaste and generously hostile to cruelty and bloodshed, he maintains the blessings of sensible government and free discussion in a world torn by political greed and religious intolerance.

"King Charles" is not so clearly pointed toward the present as most of Shaw's historical plays. The parallel between religious fanaticism in the seventeenth century and nationalistic fanaticism in the twentieth is not insisted on. In general terms, the author emphasizes the blindness of hatred, the folly of violence, and the wisdom of combining a strong authority with the calm spirit of national tolerance. Having gathered under Isaac Newton's roof King Charles, The Duke of York, Newton himself, the artist Godfrey Kneller, the Quaker George Fox, and all the King's more distinguished mistresses, Shaw illustrates how much or how little each one can learn from discussion. As a brainless zealot, the Duke is incapable of learning anything. As the Shavian spokesman, Charles has nothing to learn. As a great artist, Kneller knows all he needs to know by aesthetic intuition. Fox receives from Charles the Shavian suggestion that theaters as well as churches may have their congregations—and is much unsettled. Newton receives from Kneller the Einsteinian suggestion that the universe may be curved because the curved line is the most beautiful—and is also much unsettled. The play contains a great deal of talk and very little action. Beyond the meeting itself, no history is made. In fact, the discussion seems hardly to justify the meeting, even when Einstein and twentieth-century *post facto* historical omniscience have been called into requisition. "King Charles" is a simpler "Apple Cart," in which less vivid characters express fewer ideas with less wit and brilliance.

After the war Shaw wrote "Buoyant Billions: A Comedy of No Manners by a Fellow of the Royal Society of Literature," which was privately printed in 1947 and acted at Malvern in 1949. It is the story of a ferocious young Marxist who marries an heiress and subsides into a nonviolent vegetarian. "I tell you, if people only knew the history of their own times they would die of horror at their own wickedness." [8] This speech is assigned to the young hero, but the real speaker is the aged Shaw, who had lived to see the world he helped to create become at least more spectacularly wicked than that he helped to destroy. In one sense, his words are the scandalized comment of the nineteenth century on the twentieth.

The Preface is a significant expression, from a remarkably doctrinaire and self-conscious writer, of the naïveté and purity of his art. "When I write a play," he reiterates, "I do not foresee nor intend a page of it from one end to the other." And then he relates that when he was an "elderly man," his mother amused herself with a ouija board and planchette. The results were her "wishful writings," "her story-telling inventions, as much as the Waverley novels were Scott's. . . . Why was I doing essentially the same thing as a playwright? I do not know." He mentions "moments of inexplicable happiness." "To me they have come not oftener than once every fifteen years or so." [9] Apparently, Shaw would remind us that he is not only a socialist but an artist. This lesson the world will learn better as times goes on.

"Buoyant Billions" is, to date, Shaw's last play. It was then sixty-two years since he had begun "Widowers' Houses" in 1885.

CHAPTER FORTY-TWO

Conclusion

With increasing years Goethe became Olympian and talked common sense; Wordsworth wrote pious sonnets and looked patriarchal; Disraeli was sphinxlike and occasionally witty at dinner parties. Toryism, moderation, and silence are the virtues of old age. Of course Shaw possessed none of them. White hairs and universal reverence found him more revolutionary than ever, and hardly less Shavian. He did not grow old gracefully. He was simply a young man with a long white beard. Moreover, until well into his eighties, he talked, walked, worked, swam, gardened, and chopped wood like a man half his age. At seventy-one he fished the youthful Lawrence Langner out of the icy waters of the Lago Maggiore. At seventy-five he walked journalists to a standstill in the streets and museums of Moscow and then infuriated them with jaunty and unseemly remarks in the evening. At seventy-six he braved the rigors of a strenuous African tour, and at seventy-seven, at the Opera House in New York, he held a huge crowd spellbound for ninety minutes. Nor were these prodigies softened by any considerable accession of personal dignity. In fact, abandoning some of the Victorian propriety which had somehow graced even his most staggering offenses, he picked up not a little twentieth-century frankness and profanity. Naturally, many people have felt that his old age sat very shockingly upon him.

Throughout this period he continued to live several lives at once. Though he had long since given up the more strenuous forms of political activity, he was still regular and vocal at meetings and did a vast amount of committee work. In fact, just to go on being Bernard Shaw was sufficiently arduous. He had to be a genial, helpful, visible deity to the Malvern Festival. He had to keep a close eye on world politics and the Fabian Society. He frequently had to admonish the British Empire. He had to counteract the ill effects of British education and to explode the errors of contemporary science. He also gave more time to special projects.

An important interest of his later years was the Royal Academy of

Dramatic Artists, on the Council of which he had replaced Sir William Gilbert in 1911. Shaw found the R.A.D.A. an unimportant school, housed in what he called "the Gower Street lodgings," and left it a national institution comparable in prestige with the Royal Academies of Art and Music. Most of this development was due to the steady efforts of Sir Kenneth Barnes and other executives, yet in the interval of his incumbency, Shaw demonstrated that the decline of great literary, oratorical, and business gifts still left room for a colorful and farsighted educator.

His first action was to point out that though the student body was four-fifths women, the Council consisted entirely of men. Why should there not be at least one woman member? Shaw returned to the attack time after time, until his colleagues, apparently fearing an embattled Shaw more than a problematical female, appointed Irene Vanbrugh on the death of Edward Terry. Again, recurring to his early convictions that the theater was too little of a school and acting too little of a profession, he urged that a truly liberal training be offered, with a curriculum approximating that for the art's degree in a university. He also shrewdly insisted on accumulating all possible rubber stamps of public and government recognition. In 1913 the Academy was incorporated, and after the war he urged that it seek a Royal Charter, which was obtained. Finally, the basis of the Council was broadened, and the aged revolutionary labored to secure the appointment of bishops and earls. He contributed his hearty support, as well as five thousand pounds sterling, to the building of Malet Street Theatre, which was opened in 1921 by the Prince of Wales. Shaw now pressed for the same tax exemption which the Colleges of Music enjoyed. This the government refused on the mid-Victorian principle that acting was not a fine art, thus enabling Shaw to fight another battle with a favorite enemy and eventually, by his jovial, inverted diplomacy, to obtain the tax exemption he desired.

Practical education found Shaw thoroughly practical and therefore in some respects quite un-Shavian. He not only emphasized the value of rubber-stamp and formal education; he even went to the elderly extreme of dispensing paternal advice, suggesting in 1941 that when they received their diplomas, students be given a booklet of professional guidance from members of the Council. He himself wrote the Introduction, which proved to be a model commencement address. Whatever the effect of this didactic maneuver on the young people, Shaw was still too youthful, and indeed too dazzlingly famous and incomparably talented as a teacher, to be anything but extremely popular at the Academy. Nor did he ever refuse an invitation to superintend the rehearsal of one of his plays. Even when over eighty, he would remain standing for two or three hours, listening to every tone and observing every gesture. "His comments," says Sir Kenneth Barnes, "were gems of lucidity and humour. He had a power of bringing the best out of young people that I have never seen equalled in a long experience." [1]

The Malet Street Theatre was one of the few episodes in Shaw's life to come to a definite and indubitable end. In 1941 it was destroyed by a land mine. "He came to see the damage," writes Sir Kenneth Barnes, "and was, I think, astonished at its extent. He looked silently at it for half a minute, then turned away and said to me, 'Well, they made a good job of it.'" [2]

Shaw had always been triumphantly equal to the monsters which issued from the womb of mechanical invention. The telegraph and telephone, the bicycle, camera, automobile, and motorcycle all found him a dexterously, even a spectacularly, tool-using animal. In fact,

> he likes machines as a child likes toys, and once very nearly bought a cash register without having the slightest use for it. When he was on the verge of sixty he yielded to the fascination of a motor bicycle, and rode it away from the factory for seventy-seven miles, at the end of which, just outside his own door, he took a corner too fast and was left sprawling. [3]

The radio and the moving picture, however, met at first with just a hint of elderly contempt. But Shaw was not the man to grow old obviously. In 1924, at the invitation of the British Broadcasting Company, he gave a broadcast reading of his "O'Flaherty, V.C." He was applauded almost from the corners of the earth and thereafter, captivated by the possibilities of the new gadget, conscientiously guided, prodded, instructed, inspired, criticized, and deflated the dignitaries of the B.B.C.

The movies also he stooped to conquer with good grace. Some years ago Gabriel Pascal, then a little-known director, appeared in Shaw's flat in Whitehall Court, swiftly demonstrated his abilities, formed in the course of a few visits a delightful acquaintance, and then demanded the cinema rights to "Pygmalion" by four o'clock on Friday the thirteenth, when he would have to think of accepting an offer to make pictures in China.

"What! Is this an ultimatum?" asked Shaw.

"Yes, an ultimatum." [4]

Several days passed, and with them most of the producer's hopes. Friday came. When his watch said four o'clock, hope was extinct. A moment later Big Ben chimed. His bell rang. There was a messenger with a signed contract from Shaw. At Mr. Pascal's request, the veteran author wrote altogether nearly two dozen scenes for the cinema versions of "Pygmalion," "Major Barbara," and "Caesar and Cleopatra." The results were brilliant. As a former art critic, camera expert, stage director, dramatist, and artistic genius supremely confident of conquering any medium, Shaw was luxuriously prepared for scenario writing, in which, so far as Mr. Pascal's experience extends, he has shown more "genuine instinct for camera angles" and more "rhythmical sense for movie continuity" than any other great playwright.[5]

But even as he conquered new worlds, the old worlds were passing away. Frail and quieter now, the aged immortal stood more and more alone. In 1943 Charlotte died, leaving a jaunty will and careful instructions for a cheerful cremation. Her ashes were to be taken to London. No black clothing was to be worn. The bulk of her six-hundred-thousand dollar estate was to be used in bringing good manners and great works of art to the Irish people. Asked what he as an Irishman thought about Irish manners, the old man explained that he was really an Englishman, having spent less than a fourth of his life in the land of his birth. The hard and flippant Shavian mask to which the reporter addressed his ruthless question spoke in an idiom infinitely remote from what lay in Shaw's mind. For Charlotte's illness had been so painful and so hopeless that his friends could not mention her death to him for many months.

But time and death would not leave him in peace. In 1943 Beatrice Webb died, the Aunt Bo who fifty years before had scandalized her relatives by marrying "a seditious Cockney cad";[6] and in 1946 H. G. Wells, who forty years ago had so dazzlingly epitomized youth to a middle-aged Fabian Society. Shaw wrote about both of them of course—well and feelingly of Beatrice, rather absent-mindedly and repetitively of Wells. All that he had to say of Wells he had said brilliantly so long ago. That, perhaps, was one of the disadvantages of growing very old. Few men have had more to say than Bernard Shaw. But by now he had said it all, and so magnificently that the rest would have to be repetition and therefore less than repetition.

In 1945 Shaw wrote another Preface for "Geneva." In its renewed faith in democracy and Anglo-Saxon political tradition, it continues the trend of *Everybody's Political What's What?*. In fact, Shaw goes so far as to prefer British dullness to German cogitation. But his preference is not very strong. A tired indifference appears behind the customary vigor of expression. One feels that the author has very few illusions. Dictators are nearly always clever and usually bad. Democrats are hardly ever clever. Attlee's Labourites are just as utopian as MacDonald's were. The counterpart to this tired pessimism is a tired, deprecatory, grandfatherly optimism. The Nazi atrocities occurred through mere inefficiency. Democracy fails through sheer ignorance. The world is too shabby and mean a place to have anything very big wrong with it. It may therefore improve considerably. But Shaw seems weary of history, of having old ideas about new events. He yawns a little even over the atom bomb.

Interviewed on his eighty-ninth birthday, he once more prescribed for the ills of the world the Methuselan remedy of longer life for greater wisdom, which he declared himself to be triumphantly carrying out. Nevertheless, he concluded characteristically by suggesting that the interviewer consult a life-insurance actuary before wishing him many happy returns. William Saroyan saw him in 1946 and found him "a sweet old gentleman," extremely Victorian and inclined to put too much effort into scintillating for visitors.[7] Professor Evans of the University of California, calling on Shaw in 1947, describes him as an almost transparent and incredibly frail-looking giant, with small twinkling eyes, "tiny arms," "little stems of legs," and a soft, low voice not yet "broken." [8] Partly because he was in the company of an eminent medical scientist, partly because he suffers from anemia, Shaw was eagerly curious about the hormones and vitamins whose existence he had so scoffingly denied in print. Dr. Evans was told that the aged dramatist was much more cheerful and talkative than he had been for some time.

And yet, visiting him in the following year, his friend Mr. Charles Bolles Rogers says that "he never seems to hesitate for a name, a date, or a place in his conversation. . . . When I remarked to him . . . that I thought he looked better and younger than ever he answered, 'I don't mind telling you, being a bachelor gives one a lift.' His eyes twinkled like a young schoolboy's rather than a nonagenarian's." [9] Mr. Rogers also gives some interesting details about Shaw's diet:

> He now has the theory most . . . vegetarian foods are much richer than he needs. He has eliminated practically all starch. He thinks the protein emphasis absurd and he tells me that he lives, largely, on grated vegetables, usually raw. It is certain that he eats very, very little.[9]

In 1948 Shaw completed *Sixteen Self Sketches,* an autobiography made up of previously published fragments set in a narrative of considerable length. The first chapter portrays the infant Shaw from his father's letters. The second contains a witty demonstration that autobiography is a waste of time:

> I have had no heroic adventures. Things have not happened to me: on the contrary it is I who have happened to them; and all my happenings have taken the form of books and plays. Read them, or spectate them; and you have my whole story: the rest is only breakfast, lunch, dinner, sleeping, wakening, and washing.[10]

In earlier years Shaw did not find himself so arid a theme. *Self Sketches* show that he is bored with his biographers, if not with himself.

There are also startling revelations of "Shame and Wounded Snobbery," as well as chapters on young manhood and the Fabian Society, which soberly echo, correct, and amplify earlier writings. There are the brilliant fragments "Who I am, and what I think" and "How Frank ought to have done it," rescued from obscure publications. There are discussions of education and religion, bitter epistolary expostulations with a mysterious biographer, Professor O'Bolger, and lengthy arguments about Shavian facts with critical posterity, which ranges from Winston Churchill to Cousin Charles Shaw.

One is impressed in this, as in other later writings, with Shaw's concern for objective verity. He strives for an accurate, not an epigrammatic, account of his early life and family. He emphasizes the neglected truth that in building Fabian tradition, he was more the theorizer, and Webb, more the empiricist. He attempts to guard against the accusation of flagrant scientific error and gross philosophic naïveté. For he does not altogether "repudiate Darwin" nor fail to attach "importance to the part played in human destiny by Natural Selection and by Reason." [11] But neither again is he a mere rationalist, for rationalism "implies the belief that reason is not only method, but motive." [12] Here Shaw is writing not for the momentary crisis but for the permanent record.

And so, in this strange, noisy, unfathomable world, which he as much as any man has built, Bernard Shaw lives on, not less than a very great man grown very old. He has outlived his Victorian past, his present of midday achievement, even his future of millennial hopes, but not his fame, which is still in the first blush of youth.

FOOTNOTES

NOTE: Most of the books listed by George Bernard Shaw below as originally published by Brentano's, Inc., are now copyrighted and published by Dodd, Mead & Company, Inc., New York.

CHAPTER ONE

1. Shaw, George Bernard, "In the Days of My Youth," *Living Age,* New York, vol. cccxxii (1924), p. 325.

2. *Ibid.,* p. 323.

3. Chesterton, G. K., *George Bernard Shaw,* John Lane, The Bodley Head, Ltd., London, 1909, p. 40.

4. Mr. Shaw's additions to the author's manuscript.

5. Wilson, Edmund, "Bernard Shaw at Eighty," *The Triple Thinkers,* Harcourt, Brace and Company, Inc., New York, 1938, p. 244.

6. St. John, Christopher, editor, *Ellen Terry and Bernard Shaw: A Correspondence,* G. P. Putnam's Sons, New York, 1931, p. 157.

7. Shaw, George Bernard, Preface, *Immaturity,* Constable & Co., Ltd., London, 1931, p. xxiv.

8. *Ibid.,* pp. xx–xxi.

9. *Ibid.,* p. xi.

10. St. John, Christopher, editor, *Ellen Terry and Bernard Shaw: A Correspondence,* p. 86.

11. Shaw, George Bernard, *Sixteen Self Sketches,* Dodd, Mead & Company, Inc., New York, 1949, p. 170.

12. Shaw, George Bernard, "Who I Am, and What I Think," *The Candid Friend,* May 11, 1901, p. 58.

13. *Loc. cit.*

14. Mr. Shaw's emendation of this passage emphasizes his 'Pottsian discomfitures: "He was a quiet, portentous-browed infant who busied himself with large tomes, performed children's Christmas ceremonies of melting lead and hiding rings in pancakes with complete scepticism, repeated the

limericks of his Rabelaisian máternal uncle and imitated the anticlimaxes, and, failing in everything for want of training after expecting to do them naturally, had the conceit taken out of him almost to the extent of an inferiority complex for many years."

15. Shaw, George Bernard, Preface, *London Music in 1888–89 as Heard by Corno di Bassetto*, Constable & Co., Ltd., London, 1939, p. 13.

16. Mr. Shaw's emendation.

17. Shaw, George Bernard, *The Intelligent Woman's Guide to Socialism and Capitalism*, Brentano's, Inc., New York, 1928, p. 184.

18. Mr. Shaw's addition.

19. Mr. Shaw's emendation indìcates he does not regard himself as a hero-worshiper: "Paradoxically, he proved later that he knew the value of genius, but his geniuses were all human and all rebels like himself: and he could laugh at them all the time."

20. Shaw, George Bernard, *An Essay on Going to Church*, John W. Luce Company, Boston, 1905, p. 44.

21. Shaw, Preface, *Immaturity*, p. xix.

22. Shaw, "In the Days of My Youth," p. 324.

23. Pearson, Hesketh, *G.B.S., A Full Length Portrait*, Harper & Brothers, New York, 1942, p. 19.

24. St. John, Christopher, editor, *Ellen Terry and Bernard Shaw: A Correspondence*, p. 157.

CHAPTER TWO

1. Mr. Shaw's emendation. And yet in his *Sixteen Self Sketches* he writes: "On the whole it is safer to delegate the child's education to a conventional school, as Voltaire's was to the Jesuits, leaving it to react by its own strength, than to risk its having to learn with difficulty in its sixteenth year what it could have been taught easily in its sixth." (Shaw, George Bernard, *Sixteen Self Sketches*, Dodd, Mead & Company, Inc., New York, 1949, p. 35.)

2. Shaw, *Sixteen Self Sketches*, p. 50.

3. Mr. Shaw's emendation.

4. Shaw, George Bernard, "In the Days of My Youth," *Living Age*, vol. cccxxii (1924), pp. 325–326.

5. Shaw, George Bernard, Preface, *London Music in 1888–89 as Heard by Corno di Bassetto*, Constable & Co., Ltd., London, 1939, p. 8.

6. Mr. Shaw's emendation.

7. Shaw, *Sixteen Self Sketches*, p. 31.

8. "George Bernard Shaw As a Boy," *The Commercial Advertiser,* August 10, 1901.

9. Shaw, George Bernard, "The Religion of the Pianoforte," *The Fortnightly Review,* vol. lv (1894), p. 257.

10. Mr. Shaw's emendation.

11. Mr. Shaw's addition.

12. Pearson, Hesketh, *G.B.S., A Full Length Portrait,* Harper & Brothers, New York, 1942, p. 20.

13. Shaw, *Sixteen Self Sketches,* pp. 69–70.

14. Harris, Frank, *Bernard Shaw: An Unauthorized Biography,* Simon and Schuster, Inc., New York, 1931, p. 70.

15. Shaw, George Bernard, Preface, *Immaturity,* Constable & Co., Ltd., London, 1931, p. xxxiv.

16. Mr. Shaw's emendation.

17. Mr. Shaw's additions.

18. Shaw, Preface, *Immaturity,* p. x.

19. Mr. Shaw's emendation.

CHAPTER THREE

1. Newman, John Henry, "The Tamworth Reading Room," *Discussions and Arguments on Various Subjects,* Longmans Green & Co., Ltd., London, 1924, p. 295.

2. Shaw, George Bernard, "The Transition to Social Democracy," *Fabian Essays in Socialism,* George Bernard Shaw, editor, George Allen & Unwin, Ltd., London, 1931, p. 173.

3. Harris, Frank, *Bernard Shaw: An Unauthorized Biography,* Simon and Schuster, Inc., New York, 1931, p. 72.

4. Shaw, George Bernard, Preface, *Immaturity,* Constable & Co., Ltd., London, 1931, p. xxxvi.

5. Shaw, George Bernard, Preface, *The Irrational Knot,* Brentano's, Inc., New York, 1926, p. xx.

CHAPTER FOUR

1. Shaw, George Bernard, Preface, "Major Barbara," *John Bull's Other Island and Major Barbara,* Brentano's, Inc., New York, 1929, pp. 157–158.

2. Shaw, George Bernard, *Immaturity,* Constable & Co., Ltd., London, 1931, p. 417.

3. Shaw, George Bernard, Preface, *Cashel Byron's Profession,* Herbert S. Stone, Chicago, 1901, p. xiii.

4. Shaw, George Bernard, Preface, *London Music in 1888–89 as Heard by Corno di Bassetto,* Constable & Co., Ltd., London, 1939, p. 27.

5. *Ibid.,* p. 28.

6. Quoted by Pearson, Hesketh, *G.B.S.: A Full Length Portrait,* Harper & Brothers, New York, 1942, pp. 39–40.

7. Henderson, Archibald, *George Bernard Shaw, His Life and Works,* Stewart & Kidd, Cincinnati, 1911, p. 40.

8. Shaw, George Bernard, "Who I Am, and What I Think," *The Candid Friend,* May 11, 1901, p. 57.

9. I mean this to be understood figuratively. Shaw did not read Butler until later. See p. 408 and also C. M. Shaw, *Bernard's Brethren,* note facing p. 124.

10. Shaw, George Bernard, *The Irrational Knot,* Brentano's Inc., New York, 1926, p. 18.

11. Pearson, *op. cit.,* p. 42.

12. Shaw, George Bernard, *Love among the Artists,* Brentano's, Inc., New York, 1927, pp. 132–133.

13. Shaw, *Cashel Byron's Profession,* p. 289.

14. Shaw, George Bernard, "Mr. Bernard Shaw's Works of Fiction as Reviewed by Himself," *Tinsley's Magazine,* vol. xlviii (1892), p. 238.

15. Shaw, George Bernard, *An Unsocial Socialist,* Brentano's, Inc., New York, 1905, p. 290.

16. *Ibid.,* p. 368.

17. Shaw, "Mr. Bernard Shaw's Works of Fiction as Reviewed by Himself," p. 241.

CHAPTER FIVE

1. Shaw, George Bernard, *Sixteen Self Sketches,* Dodd, Mead & Company, Inc., New York, 1949, p. 95.

2. Harris, Frank, *Bernard Shaw: An Unauthorized Biography,* Simon and Schuster, Inc., New York, 1931, pp. 76–77.

3. Henderson, Archibald, *Bernard Shaw, Playboy and Prophet,* D. Appleton & Company, Inc., New York, 1932, p. 124.

4. Shaw, *Sixteen Self Sketches,* p. 107.

5. *Ibid.,* p. 108.

6. *Ibid.,* p. 108.

7. *Ibid.*, p. 94.

8. See p. 85.

9. Quoted by Henderson, *Playboy and Prophet*, p. 145.

10. Henderson, Archibald, *George Bernard Shaw: His Life and Works,* Stewart & Kidd, Cincinnati, 1911, p. 95.

11. A metaphor frequently used by Henry George, Jr., in his *Life of Henry George,* Doubleday & Company, Inc., New York, 1905.

12. Webb, Sidney, and Beatrice Webb, *The History of Trade Unionism,* Longmans, Green & Co., Inc., New York, 1926, p. 375.

13. Quoted from George R. Geiger, *The Philosophy of Henry George,* The Macmillan Company, New York, 1933, p. 60.

14. Henderson, *George Bernard Shaw: His Life and Works,* p. 96.

15. A letter to Hamlin Garland, as Chairman of the Committee, the *Progress and Poverty* Dinner, New York, January 24, 1905. Quoted by Henderson, *George Bernard Shaw: His Life and Works,* pp. 152–153.

16. Shaw, *Sixteen Self Sketches,* p. 97.

CHAPTER SIX

1. Hook, Sidney, *Towards the Understanding of Karl Marx, A Revolutionary Interpretation,* The John Day Company, New York, 1933, pp. 78, 84.

2. Pease, Edward R., *The History of the Fabian Society,* A. C. Fifield, London, 1916, p. 30.

3. *Ibid.*, p. 39.

4. *Ibid.*, p. 40.

5. Shaw, George Bernard, "The Fabian Society: Its Early History," *Fabian Tract No. 41,* Fabian Society, London, 1892, p. 4.

6. Shaw, George Bernard, "Who I Am, and What I Think," *The Candid Friend,* May 11, 1901, p. 57.

CHAPTER SEVEN

1. Stephen, Sir Leslie, *The English Utilitarians,* G. P. Putnam's Sons, New York, 1900, vol. ii, p. 219.

2. Menger, Anton, *The Right to the Whole Produce of Labour,* Macmillan & Co., Ltd., London, 1899, p. 52.

3. Mill, John Stuart, *The Principles of Political Economy,* W. J. Ashley, editor, Longmans Green & Co., Ltd., London, 1909, pp. 210–211.

4. *Ibid.*, p. 963.

5. *Ibid.*, pp. 933–934.

6. Stephen, *op. cit.*, vol. iii, p. 228.

7. Mill, *op. cit.*, p. 230.

8. *Ibid.*, pp. 223–228.

9. *Ibid.*, pp. 212–217, 781–794.

10. Stephen, *op. cit.*, vol. iii, p. 235.

11. Shaw, George Bernard, Preface, *Back to Methuselah*, Brentano's, Inc., New York, 1921, p. lxv.

12. Webb, Sidney, "Socialism in England," *Publications of the American Economic Association*, n.s. vol. iv, no. 2, p. 139.

CHAPTER EIGHT

1. The entire tract is also quoted by Edward R. Pease, *The History of the Fabian Society*, A. C. Fifield, London, 1916, pp. 41–43.

2. My quotations from the "Manifesto" are not complete.

3. Mill, John Stuart, *Autobiography*, World Classics, Oxford University Press, New York, 1924, p. 141.

4. Mill, John Stuart, *The Principles of Political Economy*, W. J. Ashley, editor, Longmans, Green & Co., Ltd., London, 1909, pp. 226–227.

5. Mill, John Stuart, *Socialism*, Humbolt Publishing Co., New York, 1891, pp. 77–81.

6. Mill, John Stuart, *Utilitarianism, Liberty, and Representative Government*, Everyman's Library, J. M. Dent & Sons, Ltd., 1910, p. 161; also *The Principles of Political Economy*, p. 942.

7. Mill, *The Principles of Political Economy*, p. 860.

8. Quoted by Archibald Henderson, *George Bernard Shaw: His Life and Works*, Stewart & Kidd, Cincinnati, 1911, p. 106n.

9. Pease, *op. cit.*, pp. 47–48.

10. Quoted by Hesketh Pearson, *G.B.S., A Full Length Portrait*, Harper & Brothers, New York, 1942, p. 62.

11. Quoted by Doris L. Moore, *E. Nesbit, A Biography*, Ernest Benn, Ltd., London, 1933, pp. 65–66.

12. *Ibid.*, p. 204.

13. Wells, H. G., *Experiment in Autobiography*, The Macmillan Company, New York, 1934, p. 517.

14. Moore, *op. cit.*, pp. 72–73.

15. Shaw, George Bernard, "The Fabian Society: Its Early History," *Fabian Tract No. 41*, Fabian Society, London, 1892, p. 4.

16. Shaw, George Bernard, "The Transition to Social Democracy," *Fabian Essays in Socialism*, George Bernard Shaw, editor, George Allen & Unwin, Ltd., London, 1931, p. 173.

17. Wells, *op. cit.*, p. 519.

18. Shaw, "The Transition to Social Democracy," *Fabian Essays in Socialism*, p. 173.

19. Shaw, George Bernard, *Sixteen Self Sketches*, Dodd, Mead & Company, Inc., New York, 1949, pp. 110–111.

20. All unnumerated quotations from p. 105 through p. 109 are taken from Shaw, "The Fabian Society: Its Early History," *Fabian Tract No. 41*, pp. 1–11.

21. Pearson, *op. cit.*, p. 63.

22. *Ibid.*, p. 66.

23. Shaw, "The Fabian Society: Its Early History," *Fabian Tract No. 41*, p. 17.

24. Shaw, George Bernard, "The Impossibilities of Anarchism," *Fabian Tract No. 45*, Fabian Society, London, 1895, p. 21.

CHAPTER NINE

1. Shaw, George Bernard, "The Fabian Society: Its Early History," *Fabian Tract No. 41*, Fabian Society, London, 1892, pp. 18–21, 23.

2. Shaw, George Bernard, "Fabian Economics," Appendix I in Edward Pease, *The History of the Fabian Society*, A. C. Fifield, London, 1916, pp. 260, 263.

3. Haynes, E. S. P., "Liberty and the State," *Living Age*, vol. ccc (1919), p. 396.

4. Shaw, "Fabian Economics," Appendix I in Pease, *The History of the Fabian Society*, p. 258.

5. Webb, Beatrice, *My Apprenticeship*, Longmans, Green & Co., Ltd., London, 1926, pp. 15–17.

6. Hamilton, Mary Agnes, *Sidney and Beatrice Webb*, Houghton Mifflin Company, Boston, 1929, p. 17.

7. See Sidney Webb, "Socialism in England," *Publications of the American Economic Association*, n.s. vol. iv, no. 2.

8. Webb, Sidney, "The Basis of Socialism: Historic," *Fabian Essays in Socialism*, George Bernard Shaw, editor, George Allen & Unwin, Ltd., London, 1931, p. 52.

9. Hearnshaw, F. J. C., *A Survey of Socialism: Analytical, Historical, and Critical*, Macmillan & Co., Ltd., London, 1928, pp. 307–308.

10. In "Man and Superman" and "Back to Methuselah," Shaw stands on the other side of the question.

11. Hamilton, *op. cit.*, pp. 119–137.

12. Barker, Ernest, *Political Thought in England from Herbert Spencer to the Present Day*, Home University Library of Modern Knowledge, Williams & Norgate, Ltd., London, 1915, pp. 215–219.

13. Thus Graham Wallas's *Life of Francis Place* is naturally hostile to the individualism of the Benthamites. Otherwise his attitude is friendly. They did not simply dream and agitate, like the Chartists. In a truly Fabian spirit, they were practical and got things done. Wallas eventually became something much more modern than the youthful utilitarian he had been. Like McDougall, he must be classified among those who study social phenomena from the point of view of group psychological principles. But whereas McDougall emphasizes in the life of social groups the role of instinct and emotion, Wallas emphasizes that of reason and logic —and here again it seems probable that he reveals a utilitarian bias, especially as all of his writings indicate a wide familiarity with utilitarian literature and a great, though critical, admiration for Jeremy Bentham. H. G. Wells (*Experiment in Autobiography*, The Macmillan Company, New York, 1934, p. 511) recalls that, a few years before his death, Wallas "had been reading a good deal of Bentham . . . digging out long forgotten books, and I remember his glasses gleaming appreciatively as he squatted in my lowest easy chair and dilated on the 'old boy's' abundance and breadth of range."

Mrs. Annie Besant was during the early part of her career closely linked with utilitarianism as the follower of Charles Bradlaugh, the atheist, who was influenced by Comte, Lewes, J. S. Mill, and Bentham. The martyr of Benthamism, Bradlaugh for nearly fifty years devoted his powerful mental and physical muscularity to belaboring policemen with clubs and preachers with utilitarian logic. His martyrdom had the unusual luxury of leaving him a whole skin to a fairly advanced age. Throughout his long battle Mrs. Besant remained his close ally. As he was a Benthamite in all save his fanatical enmity to Christianity, she was his disciple in all save her socialism, and on this issue they eventually parted company. Later, Mrs. Besant became a Theosophist, but the Theosophism which she learned from Madame Blavatsky and in far-off India turned out eventually to be, from the political point of view, strangely like the Fabianism which she had known all along in London. By her faith in democracy and equality, her constitutional and evolutionary socialism, and her interest in the Malthusian problem of population, she shows herself a reformer in the tradition of Bentham and Mill.

14. Shaw, George Bernard, Preface, "Androcles and the Lion," *Androcles and the Lion, Overruled, Pygmalion*, Brentano's, Inc., New York, 1916, p. xiv.

15. Webb, Sidney, and Beatrice Webb, *A Constitution for the Socialist Com-*

monwealth of Great Britain, Longmans, Green & Co., Inc., New York, 1920, pp. xiv–xv.

CHAPTER TEN

1. Marx, Karl, *Capital*, Modern Library, Inc., Random House, New York, 1936, pp. 48, 51-52, 59, 106.

2. Wicksteed, Philip H., "Das Kapital: A Criticism by Philip H. Wicksteed," *Bernard Shaw and Karl Marx: A Symposium, 1884–1889*, Richard W. Ellis, editor, Random House, New York, 1930, p. 42.

3. *Ibid.*, p. 64.

4. Marx, *Capital*, chap. xxiii; see also Karl Marx, *The Poverty of Philosophy*, Charles H. Kerr & Company, Chicago, 1910, p. 45n.

5. Shaw, George Bernard, "Bluffing the Value Theory," *Bernard Shaw and Karl Marx: A Symposium, 1884–1889*, p. 177.

6. Shaw, George Bernard, "The Jevonian Criticism of Marx: A Comment on the Rev. P. H. Wicksteed's Article by George Bernard Shaw," *Bernard Shaw and Karl Marx: A Symposium, 1884–1889*, pp. 70–71.

7. Wicksteed, Philip H., "The Jevonian Criticism of Marx: A Rejoinder by Philip H. Wicksteed," *Bernard Shaw and Karl Marx: A Symposium, 1884–1889*, pp. 96–97.

8. Quoted by Archibald Henderson, *George Bernard Shaw: His Life and Works*, Stewart & Kidd, Cincinnati, 1911, pp. 158–159.

9. *Ibid.*, p. 158n.1.

10. Eckard, E. W., *Economics of W. S. Jevons*, American Council on Public Affairs, Washington, D.C., 1940, p. 34.

11. Quoted by Archibald Henderson, *Bernard Shaw, Playboy and Prophet*, D. Appleton & Company, Inc., New York, 1932, p. 165.

12. Shaw, George Bernard, *Sixteen Self Sketches*, Dodd, Mead & Company, Inc., New York, 1949, p. 111.

13. *Ibid.*, pp. 131–132.

14. Wallas, Graham, "Socialism and the Fabian Society," *The New Republic*, June 24, 1916, p. 203.

15. This and the following quotations are from George Bernard Shaw, "Karl Marx and 'Das Kapital' [First Notice] by G. Bernard Shaw," *Bernard Shaw and Karl Marx: A Symposium, 1884–1889*, pp. 105–118.

16. Barzun, Jacques, *Darwin, Marx, Wagner; Critique of a Heritage*, Little, Brown & Company, Boston, 1941, p. 196.

17. He begins with a Jevonian definition of economics: it treats of those activities by which men attempt to satisfy their wants with the least possi-

ble exertion (Jevons, W. S., *The Theory of Political Economy,* Macmillan & Co., Ltd., London, 1888, p. 37). Continuing the theme of exertion, he demonstrates that commodities are, as Marx says, commensurable in terms of abstract labor. But they are also commensurable in terms of abstract utility. Then comes a test case. The fragment of a teacup embodies abstract labor, but it is not useful. Neither does it possess value. To be sure, this does not conclusively link value with utility, because fresh air is useful but not valuable. Shaw then explains the laws of indifference and of variable utility, concluding that value represents the final abstract utility of an article, or "the utility of the final increment that is worth producing. Or, going behind the ware to the labour, its value represents . . . the final utility of the abstract human labour socially necessary to produce it" (Shaw, George Bernard, "Karl Marx and 'Das Kapital' [Second Notice] by G. Bernard Shaw," *Bernard Shaw and Karl Marx: A Symposium, 1884–1889,* p. 144). Under normal conditions, wares containing equal quantities of labor will be equal in value when the final utilities of the labor expended are equal (*ibid.,* p. 145; also Eckard, *op. cit.,* p. 22). Wares are not valuable because they embody labor but embody labor because they are valuable (Eckard, *op. cit.,* p. 35).

Within the limits of a brief paper, Shaw is reasonably complete, although he might have entered a little more fully into the relation of labor to commodity value. Ancient masterpieces of painting, for example, are valuable not because great pains were once taken with them but because they are now both scarce and desirable.

18. Shaw, George Bernard, "Karl Marx and 'Das Kapital' [Third Notice] by G. Bernard Shaw," *Bernard Shaw and Karl Marx: A Symposium, 1884–1889,* p. 159.

19. *Ibid.,* p. 168.

20. *Ibid.,* p. 169.

21. Shaw, "Bluffing the Value Theory," *Bernard Shaw and Karl Marx: A Symposium, 1884–1889,* pp. 195–196.

22. Shaw, George Bernard, "Shaw's Economics," *G.B.S. 90,* S. Winsten, editor, Dodd, Mead & Company, Inc., New York, 1946, p. 171.

23. Shaw, George Bernard, "The Illusions of Socialism," *Forecasts of the Coming Century by a Decade of Writers,* Edward Carpenter, editor, Walter Scott, London, 1897, pp. 157–158.

24. Shaw, George Bernard, "Who I Am, and What I Think," *The Candid Friend,* May 11, 1901.

25. Shaw, George Bernard, Preface, *Back to Methuselah,* Brentano's, Inc., New York, 1921, p. lxviii.

CHAPTER ELEVEN

1. Pease, Edward R., *The History of the Fabian Society,* A. C. Fifield, London, 1916, pp. 102–104.

2. Hamilton, Mary Agnes, *Sidney and Beatrice Webb,* Houghton Mifflin Company, Boston, p. 33.

3. Shaw, George Bernard, "The Old Revolutionist and the New Revolution," *Pen Portraits and Reviews,* Constable & Co., Ltd., London, 1931, p. 132.

4. Shaw, George Bernard, "The Fabian Society: Its Early History," *Fabian Tract No. 41,* Fabian Society, London, 1892, p. 18.

5. Pease, *op. cit.,* p. 74.

6. Shaw, "The Fabian Society: Its Early History," *Fabian Tract No. 41,* p. 16.

7. *Ibid.,* p. 19.

8. Quoted by Hamilton, *op. cit.,* p. 35.

9. Pease, *op. cit.,* p. 110.

10. *Ibid.,* p. 81.

11. *Ibid.,* p. 112*n*.1.

12. Shaw, George Bernard, "Fabian Election Manifesto: 1892," *Fabian Tract No. 40,* Fabian Society, London, 1892, p. 4.

13. Shaw, George Bernard, "What Mr. Gladstone Ought to Do," *The Fortnightly Review,* vol. liii (1893), p. 276.

14. *Ibid.,* p. 277.

15. Shaw, George Bernard, *William Morris As I Knew Him,* Dodd, Mead & Company, Inc., New York, 1936, pp. 24, 25.

16. *Ibid.,* pp. 7, 19.

17. *Ibid.,* pp. 48, 51.

18. *Ibid.,* pp. 47–48, 51.

CHAPTER TWELVE

1. Shaw, George Bernard, "The Basis of Socialism: Economic," *Fabian Essays in Socialism,* George Bernard Shaw, editor, George Allen & Unwin, Ltd., London, 1931, p. 3.

2. *Ibid.,* p. 26.

3. Knowlton, Thomas, *The Economic Theory of George Bernard Shaw,* University of Maine Press, Orono, Maine, 1936, p. 45.

4. Besant, Mrs. Annie, "Industry under Socialism," *Fabian Essays in Socialism*, p. 154.

5. *Ibid.*, p. 162.

6. *Ibid.*, pp. 166, 165.

7. Shaw, George Bernard, "The Illusions of Socialism," *Forecasts of the Coming Century by a Decade of Writers,* Edward Carpenter, editor, Walter Scott, London, 1897.

8. Henderson, Archibald, *Bernard Shaw, Playboy and Prophet,* D. Appleton & Company, Inc., New York, 1932, p. 238.

CHAPTER THIRTEEN

1. Pfeiffer, Edouard, *La Société Fabienne et le mouvement socialiste anglais contemporain,* F. Giard & E. Brière, Paris, 1911, p. 85.

2. See Lord Elton, *The Life of James Ramsay MacDonald (1866–1919),* William Collins Sons & Co., Ltd., London, 1939, pp. 102–103.

3. Davies, A. Emil, "G. B. S. and Local Government," *G.B.S. 90,* S. Winsten, editor, Dodd, Mead & Company, Inc., New York, 1946, p. 204.

4. Manuscript letter, August 30, 1898.

5. Henderson, Archibald, *George Bernard Shaw: His Life and Works,* Stewart & Kidd, Cincinnati, 1911, p. 183.

CHAPTER FOURTEEN

1. Archer, C., *William Archer,* George Allen & Unwin, Ltd., London, 1931, p. 119.

2. Quoted by Hesketh Pearson, *G. B. S., A Full Length Portrait,* Harper & Brothers, New York, 1942, p. 89.

3. Bentley, Eric, *A Century of Hero-Worship,* J. B. Lippincott Company, Philadelphia, 1944, p. 264.

4. *Ibid.*, pp. 194–198.

5. Pierce, Charles, "How to Make Our Ideas Clear," *The Popular Science Monthly,* vol. xii (1877–1878), pp. 286–302, summarized by William James, *Pragmatism,* Longmans, Green & Co., Inc., New York, 1921, p. 46.

6. Quoted by Archibald Henderson, *Bernard Shaw, Playboy and Prophet,* D. Appleton & Company, Inc., New York, 1932, pp. 265–266.

CHAPTER FIFTEEN

1. Faure, Elie, *Modern Art: History of Art*, Garden City Publishing Company, Inc., Garden City, N.Y., 1924, pp. 284–285.

2. Quoted by Archibald Henderson, *George Bernard Shaw: His Life and Works*, Stewart & Kidd, Cincinnati, 1911, pp. 218–219.

3. Shaw, George Bernard, "Madox Brown, Watts, and Ibsen," *The Saturday Review*, vol. lxxxiii (1897), p. 266.

4. *Ibid.,* p. 266.

5. *Ibid.,* p. 266.

6. *Ibid.,* p. 267.

7. Henderson, *George Bernard Shaw: His Life and Works*, p. 200.

8. *Our Corner,* May, 1886, quoted by Archibald Henderson, *Bernard Shaw, Playboy and Prophet,* D. Appleton & Company, Inc., New York, 1932, p. 264.

9. Shaw, George Bernard, "Who I Am, and What I Think," *The Candid Friend,* May 11, 1901, p. 96.

10. *Loc. cit.*

11. Shaw, George Bernard, *The Sanity of Art,* Benjamin R. Tucker, New York, 1908, p. 23.

12. *Ibid.,* p. 26.

13. *Ibid.,* p. 27.

14. *Ibid.,* pp. 75–77.

15. Quoted by Henderson, *George Bernard Shaw: His Life and Works,* p. 224.

CHAPTER SIXTEEN

1. Shaw, George Bernard, *London Music in 1888–89 as Heard by Corno di Bassetto,* Constable & Co., Ltd., London, 1939, p. 391.

2. Shaw, George Bernard, *Music in London 1890–94,* Constable & Co., Ltd., London, 1932, vol. ii, p. 71.

3. *Ibid.,* vol. ii, p. 245.

4. *Ibid.,* vol. ii, pp. 229–230.

5. Shaw, *London Music in 1888–89 as Heard by Corno di Bassetto,* p. 314.

6. *Ibid.,* p. 345.

7. Shaw, *Music in London 1890–94,* vol. i, p. 130.

8. Shaw, *London Music in 1888–89 as Heard by Corno di Bassetto*, p. 228.

9. Shaw, *Music in London 1890–94*, vol. i, pp. 129, 143–144.

10. *Ibid.*, vol. ii, pp. 146–147.

11. *Ibid.*, vol. i, p. 284.

12. Shaw, *London Music in 1888–89 as Heard by Corno di Bassetto*, p. 320.

13. *Ibid.*, pp. 175–176; Shaw, *Music in London 1890–94*, vol. ii, p. 126.

14. Shaw, *Music in London 1890–94*, vol. i, p. 250.

15. *Ibid.*, vol. iii, p. 88.

16. Shaw, *London Music in 1888–89 as Heard by Corno di Bassetto*, p. 268.

17. *Ibid.*, p. 266.

18. Shaw, *Music in London 1890–94*, vol. i, p. 108.

19. Shaw, *London Music in 1888–89 as Heard by Corno di Bassetto*, p. 42.

20. Shaw, *Music in London 1890–94*, vol. i, p. 237.

21. *Ibid.*, vol. ii, p. 83.

22. *Ibid.*, vol. ii, p. 79.

23. *Ibid.*, vol. i, pp. 170–171.

24. *Ibid.*, vol. ii, p. 84.

25. Shaw, *London Music in 1888–89 as Heard by Corno di Bassetto*, p. 360.

26. Shaw, *Music in London 1890–94*, vol. i, p. 59.

27. Shaw, *London Music in 1888–89 as Heard by Corno di Bassetto*, p. 373.

28. *Ibid.*, pp. 330–331.

29. Shaw, *Music in London 1890–94*, vol. i, p. 150.

30. Shaw, *London Music in 1888–89 as Heard by Corno di Bassetto*, p. 56.

31. Shaw, *Music in London 1890–94*, vol. iii, p. 133.

32. *Ibid.*, vol. ii, p. 44.

33. *Ibid.*, vol. ii, p. 53.

34. *Ibid.*, vol. i, p. 110.

35. *Ibid.*, vol. iii, p. 145.

36. Shaw, George Bernard, *The Sanity of Art,* Benjamin R. Tucker, New York, 1908, p. 82.

37. Shaw, *Music in London 1890–94*, vol. ii, p. 86.

38. *Ibid.*, vol. iii, p. 73.

39. *Ibid.*, vol. ii, p. 52.

40. *Ibid.*, vol. iii, p. 169.

41. *Ibid.*, vol. iii, p. 150.

42. Shaw, *London Music in 1888–89 as Heard by Corno di Bassetto,* p. 323.

43. *Ibid.,* p. 388.

44. *Ibid.,* p. 390.

45. Shaw, George Bernard, "The Religion of the Pianoforte," *The Fortnightly Review,* vol. lv (1894), p. 259.

46. Shaw, George Bernard, *The Perfect Wagnerite,* Brentano's, Inc., New York, 1911, p. 32.

47. See Arthur Drews, *Der Ideengehalt von Richard Wagners "Ring des Niebelungen" in Seinen Beziehungen zur Modernen Philosophie,* Hermann Haack, Leipzig, 1898.

48. Bentley, Eric, *A Century of Hero-Worship,* J. B. Lippincott Company, Philadelphia, 1944, pp. 174–175.

49. Shaw, *The Sanity of Art,* p. 38n.

CHAPTER SEVENTEEN

1. Quoted by George Bernard Shaw, *The Quintessence of Ibsenism, Now Completed to the Death of Ibsen,* Brentano's, Inc., New York, 1913, p. 99. I quote entirely from the 1913 edition, which contains later additions and interpolations. Wherever it is important, I shall make clear the chronology of Shaw's opinions.

2. *Ibid.,* p. 11.

3. *Ibid.,* p. 8.

4. *Ibid.,* p. 40.

5. Shaw, George Bernard, *The Sanity of Art,* Benjamin R. Tucker, New York, 1908, p. 61.

6. Chesterton, G. K., *George Bernard Shaw,* John Lane, The Bodley Head, Ltd., London, 1909, p. 111. Reprinted by permission of Dodd, Mead & Company, Inc., New York. Copyright, 1909, by Dodd, Mead & Company.

7. For the general framework of Ibsen's development I am much indebted to Janko Lavrin, *Ibsen and His Creation: A Psycho-Critical Study,* William Collins Sons & Co., Ltd., London, 1921.

8. Shaw, *The Quintessence of Ibsenism, Now Completed to the Death of Ibsen,* p. 50.

9. *Ibid.,* p. 230.

CHAPTER EIGHTEEN

1. Shaw, George Bernard, *Sixteen Self Sketches,* Dodd, Mead & Company, Inc., New York, 1949, p. 175.

2. Quoted by Henry C. Duffin, "Bernard Shaw as a Critic," *The Cornhill Magazine*, vol. lvi (1924), p. 39.

3. Shaw, *Sixteen Self Sketches*, p. 176.

4. *Ibid.*, p. 177.

5. Pearson, Hesketh, *G. B. S., A Full Length Portrait*, Harper & Brothers, New York, 1942, p. 101.

6. Shaw, *Sixteen Self Sketches*, p. 178.

7. Shaw, George Bernard, *William Morris As I Knew Him*, Dodd, Mead & Company, Inc., New York, 1936, pp. 31–32.

8. *Ibid.*, p. 36.

9. Pearson, *op. cit.*, p. 79.

10. *Ibid.*, p. 93.

11. *Ibid.*, p. 94.

12. *Ibid.*, p. 97.

13. Shaw, George Bernard, "Don Giovanni Explains," *Short Stories, Scraps and Shavings*, Dodd, Mead & Company, Inc., New York, 1934, p. 105.

14. Shaw, George Bernard, Foreward, William Archer, *Three Plays*, Constable & Co., Ltd., London, 1927, pp. xxviii–xxix.

15. Bax, Clifford, editor, *Florence Farr, George Bernard Shaw, W. B. Yeats: Letters*, Dodd, Mead & Company, Inc., New York, 1942, p. 4.

16. *Ibid.*, p. 1.

17. *Ibid.*, p. 6.

18. *Ibid.*, pp. 8–9.

19. *Ibid.*, pp. 2–3.

20. *Ibid.*, p. 38.

21. *Ibid.*, p. 15.

22. *Ibid.*, p. 17.

23. Campbell, Mrs. Patrick, *My Life and Some Letters*, Dodd, Mead & Company, Inc., New York, 1922, p. 322.

CHAPTER NINETEEN

1. See Renée M. Deacon, *Bernard Shaw as Artist-Philosopher*, John Lane, The Bodley Head, Ltd., London, 1910, pp. 9–16.

2. Shaw, George Bernard, Preface, *Plays: Pleasant and Unpleasant: I, Unpleasant*, Brentano's, Inc., New York, 1910, p. xi.

3. *Ibid.*, p. v.

4. *Ibid.*, pp. v–vi.

5. *Ibid.*, p. v.

6. Shaw, "Widowers' Houses," *Plays: Pleasant and Unpleasant: I, Unpleasant,* p. 34.

7. *Ibid.*, p. 34.

8. *Ibid.*, p. 37.

9. *Ibid.*, pp. 41–42.

10. Shaw, George Bernard, "Epistle Dedicatory to Arthur Bingham Walkley," *Man and Superman,* Brentano's, Inc., New York, 1905, p. xxxii.

11. Shaw, George Bernard, *Our Theatres in the Nineties,* Constable & Co., Ltd., London, 1932, vol. i, p. 249.

12. Quoted by Archibald Henderson, *George Bernard Shaw: His Life and Works,* Stewart & Kidd, Cincinnati, 1911, pp. 295–296.

13. *Ibid.*, p. 296.

14. Bax, Clifford, editor, *Florence Farr, George Bernard Shaw, W. B. Yeats: Letters,* Dodd, Mead & Company, Inc., New York, 1942, pp. 18, 1–10.

15. Walkley, A. B., *Drama and Life,* Brentano's, Inc., New York, 1908, pp. 245–246.

16. Shaw, George Bernard, letter to *The Daily Chronicle,* August 30, 1898, quoted by Henderson, *op. cit.*, p. 305.

17. Shaw, Preface, *Plays: Pleasant and Unpleasant: I, Unpleasant,* pp. xxvi–xxvii.

18. Henderson, *op. cit.*, p. 320.

19. Butler, Samuel, *Erewhon, Or Over the Range* and *Erewhon Revisited—Twenty Years Later,* Modern Library, Random House, New York, 1927, p. 114.

20. Shaw, letter to *The Daily Chronicle,* August 30, 1898, quoted by Henderson, *op. cit.*, p. 305.

21. Shaw, "Mrs. Warren's Profession," *Plays: Pleasant and Unpleasant: I, Unpleasant,* p. 173.

22. See Wilhelm Rehbach, *George Bernard Shaw als Dramatiker,* inaugural dissertation, Robert Noske, Borna-Leipzig, 1915, p. 32.

23. Shaw, "Mrs. Warren's Profession," *Plays: Pleasant and Unpleasant: I, Unpleasant,* p. 241.

24. St. John, Christopher, editor, *Ellen Terry and Bernard Shaw: A Correspondence,* G. P. Putnam's Sons, New York, 1931, p. 154.

25. Shaw, George Bernard, *The Author's Apology for "Mrs. Warren's Profession" with an Introduction by John Corbin: The Tyranny of Police and Press,* Brentano's, Inc., New York, 1905, p. 62.

26. *Ibid.*, p. 13.

27. *Ibid.*, p. 19.

28. "Plays Pleasant And—. Mr. G. B. Shaw Gives Evidence on Censorship," *Westminster Gazette,* July 31, 1909, quoted by Hesketh Pearson, *G. B. S., A Full Length Portrait,* Harper & Brothers, New York, 1942, p. 166.

CHAPTER TWENTY

1. Shaw, George Bernard, "Arms and the Man," *Plays: Pleasant and Unpleasant: II, Pleasant,* Brentano's, Inc., New York, 1910, p. 67.

2. *Ibid.*, p. 34.

3. *Ibid.*, p. 56.

4. Shaw, "Candida," *Plays: Pleasant and Unpleasant: II, Pleasant,* p. 102.

5. *Ibid.*, p. 86.

6. *Ibid.*, p. 110.

7. Huneker, James, "The Truth about Candida," *Metropolitan Magazine,* vol. xx (1904), p. 635.

8. *Loc. cit.*

9. Chesterton, G. K., *George Bernard Shaw,* John Lane, The Bodley Head, Ltd., London, 1909, pp. 121–123. Reprinted by permission of Dodd, Mead & Company, Inc., New York. Copyright, 1909, by Dodd, Mead & Company.

10. Shaw, "Candida," *Plays: Pleasant and Unpleasant: II, Pleasant,* p. 129.

11. *Ibid.*, p. 155.

12. *Ibid.*, p. 156.

13. *Ibid.*, pp. 157–158.

14. Shaw, "The Man of Destiny," *Plays: Pleasant and Unpleasant: II, Pleasant,* p. 164.

15. *Ibid.*, p. 185.

16. St. John, Christopher, editor, *Ellen Terry and Bernard Shaw: A Correspondence,* G. P. Putnam's Sons, New York, 1931, p. 17; Shaw, Preface, *Plays: Pleasant and Unpleasant: II, Pleasant,* p. ix.

CHAPTER TWENTY-ONE

1. St. John, Christopher, editor, *Ellen Terry and Bernard Shaw: A Correspondence,* G. P. Putnam's Sons, New York, 1931, p. xx.

2. *Ibid.*, p. 4.

3. *Ibid.*, p. 16.

4. *Ibid.*, p. 16.

5. *Ibid.*, p. 19.

6. *Ibid.*, p. 28.

7. *Ibid.*, p. 57.

8. *Ibid.*, p. 60.

9. *Ibid.*, p. 34.

10. *Ibid.*, pp. 75–76.

11. *Ibid.*, p. 78.

12. *Ibid.*, p. 79.

13. *Ibid.*, p. 73.

14. *Ibid.*, p. 73.

15. *Ibid.*, p. 88.

16. *Ibid.*, p. 104.

17. *Ibid.*, p. 126.

18. *Ibid.*, p. 158.

19. *Ibid.*, p. 91.

20. *Ibid.*, pp. 94–95.

21. *Ibid.*, p. 108.

22. *Ibid.*, p. 110.

23. *Ibid.*, p. 185.

24. *Ibid.*, p. 187.

25. *Ibid.*, p. 141.

26. Shaw, George Bernard, *Our Theatres in the Nineties,* Constable & Co., Ltd., London, 1932, vol. ii, pp. 197–198.

27. St. John, editor, *op. cit.*, p. 62.

28. Shaw, *Our Theatres in the Nineties,* vol. ii, pp. 290–291.

29. St. John, editor, *op. cit.*, p. 166.

30. *Ibid.*, p. 139.

31. *Ibid.*, p. 144.

32. *Ibid.*, p. 150.

33. *Ibid.*, pp. 241, 244–245.

34. *Ibid.*, p. 246.

35. *Ibid.*, p. 251.

36. *Ibid.*, p. 281.

37. *Ibid.*, p. 256.

38. *Ibid.*, p. 282.

39. *Ibid.*, p. 291.

40. *Ibid.*, p. 308.

41. *Ibid.*, p. xxvii.

42. *Ibid.*, p. 318.

43. *Loc. cit.*

CHAPTER TWENTY-TWO

1. Shaw, George Bernard, *Our Theatres in the Nineties,* Constable & Co., Ltd., London, 1932, vol. iii, p. 16.

2. Shaw, George Bernard, "The Problem Play: A Symposium," *The Humanitarian,* vol. vi (1895), p. 350.

3. Shaw, *Our Theatres in the Nineties,* vol. iii, p. 58.

4. Shaw, George Bernard, *The Quintessence of Ibsenism, Now Completed to the Death of Ibsen,* Brentano's, Inc., New York, 1913, p. 239.

5. Shaw, *Our Theatres in the Nineties,* vol. ii, p. 167.

6. Shaw, *The Quintessence of Ibsenism, Now Completed to the Death of Ibsen,* p. 230.

7. Shaw, *Our Theatres in the Nineties,* vol. ii, pp. 182–183.

8. St. John, Christopher, editor, *Ellen Terry and Bernard Shaw: A Correspondence,* G. P. Putnam's Sons, New York, 1931, pp. 36–43.

9. Shaw, *Our Theatres in the Nineties,* vol. i, p. 24.

10. *Ibid.*, vol. iii, pp. 147–148

11. *Ibid.*, vol. iii, p. 77.

12. *Ibid.*, vol. iii, p. 201.

13. *Ibid.*, vol. iii, p. 202.

CHAPTER TWENTY-THREE

1. Shaw, George Bernard, *Dramatic Opinions and Essays,* Brentano's, Inc., New York, 1928, vol. i, p. 375.

2. Shaw, George Bernard, *Our Theatres in the Nineties,* Constable & Co., Ltd., London, 1932, vol. i, p. 211.

3. *Ibid.*, vol. ii, p. 194.

4. *Ibid.*, vol. i, p. 211.

5. *Ibid.*, vol. iii, p. 205.

6. *Ibid.*, vol. iii, p. 182.

7. *Ibid.*, vol. iii, p. 162.

8. *Ibid.*, vol. iii, p. 45.

9. *Ibid.*, vol. i, p. 94.

10. *Ibid.*, vol. ii, pp. 160–161.

11. *Ibid.*, vol. iii, pp. 76–83.

CHAPTER TWENTY-FOUR

1. St. John, Christopher, editor, *Ellen Terry and Bernard Shaw: A Correspondence*, G. P. Putnam's Sons, New York, 1931, p. 184.

2. *Ibid.*, p. 34.

3. *Ibid.*, p. 86.

4. *Ibid.*, p. 54.

5. *Ibid.*, p. 73.

6. All quotations until the next index numeral are from St. John, editor, *op. cit.*, pp. 87–89.

7. *Ibid.*, p. 88.

8. *Ibid.*, p. 91.

9. *Ibid.*, p. 93.

10. *Ibid.*, p. 94.

11. *Ibid.*, p. 99.

12. *Ibid.*, pp. 99–100.

13. *Ibid.*, p. 104.

14. *Ibid.*, p. 152.

15. *Ibid.*, p. 184.

16. *Ibid.*, p. 178.

17. *Ibid.*, pp. 154–155.

18. *Ibid.*, p. 161.

19. *Ibid.*, p. 162.

20. *Ibid.*, p. 155.

21. *Ibid.*, p. 160.

22. *Ibid.*, pp. 168–169.

23. *Ibid.*, p. 182.

24. *Ibid.*, p. 183.

25. *Ibid.*, p. 185.

26. *Ibid.*, p. 193.

27. Shaw, George Bernard, "Getting Married," *The Doctor's Dilemma, Getting Married, and The Shewing-Up of Blanco Posnet*, Brentano's, Inc., New York, 1928, p. 220.

28. St. John, editor, *op. cit.*, p. 230.

CHAPTER TWENTY-FIVE

1. Pearson, Hesketh, *G. B. S., A Full Length Portrait*, Harper & Brothers, New York, 1942, p. 291.

2. Shaw, George Bernard, *Music in London 1890–94*, Constable & Co., Ltd., London, 1932, vol. iii, p. 86.

3. Wells, H. G., *Experiment in Autobiography*, The Macmillan Company, New York, 1934, pp. 211–212.

4. Shaw, George Bernard, "Fabianism and the Empire: A Manifesto by the Fabian Society," Grant Richardson, London, 1900, p. 38.

CHAPTER TWENTY-SIX

1. Shaw, George Bernard, Preface, *Three Plays for Puritans*, Brentano's, Inc., New York, 1911, p. xx.

2. *Ibid.*, p. xxi.

3. *Ibid.*, p. xxvii.

4. Butler, Samuel, *Erewhon, Or Over the Range* and *Erewhon Revisited—Twenty Years Later*, Modern Library, Random House, New York, 1927, p. 269.

5. Maude, Aylmer, *The Life of Tolstoy, Later Years*, Constable & Co., Ltd., London, 1910, p. 641.

6. Shaw, Notes, "Caesar and Cleopatra," *Three Plays for Puritans*, p. 206.

7. Shaw, "Caesar and Cleopatra," *Three Plays for Puritans*, p. 184.

8. See George Bernard Shaw, Introduction, L. S. Woolf, *International Government: Two Reports Prepared for the Fabian Research Department together with a Project by a Fabian Committee for a Supernational Authority That Will Prevent War*, Brentano's, Inc., New York, 1916.

9. Shaw, Preface, *Three Plays for Puritans*, p. xxxiv.

10. Shaw, "Captain Brassbound's Conversion," *Three Plays for Puritans*, p. 282.

CHAPTER TWENTY-SEVEN

1. Shaw, George Bernard, "The Revolutionist's Handbook," *Man and Superman*, Brentano's, Inc., New York, 1905, p. 197.

2. *Ibid.*, p. 206.

3. *Ibid.*, p. 219.

4. Shaw, "Epistle Dedicatory to Arthur Bingham Walkley," *Man and Superman*, p. xix.

5. Shaw, *Man and Superman*, pp. 22–23.

6. Shaw, George Bernard, *Sixteen Self Sketches*, Dodd, Mead & Company, Inc., New York, 1949, pp. 199–200.

7. Strauss, E., *Bernard Shaw: Art and Socialism*, Victor Gollancz, Ltd., London, 1942, pp. 38–40.

8. Elsabeth Peper, in "George Bernard Shaws Beziehungen zu Samuel Butler der Jüngere," *Anglia*, vol. 1 (1926), p. 296, supposes Shaw did not know Butler when he wrote *Man and Superman* and points out that he did not mention that writer in the original 1903 edition. As a matter of fact, Shaw had written a review of *Luck, or Cunning?* in the *Pall Mall Gazette*, May 31, 1887.

9. St. John, Christopher, editor, *Ellen Terry and Bernard Shaw: A Correspondence*, G. P. Putnam's Sons, New York, 1931, p. 110.

10. Synopsis of "Don Juan in Hell," quoted by Archibald Henderson, *George Bernard Shaw: His Life and Works*, Stewart & Kidd, Cincinnati, 1911, p. 370.

11. Shaw, *Man and Superman*, p. 235.

12. *Ibid.*, pp. 228, 241.

13. *Ibid.*, pp. 235, 227.

14. *Ibid.*, pp. 227, 232, 235.

15. *Ibid.*, p. 91.

16. Blake, William, *The Poetry and Prose of William Blake*, Geoffrey Keynes, editor, Random House, New York, 1939, p. 132.

17. Shaw, *Man and Superman*, p. 243.

CHAPTER TWENTY-EIGHT

1. Quoted by Hesketh Pearson, *G. B. S., A Full Length Portrait*, Harper & Brothers, New York, 1942, p. 201.

2. *Ibid.*, p. 205.

3. Quoted from Lillah McCarthy, *Myself and My Friends*, E. P. Dutton &

Co., Inc., New York, 1933, p. 34. *The Saturday Review* article is apparently that of May 25, 1895.

4. McCarthy, *op. cit.*, p. 55.

5. Shaw, George Bernard, "An Aside," McCarthy, *op. cit.*, pp. 5–6.

6. Quoted by McCarthy, *op. cit.*, p. 56.

7. Pearson, *op. cit.*, p. 206.

8. Park, Julian, editor, *Some Unpublished Letters of George Bernard Shaw,* University of Buffalo Studies, vol. xvi (1939), no. 3, pp. 120–122.

9. Walkley, A. B., "The Irish National Theatre," *Drama and Life,* Brentano's, Inc., New York, 1908, pp. 310–315.

10. Shaw, George Bernard, *Our Theatres in the Nineties,* Constable & Co., Ltd., London, 1932, vol. iii, p. 81.

11. Quoted by Pearson, *op. cit.*, p. 208.

12. Quoted by Archibald Henderson, *Bernard Shaw, Playboy and Prophet,* D. Appleton & Company, Inc., New York, 1932, pp. 577–578.

13. Shaw, George Bernard, "John Bull's Other Island," *John Bull's Other Island and Major Barbara,* Brentano's, Inc., New York, 1929, p. 125.

14. *Ibid.*, p. 125.

15. *Ibid.*, p. 23.

16. Shaw, George Bernard, *How to Settle the Irish Question,* Constable & Co., Ltd., London, 1917, p. 13.

17. Shaw, "John Bull's Other Island," *John Bull's Other Island and Major Barbara,* p. 72.

18. Shaw, George Bernard, "Karl Marx and 'Das Kapital,'" *Bernard Shaw and Karl Marx: A Symposium, 1884–1889,* Richard W. Ellis, editor, Random House, New York, 1930, p. 115.

19. Shaw, "John Bull's Other Island," *John Bull's Other Island and Major Barbara,* p. 119.

20. *Ibid.*, p. 120.

21. *Ibid.*, p. 123.

22. Archer, William, *The Old Drama and the New: An Essay in Re-Valuation,* Small, Maynard, Boston, 1924, pp. 353–354.

23. Thompson, Alex M., "The Sur-Passing Shaw," *The Clarion,* December 8, 1905.

24. Bentley, Eric, *A Century of Hero-Worship,* J. B. Lippincott Company, Philadelphia, 1944, pp. 199–201.

25. Walkley, *op. cit.*, p. 238.

26. Shaw, "First Aid to Critics" (Preface), "Major Barbara," *John Bull's Other Island and Major Barbara,* p. 161.

27. Henderson, Archibald, *George Bernard Shaw: His Life and Works,* Stewart & Kidd, Cincinnati, 1911, p. 381.

28. Shaw, "Major Barbara," *John Bull's Other Island and Major Barbara,* pp. 252–253.

29. Strauss, E., *Bernard Shaw: Art and Socialism,* Victor Gollancz, Ltd., London, 1942, pp. 55–56.

30. Henderson, *George Bernard Shaw: His Life and Works,* p. 381.

31. Shaw, "Major Barbara," *John Bull's Other Island and Major Barbara,* p. 247.

32. *Ibid.,* p. 161.

33. *Ibid.,* p. 197.

34. *Ibid.,* p. 301.

35. *Ibid.,* p. 169.

36. *Ibid.,* p. 301.

37. Nietzsche, Friedrich, *Also Sprach Zarathustra,* Alfred Kroener, Leipzig, 1917, p. 12.

38. Shaw, "Major Barbara," *John Bull's Other Island and Major Barbara,* p. 307.

39. *Ibid.,* p. 167.

CHAPTER TWENTY-NINE

1. Quoted by Edward R. Pease, *The History of the Fabian Society,* A. C. Fifield, London, 1916, p. 165.

2. Shaw, George Bernard, "H. G. Wells on the Rest of Us," *Pen Portraits and Reviews,* Constable & Co., Ltd., London, 1931, p. 280.

3. Wells, H. G., *Experiment in Autobiography,* The Macmillan Company, New York, 1934, p. 213.

CHAPTER THIRTY

1. Quoted by Clara G. Stillman, *Samuel Butler: A Mid-Victorian Modern,* The Viking Press, Inc., New York, 1932, p. 287.

2. Quoted by Hesketh Pearson, *G. B. S., A Full Length Portrait,* Harper & Brothers, New York, 1942, p. 231.

3. Quoted by C. Archer, *William Archer,* George Allen & Unwin, Ltd., London, 1931, p. 296. Copyright, 1931, by Yale University Press, New Haven. Reprinted by permission of the publishers.

4. Shaw, George Bernard, "The Doctor's Dilemma," *The Doctor's Dilemma, Getting Married, and The Shewing-Up of Blanco Posnet,* Brentano's, Inc., New York, 1928, p. 102.

5. Pearson, *op. cit.,* p. 216.

6. Shaw, Preface, "Getting Married," *The Doctor's Dilemma, Getting Married, and The Shewing-Up of Blanco Posnet,* p. 148.

7. Shaw, "Getting Married," *The Doctor's Dilemma, Getting Married, and The Shewing-Up of Blanco Posnet,* p. 280.

8. *Ibid.,* p. 303.

9. Norwood, Gilbert, "Euripides and Shaw: A Comparison," *Euripides and Shaw, With Other Essays,* Methuen & Co., Ltd., London, 1921.

10. Shaw, George Bernard, Preface, "Misalliance," *Misalliance, The Dark Lady of the Sonnets, and Fanny's First Play: With a Treatise on Parents and Children,* Brentano's, Inc., New York, 1914, pp. lxxvii–lxxviii.

11. *Ibid.,* p. lv.

12. Shaw, "Misalliance," *Misalliance, The Dark Lady of the Sonnets, and Fanny's First Play: With a Treatise on Parents and Children,* p. 103.

13. Shaw, George Bernard, *Sixteen Self Sketches,* Dodd, Mead & Company, Inc., New York, 1949, p. 31.

14. Shaw, "Misalliance," *Misalliance, The Dark Lady of the Sonnets, and Fanny's First Play: With a Treatise on Parents and Children,* p. 44.

15. *Ibid.,* p. 43.

16. *Ibid.,* p. 100.

17. *Ibid.,* p. 84.

CHAPTER THIRTY-ONE

1. Shaw, George Bernard, Preface, "The Dark Lady of the Sonnets," *Misalliance, The Dark Lady of the Sonnets and Fanny's First Play: With a Treatise on Parents and Children,* Brentano's, Inc., New York, 1914, pp. 137–138.

2. *Ibid.,* p. 123.

3. Sheean, Vincent, *Between the Thunder and the Sun,* Random House, New York, 1943, p. 175.

4. Shaw, George Bernard, "To My Critics," *The New Review,* vol. xi (1894), p. 56.

5. McCarthy, Lillah, *Myself and My Friends,* E. P. Dutton & Co., Inc., New York, 1933, p. 136.

6. Shaw, George Bernard, "Androcles and the Lion," *Androcles and the Lion, Overruled, Pygmalion,* Brentano's, Inc., New York, 1916, p. 53.

7. McCarthy, *op. cit.*, p. 169.

8. Shaw, Preface, "Androcles and the Lion," *Androcles and the Lion, Overruled, Pygmalion,* p. xlii.

9. Henderson, Archibald, *Bernard Shaw, Playboy and Prophet,* D. Appleton & Company, Inc., New York, 1932, p. 564.

10. Shaw, Preface, "Pygmalion," *Androcles and the Lion, Overruled, Pygmalion,* p. 113.

11. Pearson, Hesketh, *G. B. S., A Full Length Portrait,* Harper & Brothers, New York, 1942, p. 260.

12. Shaw, George Bernard, "From the Point of View of the Playwright," *Herbert Beerbohm Tree: Some Memories of Him and of His Art,* Max Beerbohm, editor, E. P. Dutton & Co., Inc., New York, p. 250.

13. *Ibid.,* p. 245.

14. *Ibid.,* p. 246.

15. Quoted by McCarthy, *op. cit.,* pp. 162–163.

16. Quoted by Mrs. Patrick Campbell, *My Life and Some Letters,* Dodd, Mead & Company, Inc., New York, 1922, p. 323.

17. *Ibid.,* pp. 326–327.

18. *Ibid.,* pp. 342–343.

CHAPTER THIRTY-TWO

1. Henderson, Archibald, *Bernard Shaw, Playboy and Prophet,* D. Appleton & Company, Inc., New York, 1932, p. 579.

2. Shaw, George Bernard, "Heartbreak House," *Heartbreak House, Great Catherine, and Playlets of the War,* Brentano's, Inc., New York, 1919, p. 101.

3. Shaw, George Bernard, *What I Really Wrote about the War,* Constable & Co., Ltd., 1931, p. 4.

4. See Martin Ellehauge, *The Position of Bernard Shaw in European Drama and Philosophy,* Levin & Munksgaard, Copenhagen, 1931, pp. 186–239, 343–371.

5. Shaw, Preface, "Heartbreak House," *Heartbreak House, Great Catherine, and Playlets of the War,* p. xlvii.

6. Dickinson, Thomas, "Bernard Shaw and Woodrow Wilson," *The Virginia Quarterly,* vol. vii (1931), pp. 8–9.

7. Quoted by Maisie Ward, *Gilbert Keith Chesterton,* Sheed & Ward, Ltd., London, 1943, pp. 390–391. Copyright, 1943, by Sheed & Ward, Inc., New York. Reprinted by permission of publishers and of executrix of estate of G. K. Chesterton.

8. Henderson, Archibald, *Table-Talk of G. B. S.*, Harper & Brothers, New York, 1925, p. 122.

9. Shaw, *What I Really Wrote about the War*, p. 28.

10. Fay, Sidney B., *The Origins of the World War*, second edition, revised, The Macmillan Company, New York, 1930, vol. ii, p. 4.

11. Shaw, *What I Really Wrote about the War*, p. 119.

12. *Ibid.*, pp. 154–155, 182.

13. Liddell Hart, B. H., *Reputations Ten Years After*, Little, Brown & Company, Boston, 1928, p. 184.

14. See Fay, *op. cit.*, vol. ii, pp. 498–499, 321–325.

15. Shaw, *What I Really Wrote about the War*, p. 164.

16. *Ibid.*, p. 237.

CHAPTER THIRTY-THREE

1. Shaw, George Bernard, *What I Really Wrote about the War*, Constable & Co., Ltd., London, 1931, p. 240.

2. Letter of March 10, 1919, quoted in part in *Autograph Letters of Bernard Shaw*, American Art Association, Anderson Galleries, New York, 1930.

3. *Ibid.*

4. See Thomas Dickinson, "Bernard Shaw and Woodrow Wilson," *The Virginia Quarterly*, vol. vii (1931), pp. 11–16.

5. See Thomas A. Bailey, *Woodrow Wilson and the Lost Peace*, The Macmillan Company, New York, 1944, pp. 25–28.

6. Shaw, *What I Really Wrote about the War*, p. 287.

7. *Ibid.*, p. 316.

CHAPTER THIRTY-FOUR

1. Shaw, George Bernard, Preface, "Heartbreak House," *Heartbreak House, Great Catherine, and Playlets of the War*, Brentano's, Inc., New York, 1919, p. xxix.

2. Shaw, George Bernard, *What I Really Wrote about the War*, Constable & Co., Ltd., London, 1931, pp. 316–318.

3. *Ibid.*, p. 331.

4. "Mr. Shaw and Mussolini," *The Nation and Athenaeum*, vol. xlii (1927–1928), p. 106.

5. Shaw, George Bernard, Preface, *Back to Methuselah*, Brentano's, Inc., New York, 1921, p. x.

6. *Ibid.*, p. xxxiii.

7. *Ibid.*, pp. l–li.

8. Inge, W. R., "Shaw as a Theologian," *G.B.S. 90*, S. Winsten, editor, Dodd, Mead & Company, Inc., New York, 1946, pp. 143–144.

9. Stillman, Clara G., *Samuel Butler: A Mid-Victorian Modern*, The Viking Press, Inc., New York, 1932, pp. 183–184.

10. Henderson, Archibald, *Bernard Shaw, Playboy and Prophet*, D. Appleton & Company, New York, 1932, p. 536.

11. Shaw, *Back to Methuselah*, p. 107.

12. *Ibid.*, p. 284.

13. Shaw, Preface, *Back to Methuselah*, pp. c–ci.

14. Joad, C. E. M., "Shaw's Philosophy," *G. B. S. 90*.

15. *Ibid.*, p. 86.

CHAPTER THIRTY-FIVE

1. Shaw, George Bernard, Preface, *Saint Joan*, Brentano's, Inc., New York, 1924, pp. lx–lxi.

2. Barrett, W. P., editor and translator, *The Trial of Jeanne d'Arc: Translated into English from the Original Latin and French Documents*, Gotham House, Inc., New York, 1932, p. 137.

3. Shaw, *Saint Joan*, p. 92.

4. Barrett, editor, *op. cit.*, p. 116.

5. *Ibid.*, pp. 183–184.

6. *Ibid.*, p. 61.

7. Quoted by Shaw, Preface, *Saint Joan*, p. lv.

8. Henderson, Archibald, *Bernard Shaw, Playboy and Prophet*, D. Appleton & Company, Inc., New York, 1932, p. 543.

9. Shaw, *Saint Joan*, p. 85.

10. Shaw, Preface, *Saint Joan*, p. lxxx.

11. Shaw, *Saint Joan*, pp. 159, 161.

12. *Ibid.*, p. 163.

13. *Ibid.*, p. 160.

14. *Ibid.*, p. 156.

15. "Shaw Highly Honored," *The Outlook*, November 24, 1926, p. 392.

16. Quoted by Hesketh Pearson, *G. B. S., A Full Length Portrait*, Harper & Brothers, New York, 1942, p. 345.

CHAPTER THIRTY-SIX

1. Reprinted from *Bernard Shaw: An Unauthorized Biography*, by Frank Harris, published by Simon and Schuster, Inc., New York, p. 291. Copyright, 1931, by Nellie Harris.

2. Quoted by Hesketh Pearson, *G. B. S., A Full Length Portrait*, Harper & Brothers, New York, 1942, p. 238.

3. Shaw, George Bernard, Preface, *Killing for Sport*, Henry S. Salt, editor, George Bell & Sons, Ltd., London, 1915, p. xii.

4. Quoted by Harris, *op. cit.*, p. 292.

5. Quoted by Lillah McCarthy, *Myself and My Friends*, E. P. Dutton & Co., Inc., New York, 1933, pp. 86–87.

6. *Ibid.*, p. 173.

7. Bennett, Arnold, *The Journal of Arnold Bennett, 1921–1928*, The Viking Press, Inc., New York, 1932–1933, p. 188.

8. Pearson, *op. cit.*, p. 269.

9. *Ibid.*, p. 269.

10. *Ibid.*, p. 239.

11. Quoted by C. Archer, *William Archer*, George Allen & Unwin, Ltd., London, 1931, p. 242.

12. Archer, William, "The Psychology of G. B. S.," *The Bookman*, vol. lxvii (1924), p. 139.

13. Quoted by Maisie Ward, *Gilbert Keith Chesterton*, Sheed & Ward, Ltd., London, 1943, p. 238. Copyright, 1943, Sheed & Ward, Inc., New York. Reprinted by permission of publishers and of executrix of estate of G. K. Chesterton.

14. Shaw, George Bernard, Preface, W. H. Davies, *The Autobiography of a Super-Tramp*, Alfred A. Knopf, Inc., New York, 1924, p. viii.

15. *Ibid.*, p. xii.

16. *Ibid.*, p. xiv.

17. Margrie, William, "Bernard Shaw's Advice to Me," *The Bermondsey Book*, vol. i (1924), p. 15. Mr. Margrie's comment: "Shaw's letter referred to a play I wrote nearly 40 years ago. It was about a British filibuster something like Hitler. In a second letter Shaw said 'damned fool' was a term of endearment! I have been nicknamed 'G.B.S. of Camberwell!' "

18. *Ibid.*, pp. 15–18.

19. Kingsmill, Hugh, *Frank Harris: A Biography,* Jonathan Cape, Ltd., London, 1932, p. 164.

20. Quoted by Harris, *op. cit.,* p. 285.

21. Letters of March 5, 1918, and February 15, 1923, quoted in part in *Autograph Letters of Bernard Shaw,* American Art Association, Anderson Galleries, New York, 1930.

22. Shaw, George Bernard, Preface, "The Dark Lady of the Sonnets," *Misalliance, The Dark Lady of the Sonnets, and Fanny's First Play: With a Treatise on Parents and Children,* Brentano's, Inc., New York, 1914, p. 115.

CHAPTER THIRTY-SEVEN

1. Ward, Maisie, *Gilbert Keith Chesterton,* Sheed & Ward, Ltd., London, 1943, pp. 223–225. Copyright, 1943, by Sheed & Ward, Inc., New York. Reprinted by permission of publishers and of executrix of estate of G. K. Chesterton.

2. *Ibid.,* p. 154.

3. McCarthy, Lillah, *Myself and My Friends,* E. P. Dutton & Co., Inc., New York, 1933, p. 67.

4. Chesterton, G. K., *The Autobiography of G. K. Chesterton,* Sheed & Ward, Ltd., London, 1936, p. 229. Reprinted by permission of Dodd, Mead & Company. Copyright, 1909, by Dodd, Mead & Company, Inc.

5. Ward, *op. cit.,* p. 367.

6. *Ibid.,* pp. 178–180.

7. Shaw, George Bernard, article in *The* [London] *Nation,* August 28, 1909, p. 787.

8. Ward, *op. cit.,* p. 365. Copyright, 1943, by Sheed & Ward, Inc., New York. Reprinted by permission of publishers and of executrix of estate of G. K. Chesterton.

9. *Ibid.,* p. 366.

10. *Do We Agree? A Debate between G. K. Chesterton and Bernard Shaw, with Hilaire Belloc in the Chair,* Cecil Palmer, London, 1928, p. 8.

11. Pearson, Hesketh, "G. B. S. versus G. K. C.," *Living Age,* vol. cccxix (1923), pp. 35–36.

12. Ward, *op. cit.,* p. 441.

13. *Ibid.,* pp. 489–490.

14. Pearson, Hesketh, *G. B. S., A Full Length Portrait,* Harper & Brothers, New York, 1942, p. 340.

15. Shaw, George Bernard, *Short Stories, Scraps and Shavings,* Dodd, Mead & Company, Inc., New York, 1934.

16. Ward, *op. cit.,* p. 595.

CHAPTER THIRTY-EIGHT

1. Shaw, George Bernard, *An Unsocial Socialist,* Brentano's, Inc., New York, 1905, p. 308.

2. Shaw, George Bernard, *The Intelligent Woman's Guide to Socialism and Capitalism,* Brentano's, Inc., New York, 1928, p. 20.

3. *Ibid.,* pp. 69–70.

4. *Ibid.,* p. 68.

5. *Ibid.,* pp. 325–326.

6. Shaw, George Bernard, "Too True to Be Good," *Too True to Be Good, Village Wooing, and On the Rocks,* Brentano's, Inc., New York, 1934, p. 76.

7. Shaw, *The Intelligent Woman's Guide to Socialism and Capitalism,* p. 377.

8. Pearson, Hesketh, *G. B. S., A Full Length Portrait,* Harper & Brothers, New York, 1942, p. 347.

9. Quoted by George Bernard Shaw, Foreword, William Archer, *Three Plays,* Constable & Co., Ltd., London, 1927, p. xxxix.

10. Shaw, George Bernard, Preface, *The Apple Cart,* Constable & Co., Ltd., London, 1930, p. v.

11. Shaw, *The Apple Cart,* p. 38.

12. *Ibid.,* p. 49.

13. *Ibid.,* p. 51.

14. *Ibid.,* p. 54.

15. *Ibid.,* p. 53.

16. *Ibid.,* p. 55.

CHAPTER THIRTY-NINE

1. Shaw, George Bernard, "On the Rocks," *Too True to Be Good, Village Wooing, and On the Rocks,* Brentano's, Inc., New York, 1934, pp. 341–342.

2. Quoted by H. W. L. Dana, "Shaw in Moscow," *The American Mercury,* vol. xxv (1932), p. 346.

3. Lyons, Eugene, "Bernard Shaw in Moscow," *Assignment in Utopia*, Harcourt, Brace & Company, Inc., New York, 1927, p. 429.

4. *Ibid.*, p. 430.

5. Dana, *op. cit.*, p. 348.

6. *Ibid.*, pp. 348–349.

7. "Shaw Discovers the Almost Perfect State," *The New York Times*, August 30, 1931, p. 20; "Shaw Twits America on Reds' 'Prosperity,'" *The New York Times*, October 12, 1931, p. 30.

CHAPTER FORTY

1. Barzun, Jacques, "Bernard Shaw in Twilight," *The Kenyon Review*, vol. v (1943), pp. 326–327.

2. Shaw, George Bernard, *Everybody's Political What's What?*, Dodd, Mead & Company, Inc., New York, 1944, pp. 228–229.

3. Shaw, George Bernard, *The Future of Political Science in America*, Dodd, Mead & Company, Inc., New York, 1933.

CHAPTER FORTY-ONE

1. Shaw, George Bernard, "Too True to Be Good," *Too True to Be Good, Village Wooing, and On the Rocks*, Brentano's, Inc., New York, 1934, pp. 87, 116.

2. *Ibid.*, p. 103.

3. Shaw, George Bernard, "Again the Dean Speaks Out," *The Nation and Athenaeum*, vol. xxxii (1922), p. 422.

4. Shaw, "Too True to Be Good," *Too True to Be Good, Village Wooing, and On the Rocks*, p. 104.

5. Shaw, George Bernard, Preface, "The Simpleton of the Unexpected Isles," *The Simpleton, The Six, The Millionairess*, Dodd, Mead & Company, Inc., New York, 1936, pp. 18–19.

6. Shaw, "The Simpleton of the Unexpected Isles," *The Simpleton, The Six, and The Millionairess*, p. 56.

7. *Ibid.*, p. 83.

8. Shaw, George Bernard, *Buoyant Billions*, privately printed, 1947, p. 13.

9. Shaw, Preface, *Buoyant Billions*, pp. 4–5.

1. Barnes, Sir Kenneth, "G. B. S. and the Royal Academy of Dramatic Arts," *G. B. S. 90*, S. Winsten, editor, Dodd, Mead & Company, Inc., New York, 1946, pp. 237–238.

2. *Ibid.*, pp. 236–237.

3. Shaw, George Bernard, *Sixteen Self Sketches*, Dodd, Mead & Company, Inc., New York, 1949, pp. 196–197.

4. Pascal, Gabriel, "Shaw as a Scenario Writer," *G. B. S. 90*, p. 259.

5. *Ibid.*, p. 257.

6. Shaw, George Bernard, "The Webbs and Social Revolution," *The New York Times Book Review*, November 18, 1945, p. 1.

7. Saroyan, William, "My Visit with G. B. S.," *New Republic*, July 2, 1946, p. 80.

8. Evans, Herbert M., and Dorothy A. Evans, *A Visit with G. B. S.*, Berkeley, Calif., 1947, p. 11.

9. Rogers, Charles Bolles, letter to the author, September 7, 1948.

10. Shaw, *Sixteen Self Sketches*, p. 18.

11. *Ibid.*, p. 125.

12. *Ibid.*, p. 122.

BIBLIOGRAPHY

Note: Most of the books listed by George Bernard Shaw below as originally published by Brentano's, Inc., are now copyrighted and published by Dodd, Mead & Company, Inc., New York.

WORKS BY SHAW: CORRESPONDENCE

Autograph Letters of Bernard Shaw, American Art Association, Anderson Galleries, New York, 1930.

Ellen Terry and Bernard Shaw: A Correspondence, Christopher St. John, editor, G. P. Putnam's Sons, New York, 1931.

Florence Farr, George Bernard Shaw, W. B. Yeats: Letters, Clifford Bax, editor, Dodd, Mead & Company, Inc., New York, 1942.

Some Unpublished Letters of George Bernard Shaw, Julian Park, editor, University of Buffalo Studies, vol. xvi, no. 3, 1939.

WORKS BY SHAW: CRITICAL

The Author's Apology for "Mrs. Warren's Profession" with an Introduction by John Corbin: The Tyranny of Police and Press, Brentano's, Inc., New York, 1905.

"Darwin Denounced" (a review of Samuel Butler's *Luck, or Cunning?*), *Pall Mall Gazette,* May 31, 1887.

Dramatic Opinions and Essays, 2 vols., Brentano's, Inc., New York, 1928.

Foreword, William Archer, *Three Plays,* Constable & Co., Ltd., London, 1927.

London Music in 1888–1889 as Heard by Corno di Bassetto, Constable & Co., Ltd., London, 1939.

"Madox Brown, Watts, and Ibsen," *The Saturday Review,* vol. lxxxiii (1897), pp. 266–267.

"Mr. Bernard Shaw's Works of Fiction as Reviewed by Himself," *Tinsley's Magazine,* vol. xlviii (1892), p. 238.

Music in London 1890–94, 3 vols., Constable & Co., Ltd., London, 1932.

Our Theatres in the Nineties, 3 vols., Constable & Co., Ltd., London, 1932.

[417]

Pen Portraits and Reviews, Constable & Co., Ltd., London, 1931.

The Perfect Wagnerite: A Commentary on the Niblung's Ring, Brentano's, Inc., New York, 1911.

Preface, Eugène Brieux, *Three Plays,* Mrs. Bernard Shaw, St. John Hankin and John Pollock, translators, Brentano's, Inc., New York, 1913.

"The Problem Play: A Symposium," *The Humanitarian,* vol. vi (1895), p. 350.

The Quintessence of Ibsenism, Now Completed to the Death of Ibsen, Brentano's, Inc., New York, 1913.

"The Religion of the Pianoforte," *The Fortnightly Review,* vol. lv (1894), pp. 255–266.

The Sanity of Art: An Exposure of the Current Nonsense about Artists Being Degenerate, Benjamin R. Tucker, New York, 1908.

"To My Critics," *The New Review,* vol. xi (1894), p. 56.

WORKS BY SHAW: DRAMATIC

Androcles and the Lion, Overruled, Pygmalion, Brentano's, Inc., New York, 1916.

The Apple Cart: A Political Extravaganza, Constable & Co., Ltd., London, 1930.

Back to Methuselah: A Metabiological Pentateuch, Brentano's Inc., New York, 1921.

Buoyant Billions: A Comedy of No Manners by a Fellow of the Royal Society of Literature, privately printed, 1947.

The Doctor's Dilemma, Getting Married, and the Shewing-Up of Blanco Posnet, Brentano's, Inc., New York, 1928.

Geneva, Dodd, Mead & Company, Inc., New York, 1947.

Heartbreak House, Great Catherine, and Playlets of the War, Brentano's, Inc., New York, 1919.

In Good King Charles Golden Days, A History Lesson, Constable & Co., Ltd., London, 1939.

John Bull's Other Island and Major Barbara, Brentano's, Inc., New York, 1929.

Man and Superman: A Comedy and a Philosophy, Brentano's, Inc., New York, 1905.

Misalliance, The Dark Lady of the Sonnets, and Fanny's First Play: With a Treatise on Parents and Children, Brentano's, Inc., New York, 1914.

Plays: Pleasant and Unpleasant: I, Unpleasant, Brentano's, Inc., New York, 1910.

Plays, Pleasant and Unpleasant: II, Pleasant, Brentano's, Inc., New York, 1910.

Saint Joan: A Chronicle Play in Six Scenes and an Epilogue, Brentano's, Inc., New York, 1924.

The Simpleton, The Six, The Millionairess, Dodd, Mead & Company, Inc., New York, 1936.

Three Plays for Puritans, Brentano's, Inc., New York, 1911.

Too True to Be Good, Village Wooing and On the Rocks, Brentano's, Inc., New York, 1934.

WORKS BY SHAW: FABIAN PUBLICATIONS

"Fabian Election Manifesto of 1892," *Fabian Tract No. 40,* Fabian Society, London, 1892.

(Editor) *Fabian Essays in Socialism,* George Allen & Unwin, Ltd., London, 1931.

"The Fabian Society: Its Early History," *Fabian Tract No. 41,* Fabian Society, London, 1892.

"Fabianism and the Empire: A Manifesto by the Fabian Society," Grant Richardson, Ltd., London, 1900.

"The Impossibilities of Anarchism," *Fabian Tract No. 45,* Fabian Society, London, 1895.

"A Manifesto," *Fabian Tract No. 2,* Fabian Society, London, 1884.

WORKS BY SHAW: MISCELLANEOUS

"Again the Dean Speaks Out," *The Nation and Athenaeum,* vol. xxxii (1922), pp. 421–422.

Bernard Shaw and Karl Marx: A Symposium, 1884–1889, Richard W. Ellis, editor, Random House, New York, 1930.

"In the Days of My Youth," *Living Age,* vol. cccxxii (1924), pp. 323–326.

An Essay on Going to Church, John W. Luce Company, Boston, 1905.

Everybody's Political What's What?, Dodd, Mead & Company, Inc., New York, 1944.

The Future of Political Science in America, Dodd, Mead & Company, Inc., New York, 1933.

How to Settle the Irish Question, Constable & Co., Ltd., London, 1917.

"The Illusions of Socialism," *Forecasts of the Coming Century by a Decade of Writers,* Edward Carpenter, editor, Walter Scott, London, 1897.

The Intelligent Woman's Guide to Socialism and Capitalism, Brentano's Inc., New York, 1928.

Preface, W. H. Davies, *The Autobiography of a Super-Tramp,* Alfred A. Knopf, Inc., New York, 1924.

Preface, *Killing for Sport: Essays by Various Writers,* Henry S. Salt, editor, George Bell & Sons, Ltd., London, 1915.

Short Stories, Scraps and Shavings, Dodd, Mead & Company, Inc., New York, 1934.

Sixteen Self Sketches, Dodd, Mead & Company, Inc., New York, 1949.

Unpublished notes and corrections upon the first two chapters of *The Universe of G. B. S.*

"The Webbs and Social Revolution," *The New York Times Book Review,* November 18, 1945, p. 1.

What I Really Wrote about the War, Constable & Co., Ltd., London, 1931.

"What Mr. Gladstone Ought to Do," *The Fortnightly Review,* vol. liii (1893), pp. 276–280.

"Who I Am, and What I Think," *The Candid Friend,* May 11, 1901, pp. 56–58.

William Morris As I Knew Him, Dodd, Mead & Company, Inc., New York, 1936.

WORKS BY SHAW: NOVELS

Cashel Byron's Profession Newly Revised, with Several Prefaces and an Essay on Prizefighting: Also, The Admirable Bashville, or Constancy Unrewarded, Being the Novel of Cashel Byron's Profession Done into a Stage Play in Three Acts and in Blank Verse, Herbert S. Stone, Chicago, 1901.

Immaturity, Constable & Co., Ltd., London, 1931.

The Irrational Knot, Brentano's, Inc., New York, 1926.

Love among the Artists, Brentano's, Inc., New York, 1927.

An Unsocial Socialist, Brentano's, Inc., New York, 1905.

WORKS BY OTHER AUTHORS

ARCHER, C., *William Archer,* George Allen & Unwin, Ltd., London, 1931.

ARCHER, WILLIAM, *The Old Drama and the New: An Essay in Re-Valuation,* Small, Maynard, Boston, 1924.

———, "The Psychology of G. B. S.," *The Bookman,* vol. lxvii (1924), pp. 139–144.

BAILEY, THOMAS A., *Woodrow Wilson and the Lost Peace*, The Macmillan Company, New York, 1944.

BARKER, ERNEST, *Political Thought in England from Herbert Spencer to the Present Day*, Home University Library of Modern Knowledge, Williams & Norgate, Ltd., London, 1915.

BARRETT, W. P., editor and translator, *The Trial of Jeanne d'Arc: Translated into English from the Original Latin and French Documents*, Gotham House, Inc., New York, 1932.

BARZUN, JACQUES, "Bernard Shaw in Twilight," *The Kenyon Review*, vol. v (1943), pp. 321–346.

———, *Darwin, Marx, Wagner: Critique of a Heritage*, Little, Brown & Company, Boston, 1941.

BEERBOHM, MAX, editor, *Herbert Beerbohm Tree: Some Memories of Him and of His Art*, E. P. Dutton & Co., Inc., New York, [n.d.]

BENNETT, ARNOLD, *The Journal of Arnold Bennett, 1921–1928*, The Viking Press, Inc., New York, 1932–1933.

BENTLEY, ERIC, *A Century of Hero-Worship*, J. B. Lippincott Company, Philadelphia, 1944.

———, *Shaw: A Reconsideration*, The Makers of Modern Literature Series, New Directions, Norfolk, Conn., 1947.

BERGSON, HENRI, *L'Evolution Créatrice*, Felix Alcan, editor, Felix Alcan et Guillaumin, Paris, 1908.

BLAKE, WILLIAM, *The Poetry and Prose of William Blake*, Geoffrey Keynes, editor, Random House, New York, 1939.

BUTLER, SAMUEL, *Erewhon, Or Over the Range* and *Erewhon Revisited— Twenty Years Later*, Modern Library, Random House, New York, 1927.

CAMPBELL, MRS. PATRICK, *My Life and Some Letters*, Dodd, Mead & Company, Inc., New York, 1922.

CHESTERTON, G. K., *The Autobiography of G. K. Chesterton*, Sheed & Ward, Inc., New York, 1936.

———, *Do We Agree? A Debate between G. K. Chesterton and Bernard Shaw, with Hilaire Belloc in the Chair*, Cecil Palmer, London, 1928.

———, *George Bernard Shaw*, John Lane, The Bodley Head, Ltd., London, 1909.

Current Literature, vol. xl (1906), pp. 191–193, "Bernard Shaw's 'Discussion' —'Major Barbara.' "

DANA, H. W. L., "Shaw in Moscow," *The American Mercury*, vol. xxv (1932), pp. 343–352.

DEACON, RENÉE M., *Bernard Shaw as Artist-Philosopher: An Exposition of Shavianism*, John Lane, The Bodley Head, Ltd., London, 1910.

DICKINSON, THOMAS, "Bernard Shaw and Woodrow Wilson," *The Virginia Quarterly*, vol. vii (1931), pp. 1–17.

DREWS, ARTHUR, *Der Ideengehalt von Richard Wagners "Ring des Niebelungen" In Seinen Beziehungen Zur Modernen Philosophie*, Hermann Haacke, Leipzig, 1898.

DRUCKER, PETER F., *The End of Economic Man: A Study of the New Totalitarianism, with an Introduction by H. N. Brailsford*, The John Day Company, New York, 1939.

DUFFIN, HENRY C., "Bernard Shaw as a Critic," *The Cornhill Magazine*, n.s. vol. lvi (1924), pp. 31–40.

ECKARD, E. W., *Economics of W. S. Jevons*, American Council on Public Affairs, Washington, D.C., 1940.

ELLEHAUGE, MARTIN, *The Position of Bernard Shaw in European Drama and Philosophy*, Levin & Munksgaard, Copenhagen, 1931.

ELTON, LORD, *The Life of James Ramsay MacDonald (1866–1919)*, William Collins Sons & Co., Ltd., London, 1939.

EVANS, HERBERT M., and DOROTHY A. EVANS, *A Visit with G. B. S.*, Berkeley, Calif., 1947.

FAURE, ELIE, *Modern Art: History of Art*, Garden City Publishing Company, Inc., Garden City, N.Y., 1924.

FAY, SIDNEY B., *The Origins of the World War*, second edition, revised, 2 vols. in one, The Macmillan Company, New York, 1930.

FILON, AUGUSTIN, "M. Bernard Shaw et son Théâtre," *Revue des Deux Mondes*, 15 novembre, 1905, p. 424.

FREUD, SIGMUND, *Der Witz und Seine Beziehung zum Unbewuessten*, F. Deutiche, Leipzig, 1905.

GEIGER, GEORGE R., *The Philosophy of Henry George*, The Macmillan Company, New York, 1933.

GEORGE, HENRY, *Progress and Poverty, An Inquiry into the Causes of Industrial Depressions, and of Increase of Want with Increase of Wealth*, Modern Library, Random House, New York, 1938.

GEORGE, HENRY, JR., *Life of Henry George*, Doubleday, Page, New York, 1905.

HACKETT, J. P., *Shaw: George vs. Bernard*, Sheed & Ward, Ltd., London, 1939.

HAMILTON, MARY AGNES, *J. Ramsay MacDonald*, Jonathan Cape, Ltd., London, 1929.

———, *Sidney and Beatrice Webb: A Study in Contemporary Biography*, Houghton Mifflin Company, Boston. [n.d.]

HARRIS, FRANK, *Bernard Shaw: An Unauthorized Biography Based on First Hand Information, with a Postscript by Mr. Shaw*, Simon and Schuster, Inc., New York, 1931.

HAYNES, E. S. P., "Liberty and the State," *Living Age*, vol. ccc (1919), p. 396.

HEARNSHAW, F. J. C., *A Survey of Socialism: Analytical, Historical, and Critical*, Macmillan & Co., Ltd., London, 1928.

HENDERSON, ARCHIBALD, *Bernard Shaw, Playboy and Prophet*, D. Appleton & Company, Inc., New York, 1932.

————, *George Bernard Shaw: His Life and Works: A Critical Biography*, Stewart & Kidd, Cincinnati, 1911.

————, *Table-Talk of G. B. S.: Conversations on Things in General between George Bernard Shaw and His Biographer*, Harper & Brothers, New York, 1925.

HOOK, SIDNEY, *Towards the Understanding of Karl Marx, A Revolutionary Interpretation*, The John Day Company, New York, 1933.

HUNEKER, JAMES, "The Truth about Candida," *Metropolitan Magazine*, vol. xx (1904), p. 635.

JAMES, WILLIAM, *Pragmatism: A New Name for Some Old Ways of Thinking*, Longmans, Green & Co., Inc., New York, 1921.

JEVONS, W. S., *The Theory of Political Economy*, Macmillan & Co., Ltd., London, 1888.

KINGSMILL, HUGH, *Frank Harris: A Biography*, Jonathan Cape, Ltd., London, 1932.

KNOWLTON, THOMAS, *The Economic Theory of George Bernard Shaw*, University of Maine Press, Orono, Maine, 1936.

LAVRIN, JANKO, *Ibsen and His Creation: A Psycho-Critical Study*, William Collins Sons & Co., Ltd., London, 1921.

LIDDELL HART, B. H., *Reputations Ten Years After*, Little, Brown & Company, Boston, 1928.

LYONS, EUGENE, "Bernard Shaw in Moscow," *Assignment in Utopia*, Harcourt, Brace & Company, Inc., New York, 1927.

MARGRIE, WILLIAM, "Bernard Shaw's Advice to Me," *The Bermondsey Book*, vol. i (1924), pp. 15–18.

MARX, KARL, *Capital*, Modern Library, Random House, New York, 1936.

————, *The Poverty of Philosophy*, Charles H. Kerr & Company, Chicago, 1910.

MAUDE, AYLMER, *The Life of Tolstoy, Later Years*, Constable & Co., Ltd., London, 1910.

McCARTHY, LILLAH, *Myself and My Friends*, E. P. Dutton & Co., Inc., New York, 1933.

MENGER, ANTON, *The Right to the Whole Produce of Labour: The Origin and Development of the Theory of Labour's Claim to the Whole Product of Industry*, Macmillan & Co., Ltd., London, 1899.

[423]

MILL, JOHN STUART, *Autobiography,* World Classics, Oxford University Press, New York, 1924.

————, *The Principles of Political Economy, with Some Applications to Social Philosophy,* W. J. Ashley, editor, Longmans, Green, Ltd., London, 1909.

————, *Socialism,* Humbolt Publishing Co., New York, 1891.

————, *Utilitarianism, Liberty, and Representative Government,* Everyman's Library, J. M. Dent & Sons, Ltd., London, 1910.

MOORE, DORIS L., *E. Nesbit, A Biography,* Ernest Benn, Ltd., London, 1933.

The Nation and Athenaeum, vol. xlii (1927–1928), 106–107, "Mr. Shaw and Mussolini."

NEWMAN, JOHN HENRY, "The Tamworth Reading Room," *Discussions and Arguments on Various Subjects,* Longmans, Green, Ltd., London, 1924.

The New York Times, August 30, 1931, p. 20, "Shaw Discovers the Almost Perfect State."

————, October 12, 1931, p. 30, "Shaw Twits America on Reds' 'Prosperity.' "

NIETZSCHE, FRIEDRICH, *Also Sprach Zarathustra: Ein Buch für Alle und Keinen,* Alfred Kroener, Leipzig, 1917.

NORWOOD, GILBERT, *Euripides and Shaw, With Other Essays,* Methuen & Co., Ltd., London, 1921.

The Outlook, November 24, 1926, p. 392, "Shaw Highly Honored."

PEARSON, HESKETH, *G. B. S., A Full Length Portrait,* Harper & Brothers, New York, 1942.

————, "G. B. S. versus G. K. C.," *Living Age,* vol. cccxix (1923), pp. 35–39.

PEASE, EDWARD R., *The History of the Fabian Society,* A. C. Fifield, London, 1916.

PEPER, ELSABETH, "George Bernard Shaws Beziehungen zu Samuel Butler der Jüngere," *Anglia,* vol. l (1926), 295–316.

PFEIFFER, EDOUARD, *La Société Fabienne et le Mouvement socialiste anglais contemporain,* F. Giard & E. Brière, Paris, 1911.

PIERCE, CHARLES, "How to Make Our Ideas Clear," *The Popular Science Monthly,* vol. xii (1877–1878), pp. 286–302.

REHBACH, WILHELM, *George Bernard Shaw als Dramatiker,* inaugural dissertation, Robert Noske, Borna-Leipzig, 1915.

SAROYAN, WILLIAM, "My Visit with G. B. S.," *The New Republic,* July 2, 1946, p. 80.

SCHOPENHAUER, ARTHUR, *Sämmtliche Werke,* 5 vols. Inselverlag, Leipzig, 1919.

SHAW, C. M., *Bernard's Brethren; with Comments by Bernard Shaw,* Constable & Co., Ltd., London, 1939.

SHEEAN, VINCENT, *Between the Thunder and the Sun*, Random House, New York, 1943.

STEPHEN, SIR LESLIE, *The English Utilitarians*, 3 vols., G. P. Putnam's Sons, New York, 1900.

STILLMAN, CLARA G., *Samuel Butler: A Mid-Victorian Modern*, The Viking Press, Inc., New York, 1932.

STRAUSS, E., *Bernard Shaw: Art and Socialism*, Victor Gollancz, Ltd., London, 1942.

THOMPSON, ALEX M., "The Sur-Passing Shaw," *The Clarion*, December 8, 1905.

WALKLEY, A. B., *Drama and Life*, Brentano's, Inc., New York, 1908.

WALLAS, GRAHAM, *Life of Francis Place*, Alfred A. Knopf, Inc., New York, 1919.

———, "Socialism and the Fabian Society," *The New Republic*, June 24, 1916, pp. 203–204.

WARD, MAISIE, *Gilbert Keith Chesterton*, Sheed & Ward, Inc., New York, 1943.

WEBB, BEATRICE, *My Apprenticeship*, Longmans, Green, Ltd., London, 1926.

WEBB, SIDNEY, "English Progress towards Social Democracy," *Fabian Tract No. 15*, Fabian Society, London, 1893.

———, "Facts for Socialists," *Fabian Tract No. 45*, Fabian Society, London, 1887.

———, "Socialism in England," *Publications of the American Economic Association*, n.s. vol. iv, no. 2, pp. 77–143.

WEBB, SIDNEY, and BEATRICE WEBB, *A Constitution for the Socialist Commonwealth of Great Britain*, Longmans, Green & Co., Inc., New York, 1920.

———, *The History of Trade-Unionism*, Longmans, Green & Co., Inc., New York, 1926.

WELLS, H. G., *Experiment in Autobiography: Discoveries and Conclusions of a Very Ordinary Brain (since 1866)*, The Macmillan Company, New York, 1934.

———, "Faults of the Fabian," privately printed, 1908 [?].

WILSON, EDMUND, "Bernard Shaw at Eighty," *The Triple Thinkers*, Harcourt, Brace and Company, Inc., New York, 1938.

WINSTEN, S., editor, *G. B. S. 90: Aspects of Bernard Shaw's Life and Work*, Dodd, Mead & Company, Inc., New York, 1946.

WOOLF, L. S., *International Government: Two Reports Prepared for the Fabian Research Department together with a Project by a Fabian Committee for a Supernational Authority That Will Prevent War*, Brentano's, Inc., New York, 1916.

INDEX

O

O'Connor, T. P., 125
"O'Flaherty, V. C.," 304, 379
O.G.P.U., 357, 361
Olivier, Sidney, 39, 62, 69, 78–79, 86, 96, 98–99, 103, 111
"On the Rocks," 354–355, 361–362, 368
Opera, 129–130, 132–135
Our Corner, 111, 149
Our Theatres in the Nineties, 201
"Overruled," 288–289
Owen, Robert, 48, 62, 70

P

Pall Mall Gazette, 65, 111
Parliament, 18, 36, 92, 100, 104, 229, 243, 269, 316, 343, 347, 350, 355
Pascal, Gabriel, 379
Pater, Walter, 113, 124
Patriotism, 157, 172, 219, 297–298, 302, 304, 325
Patterson, Jenny, 151–152
Patti, Adelina, 127
Payne, Iden, 252
Payne-Townshend, Charlotte (*see* Shaw, Mrs. George Bernard)
"Peace Conference Hints," 306–308
Pearson, Hesketh, 9, 24, 149, 275, 287, 290, 330, 331, 334, 340, 358
Pease, Edward, 61, 63, 104, 105, 266
The Perfect Wagnerite, 134–136, 217
Pfeiffer, Edouard, 103
"Philanderer," 105, 151–152, 162, 180, 181
"Philharmonic," 127, 130
Phillips, W. L., 49
Phonetics, 28, 131, 234, 289
Photography, 120, 124, 379
Pierce, Charles, 115
Pinero, Sir Arthur W., 139, 156, 158, 167, 201–202, 332

Place, Francis, 86, 89, 103
Plato, 14, 230, 243, 318
"Playlets about the War," 304
Plays for Puritans, 224–234
Podmore, Frank, 61, 64
Political leadership, 74, 89, 115, 164, 230, 295, 298, 300, 308, 316, 325, 349–351, 367
(*See also* Superman)
Potter, Beatrice (*see* Webb, Beatrice)
Poverty, 42–43, 94, 160, 244
Shaw's attitude toward, 8, 26, 31, 43, 94, 159, 166, 257, 259–264
widespread in 1880's, 19, 35, 40, 64
Pragmatism, 115–116, 233, 314
of Shaw, 120, 126, 242–243, 288, 302, 311, 319, 346, 361–362, 382
Pre-Raphaelites, 122
Press, 18, 86–87, 89, 108, 164, 220, 221, 232, 237, 274, 300, 304, 308, 311, 312, 337
Prophet (*see* Genius)
Protestants, 2, 3, 9, 321–323
Prostitution, 164, 166–168, 186
Proudhon, Pierre J., 45, 62
Publishers, 331–332, 338
Puritanism, 137, 224–229, 233, 285
of Shaw, 3, 10, 13, 21, 43, 45, 84, 119, 147–148, 178, 207, 226, 229, 260, 287, 298, 306, 311, 318, 327, 361
"Pygmalion," 151, 289–291, 379

Q

Quicherat, Jules, 320, 321
Quintessence of Ibsenism, 73, 88, 137–146, 185, 195, 201, 247

R

Radical Party, 57, 66, 69, 70, 85, 86, 88–90, 100, 102

Women, Shaw's theory of, mother-woman, 175–176, 233, 238
    womanly, 142, 158–159, 163, 239, 245
Woolf, L. S., 306
Wordsworth, William, 337
Workers' Educational Association *Yearbook* for 1918, 279
World, 110, 118, 125, 129
World War I, 173, 179, 237, 296–300, 303–304, 310, 313, 316, 319, 325, 355
    peace settlement, 300, 305–309

World War II, 301, 365–366, 368, 371
Wright, Sir Almroth, 271–272

Y

Yeats, W. B., 154, 250
"You Never Can Tell," 162, 180–181, 208–209, 212, 234, 276

Z

Zetetical Society, 36, 38–39
Zinoviev Letter, 343
Zola, Émile, 201

COLLEGE OF MARIN

3 2555 00100847 8